SEXUALITY ACROSS THE LIFE COURSE

Edited by

Alice S. Rossi

The University of Chicago Press
Chicago and London

THE UNIVERSITY OF CHICAGO PRESS, CHICAGO 60637
The University of Chicago Press, Ltd., London

© 1994 by The University of Chicago
All rights reserved. Published 1994
Paperback edition 1999
Printed in the United States of America

03 02 01 00 99   5 4 3 2

ISBN: 0–226–72833–1 (cloth)
ISBN: 0–226–72870–6 (paperback)

The University of Chicago Press gratefully acknowledges a subvention from the John D. and Catherine T. MacArthur Foundation in partial support of the costs of production of this volume.

Library of Congress Cataloging-in-Publication Data

Sexuality across the life course / edited by Alice S. Rossi.
    p. cm. — (The John D. and Catherine T. MacArthur Foundation series on mental health and development. Studies on successful midlife development)
   Includes bibliographical references and indexes.
   ISBN 0-226-72833-1
   1. Sex.   2. Intimacy (Psychology)   I. Rossi, Alice S., 1922–   .
II. Series.
HQ21.S4756   1994
306.7—dc20   93-41706
                                       CIP

CONTENTS

BACKGROUND

This volume is the product of a project supported by the Research Network on Successful Midlife Development, one of several networks sponsored by the health program of the John D. and Catherine T. MacArthur Foundation. All the MacArthur Foundation research networks are multidisciplinary groups of scholars, including biomedical, behavioral, and social scientists, who seek to promote an exchange of concepts and methods and to develop new research on substantive issues on which the network members share intellectual and policy concerns.

Gilbert Brim, former president of the Russell Sage Foundation and the Foundation for Child Development, chairs the midlife research network, which was formed in 1989. Paul Baltes (Max Planck Institute for Human Development and Education, Berlin), Margie Lachman (Brandeis University), and Carol Ryff (University of Wisconsin) represent psychology on the network; David Featherman (Social Science Research Council) and I, Alice Rossi (University of Massachusetts), sociology; Paul Cleary (Harvard Medical School) and Ronald Kessler (University of Michigan), medical sociology; Larry Bumpass (University of Wisconsin), demography; Richard Shweder (University of Chicago), anthropology; and William Hazzard (Bowman Gray School of Medicine) and Michael Marmot (Middlesex Hospital Medical School, London), medicine.

Over the course of the four years since we formed the midlife network, we have explored a variety of topics on development during the middle years of the life course (pragmatically defined as ages 35–60). All the research conducted by network members shares a concern for three primary criteria relevant to adult development: physical health, psychological well-being, and social responsibility. Our ultimate goal is to encourage an integration of biological, psychological, and sociological constructs and by so doing to demonstrate through our research the power and insight potential of an integrated, multidisciplinary framework for understanding successful development in midlife.

Toward this goal, the network has followed a variety of approaches: network members have conducted a wide array of pilot research—for example, images of midlife held by adults at various points of the life course, peak psychological experiences of middle-aged adults, cultural differences in defining the life course, the effect on middle-aged parents' well-being of how their adult children are faring, and management strategies in dealing with midlife issues. Other approaches by the mid-life network include establishing collaborative links to ongoing longitudinal studies whose subjects include middle-aged adults, inviting specialists from a wide array of fields to join us at our network meetings, and sponsoring commissioned papers for conferences and workshops on topics the network members consider to be in need of focused reviews.

This volume had its source in network discussions concerning physical health and psychological well-being. During the course of such discussions, we made frequent reference to sexual functioning and interpersonal intimacy, their relationship to health and well-being, and what changes—if any—take place in sexual functioning across the life course. We noted, for example, that coital frequency among married couples shows a linear decline with age, but, when it came to explaining why this was the case, we were hard-pressed to assess the balance of potential explanatory factors: changed health status, the press of multiple responsibilities in midlife, declining hormonal secretion levels, age-graded social expectations about sex, cohort differences masked in cross-sectional age distributions, or a lack of sexual variety and stimulation.

By spring 1991 it was clear that the topic of sexuality was a candidate for a special project. Because none of the network members had themselves conducted research on sexuality in midlife, a useful first step was to commission papers on an array of topics concerning sexuality, and to bring together the authors of such review papers at a seminar-type meeting. If the quality of the work justified it, we would take the next step of revising the papers by taking into account the workshop discussions and to publish a volume of some, if not all, the commissioned papers. I agreed to serve as organizer of the project and editor of the potential volume of commissioned papers.

Topic Coverage and Omissions

Several considerations dictated the selection of topics for the commissioned papers. The first was to broaden the focus from only the middle years to the full age range of sexual life from adolescence to old age. This enlargement was considered important for two reasons: First, a life course perspective has rarely guided prior work in research on sexual behavior, and hence we could not know in advance what was special to the middle years without an age-comparative framework. Second, sexuality had not been a high priority on the agenda of other health program research networks sponsored by the MacArthur Foundation (i.e., neither the old-age network nor the adolescence-youth network had earmarked sexual functioning as among their major research topics). A volume that included youth, midlife, and old age would therefore be of interest to all the MacArthur Foundation networks and would contribute to the foundation's interest in establishing linkages across the networks whose work they sponsor.

One could easily raise a question concerning the omission of childhood and puberty or the related question, What childhood precursors are significant predictors of sexual functioning in adulthood? We gave this serious consideration but opted against such an inclusion for several reasons: First, even the expansion from midlife to sexual initiation in adolescence and sexual experience in old age implied a lengthy volume, and it seemed more appropriate to exclude the phases of the life course prior to sexual maturation than any other. Second, the research literature on childhood sexuality is very sparse (apart from the current interest in child sexual abuse) in developmental psychology. Indeed, to our surprise the sexual self has not even been defined as salient in adult personality research on self schemas. Third, the theory and research on childhood precursors of adult sexual functioning is in the clinical tradition in medicine and psychiatry, which is outside the scope of this project. For the aspect of the plan that included psychiatric and medical expertise, we deemed it more important to focus on changes in sexual problems and sexual therapies and on the effect of disease and medication on sexual functioning.

As a second criterion at the planning stage of the sexuality project, and in keeping with the multidisciplinary nature of all MacArthur research network agendas, we sought a diversity of disciplinary perspectives and methods among the scholars invited to participate. We knew in advance, of course, that as a consequence of disciplinary specialization there were few individual researchers whose work embraced biomedical, psychological, and social behavioral variables, although we would give priority in extending invitations to the rare individuals whose work did represent such an integration. The research reported in the chapters by myself, Jane Lancaster, John McKinlay and Henry Feldman, and Richard Udry and Ben Campbell represent such integrated approaches. For the most part, however, the current state of knowledge predicted the more modest goal of bringing together specialists from diverse fields so that any final volume would be a rich mix of perspectives and methods relevant to an understanding of the many-sided aspects of human sexual functioning.

The most important gap to be bridged, in our judgment, was the gap between biomedical specialties on sexual functioning and the social-behavioral disciplines. There is perhaps no area of human life in which the physical body and the social self are more inherently connected than in sexual functioning; yet the research literature on sexuality is polarized in such a way that biomedical specialists rarely focus on the social relationship within which sex takes place and social scientists rarely incorporate physiological factors. Many universities even house these two bodies of research literature in separate libraries: to read about normal and abnormal genital structure, sex steroid levels, or erectile dysfunction takes us to journals totally different from those in which we read about the social relationship between sexual partners or the cultural or historical context within which sexual behavior takes place.

We therefore deemed it desirable to include chapters from both polarized sets of disciplines in one comprehensive volume, with particular attention to providing solid bibliographies that facilitate a reader's easy access to other related materials.

In light of the very great potential scope of a project that would bridge the biomedical and social disciplines and the full range of the life course from adolescence to old age, we found the choice of specific topics difficult to make. From the biomedical side, we chose two important topics. In light of the fact that ours is an aging society with an advanced medical technology, we felt it important to bring together what evidence exists on how chronic disease and medication affects sexual functioning. Such a review would be of interest in its own right but would also serve as a corrective to premature interpretive closure by social scientists and gerontologists concerning age-related declines in sexual activities and performance. Raul Schiavi's chapter makes this complex biomedical knowledge accessible to readers with primary interest and expertise in the social-behavioral disciplines.

The second biomedical topic we chose is sexual problems and sexual therapies. We are all aware of (or assume there have been) highly significant changes in sexual attitudes and behavior over the last half century: sex is restricted to marriage far less than in the past; cohabitation by unmarried, divorced, and widowed adults is more prevalent; female sexual gratification is a more widely held expectation among men as well as women, and almost all aspects of sex are more publicly displayed and discussed. Nonmarital as well as marital sex figure large in widely viewed TV dramas such as *Dallas* and in TV talk shows, and by all reports VCR rentals of X-rated movies with graphic scenes of sexual intercourse are high on the list of popular rentals. We deemed it important to pose to clinicians the question of whether changes in sexual expectations and behavior are reflected in changes in the nature of medical and psychiatric problems brought to them for treatment and whether the health professions have themselves changed their diagnosis and therapies in recent decades. These are the issues psychiatrist Richard Green addresses in his chapter. Sex therapists today report fewer cases of female frigidity and more cases of male impotence. This change may well reflect a better understanding of female sexuality and a more equitable balance in who initiates sexual encounters: when and if such initiative was largely a male prerogative, male impotence is not likely to be pervasive for the simple reason that men with little or no desire for sex would not initiate a sexual encounter; when the sexual script allows more female initiative, one would expect more performance failures among men and fewer failures among women than in earlier decades.

We also had to be highly selective in the topics on which social scientific expertise was relevant. High on our list was the question whether the far greater public display of sex in the media, as in art and literature, was matched by change in sexual attitudes and behavior in the population at large. We have become far less gullible when the media proclaim the emergence or the demise of anything worthy of the construct label *revolution,* whether feminism, conservatism, or sexual life. It was therefore important to review the empirical evidence on the extent to which sexual attitudes have changed over the past several decades and whether attitudes are translated into actual sexual behavior. As we know, what we say is often at odds with what we do. Numerous public surveys over the years have charted trends in attitudes toward several aspects of sexuality; Tom Smith summarizes these trends in his chapter. Public attitudes have changed far less than one would expect on the basis of media attention to sex.

Unfortunately, there exist no counterpart data banks on trends in sexual behavior to match those available on sexual attitudes. The Kinsey volumes on male and female sexual behavior, published in the late 1940s and early 1950s, continue to be a primary source to researchers. Short-sightedness and political resistance from the Reagan and Bush administrations have precluded an updating of the Kinsey findings, despite the growing importance of such knowledge to public health workers in light of the AIDS epidemic. In fact, funds were withheld from two major studies of sex behavior in 1990, projects that had already received high ratings by peer review committees, because of political intrusion into federal agency decisions on appropriations.

This does not mean that no sex behavior research has been conducted in recent decades. It implies only that there is no full-scale survey of sexual behavior examined in depth and based on national probability samples. In fact there have been many interesting research projects whose foci were on topics other than sexuality but which also included data on sexual behavior. Studies of marital instability and divorce typically include measures on the quality of the sexual bond; developmental research on puberty and adolescence often includes the timing of sexual initiation; studies of the menopausal transition occasionally include measures of sexual pleasure, coital frequency, or pain during intercourse. It is from studies such as these that we invited many authors in this volume to share their findings, as Udry and Campbell do on the timing of sexual initiation in their study of youths in North Carolina, or McKinlay and Feldman on sexual behavior and satisfaction in a Boston area sample of men between ages 40 and 70, or Edwards and Booth on sex as a dimension of the quality of the marital relationship among middle-aged married couples. Even in the chapter summarizing trends in sexual attitudes, Tom Smith reports the correlation between attitudes and sexual behavior and explores to the limit of available data the effect on well-being when attitudes and behavior are discordant.

Another topic we deemed important was possible ethnic and racial diversity in sexual behavior and attitudes, a topic subject to much speculation but little empirical evidence. We were fortunate to locate two social scientists who were conducting qualitative research with small samples of African-American men and women: anthropologist Claire Sterk-Elifson, who was studying African-American women in Atlanta, and sociologist Benjamin Bowser, who did research with African-

American men in California. It was with disappointment that we had to exclude any attention to sexuality in the Hispanic population. Sterk-Elifson had planned to conduct interviews with Hispanic women in Atlanta that would have provided a comparative dimension to her findings on African-American women, but she reported extreme resistance among Hispanic women in pilot interviews to any discussion of the sexual side of their lives. My networking efforts in conversations with other researchers on Hispanic groups only confirmed this resistance. It seems likely that ethnic diversity in sexual functioning must await future research agendas, in all likelihood in studies that include sexual issues as a minor component of a larger topic such as health.

Marriage is so dominant a pattern among adults that the concept is retained even when referring to sex outside of marriage—for example, the words *premarital* and *extramarital*. This blurs awareness of the extensive periods in a life course when we are not bound by marital relationships: the prolonged period between completing schooling and marriage, now that the marriage age is creeping upward; the period of separation or divorce between marriages; and, especially for women, the increasing number of years as widows after the death of a spouse. In addition, an increasing proportion of adults remain unmarried or do not marry again following a divorce. These partnerless periods of time across the lifeline undoubtedly involved far more adults than those with persistent sexual orientations as gay men or lesbian women. It seemed appropriate, therefore, to charge one of the authors to focus not merely on homosexual lifestyles but on nonmarital lifestyles of heterosexual singles as well. This is the focus of Martha Fowlkes's chapter.

Another rather special topic was worth inclusion in the project: sexual deviance. Again, the charge to the authors (Richard Gelles and Glenn Wolfner) was to provide an overview of this body of knowledge on sexual abuse of children, sexual molestation, incest, and rape, with attention to both the offenders and the victims of such unwanted sexual experiences.

As our last criterion for topic selection, we considered it important to view human sexuality as a fundamental species characteristic that subserves reproductive ends. It is all too easy in contemporary Western societies to overlook the fact that above all else sexuality is the proximate cause of reproduction. Our greatly expanded longevity means childbearing and rearing occupy a small proportion of the life course, and our ability to differentiate between procreative and recreative sex can easily lead us to view our sex lives as sharply differentiated from bearing and rearing children. The female breast is more likely to be an erotic than a nurturant symbol. But contemporary human males and females have the same genetic characteristics as did their ancestors of many thousands of years ago, and internal physiology, as much as cultural norms governing social and sexual behavior, primes sexual attraction. Tracing the implications of our biological heritage was the charge put to Jane Lancaster in her chapter on human sexuality, life strategies, and evolutionary biology.

It was not part of the original design, for either the workshop or the volume, for the editor to write a first chapter. But when we reviewed the revised papers, we felt it appropriate to enlarge the bioevolutionary framework that governs Lancaster's chapter and to attempt a synthesis of research findings that are typically left as discrete and unconnected bodies of knowledge. This I attempted in the first chapter by drawing on evolutionary biology, behavior genetics, psychological studies of physical attractiveness, and studies of gender differences in personal attributes and personality. I intended the metaphors referred to in the chapter's title, _eros_ and _caritas,_ to join the contemporary view of sexuality as referring to lust and romantic love _(eros),_ a view that is important to mate selection, with the loving attachment to our children and the loving concern for the other above the self, an attachment that marks mature marital relationships _(caritas)._

To this point, I have sketched the criteria for topic selection for those chapters included in the present volume. But in endeavors of this kind, compromise is always a fact of life. We could not include every topic we wished to cover in the volume. Indeed, there were topics for which we could not locate an appropriate author, as instanced by the absence of any focus on ethnic diversity. On other topics, we learned, the literature was too sparse to merit a review. Omitted are papers we had hoped to have that gave a fine-grained, in-depth analysis of intimate sexual relationships; an overview of changes in sexual and reproductive norms across history; the sexual self in the array of domains and roles that figure in self schemas; a comparative analysis of changing sexual images in novels written during the decades since World War II; an analysis of changes in how movies first produced in one decade and then redone in later decades portrayed sexuality; a sociographic analysis of pioneer couples in earlier times—for example, the New Moralists at the turn of the twentieth century, who attempted to live creative and productive professional or artistic lives while sustaining long-standing intimate sexual relationships; and an analysis of needed gender role renegotiation to minimize the risk of exposure to the AIDS virus.

We hope, despite these omissions, that readers find that the topics covered in this volume far outweigh in their contributions what had to be abandoned. Diversity of disciplinary background and research methodology is amply demonstrated. In terms of disciplinary representation, sociology is most heavily represented, with eight authors, although from numerous specialty fields within the discipline: these are the chapters by John Edwards and Alan Booth (family sociology); Benjamin Bowser (ethnic studies); Richard Gelles (family violence); Richard Udry (biosociology and demography); Martha Fowlkes (psychoanalytic sociology and gender studies); Tom Smith (survey research specialist); and myself (family and kinship and adult development). Three authors represent anthropology: Jane Lancaster (bioevolutionary perspective); Claire Sterk-Elifson (ethnic studies); and Benjamin Campbell (biological anthropology). Medical sociology is the primary forte of two authors, Judith Levy and John McKinlay; Raul Schiavi and Richard Green represent medicine and psychiatry; and Glenn Wolfner, clinical psychology. Sharon Thompson has a background in comparative literature and has branched out to qualitative ethnographic scholarship in a recent study of teenage girls' narratives about their initiation into sex and romance. Henry Feldman was trained in statistics.

Research methodology is similarly diverse: five chapters rely primarily on quantitative survey research: the chapters by Smith, Udry and Campbell, Gelles and Wolfner, McKinlay and Feldman, and Edwards and Booth. Three chapters rely primarily on qualitative data from intensive interviews and focused group discussions: Sterk-Elifson, Bowser, and Thompson. The remaining six chapters are essentially reviews that summarize extensive findings on their special topics: those by Rossi, Lancaster, Fowlkes, Levy, Schiavi, and Green.

Qualitative research methods serve ends quite different from those of quantitative survey methods. The former are appropriate in approaching topics or population groups that have had scant attention in the past: they are more descriptive than analytic and often provide a pool of relevant items for subsequent efforts to quantify a particular construct. Qualitative research also provides in-depth windows into individual and cultural meanings, the diversity of motivations that may underlie a given behavior, or the variance within gender or class or race often not seen when such sociodemographic variables are approached in survey design and analysis. By contrast, the best use of quantitative techniques provides reliable and valid measurement of major constructs, the statistical ability to disentangle the myriad ways in which major variables are significant but correlated predictors of the phenomenon being studied, and results whose generalizability is known on the basis of the sampled population. These two major research approaches are not contradictory but complementary: one (qualitative) provides depth; the other (quantitative) provides scope. If statistical analysis may be said to provide the skeleton, qualitative data adds the flesh.

We believe, and reviewers of the manuscript concurred, that the topic coverage is comprehensive, the prose clear and lively, the bibliographies rich with linkages to additional materials for those interested in one or another of the topics covered, and the multidisciplinary approach stimulating to those planning to undertake research of their own on human sexual functioning.

Organization of the Volume

The fourteen chapters in this volume are organized into four substantive sections. The first section consists of only one chapter, by the editor, which models an integrated biopsychosocial approach to an understanding of both sexuality and reproduction. The second section, with five papers, demonstrates the great diversity of perspectives on sexuality and illustrates the differences in humankind as a function of *history* (Lancaster in an evolutionary time frame, Smith in the last thirty years of American history); *culture* (the qualitative chapters on African-American sexuality by Sterk-Elifson [African-American women], and Bowser [African-American men]); and *opportunity and sexual orientation* (Fowlkes on intimacy and sexuality among single adults and homosexual lifestyles).

The third substantive section contains five chapters that focus on selected phases of the life course: sexual initiation in *adolescence* (Richard Udry and Ben Campbell on boys but with some data on girls as well, and Sharon Thompson on teenage girls); the *middle years* (John McKinlay and Henry Feldman on sex and aging among men, and John Edwards and Alan Booth on sexuality and well-being among married couples in midlife); and *old age* (Judith Levy).

The last section consists of three chapters on health-related issues in sexuality: Raul Schiavi compresses an extensive literature on the effect of chronic disease and medication on sexual functioning. Richard Green sketches changes over the past quarter century in the nature of sexual problems and the variety of therapies used to deal with them. The volume ends with the chapter by Richard Gelles and Glenn Wolfner, which summarizes research on sexual deviance and victimization.

Notes of Appreciation and Gratitude

I would like to thank a number of people whose help and support were of great significance during the history of the sexuality project. First, I am grateful for the support from the John D. and Catherine T. MacArthur Foundation, and in particular the Research Network on Successful Midlife Development. Idy Gitelson of the foundation health program staff, and Gilbert Brim, director of the research network on midlife development, were enthusiastic supporters throughout the history of the project. My colleagues on the research network were invariably helpful with suggestions and commentary when I reported on the progress of the project during 1991 and 1992. In the early stages of the project, when plans for topics and potential authors were underway, many people gave wise and fruitful suggestions, including Paul Cleary, Anke Ehrhardt, David Featherman, Carolyn Heilbrun, Ron Kessler, Richard Jessor, Joan Moore, Marcia Ory, Jack Rowe, Carol Ryff, Edward Schneider, Ann Snitow, and Marta Tienda. From start to finish, I am indebted to my administrative assistant on the project, Karen Mason, who handled endless paperwork details throughout the process. Very special thanks are due to all the participating authors, whose enthusiasm, patience, and performance were outstanding from start to finish.

Special thanks are also due to the two poets whose poems grace my own chapter: Sharon Olds, who granted permission to republish her poem, "True Love" (which first appeared in the *American Poetry Review* in 1985) and Anselm Hollo, who granted permission to republish his poem, "The One" (which first appeared in a poetry collection, *The Coherences,* in 1968).

Last, but as always far from least, my special gratitude to my colleague and husband, Peter Rossi, whose advice and support were always there when needed and were given most generously.

Alice S. Rossi

I THE BIOPSYCHOSOCIAL
PERSPECTIVE

Eros and Caritas: A Biopsychosocial Approach to Human Sexuality and Reproduction

Alice S. Rossi

The major aim of this chapter is to demonstrate that a multidisciplinary approach enriches our understanding of sexuality, mate choice, and reproduction. First I describe the biosocial or biopsychosocial perspective and argue for its greater explanatory potential compared to the polarized dichotomy in contemporary research and theory concerning sexuality and reproduction implicit in the biomedical approach on the one hand, and the social constructionist approach on the other. Second, I sketch a bioevolutionary perspective that alerts us to the unique species characteristics of human compared to nonhuman primate mammals and discuss its relevance to an understanding of sexual behavior. Third, I review social psychological research on physical appearance and attractiveness to demonstrate the applicability of bioevolutionary theories to contemporary social life, and in particular to gender differences in sexual behavior and mate choice. Lastly, I argue the thesis that differences between men and women in the sexual domain reflect fundamental personality modalities associated with gender.

The underlying thesis of my analysis is that *eros* (infatuation and youthful passion) is a necessary stage in the development of sexual attraction to the point of mate choice and reproduction; *caritas* (loving kindness and attachment) is the more enduring and mature quality necessary to assure the care and protection of human young through the uniquely long human stage of youthful dependency. The metaphor of *eros* carries a widely shared meaning; by contrast there is great cultural and historical variation in the metaphors that refer to enduring attachment of any kind. The Greeks contrasted *eros* with *agape* and *philia;* Aquinas called it *benevolentia,* wishing the very best for others. The distinguished modern physicist, Freeman Dyson, titled his latest book, *From Eros to Gaia* (Dyson 1992), Gaia being the goddess of motherhood and of caring for all life's creatures (Penrose 1993).

I have chosen *caritas* because it is aesthetically pleasing and because it is associated with charity in the sense of altruistic concern for others on a par with—if not above—concern for self. I realize that for some,

3

the term *caritas* has religious or spiritual connotations. Psychologists may associate it with altruism or generativity. For me, it is associated with a core gender difference rooted in human evolution, with valued attributes of being female, and with a commitment to a communitarian ideal of a socially cohesive society and responsive polity.

THE BIOSOCIAL PERSPECTIVE

The terms *biosocial* or *biopsychosocial* are used to emphasize the functional unity of biological, psychological, and socioenvironmental factors. (I shall use the shorter term *biosocial* throughout, but this should be understood to embrace the psychological domain as well as the biological and social-environmental). Human beings are embodied creatures; our thoughts and feelings find expression through physical and chemical processes internal to our bodies, and, despite enormous cultural diversity across all known societies in the human record, all societies accommodate key characteristics of the human species. Our needs for sleep, for nourishment, for social relations, for sexual expression, and for reproduction involve basic biological needs that our various social arrangements are designed to meet. Below some minimal level of social provision to meet these needs, individuals or societies could not survive. Any approach to the study of human sexuality that sets biology and social behavior in competition, or that stresses only one dimension to the neglect of the other, is counterproductive. It is futile to study human behavioral systems without integrating all significant levels of causation. Hence our goal ought to be an integration of all relevant systems and all relevant disciplines involved in sexual and reproductive functioning.

These points may seem transparently true where reproduction is concerned. Clearly there are unique aspects of human pregnancy, birth, and child rearing that have had to be accommodated in all human societies, as I discuss below. It is worth underlining the basic point that, whatever else sexual behavior symbolizes and whatever range of complex and variant motivations lie behind sexual behavior, sexuality is the proximate cause of reproduction. That this point requires emphasis today stems from the fact that it is a relatively recent historical development over the past century for the human population to be of such a size, with such powerful means to prevent infant and maternal mortality, and with such effective tools to prevent unwanted pregnancies, that it is now possible to conceptualize and to experience sex in purely recreational terms, clearly distinct from its reproductive consequences. At the end of the twentieth century, there is no pressing social need for human societies to be strongly pronatalist any longer, and, with greatly increased longevity, a much smaller proportion of the female life span involves pregnancy, birth, and child rearing. This profound demographic transition in Western societies is the background to the predominance of sexual images over fertility images in our culture: the breast is rarely the symbol of fertility that it is in primitive and early Western art; rather it is a symbol of eroticism.

Social Constructionist versus Medical Models of Sexuality

I believe it is this underlying demographic shift from a pronatalist to a fertility-neutral—if not antinatalist—situation that has encouraged a widened gap in studies of sexuality between the biological and social science disciplines rather than an advance toward an integrated discipline that draws on and integrates relevant constructs and variables from evolutionary biology, physiology, and endocrinology, and the social-behavioral sciences. The same barriers and prejudices hold in contemporary studies of gender. I am referring of course to the penetration of a social constructionist theoretical perspective in anthropology, sociology, and psychology (Stein 1992), as well as in literary and historical analyses. Social constructionists argue that there is no such thing as a value-free science, that the concepts we use are popular or persistent not because they are valid but because they are socially and politically useful. In the case of sexuality, following the lead of Michel Foucault (1978), the social constructionist argues that the modern idea of sexuality was constructed in a particular social-historical context. Hence, Foucault argues that, contrary to popular belief, sexuality was not repressed in the Victorian era and gradually reawakened in the twentieth century era of permissiveness because there is no essential human quality or drive to sexuality that can be repressed at one point in history and liberated in another. Instead, he claims there are sexualities that are constantly produced, changed, and modified by social forces, forces that have an effect as much on the scholar-researcher as on the public at large.

In an essay that very pointedly argues this perspective, Kenneth Plummer (1982) asks whether sexuality draws on a powerful universal biological drive that can be shaped by cultural forces and instilled through varying socialization practices, or whether it is more like a learned script that varies by historic time and place. He comes down of course on the side of a socially constructed sexual script, a dramaturgic metaphor first elaborated by John Gagnon and William Simon (1973). In this view, sex is not a universal human potential but an emergent possibility dependent on social-historical circumstances and life history. What is ironic is that social constructionists simultaneously espouse an emphasis on a person's active role in structuring reality, guided only loosely by his or her culture (Gergen 1985; Tiefer 1992). Clearly social constructionists view themselves as independent actors, and by implication they presumably possess the unique ability to analyze sexual patterns unbound by their own personal histories or the constraints of their own time and culture. Note, however, that the social constructionist models of sexuality include no reference to reproduction, revealing by that omission their acceptance of the contemporary focus on recreational rather than procreative sex. They are, in the final analysis, almost as time bound and culture bound as the earlier theorists they criticize.

This is not to argue that a social constructionist perspective cannot illuminate our thinking. It is in the tradition of work in the sociology of knowledge, and, held with some reservations, it encourages us to be critical of the assumptions we may unwittingly bring to whatever subject we investigate. To avoid intellectual sterility, it is wise to periodically reexamine our most deeply held presuppositions. In our era of high levels of knowledge specialization, this is difficult to do; we feel more comfortable remaining in the grooves of the narrower disciplines in which we were trained. It is a wrenching experience for social scientists trained in the past twenty years and more to think in terms of the physiological pathways through which the variables with which we are concerned operate to produce the outcomes of interest to us. I am persuaded, nonetheless, that the wave of the future is to attempt an integration of previously sharply separated disciplines. There is everything to gain and nothing to lose by doing so.

What is it, for example, that intervenes between a sociological variable like social isolation (the absence of a supportive social network) or a traumatic life event (divorce, death of a spouse, prolonged unemployment) and psychological stress, depression, and even heart disease? The correlation between social isolation and depression in a study of women whose husbands died recently might be in the range of .30–.50, significant but hardly overwhelming. The power of our explanatory models might well be increased were we to tap individual variance in the biochemical processes that are at work during difficult life transitions. Stress, for example, causes chronic secretion of neuroendocrine hormones (epinephrine, norepinephrine, cortisol) that result in elevated blood pressure, blood sugar, and cholesterol (McNeil 1988). Norepinephrine is a potent vasoconstrictor that can raise blood pressure, so changes in endocrine secretions may in turn affect vascular function (Abell 1992) and pave the way for psychological depression, or, if life turmoil persists for a period of time, cardiac disease. A multifactor causal model that embraces social, psychological, and biological factors takes nothing away from the importance of the social-behavioral elements of the model, but the inclusion of the biological factors may be of critical importance in the policy recommendations that flow from such research, for example, to monitor blood pressure or to prescribe particular medications, along with efforts to involve grieving women in support groups of others undergoing similar painful life transitions.

An integration of biological and social-behavioral variables in studies of human behavior cannot only enrich the knowledge being developed in the social sciences; it can also inform the biomedical fields of the importance of social-environmental factors and impose some break on the tendency toward a narrow medical approach to the solution of numerous sexual and reproductive problems. (See Riessman [1983] and Tiefer [1986, 1992] for two good analyses relevant to such medicalization.) At our sexuality workshop Raul Schiavi (author of chap. 12, this volume) sketched the changes that have taken place in sex therapy over the past few decades: in the 1970s, the prevailing notion was that 90 percent of sexual problems were due to psychological reasons, whereas in the 1990s, we are confronted with the equally undocumented claim that 60–80 percent of sexual problems have organic origins. By contrast, Schiavi urged a complex therapeutic model that considers the contribution of both organic and psychological causal factors.

A similar trend has been observed where menopause is concerned. Many years ago, psychoanalytic interpretations were dominant in explaining menopausal distress in women, rooted in the notion that, as Helene Deutsch put it, woman has ended her existence as bearer of future life and has reached her natural end—her partial death as servant of the species (Deutsch 1945). Today, a very different theory predominates, a medical model premised on the effect of declining hormonal levels, and the solution is sought in hormone-replacement therapy. Indeed, hormone replacement is increasingly being advocated not merely for a few years during the menopausal transition but as a permanent preventive treatment for all the years remaining in a woman's life after menopause at fifty, to minimize the probability of developing osteoporosis and heart disease (Bush 1992; Rossi 1992). Hormone replacement therapy has been described by John McKinlay (1989) as a "treatment in search of a disease." McKinlay also predicts that a counterpart development is likely to be treatment of midlife men presumed to be suffering from a midlife "viropause" or "andropause," as some British physicians describe it (Langan 1992), with testosterone replacement (Rossi 1992).

An important contribution to the disease model so prevalent today in the treatment of sexual dysfunction was the narrow physiological approach to sexuality that characterized the work of major sexologists in this century: Alfred Kinsey in the 1940s and 1950s (Kinsey, Pomeroy, and Martin 1948; Kinsey et al. 1953), followed by Masters and Johnson (1966) in the 1960s and 1970s. Theories concerning sexuality in Europe have tended toward multicausal models, drawing on psychology as well as biology, and have been sensitive to the effect of historical period (cf., e.g., Ariès and Béjin 1985). As Paul Robinson (1976) has suggested, a change occurred as sex research crossed the Atlantic: Alfred Kinsey and his associates' primary unit of analysis was the orgasm, from whatever source—masturbation, heterosexual intercourse, or homosexual coupling. Although the Kinsey studies contributed to demystifying sexuality by undermining notions of so-called sexual normality, Kinsey retained the same assumption that guided Freud's psychosexual developmental theories—that is, an evolution-related universal sex drive. Masters and Johnson's work in the laboratory further contributed to a focus on physiological sexual functioning of the individual in a social vacuum: using a homogeneous sample of individual subjects, they focused on vaginal and penile blood flow; on anal, clitoral, and vaginal contractions during orgasm; and on the histochemistry of the clitoris and claimed to have empirically found a common sexual response cycle—a fixed four-stage cycle they argued was identical in men and women. As Robinson (1976) and Leonore Tiefer (1992) have suggested, the use of a homogeneous sample of men and women engaging in masturbation in a laboratory setting encouraged the conception of sexuality as individual behavior subject to biological processes rather than a social experience with a partner, and hence subject to the nature and history of a social relationship.

It is an ironic twist that feminists, commonly opposed to theories of biologically grounded sex differences, have embraced the medical model of sexuality implicit in Masters and Johnson's research because it "proved" that women's biology entitled them to sexual activity, pleasure, and orgasm. Much was made of the laboratory reports that women were if anything more highly sexed than men because women are capable of multiple orgasms during one sexual episode (Barbach 1975; Hite 1976; Sherfey 1972). Freud was surely mistaken in the belief that a vaginal orgasm was distinguishable from a clitoral orgasm, much less in his view that vaginal orgasm was the mature female response, whereas a clitoral orgasm indicated an immature adolescent sexual response. On the other hand, there is a tendency in contemporary feminist writings on female sexuality to swing strongly to the opposite view that penile penetration reflects patriarchal dominance of women, and clitoral orgasm is women's path to sexual freedom (Barbach 1975; Cartledge and Ryan 1985; Hite 1976), a view also congenial to lesbian sexuality. The focus in these writings is on masturbation and autoeroticism (cf. especially Barbach 1975; Hite 1976): as Pat Whiting put it, women can learn through masturbation "where their male-inspired hangups end and their real sexual feelings begin" (Wandor 1972, 189). Like their mentors, William Masters and Virginia Johnson, such feminists have adopted a physicalist view of sexuality, sex understood simply as a physical response to a physical stimulation. Lynne Segal makes this point well: "In this individualistic psychology sexual liberation is not about social relations or subjective experience, but about individual sensation. And sexual desire is understood not in terms of a person's relation to the object desired, but as some bodily state" (Segal 1985, 34). Segal goes on to suggest that feminists have exposed the myth of a liberated sexuality, typified by novels from the pens of Lawrence, Miller, and Mailer, as little more than a homage to masculinity but now seem to be "in danger of coming up with a new version of the same myth" (Segal 1985, 40).

The sex-therapy profession also built on Masters and Johnson's work in the emphasis placed on learning sexual skills via masturbation even in the treatment of sexual dysfunction among married couples, and a narrow focus on male sexual potency in terms of regular, resilient, rigid penile erections. Little wonder, then, that treatment of male sexual dysfunctions such as impotence in recent years so often involves mechanical solutions via penile prostheses or chemical solutions via hormonal supplements.

BIOEVOLUTIONARY PERSPECTIVE ON HUMAN SEXUALITY

The medical disease model in the case of menopause provides a good example of the interpretive enrichment possible when evolutionary biology is resorted to (Hill and Hurtado 1991). The medical assumption is that lowered estrogen levels associated with menopause are indicators of a disease state that can be treated with exogenous hormone replacement. What is taken as normal are the high levels of estrogen secretion during the reproductive years (a rise in estrogen level triggers ovulation and, in the absence of fertilization, leads to menstruation). But evolutionary biology suggests quite a different view. For 99 percent of our history as a species, the human female rarely ovulated or menstruated because our female hunter-gatherer ancestors matured at a later age, underwent a period of adolescent sterility following menarche, and nursed their young for three to four years, which suppressed the resumption of ovulation and menstruation following each birth (Lancaster and King 1985; Short 1984, 1987). This also implies low levels of endogenous estrogen across the reproductive years of hunter-gatherer women. By contrast, modern women have few babies and, if they nurse them, do so for very short time periods. Hence they menstruate ten to twelve times a year for some thirty-five years during which they are subject to high levels of endogenous estrogens. In addition, over the past thirty years, countless thousands of women have been exposed to exogenous estrogen as a result of contraceptive pill usage. What is unusual in an evolutionary framework, therefore, is not the low estrogen levels postmenopausally but the fact that contemporary women have so persistent a high level of estrogen exposure during their fertile years.

But now let us take a longer time perspective on the development of bioevolutionary thinking since the publication of Darwin's *Origin of Species*. In the decades following this publication, those attracted to his theories took pleasure in finding similarities between human behavior and that of the great apes. Much of what was reported were more anthropomorphic projections of human assumptions and cultural prejudices than accurate observations and interpretations of animal behavior: the aggressive, dominant male fighting other males for sexual access to females and monogamously bonded dyads or dominant males with a harem of females were commonly reported. By contrast, field research by primatologists over the past several decades has gradually documented a very different profile of monkey and ape societies, and women field researchers have played an important part in this research: Jane Goodall's work with chimpanzees, Thelma Rowell and Jeanne Altmann on baboons, Dian Fossey on the gorilla are widely known, and well summarized and analyzed in Donna Haraway's overview, *Primate Visions* (1989). Women researchers have looked most closely at the ongoing social organization of primate groups, with particular attention to male-female sexual courting, reproductive behavior, and the socialization of the young. Far from the image of dominant males and submissive females as the keynote of monkey societies, this work often reports that female-status hierarchies provide the stable social cohesion for the group, with high male turnover and migration (Wolfe 1991; Wrangham 1980). Rather than docile monogamous creatures, females were frequently observed to copulate with numerous males even during estrus. As Jane Lancaster (chap. 2, this vol.) and Sarah Hrdy (1981) report, females often form alliances with multiple males with which they copulated during estrus, and even the males who were not progenitors show protective behavior toward the infants and their mother. So, too, female primates are fierce fighters in protecting infants from harm (Altmann 1980; Hrdy and Whitten 1987).

A similar trend can be seen in research over the past several decades on the earliest human social groups of hunters and gatherers, research that has corrected earlier assumptions about our distant ancestors. Man the hunter has had to share center stage with woman the gatherer, when it became clear that hunting was a precarious enterprise with uncertain yield, more often than not underwritten by the more reliable provision of plant and root food gathered by the women, which often accounted for more than half the food available to the group (Hurtado et al. 1985; Lee 1979). It should be noted, however, that the often-quoted 50-percent contribution of women to diet in foraging societies has undergone some recent qualification; the equitable 50-percent figure masks variation in food acquisition by women as a function of lactation status, ecological setting, and number of dependent children. For example, among the Hiwi and Ache foragers in Venezuela and Paraguay, Hurtado and her associates (1992) report a drop to as low as 20 percent of the food acquisition when women are nursing infants, compensated by higher rates among postreproductive women and husbands.

There has also been a significant shift in theoretical approaches to human evolution, stimulated by major work in sociobiology, in particular constructs of parental investment strategies and inclusive fitness (Daly and Wilson 1978; Fedigan 1986; Symons 1979; Trivers 1972). Jane Lancaster has written extensively on this topic (see chap. 2, this vol.). Her current emphasis is on tracing the significance of the *differences* between human and nonhuman primates, and the *differences* between males and females in the evolution of their reproductive strategies. I will summarize some key features of this perspective and illustrate how they apply not only to an understanding of our evolutionary origins but also to contemporary sexual and reproductive strategies of men and women in the 1990s.

The most important characteristics that differentiate the human from the nonhuman primates are the following:

An enlarged brain and bipedalism. The constraints imposed on human birth by the shift to bipedalism simultaneously with enlarged brains resulted in the premature birth of human infants compared to our closest genetic relative, the chimpanzee: the brain of a human infant at birth is only 25 percent of its adult size, compared to 45 percent for a chimp infant (68 percent for the rhesus monkey). The human infant does not reach the chimp's at-birth brain volume until six or seven months; it takes four years for the human child's brain to reach 95 percent of adult brain volume. The critical implication of this slow growth is a prolonged and fragile human infancy, requiring constant care and feeding.

Juvenile dependency. Almost all mammals feed themselves once they are weaned. Human children are unique in the prolonged postweaning period during which adults feed them. Over historic time the period of postweaning juvenile dependency has extended considerably, most markedly in the past century as the training required for jobs in a modern economy call for higher levels of educational attainment, well beyond the age by which sexual maturation has been reached.

Timing of pubertal development. Many female mammals ovulate with their first estrous cycle. The human female is unique in undergoing pubertal change and attainment of most of her eventual stature before ovulation starts, typically some period of time after the first menses. Lancaster (1989a) suggests this was an evolutionary adaptation among human females: precisely because parental investment would take a high toll of the female during pregnancy and prolonged nursing, sexual maturation to the point of ovulation was postponed so that human females would be unlikely to become pregnant during adolescent growth, thus avoiding any maternal competition for energy with a developing fetus or a nursing infant. One reason for the increase in teenage pregnancy in recent decades is a consequence of the change in the timing of pubertal development. When girls first menstruated at fifteen or sixteen, adolescent subfertility provided a cushion of time after the first menstruation, during which sexual intercourse had little likelihood of resulting in a pregnancy because the girl did not ovulate regularly for up to two years following the first menses. With age at menarche now averaging 12.6 years, by fifteen most girls are ovulating regularly and hence have a high probability of conceiving in the absence of contraceptive protection.

Sexual dimorphism. The human primate has fewer differences in body size and bulk by sex than many other mammals, but there are nonetheless several striking differences between the human male and female bodies. To carry a fetus to term in an upright mammal involves gravitational pressure against the pelvic floor that could lead to miscarriage or premature birth. The elevated sex hormone levels of the human female guards against this through higher levels of progesterone during pregnancy. But because hormones tend to have a harmonious relation to each other, humans also have comparatively higher levels of other sex hormones, estrogens and androgens. Clearly there are several striking features of human males and females compared to nonhuman primates: prominent and permanent breasts and greater fat deposits in the buttock and thigh zones of the female body, larger penises and greater muscle strength in the upper arms and shoulders of the male body. Elevated androgen levels also increase sexual arousability in both sexes and contribute to the loss of seasonally bound sexual interest and availability of men and women compared to other mammals. Humans are easily turned on sexual creatures year round. One must be cautious here because the image of ourselves as highly sexual creatures is so congenial to adults in contemporary Western societies. As Short (1976) and more recently Small (1992) have pointed out, compared to many male mammals, the human male has small testes and low sperm counts. In addition, for most of human history, there have been numerous cultural prohibitions of sexual activity—for example, during pregnancy and lactation, seasons of the year, or a large proportion of the life span.

The combination of prematurely born fragile human infants and a prolonged period of juvenile dependency is considered by evolutionary biologists to be critical to mate-selection criteria and the structure of the human family. What the female (or her family on her behalf) sought was a mate with sufficient resources (strength, worldly goods—or competence in obtaining them—and social status) to assure that she could bear children and carry responsibility for them for the long years until they were mature and capable of reproduction themselves. By contrast, what the male sought (or his family for him) was a mate with good health, sexual attractiveness by the standards culturally deemed desirable, and some promise of fertility. The widespread restrictions on young females via cultural preferences for chastity or patterns of chaperonage of sexually mature unmarried girls and women compensate for the fact that paternity is not readily determined but a matter of trust or circumstantial evidence. The further implication is greater sexual con-

servatism of the female than the male where sexual contacts are concerned. Because the consequences of a possible pregnancy are largely
the female's to bear, women are less likely to engage in casual sexual
encounters than are men.

Once again, a word of caution is called for concerning this gender
difference. Evolutionary analysis does not imply greater male interest in
sexual variety and greater female interest in stable monogamy. For one
thing, females are only fertile for a restricted time period (ovulation);
males are always potentially fertile. More important, evolutionary reasoning centers not on sex but on successful reproduction. In this context, male reproductive success is as dependent on parental care of dependent young as female reproductive success is (Small 1992). As Irons
(1983) and Lancaster and Lancaster (1983) have argued, the human
mating system evolved as one of reciprocity, with both male and female
cooperating in procreation and the rearing of dependent offspring.

It might be argued that this profile may have applied to earlier stages
of human evolution, but surely it no longer applies to a modern society
where women are capable of supporting themselves, can use effective
contraception, and have several options if faced with an unwanted pregnancy (abortion, adoption, welfare dependency, or support from family
and kin in rearing the child, if not marriage to the father). I suggest
there is a variety of evidence that there continue to be long-standing
sex differences and mate-selection preferences in support of the general
evolutionary thesis. It is to an array of such evidence that I now turn.

Physical Appearance and Attractiveness

Relatively little research was conducted on physical appearance and
attractiveness prior to the 1970s. Linda Jackson points to Gardner Lindzey's presidential address in 1965 to the division of personality and social psychology of the American Psychological Association on physical
morphology and social behavior as a critical marker of a new era of
research attention to physical appearance (Jackson 1992; Lindzey 1965).
Lindzey suggested that physical appearance and body characteristics
might have been more important influences on personality and social
behavior than the psychological variables with which personality psychologists were preoccupied in the 1960s. Eliot Aronson (1969) suggested one reason for the research neglect of physical attractiveness
might be that it was somehow undemocratic because body shape and
sexual attractiveness are more likely to be governed by one's genes than
by social variables that allowed for change, and one's looks ought not

to be relevant in a democratic society premised on merit and individual competence.

Whatever the complex of reasons for the earlier neglect of the topic, there has been an exponential growth of studies of physical appearance and attractiveness in the past two decades. Indeed, several volumes have been published that summarize research findings on the topic: in order of their appearance, Mark Cook and George Wilson's *Love and Attraction* (1979), Gordon Patzer's *The Physical Attractiveness Phenomena* (1985), Elaine Hatfield and Susan Sprecher's *Mirror, Mirror . . . The Importance of Looks in Everyday Life* (1986), and, most recently, Linda Jackson's *Physical Appearance and Gender: Sociobiological and Sociocultural Perspectives* (1992). Among the most general findings from this genre of research are the following:

1. There is very high social consensus in ratings of attractiveness at any stage of life, ratings unaffected by either the age of the subjects rated (young children vs. older adults) or by the age of the raters themselves (from school-age children to elderly adults over sixty-five years).

2. Young adults are rated higher on attractiveness than older adults.

3. Age has a greater role in attractiveness ratings of women than of men. Women are seen as maximally attractive in the age range of maximal reproductive potential (Jackson 1992; Nowak 1977). By contrast, from youth to midlife, aging has a more favorable effect on the attractiveness ratings of men: older men are seen as having more character and as being more conscientious, responsible, and distinguished than younger men (Alley 1988).

4. Facial attractiveness ratings are more stable across the life span than body attractiveness ratings (Cross and Cross 1971; Jones and Adams 1982). In one interesting study, Gerald Adams (1977) had students dig up old family photos of their parents wearing swimsuits at three stages of their lives: as adolescents (sixteen to twenty), as young married adults (thirty to thirty-five), and as middle-aged adults (forty-five to fifty). When random sets of photos were rated on an attractiveness scale, Adams found much less stability in *body* attractiveness across the three phases of the life span than *facial* attractiveness: once a pretty (or handsome) face, always a pretty (or handsome) face, but body shape is subject to far greater change in attractiveness with increasing age.

5. There is high social consensus on the importance of physical attractiveness for friendship formation, marriage selection, marital happiness, and general success in life. In fact, older people were more likely to believe physical attractiveness was important to life chances than were

younger people. Hatfield and Sprecher comment that "possibly as men and women get older they encounter more and more experiences demonstrating the importance of physical attractiveness" (Hatfield and Sprecher 1986, 287).

6. There has been little change over the past several decades in the role of physical attractiveness for judgments of desired qualities in a cross-sex partner (for dating, as for marriage). On the basis of five decades of research on this topic, Hatfield and Sprecher (1986) found a stable tendency for physical attractiveness to be considered of greater importance to women than to men, particularly in ratings by men concerning women. They suggest that, if anything, men consider physical attractiveness in potential dates and mates more important now than in the past, perhaps because other mate characteristics such as being a good cook or seamstress have become less important considerations in marriage than they used to be.

7. The appeal of attractiveness begins at an extremely young age. As early as three months, infants look longer at faces rated by adults as high on attractiveness than they do at faces rated as unattractive (Hildebrandt 1982; Langlois et al. 1987). By twelve months infants show more negative affect (by withdrawal or less involvement in play) toward strangers wearing unattractive masks than toward those wearing attractive masks (reported in Jackson [1992, 75]). Langlois and Roggman (1990) underline the importance of these results with babies under a year old because they clearly have not yet been exposed to cultural standards of beauty. The reciprocal also holds—namely, that adults gaze longer at babies seen as cute than at less attractive babies. Indeed, ethologist Konrad Lorenz (1943) argued that facial features associated with infant cuteness (large forehead, eyes, and pupils; small features and narrow faces below eye level) trigger very positive responses from adults that in turn promote caregiving behavior.

8. Women are less satisfied with their bodies than men are, and being unattractive in their own self-ratings has a greater effect on their self-esteem than is the case with men (Jackson 1992). The pervasive concern shown by female adolescents as well as adult women with their weight is a major source of self-dissatisfaction.

Concern among women about weight, and hence with food intake, is nothing new. In fact women's association with food—its growth or purchase and preparation—is universal across time and culture, to say nothing of the association of the female with the nursing of infants. But in Western history, there has been a significant change in the meaning and purpose of fasting and dieting. In the past, religious fasting aimed at the attainment of personal salvation through an internal spiritual state, for example, nineteenth-century *anorexia mirabilis;* food abstention was often a necessary preparation for tasting the spiritual food of the Eucharist (Bynum 1987). Extreme fasting today pursues the same goal of perfection, but the locus has been displaced from an internal state of grace to a focus on external bodily configuration, and a cultural standard of extreme thinness, for example, twentieth-century *anorexia nervosa* (Bell 1985; Brumberg 1988).

The emergence in recent years of a fitness and exercise cult adds further to public preoccupation with weight: both parsimonious eating and habitual exercise is increasingly sanctioned among middle- and upper-class followers of the new religion of health. It has been estimated that upward of 80 percent of American women periodically subject themselves to one diet plan or another, almost all of which are unsuccessful (Bray 1987; Brown 1991). Once a diet is abandoned, weight is quickly gained back. Yet in 1991, eight million people enrolled in commercial weight-loss programs, generating revenues in excess of two billion dollars. Concern for excessive dieting led the National Institute of Health to sponsor a conference on the issue. Its panel of experts noted the widespread recourse to dieting and its poor outcome; the experts argued that it could not be otherwise because there is increasing evidence that being overweight is not a matter of lack of willpower but is to a large extent governed by physiological, biochemical, and genetic influences. Thomas Wadden, a weight specialist at Syracuse University, believes the human body is programmed to defend a particular weight range or a certain amount of stored body fat, a set point difficult to alter by conscious efforts at weight reduction (See three-part series on fatness in *New York Times* [1992]).

Despite the greater concern for being overweight and more frequent recourse to dieting among women than among men, data from a U.S. Health and Nutrition Examination survey shows that at all ages, the percent of women who exceed so-called acceptable weight by 20 percent or more is significantly greater than the comparable percent among men, and the gender difference increases with age (Abraham and John 1979; cited in Hatfield and Sprecher 1986, 206). For example, among adults between thirty-five and forty-four, 17 percent of the men but 24 percent of the women exceeded weight norms for their age and gender by 20 percent or more; among those fifty-five to sixty-four, the counterpart figures were 15 percent of the men and 35 percent of the women.

It is also the case that what women seek in efforts to change their bodies varies by the part of the body involved: most women seek a smaller waistline, narrower hips, and slimmer thighs, but some women seek to enlarge the size of their breasts by silicone implants or exercise. In evolutionary terms, fat storage in the buttocks and thighs clearly subserve reproductive functions, not so much for fetal growth as for lactation purposes. Lancaster (1989a) and Peacock (1991) suggest an evolutionary selection for building up lactation stores first, before energy used for fetal growth can be released, the rationale being that in early human evolution, there was no reason to give birth to a newborn if there would be inadequate lactation for infant survival (Abell 1992). There are, in other words, genetic reasons rooted in our evolutionary heritage, for the great difficulty of losing weight today. In the past, human preferences for dietary fat and sugar permitted fat storage in the context of severe periodic food scarcities (Brown 1991). In Western societies today, with their economic affluence and constant food surpluses, such genetic residues are maladaptive but extremely difficult to overcome. Hence, contemporary women have less need of fat storage for lactation purposes but may well be running up against a phylogenetic brick wall in excessive attempts to attain very slim hips and thighs.

The same phylogenetic barrier may also exist where the timing of pregnancies is concerned. I noted earlier that prolonged nursing of infants in hunter-gatherer societies suppressed ovulation and assured an adequate recovery and replenishment of women's bodies before another pregnancy imposed a period of drain on physical resources. With greatly increased nutrition and improved general health, one might think modern women can safely time their births far more closely together. Indeed, many contemporary professional women do precisely this in order to restrict early childbearing and rearing to a short period of their adult lives. But Taffel's study (1989) of U.S. data found the largest single risk factor for low-birth-weight infants was birth interval: the shorter the interval, the higher the incidence of low-birth-weight babies. This is particularly true for African-American women, who are twice as likely as European and American white women to have birth intervals of less than twelve months. For all our improved nutrition and health care, the female body requires time to regain normal physiological processes and general stamina that pregnancy alters dramatically (Abell 1992).

Evolutionary biology has relevance as well to the *timing* of childbearing in the life span of women. The biggest risk factor for breast cancer in women is remaining childless or having a first child over the age of thirty. The fact that ovulation and menstruation averaged only two years among hunter-gatherer women compared to the thirty-five years of modern women suggests that the control mechanisms for ovulation did not evolve in the context of consecutive unfertilized menstrual cycles but in the hormonal and environmental context of pregnancy, birth, and lactation and during the maximally fertile phases of the reproductive years, the early twenties. Indirect evidence can be inferred where breast cancer is concerned from animal studies, which show that pregnancy alters breast tissue, making it less susceptible to cancerous changes. Walter Willett of the Harvard School of Public Health suggests that one way to reduce the risk of breast cancer for women who remain childless or want to time their pregnancies in their thirties would be to develop synthetic hormones that mimic the physiological conditions of pregnancy, a kind of false pregnancy (Allison 1992). We are a long way from developing such a chemical compensation, and the example is offered here only to underline the point that there are limits to the biological capacities of human males and females to adapt, without cost, to dramatic changes in social and economic circumstances.

GENDER, SEXUAL BEHAVIOR, AND MATE CHOICE

I suggest it is precisely in matters bearing on sexual and reproductive functions that we may be witnessing a growing gap between what our hearts and minds desire and what our bodies predispose us to. The review above on the role of physical attractiveness is further buttressed by gender differences in sexual behavior and mate preferences. Despite the very extensive political pressures to changes in the relations between men and women in the direction of greater equality of options and minimization of differences thought to be rooted in social custom and personal habit, there continue to be differences by gender in sexual behavior and mate choice. Height differences provide an interesting example. Women prefer men who are taller than themselves, and men prefer women shorter. In fact, Gillis and Avis (1980) report a difference of 6 inches in women's preferences for a mate's height compared to their own height, and 4.5 inches in men's preferences for a wife's height compared to their own. Nor is this a matter just of preferences rather than behavior. The same researchers examined bank applications for accounts that included information on the height of husbands and wives applying for joint checking accounts. If paired up randomly, one couple in twenty-nine would have a wife taller than her husband, but Gillis and

Avis report the bank records showed only one in 720 couples that included a woman taller than her husband.

Why should this height difference continue to be shown in contemporary data? And why do we continue to find age differences between husbands and wives, age differences that increase in marriages contracted following divorce? (Davis and van den Oever 1982). And why do we continue to find the highest proportion of never-married and divorced women among the most well-educated women; whereas the highest proportion of never-married men are found among those with the least education and the most erratic employment history? There are no doubt many sociocultural factors at work in producing these patterns, but it also seems likely that sociobiological factors are relevant: greater size, older age, more education, and higher income are indices of precisely the male resources needed to provide for the long period of infant fragility and juvenile dependency that follows when sexual attraction is translated into marriage formation and childbearing. Now that the majority of women are cobreadwinners along with men, female economic dependency plays a lesser role in marriage formation, and more women may opt to have children out of wedlock and in time, perhaps to marry men younger, shorter, and less capable of higher earnings than themselves, but for the foreseeable future, old preference patterns in mate choice are likely to persist, and those pioneers who depart from traditional customs may pay a price, in the form of fewer appropriate mates, marital discord, and divorce. A generation ago, social pressures opposed married women's employment except on a contingency basis (wartime, or when husbands are ill, unemployed, or dead). Today, cobreadwinning is taken for granted, although typically with wives earning far less than their husbands. It may be a long time before higher job status and earnings by a wife compared to her husband will be desired rather than experienced as threatening to male self-esteem (Rossi 1993).

The contemporary pattern of African-American fertility is a good example of the departure from the traditional confinement of births to marriage. Social concern for the fact that the majority of African-American births take place outside marriage has been widely discussed and analyzed. But to urge African-American teenage girls to postpone sexual initiation and pregnancies to an older age is shortsighted and neglects the fact that such postponement does not necessarily improve an African-American woman's life chances or even assure greater maternal health. Compared to a white woman, an African-American woman does not significantly increase her chances for a stable marriage to a man who commands good material resources if she postpones marriage and pregnancies. Unemployment, early death, and imprisonment reduce the pool of available African-American men capable of making the parental investment African-American women seek in a husband. Furthermore, infant mortality is actually *lower* for infants born to African-American mothers during their teenage years than at any other age. Infant mortality in fact rises in a unilinear fashion with increasing maternal age among African-American women. Geronimus (1987, 1991) and Lancaster (1989b, and chap. 2, this volume) suggest maternal age is a surrogate measure for the progressive deterioration of maternal health resulting from the poor nutrition, social and psychological stress, and inadequate health care that are associated with poverty in today's African-American communities.

But out of wedlock births are not restricted to the bottom of the socioeconomic hierarchy. Although the evidence is less firm, there are numerous hints of well-educated career women seeking pregnancies outside of marriage, a pattern made possible in our day by new methods of artificial reproduction via known sperm donors, resorting to sperm banks, or simply engaging in coitus for the purpose of pregnancy with no intention of marriage. I have known several professional women who sought to become pregnant by timing their trips abroad to include the ovulatory phase of their menstrual cycles and who traveled to countries where men possessed physical characteristics they valued. Interestingly, height was one such consideration, and Scandinavian countries were among their destinations.

These are clearly revealing but exceptional cases. For the majority of women and men, an important life goal in their youth is a heterosexual marriage, and preferences in the choice of a sexual partner and eventually a marital partner continue to show persistent gender differences. Men and women both seek responsible, healthy, sociable, and attractive partners, but the balance in their preferences continues to show significant differences as well. As reported above, physical attractiveness of a partner is deemed more important to men, and resources and status are more important to women (cf. also, Berscheid and Walster 1972, 1978; Feingold 1988, 1990). Beauty queens, models and actresses frequently marry men of wealth and status, but few women of independent wealth they earn themselves marry men of a lower status than their own, Elizabeth Taylor's current spouse notwithstanding.

There are of course many differences across cultures in the symbols of beauty as there are of wealth: shells, cows, land, or bonds in the latter case; breasts, buttocks, skin color, hair in the former case. But beneath such cultural specifics, the linkage in preference and behavior among women is to male resources, and among men to female beauty and health, for which youth is often a proxy (Buss 1985, 1989; Cook and Wilson 1979; Kenrick 1989, Kenrick and Trost 1986; Rosenblatt and Anderson 1981; Small 1992). As I argued in an earlier section, this contrast is rooted in sex differences in reproductive strategies, and, like losing weight, there are long-standing, genetically based tendencies that resist or make difficult societal and individual efforts at change.

Women are also by far the more conservative of the two sexes where casual sex encounters are concerned. The most dramatic example of this contrast that I have found is an unpublished study conducted by Russell Clark and Elaine Hatfield in 1981 (reported in Hatfield and Sprecher [1986, 136–37]). The study involved selecting college men and women to help run an experiment in which they were to approach members of the opposite sex on campus and strike up a conversation that began with "I have been noticing you around campus and I find you very attractive." That said, the experiment involved asking one of three questions: "Would you go out with me tonight?" or "Would you come over to my apartment tonight?" or "Would you go to bed with me tonight?"

Hatfield reports no significant differences in positive responses to an invitation to a date that evening: 56 percent of the women approached by men complied, and 50 percent of the men approached by women. But dramatic gender differences were found for compliance to the other two invitations: 69 percent of the men approached by a women agreed to visit her apartment, but only 6 percent of the women approached by a man would comply in this way. And on the boldest approach, an invitation to bed down together that night, no woman accepted the invitation, but 75 percent of the men accepted the women's invitation.

I think there are deep psychobiological factors at play in results such as these consistent with a fundamental sex difference: it is women who bear the burden of pregnancies that may result from sexual behavior, and, despite the availability of effective contraception, conservative choices in sex behavior are more prevalent among women than among men. We should not frame the issues in sexual research in too narrow a framework. Clearly there have been significant trends toward narrowing the gap between men and women in acceptance of and indulgence in nonmarital sex (both pre- and extramarital), as Tom Smith reports in this volume (chap. 3). But long-standing sex and gender differences in psychological characteristics may be of greater significance, evidence for which comes far more in research on topics *other than* sexuality than in sex research more narrowly defined. It is to such issues that I now turn.

FROM EROS TO CARITAS

I shall begin this discussion of gender differences in the experience of intimacy and sexuality with two poems. See whether you share my sense of the similarities and differences between them.

The One
the one
long hair in my beard
this morning
makes me smile:
it's yours
(Anselm Hollo [1968], quoted in Chester [1992], 82)

True Love
In the middle of the night, when we get up
after making love, we look at each other
in total friendship, we know so fully
what the other has been doing. . . .
. . . we weave through the dark
soft air, I know where you are
with my eyes closed, we are bound to each other with the
huge invisible threads of sex, though our
sexes themselves are muted, dark and
exhausted and delicately crushed, the whole
body is sex—surely this
is the most blessed time of life,
the children deep asleep in their beds like a
vein of coal and a vein of gold
not discovered yet. I sit on the
toilet in the dark, you are somewhere in the room, I
open the window and the snow has fallen in a
deep drift against the pane, I
look up into it, a
world of crystals, silent and
glistening so I call out to you and you

come and hold my hand and I say
I cannot see beyond it! I cannot see beyond it!

(Sharon Olds, quoted in Chester [1992], 244)

Both poems refer to the aftermath of sex and provide subtle hints of joy and physical pleasure in a sexual encounter. No graphic sexual gymnastics are portrayed as they are in much current literature and TV dramas; no slurpy sounds nor orgasmic gasps, and no conquests. Both offer a window on an intimate relationship between a man and a woman. But there are differences as well, and I suggest they are rooted in the fact that the first poem is written by a man and the second by a woman. Anselm Hollo uses a physical metaphor for the woman in his life, her long hair in his beard, and smiles with pleasure in a recollection of how it got there. But the experience is *his* experience, with no hint of what might be shared with his lover apart from the sexual bond. Sharon Olds, by contrast, places her primary emphasis on the relationship: *we* made love, *we* weave down the hall, *we* are bound to each other and to our two children—the "vein of coal" and a "vein of gold"—and beyond that snug family unit on a winter's night, some unknown, or unknowable linkage to a mysterious beyond—"I cannot see beyond it." *Eros*—romantic love—is present in both poems. *Caritas*—loving kindness and attachment—predominates only in Sharon Olds' poem.

Two such highly selected single examples hardly provide any firm evidence concerning more general sex differences. They were selected to *illustrate,* in a very parsimonious way, what a literature review continues to show, not only about intimacy and sexuality but also of general personality characteristics and developmental issues confronted by men and women in adulthood, sex differences grounded in a more general tendency for men to value independence and autonomy and women to value relationships and connections. The construct labels vary from one specialty to another: independence, dominance, autonomy, instrumentality, agency, masculinity in one direction; dependence, relatedness, expressivity, affiliation, connections, nurturance, communion and femininity in the other direction. As many recent psychologists have suggested, there was in the past a tendency to equate maturity in adulthood with the qualities associated with men—independence and autonomy. By contrast, current developmental theories stress the importance of a balance between autonomy and affiliation (Belenky et al. 1986; Gilligan 1982; Gilligan, Ward, and Taylor 1988; Gilligan, Lyons, and Hanmer 1990; Henry 1988; McAdams 1985; Reinisch, Rosenblum, and Sanders 1987; Waterman and Whitbourne 1982). In one recent re-formulation, Margret Baltes and Susan Silverberg describe the current emphasis on *interdependence,* a balance of dependency and indepen-dence: "Being dependent here means that one has an effect on others as the others on oneself; it does not imply being helpless, powerless or without control. In this sense, interdependence—the willingness to help and to care and be helped and cared for—empowers both the self and the other" (Baltes and Silverberg 1992, 33).

But although it is inspiring to observe psychologists getting their conceptual house in order in this way, in the real lives of men and women in the 1990s, it is no easy matter to resocialize themselves away from the traditional equations of dominance and autonomy = male and nurturance and affiliation = female. The most ardent feminist and the tenderest of men carry residues of the old traditional ways, and we cannot yet know to what extent our cognitive reformulations can con-trol and redirect the quite different messages that stem from earlier emotional layers of our personalities, resist the pressures imposed by external roles we need to fill in society, or cope with opposing predispo-sitions laid down in the biology we have inherited. Judith Bardwick sen-sitively captured the transitional quality of gender role change taking place some fourteen years ago (Bardwick 1979), in a discussion of the reassurance today's men and women may need about their masculinity and femininity, as they move toward greater acceptance of interdepen-dence. Although rejecting anything approximating "motorcycle ma-chismo," she suggests that men may need room to express some "male initiative, some particular responsibility which conveys the message, 'I am protecting you,'" which affirms the "masculinity of the male and the femininity of the female and are therefore sexy" (Bardwick 1979, 117).

There are also larger societal issues involved. Physical strength no longer matters in the worlds of work and politics as it once did, and with the increasing technical complexity of the machinery of war, physical strength is less important in the military as well. The fall from grace and status that male physical strength has undergone may partially explain the increasing attraction professional sports have to the American imag-ination, one of the few arenas in which strength and agility remain of primary importance. As Elizabeth Fox-Genovese points out, many men, frustrated by a world in which they have lost a good deal of control through an erosion of their socioeconomic advantages and the social irrelevance of their physical superiority, may be increasingly tempted to use that strength in the one situation in which it still clearly gives them an advantage—their personal and sexual relations with women. Were that to develop, Fox-Genovese suggests, we would face a "tragedy of massive proportions" (Fox-Genovese 1991, 255).

This takes on very special significance in a society still hesitant to engage in frank and open discussions of sexuality, a tragedy in the case of public education on how to avoid exposure to the AIDS virus, and a barrier to solving problems in intimate sexual relationships. Having taught undergraduate courses on human sexuality for more than a dozen years, I know firsthand how difficult communication about personal sexual issues is for even today's young adults. On numerous occasions, students discussed with me, aspects of sexuality that they did not feel free to discuss with their partners.

We know very little about either the verbal or nonverbal signals partners rely on to indicate sexual interest or unavailability. From several studies it seems clear that nonverbal cues are often relied on, though in stable marital relationships open verbal suggestions are more common. All evidence to date suggests men initiate sexual interaction in both marital and cohabiting relationships more frequently than women do (Blumstein and Schwartz 1983; Brown and Auerback 1981; Byers and Heinlein 1989), although it is not known whether this is purely a cultural sexual script or an indication of stronger sex drives in men. In one sensitive story, John Fante mused about the change in his wife following the birth of their first child, remembering, "She used to use some magic called Fernery at Twilight. It was like breathing Chopin and Edna Millay, and when its fragrance rose from her hair and shoulders I knew *the flag was up and that she had chosen to be pursued*" [emphasis added] (Fante [1988], in Chester [1992], 91). Note the nonverbal cue provided by the wife and the fact that she was inviting pursuit, not playing the overt role of pursuer. Several sex researchers have suggested that such nonverbal signals do not necessarily reflect embarrassment about communication concerning sex, but are a gentle way to indicate or to accept rejection by merely not recognizing that the "flag was up" (Cupach and Metts 1986, 1991; O'Brien 1981). Overall, however, the bulk of research on intimate sexual relationships has been limited to small samples of dating among college students, or the data were obtained from only one partner in the relationship (Cook and Wilson 1979; Peplau and Gordon 1985; Rubin 1973). The first edited volume of papers explicitly focused on sexuality in close relationships was published only in 1991 (McKinney and Sprecher 1991).

One interesting small study by Sandra Metts and William Cupach

(1991) did ask married individuals to describe the sexual aspect of their marriages. They report that women were more likely than men to mention comfort, responsiveness, specialness, and communication associated with sex; whereas men were more likely than women to speak in terms of frequency and arousal, suggesting that men thought of their sexual relationship in physical terms while women saw sexual gratification tied closely to relationship intimacy. Here we see yet again the familiar distinction between the female's stress on the emotional relationship and the male's stress on performance. Little wonder, then, that one often hears the view that men want to make love as a means of making up after a quarrel; whereas women want to discuss the problem through to a solution before they make love.

In a qualitative study of sexual experiences in England, Jackie Gilfoyle and her colleagues (Gilfoyle, Wilson, and Brown 1992) provide some dramatic current examples of the male stress on sexual performance: asked about the importance of a woman experiencing an orgasm, one young man reported he didn't like to "leave a job half finished"; a woman reported in similar terms that her partner was upset if she didn't have an orgasm because "he didn't feel he had done a good enough job." Gilfoyle points out that even in the new sexual script—described as a "reciprocal gift pattern" in which female as well as male gratification is the goal of a sexual encounter—the male is the active initiator, abrogating to himself even the power to *give* a woman an orgasm.

In this same study, the researchers asked their informants to fill in the blank in a sentence that read, "A penis is to a man what a____ is to a woman." Men had no trouble with the task, almost all referring either to a clitoris or a vagina. Women, by contrast, resisted giving any simple answer, objecting that it was not a matter of one tiny organ but far more diffuse—that is, for them sex was only one outlet to express and experience a better, deeper feeling of intimacy. No man in the study spoke in terms of intimacy: sex for them was a matter of drive, vigor, and technique.

One other research finding illustrates the persistence of the underlying distinction between control and autonomy on the one hand and affiliation and connection on the other that differentiates men from women. In this instance, it is a study of work and stress: Cynthia Piltch (1992a, 1992b) studied 2,000 men and 670 women industrial workers in a large New England manufacturing firm, to compare work-related factors associated with increased mental distress symptoms such as depression, anxiety, and sleep disorder. She found that for *both* men and women, job stress and an imbalance between work and outside obligations were strongly associated with increased mental distress. But beyond this, there were significant gender differences. What triggered work stress for men was a *lack of control* over what they did on their jobs; for women it was minimal or *no social support* on the job that triggered work stress. Further, men and women differed in how they coped with job stress: Men sought help from supervisors at work (presumably in an effort to obtain more control over what they did) more than support from their wives; whereas women considered spousal support, together with talking with friends and relatives, as the best coping device to reduce stress induced by their jobs.

One last example comes from a longitudinal study of men and women in medical school at the University of Michigan (Inglehart and Brown 1990; Inglehart, Brown, and Malanchuk 1993): the more men perceived the medical school environment as competitive early in the program, the *better* they performed later on, but the more women saw the program as competitive, the *worse* they performed in the long run. The researchers report that the reason for this pattern is that men and women link different issues with competition: men saw competitive situations as a challenge and an opportunity to demonstrate their skills; women associated competitive situations with a lack of social support that made them more uncomfortable and hence impaired their performance.

Results such as these strongly suggest that there is a long way to go before men and women show an equitable balance between autonomy and affiliation to approximate the interdependence or androgyny model of healthy, mature adult development currently being stressed by developmental psychologists. Despite some social change in this direction, there continue to be significant differences between the sexes in what they seek in sexual relations, and in their definitions of intimacy or emotional closeness. As Harry Brod put it (1987; cited in Fisher [1992]), men define emotional closeness as working or playing side by side; women view it as talking face to face.

We should perhaps also take into consideration, some underlying biological predispositions that may play a role in this distinction between men's emphasis on activity and women's on talk as the mark of emotional closeness because activity draws on a persistent male edge in spatial skills and shoulder strength, and talk on a persistent female edge in verbal skills. There is more than socioenvironmental factors involved in this gender difference. In tests 'of verbal abilities, women perform better during the ovulatory phase of their menstrual cycles, when estrogen is at a peak, and least well directly after menses, when estrogen levels are low (Fisher 1992, especially 155–56; Kimura 1983, 1989; Moir and Jessel 1989). And among males, pubescent boys with low testosterone levels do poorly on spatial tasks, and men with an extra X or Y chromosome show similar effects of testosterone level upon performance on spatial (and math) tasks: Men with an extra Y chromosome (XYY), hence with *higher* levels of testosterone than normal men, score *higher* on these tests; men with a extra X chromosome (XXY), hence with *lower* testosterone levels than normal men, score significantly *lower* on these spatial tests. Although there is no reason to think such differences cannot be minimized by special compensatory training, it is probably unrealistic to anticipate any change in school curricula for such a purpose in the near future.

Basic brain chemistry may also be a factor in what has been endlessly discussed in purely social and psychological terms: the difference between *attraction* and *infatuation* (the *eros* metaphor in this chapter's title) early in the development of an intimate relationship, typically of rather short duration, and the more long lasting emotion of *attachment* (the *caritas* metaphor in the chapter's title). Michael Liebowitz (1983) claims there are distinctly different chemical processes in the brain in these two feeling states: the euphoria, excitement, and energy involved in the early stages of an infatuation, when we find it difficult to think of anything else but the one we love, and when we have the energy to spend whole nights in intimate exchange and yet put in a regular day's work, are an experience probably facilitated by the production of endogenous *amphetamines* in the brain's emotional centers in the limbic system. By contrast, as infatuation wanes, and attachment predominates, *endorphins* in the brain undergo a surge. These natural morphinelike substances may have a calming effect we associate with the emotions of attachment, and sensations of security and peace.

These two quite distinct neural processes are critical for human survival, so once again, we can make a linkage from contemporary biology and socioemotional behavior to our evolutionary heritage as a mammalian species: the *infatuation* of males and females attracted to each other long enough to have sex and reproduce; and *attachment* to each other and their offspring to provide the stability necessary for the provision of food and protection of the young until they reach maturity. As John McKinlay and Henry Feldman report (chap. 10, this volume), the frequency of sexual intercourse goes down linearly across the life course; satisfaction with sex does not. What we earlier viewed as a potential disjuncture between sexual experience and satisfaction among older adults may be explained in part by the calming effect of brain endorphins among long-married couples. By the same process, the loss of a loved partner and hence of a deep attachment means a reduction of the endogenous endorphins that had bathed and calmed our nervous system. This may also help explain why many married adults find themselves edgy and irritable when separated from each other for more than a few days.

Conclusion

Throughout this chapter I have stressed the importance of bringing together all levels of potential relevance to issues we wish to understand: from biology, psychology, sociology, history, and literature. Biological and sociobehavioral factors are in no sense opposed to each other; they are intertwined and inseparable as factors in real life and ought to be viewed as complementary rather than contradictory.

At the same time, one must cope with the fact that political and ideological commitments often motivate research and scholarship. Sex and gender are not merely of deep personal concern to us all but are also of great political and economic salience. Gender is on the way to becoming irrelevant in work and politics, and widened options for choice may lead eventually to little or no difference in the participation, rank, and salary of women and men in the workplace and in politics. On the other hand, I agree with those who believe that much of the richness and joy of life come from the differences between men and women, and our goal might better be an appreciation of each sex for the other. Feminist scholarship and politics come in many stripes. In the best of it, in my judgment, we are trying to define, as Elizabeth Fox-Genovese put it, the spaces between the similarities and the differences between men and women, spaces within which we can criticize the excesses of individualism and urge a new conception of community (Fox-Genovese 1991, 256). It is toward that end that an integration of all the relevant sciences to an understanding of sex and gender, sexuality and reproduction, is aimed. *Caritas* may remain more congenial to the female of the species than to the male, but differences such as these ought not to be repudiated; rather, they should be used to understand how their consequences can be made equitable and just.

REFERENCES

Abell, T. D. 1992. Low birth weight, intra-uterine growth-retarded, and pre-term infants. *Human Nature* 3:335–78.

Abraham, S. and C. L. John. 1979. Overweight adults in the United States. *Advanced Data from Vital and Health Statistics of the National Center for Health Statistics.* (U.S. Department of Health, Education, and Welfare) 51 (August 30): 1–10.

Adams, G. R. 1977. Physical attractiveness, personality, and social reactions to peer pressure. *Journal of Psychology* 96:287–96.

Alley, T. R. 1988. The effects of growth and aging on facial aesthetics. In *Social and applied aspects of perceiving faces,* ed. T. R. Alley, 51–62. Hillsdale, N.J.: Erlbaum.

Allison, M. 1992. Breast cancer: Moving toward prevention. *Harvard Health Letter* 17 (August): 4–6.

Altmann, J. 1980. *Baboon mothers and infants.* Cambridge, Mass.: Harvard Univ. Press.

Ariès, P., and A. Béjin, eds. 1985. *Western sexuality: Practice and precept in past and present times.* New York: Blackwell.

Aronson, E. 1969. Some antecedents of interpersonal attraction. Volume 17 of *Nebraska Symposium on Motivation,* ed. W. J. Arnold and D. Levine. Lincoln: Univ. of Nebraska.

Baltes, M. M., and S. B. Silverberg. 1992. The dynamics between dependency and autonomy across the life-span. Unpublished.

Barbach, L. 1975. *For yourself: The fulfillment of female sexuality.* New York: Signet.

Bardwick, J. 1979. *In transition: How feminism, sexual liberation, and the search for self-fulfillment have altered America.* New York: Holt, Rinehart & Winston.

Belenky, M. F., B. M. Clinchy, N. R. Goldberg, and J. M. Tarule. 1986. *Women's ways of knowing: The development of self, voice, and mind.* New York: Basic.

Bell, R. M. 1985. *Holy Anorexia.* Chicago: Univ. of Chicago Press.

Berscheid, E., and E. H. Walster. 1972. Beauty and the best. *Psychology Today* 5:42–46.

———. 1978. *Interpersonal attraction.* 2d ed. Menlo Park, Calif.: Addison-Wesley.

Blumstein, P., and P. Schwartz. 1983. *American couples.* New York: Pocket.

Bray, G. A. 1987. Overweight is risking fate: Definition, classification, prevalence, and risks. *Human Obesity (Annals of the New York Academy of Sciences)* 499: 14–28.

Brod, H. 1987. Who benefits from male involvement in wife's pregnancy? *Marriage and Divorce Today* 12:3.

Brown, M., and A. Auerback. 1981. Communication patterns in initiation of marital sex. *Medical Aspects of Human Sexuality* 15:105–17.

Brown, P. J. 1991. Culture and the evaluation of obesity. *Human Nature* 2:31–58.

Brumberg, J. J. 1988. *Fasting girls: The emergence of anorexia nervosa as a modern disease.* Cambridge, Mass.: Harvard Univ. Press.

Burton, L. M. 1990. Teenage childbearing as an alternative life-course strategy in multigenerational black families. *Human Nature* 1:123–44.

Bush, T. L. 1992. Feminine forever revisited: Menopausal hormonal therapy in the 1990s. *Journal of Women's Health* 1:1–4.

Buss, D. M. 1985. Human mate selection. *American Scientist* 73:47–51.

———. 1989. Sex differences in human mate preferences: Evolutionary hypotheses tested in 37 cultures. *Behavioral and Brain Science* 12:1–49.

Byers, E. S., and L. Heinlein. 1989. Predicting initiations and refusals of activities in married and cohabiting heterosexual couples. *Journal of Sex Research* 26:210–31.

Bynum, C. W. 1987. *Holy feast and holy fast: The religious significance of food to medieval women.* Los Angeles: Univ. of California Press.

Cartledge, S., and J. Ryan. 1985. *Sex and love: New thoughts on old contradictions.* London: Woman's Press.

Chester, K., ed. 1992. *The unmade bed: Sensual writings on married love.* New York: HarperCollins.

Cook, M., and G. Wilson, eds. 1979. *Love and attraction.* Oxford: Pergamon.

Cross, J. F., and J. Cross. 1971. Age, sex, race, and the perception of facial beauty. *Developmental Psychology* 5:433–59.

Cupach, W. R., and S. Metts. 1986. Satisfaction with sexual communication in marriage: Links to sexual satisfaction and dyadic adjustment. *Communication Monographs* 53:311–34.

———. 1991. Sexuality and communication in close relationships. In *Sexuality in close relationships,* ed. K. McKinney and S. Sprecher, 93–110. Hillsdale, N.J.: Erlbaum.

Daly, M., and M. Wilson. 1978. *Sex, evolution, and behavior.* North Scituate, Mass.: Duxbury.

Davis, K., and P. van den Oever. 1982. Demographic foundations of new sex roles. *Population and Development Review* 8:495–511.

Deutsch, H. 1945. *The psychology of women.* Vol. 2, *Motherhood.* New York: Grune & Stratton.

Dyson, F. 1992. *From Eros to Gaia.* New York: Pantheon.

Fante, J. 1988. *Full of life.* Santa Rosa, Calif.: Black Sparrow.

Fedigan, L. M. 1986. The changing role of women in models of human evolution. *Annual Review of Anthropology* 15:25–66.

Feingold, A. 1988. Matching for attractiveness in romantic partners and same-sex friends: A meta-analysis and theoretical critique. *Psychological Bulletin* 104:226–35.

———. Gender differences in physical attractiveness on romantic attraction: Comparison across five research domains. *Journal of Personality and Social Psychology* 59:981–93.

Fisher, H. E. 1992. *Anatomy of love: The natural history of monogamy, adultery, and divorce.* New York: Norton.

Foucault, M. 1978. *The history of sexuality.* Vol. 1, *An introduction.* New York: Pantheon.

Fox-Genovese, E. 1991. *Feminism without illusions: A critique of individualism.* Chapel Hill, N.C.: Univ. of North Carolina Press.

Gagnon, J. H., and W. Simon. 1973. *Sexual conduct: The social sources of human sexuality.* Chicago: Aldine.

Gergen, K. J. 1985. The social constructionist movement in modern psychology. *American Psychologist* 40:266–75.

Geronimus, A. T. 1987. On teenage childbearing and neonatal mortality in the United States. *Population and Development Review* 13: 245–79.

———. 1991. Teenage childbearing and reproductive disadvantage: The evolution of complex questions and the demise of simple answers. *Family Relations* 40:463–71.

Gilfoyle, J., J. Wilson, and Brown. 1992. Sex, organs, and audiotape: A discourse analytic approach to talking about heterosexual sex and relationships. *Feminism and Psychology* 2:209–30.

Gilligan, C. 1982. *In a different voice.* Cambridge, Mass.: Harvard Univ. Press.

Gilligan, C., N. P. Lyons, and T. J. Hanmer. 1990. *Making connections: The relational worlds of adolescent girls at Emma Willard School.* Cambridge, Mass.: Harvard Univ. Press.

Gilligan, C., J. V. Ward, and J. M. Taylor. 1988. *Mapping the moral domain.* Cambridge, Mass.: Harvard Univ. Press.

Gillis, J. S., and W. E. Avis. 1980. The male-taller norm in mate selection. *Personality and Socal Psychology Bulletin* 6:396–401.

Haraway, D. 1989. *Primate visions: Gender, race, and nature in the world of modern science.* New York: Routledge.

Hatfield, E., and S. Sprecher. 1986. *Mirror, mirror . . . The importance of looks in everyday life.* Albany: State Univ. of New York Press.

Henry, J. P. 1988. The archetypes of power and intimacy. In *Emergent theories of aging,* ed. J. Birren and V. Bengtson, 269–98. New York: Springer.

Hildebrandt, K. A. 1982. The role of physical appearance in infant and child development. In *Theory and research in behavioral pediatrics.* Vol. 1, ed. H. E. Fitzgerald, B. M. Lester and M. W. Vogman, 181–219. New York: Plenum.

Hill, H., and A. M. Hurtado. 1991. The evolution of premature reproductive senescence and menopause in human females: An evaluation of the "grandmother" hypothesis. *Human Nature* 2:313–50.

Hite, S. 1976. *The Hite report.* New York: Dell.

Hrdy, S. B. 1981. *The woman who never evolved.* Cambridge, Mass.: Harvard Univ. Press.

Hrdy, S. B., and P. L. Whitten. 1987. Patterning of sexual activity. In *Primate Societies,* ed. B. Smuts, D. Cheney, R. Seyfarth, R. Wrangham, and T. Struhsaker, 370–84. Chicago: Univ. of Chicago Press.

Hurtado, A. M., K. Hawkes, K. Hill, and H. Kaplan. 1985. Female subsistence strategies among Ache hunter-gatherers in eastern Paraguay. *Human Ecology* 13:1–28.

Hurtado, A. M., K. Hill, H. Kaplan, and I. Hurtado. 1992. Trade-offs between female food acquisition and child care among Hiwi and Ache foragers. *Human Nature* 3:185–216.

Inglehart, M., and D. R. Brown. 1990. Professional identity and academic achievement: Considerations for the admission process. *Journal of Academic Medicine* 65:S3–4.

Inglehart, M., D. R. Brown, and M. O. Malanchuk. 1993. University of Michigan Medical School graduates of the 1980s: The professional development of women physicians. In *Women's lives through time: Educated American women of the twentieth century,* ed. K. D. Hulbert and D. T. Schuster, 374–92. San Francisco: Jossey-Bass.

Irons, W. G. 1983. Human female reproductive strategies. In *Social behavior of female vertebrates,* ed. S. W. Wasser, 169–213. New York: Academic Press.

Jackson, L. A. 1992. *Physical appearance and gender: Sociobiological and sociocultural perspectives.* Albany: State Univ. of New York Press.

Jones, R. M., and G. R. Adams. 1982. Assessing the importance of physical attractiveness across the life-span. *The Journal of Social Psychology* 118:131–32.

Kenrick, D. T. 1989. Bridging social psychology and sociobiology: The case of sexual attraction. In *Sociobiology and the Social Sciences,* ed. R. W. Bell and N. J. Bell, 5–24. Lubbock, Tex.: Texas Tech Univ. Press.

Kenrick, D. T., and M. R. Trost. 1986. A biosocial model of heterosexual relationships. In *Males, females, and sexuality,* ed. D. Byrne and K. Kelley, 59–100. Albany: State Univ. of New York Press.

Kimura, D. 1983. Sex differences in cerebral organization for speech and praxic functions. *Canadian Journal of Psychology* 37:19–35.

———. 1989. How sex hormones boost or cut intellectual ability. *Psychology Today,* November, 63–66.

Kinsey, A. C., W. B. Pomeroy, and C. E. Martin. 1948. *Sexual behavior in the human male.* Philadelphia: Saunders.

Kinsey, A. C., W. B. Pomeroy, C. E. Martin, and P. H. Gebhard. 1953. *Sexual behavior in the human female.* Philadelphia: Saunders.

Lancaster, J. B. 1989a. Woman in biosocial perspective. In *Gender and anthropology: Critical reviews for research and teaching,* ed. S. Morgan, 95–115. Washington, D.C.: American Anthropological Association.

———. 1989b. Evolutionary perspectives on single parenthood. In *Sociobiology and the social sciences,* ed. R. B. Bell, 63–72. Lubbock, Tex.: Texas Tech Univ. Press.

Lancaster, J. B, and B. J. King. 1985. An evolutionary perspective on menopause. In *In her prime: A new view of middle aged women,* ed. J. K. Brown and V. Kerns, 13–20. South Hadley, Mass.: Begin and Garvey.

Lancaster, J. B., and C. S. Lancaster. 1983. Parental investment: The hominid adaptation. In *How humans adapt,* ed. D. J. Ortner, 33–65. Washington, D.C.: Smithsonian Institution Press.

Langan, S. 1992. Male menopause? Take a pill. *The London Sunday Times,* 28 June.

Langlois, J. H., and L. A. Roggman. 1990. Attractive faces are only average. *Psychological Science* 1:115–21.

Langlois, J. H., L. A. Roggman, R. J. Casey, J. M. Ritter, L. A. Reiser-Danner, and V. Jenkins. 1987. Infants preferences for attractive faces: Rudiments of a stereotype? *Developmental Psychology* 23:363–69.

Lee, R. B. 1979. *The !Kung San: Men, women, and work in a foraging society.* New York: Cambridge Univ. Press.

Liebowitz, M. R. 1983. *The chemistry of love.* Boston: Little, Brown.

Lindzey, G. 1965. Morphology and behavior. In *Theories of personality: Primary sources and research,* ed. G. Lindzey and C. S. Hall, 344–53. New York: Wiley.

Lorenz, K. 1943. Innate forms of possible experience. *Zeitschrift für Tierpsychologie* 5:233–409.

Masters, W. H., and V. E. Johnson. 1966. *Human sexual response.* Boston: Little, Brown.

McAdams, D. P. 1985. *Power, intimacy, and the life story.* Homewood, Il.: Dorsey.

McKinlay, J. B. 1989. Is there an epidemiologic basis for a male climacteric syndrome? The Massachusetts aging study. In *Menopause: Evaluation, treatment, and health concerns,* ed. C. B. Hammond, F. P. Haseltine, and I. Schiff, 163–92. New York: Liss.

McKinney, K., and S. Sprecher, eds. 1991. *Sexuality in close relationships.* Hillsdale, N.J.: Erlbaum.

McNeil, C. 1988. The dimensions of stress. *Perspective on Prevention* 2:695–98.

Metts, S., and W. R. Cupach. 1991. The role of communication in human sexuality. In *Human sexuality: The societal and interpersonal context,* ed. M. McKinney and S. Sprecher, 139–61. Norwood, N.J.: Ablex.

Moir, A., and D. Jessel. 1989. *Brain sex: The real differences between men and women.* London: Joseph.

New York Times. 1992. Articles on fatness by Gina Kolata (Nov. 22, 1, 38); Jane Brody (Nov. 23, 1, 12), and Elizabeth Rosenthal (Nov. 24, 1, C12).

Nowak, C. A. 1977. Does youthfulness equal attractiveness? In *Looking ahead,* ed. L. E. Troll, J. Israel and K. Israel, 59–64. Englewood Cliffs, N.J.: Prentice-Hall.

O'Brien, C. P. 1981. Commentary. *Medical Aspects of Human Sexuality* 15:117.

Patzer, G. L. 1985. *The physical attractiveness phenomena.* New York: Plenum.

Peacock, N. 1991. An evolutionary perspective on the patterning of maternal investment in pregnancy. *Human Nature* 2:351–85.

Penrose, R. 1993. The great diversifier. *New York Review of Books* 40 (March 4): 5–7.

Peplau, L. A. and S. L. Gordon. 1985. Women and men in love: Gender differences in close heterosexual relationships. In *Women, gender, and social psychology,* ed. V. E. O'Leary, R. K. Unger, and B. S. Wallston, 257–291. Hillsdale, N.J.: Erlbaum.

Piltch, C. 1992a. Work and stress. *The Radcliffe Quarterly* 78 (December): 6–7.

———. 1992b. *Work and mental distress: A comparative analysis of the experience of women and men.* Ph.D. diss. Boston University.

Plummer, K. 1982. Symbolic interactionism and sexual conduct: An emergent perspective. In *Human sexual relations: Towards a redefinition of sexual politics,* ed. K. Howells, 223–41. Oxford: Blackwell.

Reinisch, J. M., L. A. Rosenblum, and S. A. Sanders, eds. 1987. *Masculinity/femininity: Basic perspectives.* New York: Oxford Univ. Press.

Riessman, C. K. 1983. Women and medicalization: A new perspective. *Social Policy,* 14:3–18.

Robinson, P. 1976. *The modernization of sex.* New York: Harper & Row.

Rosenblatt, P. C. and R. M. Anderson. 1981. Human sexuality in cross-cultural perspective. In *The bases of human sexual attraction,* ed. M. Cook, 215–50. New York: Academic Press.

Rossi, A. S. 1992. Closing the gap: Bio-medical vs. social-behavioral factors in the experience of women and research on the menopausal transition. Paper presented to the American Psychological Association symposium of Development in Midlife: Bio-psychosocial perspectives, Washington, D.C., August 1992.

———. 1993. The future in the making: Recent trends in the work/family interface. *American Journal of Orthopsychiatry* 63:166–76.

Rubin, Z. 1973. *Liking and loving: An invitation to social psychology.* New York: Holt, Rinehart & Winston.

Segal, L. 1985. Sexual uncertainty, or why the clitoris is not enough. In *Sex and love: New thoughts on old contradictions,* ed. S. Cartledge and J. Ryan, 30–47. London: Woman's Press.

Sherfey, M. J. 1972. *The nature and evolution of female sexuality.* New York: Random House.

Short, R. V. 1976. The evolution of human reproduction. *Proceedings of the Royal Society of London,* ser. B, 195:3–24.

———. 1984. The role of hormones in sexual cycles. In *Hormones in reproduction,* vol. 3, ed. C. R. Austin and R. V. Short, 42–72. Cambridge: Cambridge Univ. Press.

———. 1987. The biological basis for the contraceptive effects of breast feeding. *International Journal of Gynaecology and Obstetrics Supplement* 25:207–17.

Small, M. F. 1992. The evolution of female sexuality and mate selection in humans. *Human Nature* 3:133–56.

Stein, E. 1992. *Forms of desire: Sexual orientation and the social constructionist controversy.* New York: Routledge, Chapman & Hall.

Symons, D. 1979. *The evolution of human sexuality.* Oxford: Oxford Univ. Press.

Taffel, S. M. 1989. *Trends in low birth-weight: United States, 1975–1985.* Vital and Health Statistics, DHHS publication no. (PHS) 89-1926. Hyattsville, Md.: U.S. Department of Health and Human Services.

Tiefer, L. 1986. In pursuit of the perfect penis: The medicalization of male sexuality. *American Behavioral Scientist* 29:570–600.

———. 1992. Social constructionism and the study of human sexuality. In *Forms of desire: Sexual orientation and the social constructionist controversy,* ed. E. Stein, 295–324. New York: Routledge, Chapman & Hall.

Trivers, R. L. 1972. Parental investment and sexual selection. In *Sexual selection and the descent of man: 1871–1971,* ed. B. Campbell, 136–79. Chicago: Aldine.

Wandor, M. 1972. *The body politic.* London: Stage One.

Waterman, A. S., and S. K. Whitbourne. 1982. Androgyny and psychosexual development among college students and adults. *Journal of Personality* 50:121–33.

Wolfe, L. D. 1991. Human evolution and the sexual behavior of female primates. In *Understanding Behavior,* ed. J. D. Loy and C. B. Peters, 121–51. Oxford: Oxford University Press.

Wrangham, R. W. 1980. An ecological model of female-bonded primate groups. *Behaviour* 75:262–300.

II Sexual Diversity: History, Culture, and Lifestyle

Human Sexuality, Life Histories, and Evolutionary Ecology

Jane B. Lancaster

The task of this chapter is to set the issues of human sexuality in midlife in the broader context of the evolution of human reproductive behavior. It is written from the belief that many very important dimensions of human behavior and biology can best be understood from the perspective of evolutionary biology and human behavioral ecology. This is especially true of human sex roles and reproduction, an area of biology and behavior closely linked to evolutionary measures of fitness. Just as we recognize that humans have evolved distinctive patterns of bipedalism, feeding, tool using, intelligence, and social groupings, so, too, evolutionary processes have left a mark on human sexual behavior and reproductive biology in terms of sex differences in patterns of growth, reproductive maturation, sexuality, fertility, birth spacing, lactation, length of reproductive career, and parental investment in children.

Two important concepts emerge from a perspective based on human evolutionary biology. The first is the concept of the *environment of adaptation*. The environment of adaptation simply refers to the conditions under which particular patterns of behavior and biology evolve. This is a crucial concept in thinking about human beings because we know that our own evolutionary history has been very rapid and that there have been major, fundamental changes in the context of human experience in recent history. In some senses humans should be thought of as hunter-gatherers (a lifestyle in which we spent 99 percent of our history) now living under an incredible variety of conditions in terms of nutrition, disease, life course parameters, social density and organization, and level and distribution of resources. How much such contrasts between the environment of adaptation and current context are relevant to understanding human behavior today is open to serious question. Some scientists identify behavioral differences between human groups as environmentally induced variation in the expression of a basically similar genotype and see facultative responses to environmental differences as the essential human adaptation to socioecological variation. Others see human behavior as constrained by structures of the mind that evolved under very different environmental conditions (for a full discussion of this debate between evolutionary behavioral ecology and Darwinian psychology, see Blurton Jones, McGrew, and McGuire [1990]).

The second basic concept drawn from evolutionary biology is that the reproductive interests and strategies of males and females are not identical. The biological and behavioral adaptations of male and female can best be understood *not* as fundamentally complementary and linked in nature but as separate sets that serve the reproductive interests of each sex. This paper emphasizes the view that a species does not evolve as a single unit but rather that the adaptations of the two sexes must be understood independently of each other and not in terms of binary complementarity. This perspective also emphasizes the active involvement of individuals in the unfolding of their life histories in terms of the timing and distribution of reproductive effort over the life course and in the choice of reproductive partners.

SEXUALITY AS PROXIMATE MECHANISM

Tinbergen (1963) states that there are four great problems common to all areas of biology, including behavior, and that each deserves equal attention if we are truly to understand causation. These are proximate causation, ultimate causation, ontogeny, and phylogeny. For each subject of inquiry we decide which levels of explanation are most applicable to answering the questions we ask about why? Yet, the true answer to such questions of causality can never fully be given at a single level of explanation in spite of the confidence of defenders of one or another of these modes. Reproductive behavior is a prime example of such multiple levels of causation. Its proximate cause, human sexuality, is closely related to its ultimate cause, evolutionary fitness. Its expression is founded on both personal developmental history (such as nutrition and experience during the ontogeny of the individual) and on the constraints placed on that history by the genetics of both the individual and the adaptations of the species. No matter how many other roles sexuality plays in the life course of individuals, in the status systems of social groupings, or in the belief systems of cultures, the link between sexuality and reproduction is indisputable. This is true in spite of the clear evidence that for humans this link has been and can be disengaged by many factors such as by the emancipation of sexual activity from estrus and ovulation in the course of human evolution, or most recently by the development of various birth-control techniques that permit sexuality without exposure to conception, which in turn permits men and women to seek and experience recreational sex with no desire for procreation.

Sexuality, then, must be understood as a proximate mechanism of reproduction, and reproduction is the best and most easily measured coin we have of evolutionary fitness. Furthermore, because reproduction is so closely linked to the ultimate measure of evolutionary fitness, it leads us to ask whether the expression in the individual of the proximate mechanism, human sexuality, may be shaped or altered by the ultimate causation that it serves. Nonreproductive sex—that is, sex with nonfertile partners, such as outside of the ovulatory period or sex with members of the same sex—is not a phenomenon restricted to the modern context. As Hrdy (1981) and later Small (1992) argue, sexuality is used by many female primates to form alliances with multiple males, ones who may not be the progenitor of a particular infant but who mated with the mother around the time of conception and hence have some limited probability of paternity or who might anticipate paternity of future offspring. DeWaal (1987) also notes the widespread use of hetero- and homosexuality to forge social alliances among pygmy chimpanzees, comparable to the use of grooming in other primates. The presence of sexuality in a nonreproductive context is a given among many higher primates. The question raised here is whether the expression of sexuality in political, recreational, and social contexts might still be influenced by its original evolution as a proximate mechanism for reproduction.

LIFE-HISTORY STRATEGIES

The past fifteen years have witnessed major theoretical advances in the theory of the evolutionary biology of behavior as well as a wealth of empirical studies on animal and human populations. It is clear that all animals acquire resources from the environment to survive and reproduce and that the ways in which these resources are distributed in space and time are critical to animal systems of mating and rearing offspring (Clutton-Brock and Harvey 1978; Dunbar 1984, 1988; Kirkwood and Rose 1991; Standen and Foley 1989; Wittenberger and Tilson 1980; Wrangham 1979, 1980). Furthermore, individual organisms respond to variability in the distribution of resources in the environment with adjustments in their own behavior and life course (Charlesworth 1980; Charnov 1991; Harvey, Partridge, and Southwood 1991; Stearns 1976; Stearns and Koella 1986; West-Eberhard 1987). Life-history theory is based on the recognition that every individual organism, whether rad-

ish, rabbit, or human, has limited resources with which to live and reproduce. These resources include time, risk, energy, and health, as well
as more complex personal holdings such as territory or social estates
and monetary wealth. Whatever these resources are composed of, they
are never limitless, and this reality forces individual organisms to make
an unending chain of behavioral decisions about how to acquire and
invest such assets during the life course. Each decision once made, opens
up a new set of options and a further node of decision, virtually to the
end of the life course (Dunbar 1984, 1988).

It is particularly interesting that one dimension of human memory,
the storage of information about the frequency of occurrence of events
in the environment, does not show variability among humans along
the expected dimensions of socioeconomic status, age, sex, conscious
attention, or previous training, as do so many other aspects of learning
(Hasher and Zacks 1984). This lack of inter- and intragroup variability
in ability suggests that the monitoring of the frequency of environmental occurrences may be an automatic process that provides the basic data
informing about probabilities most critical to life-history strategies and
tactics regardless of whether or not or how consciously they are held.
Such questions as, Am I likely to survive to reproduce if I delay the
onset of reproduction? Will mates be scarce or abundant when I reach
maturity? and Will my investment in offspring increase their probability
of survivorship? must be answerable if behaviors are to be more than
random responses to environmental stimuli or strictly guided by cultural rules. It is the fundamental stuff of what Rogers (forthcoming)
refers to as time preference in life-history strategies. Rogers notes that
behavioral disciplines such as psychology and economics have long concerned themselves with aspects of time preference under the labels of
intertemporal choice, impulsiveness, delayed gratification, and discount
rates; these are all forms of time preference in which the value of a present good is measured against possible returns in the future that might
be greater but also possibly never attained. Humans, as well as animals,
behave as if they have time preferences at least partially informed by the
probability of future payoffs.

The evolutionary arena best served by time preference is reproduction. Natural selection has and will always favor individuals most able
to convert resources effectively into reproduction compared to the performance of their peers. Because of this succession of behavioral decisions made during the life course about the investment of environmental resources into reproduction, modern evolutionary biologists have

adopted a vocabulary sounding very much like that of economists in which they speak of investment, costs and benefits, trade-offs, assets, bet hedging, opportunity costs, and discounting. This usage by evolutionary biologists differs, however, from that of economists in one essential respect—the value of their coin is measured in successful reproduction.

Trade-offs

Each individual approaching reproduction is faced with a series of alternatives for the allocation of resources for which the ultimate payoff will be reproductive fitness. Such decisions about investment make up life-history strategies and tactics. Inherent in all decision is the concept of trade-offs; that is, all benefits cannot be simultaneously acquired (Partridge and Sibley 1991). They must be prioritized, and some given more investment than others on the basis of their relative costs and benefits in regards to the ultimate goal. Even in the most abundant of environments, rarely can an individual do two things at once, such as feed and mate simultaneously, so there will always be opportunity costs if nothing else. In all life histories certain inevitable trade-offs occur (fig. 1). The first of these is the distinction between somatic effort (investment in growth and maintenance of the individual) and mating effort (any investment that increases fertility at the cost of other fitness components) and parental investment (any investment in an offspring that increases the offspring's fitness at a cost to the parent's ability to invest in other offspring)(Clutton-Brock 1991; Trivers 1972; Williams 1966). Such life-history parameters as the timing of reproduction in the life course, temporal spacing between reproductive acts, the number and quality of offspring produced, and the differential allocation of energy and risk between acquiring mates and raising offspring will be affected

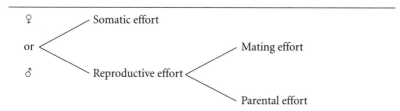

FIGURE 1 Trade-offs for sexually reproducing organisms in the allocation of resources toward somatic effort and reproductive effort and between mating effort and parental investment.

by whether resources are scarce or abundant, clumped or distributed, monopolizable or indefensible, and certain or erratically available.

Sex Differences in Reproductive Strategies

The features of resource distribution in time and space present themselves differently to individual males and females. Most theoreticians begin by analyzing sex differences in access to the resources that members of each sex need to maximize fitness. This basic theory permits comparisons between sexes and between species in mating and reproductive strategies. For the purposes of analyzing human behavioral evolution, the most fundamental contributions have been Trivers's (1972) germinal paper on parental investment strategies and sexual selection, and the papers by Clutton-Brock and Harvey (1978) and Wrangham (1979) on how individuals map behavioral strategies onto environmental resources. Although both sexes are faced with trade-offs in the allocation of resources between mating effort and parental investment, there are fundamental differences between male and female mammals in their reproductive strategies, with males tending to seek as many fertilizations as possible without paying too high a cost in risk and competition; females must seek access to resources to raise their fertilized eggs to adulthood. This means that females will tend to map their reproductive strategies onto the distribution of the resources they need to rear offspring, and males will tend to map onto the distribution of females, either directly or indirectly by controlling resources that females want.

With regard to the reproductive strategies of female mammals, evolutionary theory predicts that, because females bear the very heavy biological burden of gestation, birth, and lactation, they should inevitably link their reproductive behavior to the availability of resources to carry the fertilized egg to the status of an independent adult capable of reproduction (Clutton-Brock and Harvey 1978; Hrdy and Williams 1983; Wrangham 1980). In comparison to other large-bodied mammals, the higher primates in general give birth to offspring at a later age, have longer gestation periods, produce fewer young with each gestation, have longer periods of lactation, experience longer intervals between successive births, and produce fewer young during the life span of the adult female (Altmann 1987). The fact that higher primates and especially the great apes and humans produce high-quality, highly invested young, reflects both great cost and great value to the investing parent. The major burden of producing such valuable, costly offspring falls almost completely on the shoulders of adult females among monkeys and apes. For them, wide spacing between births allows the adult female to support a single nutritionally dependent infant at the same time that she can foster and protect a second, nutritionally independent juvenile (Lancaster and Lancaster 1983). In contrast to the other primates, human women have the burden of supporting additional nutritionally dependent young of differing ages because human children are not nutritionally independent when they are weaned but often remain dependent for ten or more additional years. The support of multiple, dependent young of various ages is rarely born by the woman alone, and so a critical modifier of this basic theoretical dichotomy between male and female reproductive strategies is whether females require aid from others to rear offspring and, if so, whether they turn to their mates, to their kin, or to cooperative nonrelatives for such assistance.

The human family represents a specialized and very basic adaptation that greatly extended the investment parents could make in their offspring, especially furthering the survivorship of weaned juveniles (Lancaster and Lancaster 1983, 1987). The investment necessary to transform a zygote into an adult is especially heavy for humans because human children are large, develop slowly, and in many societies need access to specialized resource bases (such as bride wealth, dowry, a homestead, or regular employment) in order to begin reproduction themselves. Hence, women face an even heavier burden than other female mammals in their need for reproductive resources. Given these species-typical constraints, in such elemental human behavioral patterns as the division of labor, family-formation strategies, and parental investment patterns, women should be active decision makers in optimizing their access to resources and their ability to produce healthy, competitive offspring. Men should seek healthy, fertile mates and should resist investing in offspring not their own unless such investment brings major benefits.

This dramatic evolutionary shift in the cost of raising human children has had a major effect on the reproductive strategies of both men and women that takes them beyond the simple mammalian dichotomy of males seeking mating opportunities and females seeking resources so often quoted as the fundamental differences between the sexes (Hill and Kaplan 1988). For women it means seeking assistance from others to

help rear children, which sometimes involves trading personal autonomy for access to resources (Lancaster 1989a, 1989b; Smuts 1992). For
men it means that access to mates may often be limited by a male's
ability to give parental investment (Lancaster and Kaplan 1992).

Optimality and Facultative Adjustments

One final point needs consideration before proceeding to a discussion of sexuality and life-history strategies. Natural selection favors individuals most able to translate resources into reproduction, but this
does not mean that it favors the best conceivable life-history strategy
above all others. Optimality is a concept that can be understood only in
its context and in the constraints defining available options. This means
that a given optimal life-history strategy is the best available among a
given set of options or may be even the best-of-a-bad-lot strategy in a
given physiological, genetic, social, developmental, and environmental
context and, furthermore, only in comparison with the strategies pursued by peers. Optimality, then, predicts variability in life-history strategies and tactics not normative conformity with compromised deviation.

We know also that humans are a species that have occupied more
environmental niches and a wider geographic distribution than those
of any known species. The cross-cultural record also tells us that humans exhibit a richer diversity in social organization, family-formation
strategies, and ecological conditions than any other species and that this
behavioral variability in relation to socioecological variability must be
in itself a core feature of human adaptation. Our task then as students
of human behavior is not to define an essentialist position about human
nature, nor to determine whether humans are competitive or cooperative, altruistic or self-interested, peaceful or aggressive, or whether men
are in essence highly sexed philanderers or devoted fathers or whether
females are acquisitive or self-sacrificing. The range of human behavior
encompasses all these dualisms and many more, as well as all the behavioral ground that lies between. Rather, our task is to identify the
context-dependent nature of human behavior—that is, the socioecological conditions most conducive to certain behavioral or life-history
patterns and not to others. The past decade has witnessed a wealth of
new publications documenting cultural variation in reproductive strategies and their socioecological contexts (Belsky, Steinberg, and Draper
1991; Betzig, Borgerhoff Mulder, and Turke 1988; Borgerhoff Mulder
1992; Lancaster 1989a, 1989b; Rasa, Vogel, and Voland 1989).

LIFE-HISTORY PARAMETERS OF HUMAN SEXUALITY

We know that for humans environments are not and have never been stable or homogeneous through time, space, or society. We can predict that for such an essential feature of human reproduction as sexuality variability will go far beyond simple independent variables such as age and sex to encompass all sorts of measures of individual condition, previous reproductive history, and future options for investment of mating effort and parental investment.

Mate Choice

One of the first and most critical decisions that any sexually reproducing organism has to make is in the choice of mate. For humans, this choice is even more critical because of the relatively long lives of spouses, the few numbers of offspring produced, the commitment to long-term investment in children throughout the juvenile years and even longer in complex, stratified societies, and the unusually high levels of commitment to parental investment demanded from both sexes.

Sex differences in criteria. The scientific study of human mate choice from the perspective of reproduction and socioecology is a comparatively recent endeavor. This field has been reviewed recently by Buss (1987, 1988, 1990) and by Kenrick and Trost (1987). Generally speaking, although most of the empirical data is biased against nonyouthful, rural, less educated and lower socioeconomic groups, they do show quite remarkable similarity across a wide variety of cultures in Africa, Asia, Australia, Europe, South America, and North America. The results of these studies confirm many predictions that we would derive from evolutionary theory. Although both sexes tended to list the same basic qualities for an ideal mate, they prioritized them very differently. Men listed indicators of fecundity (youth, beauty, and health) and paternity confidence (chastity for spouses but not for the ideal weekend partner) as the most important qualities for a mate likely to elicit long-term commitment. Women tended to prioritize factors indicating present or future access to resources such as earning capacity, ambition and industriousness, and education or training. Moreover, measures of reproductive value (the future likelihood of successful reproduction for an individual) are linked to age more closely for women than for men because of the male potential to father children into old age. Consequently, youthfulness as a quality of mates is much more highly valued by men than by women. As such, these results follow most directly on simple predictions from evolutionary biology that males value fertile females who (for humans) will give paternity confidence and females value access to resources to rear offspring. However, although Buss's sample includes thirty-seven different societies (1990), the fundamental bias in all the modern cross-cultural research on mate choice is crucial in understanding the limited generalizability of the findings.

Nowhere in the current literature on mate choice do we find scientific studies of mate preference from societies in which resources in the environment are not accessed on the basis of social stratification, where there is low variance in male ability to access resources, where access to resources are based on male risk taking rather than inheritance or ability, where females access their own resources, or where what males have to offer is not resources but protection, even though we know that these various conditions are very significant in the variability found in the cross-cultural record of family-formation strategies (Lancaster and Kaplan 1991). These factors, of course, contrast with the conditions described for the samples referenced above, and they represent reproduction planned in very different socioecological contexts. For example, female preference for a man with resources should not be expected in social groupings where there is low male variance in resource access or independent female access to resources or where the principal contribution a male can give to further female reproduction is protection of a woman and her children. So we should find that, in societies practicing subsistence horticulture (in which women feed themselves and their children) and where warfare and bride capture are endemic, women prefer men who are fierce and uncompromising (Chagnon 1988; Daly and Wilson 1988; Divale and Harris 1976). We can also expect that in highly stratified social systems where men at the bottom have very low access to resources, that females at the bottom might prefer males willing to sustain high levels of risk in competition and violence (Daly and Wilson 1988, 1990; Wilson and Daly 1985) or in expropriative crime (Cohen and Machalek 1988).

Furthermore, we have no data on how mate-choice preferences may change for men and women during their life histories on the basis of past reproductive success and future reproductive potential. But we should expect that, under conditions where the most that men can offer are their good genes and fit physical condition, women should be more interested in indicators such as handsomeness, muscularity, and athletic ability but not particularly in youthfulness because male reproductive potential deteriorates much more slowly and is not limited by menopause. These socioecological conditions are not restricted to small-scale societies practicing horticulture and pastoralism but are also often found on modern frontiers and in urban underclasses. We might also find that female access to resources on the basis of education and earning power (but not on access to kin or governmental support systems) should be more highly valued by middle-status men who have neither very much nor very little personal access to resources.

How might such variability in the socioecological context of reproduction and mate-choice criteria affect the sexuality of individuals? We can assume that individual sexuality is often based on how closely the person matches preferred mate criteria both because of higher self-esteem and because of having greater access to a quality mate and to multiple mates. Male sexuality, therefore, might be much more vulnerable on the basis of individual condition (both physical and resource based) and female sexuality on the basis of aging, or more specifically the closing of her reproductive career by menopause. We might predict also that in populations where older males limit their reproductive careers because of the high cost of rearing children, that postreproductive women should have higher levels of self-esteem and sexuality than in societies where men increase the number of lifetime mates as they age, and each successive marriage encompasses a wider age gap between spouses. We should also find that men of low socioeconomic status should find aging or disability much more threatening to self-image and sexuality than do men who control wealth or are highly valued for their parental investment. Each of these is a testable prediction but to my knowledge little work has been done by evolutionary biologists to try to explain differences in sexuality on the basis of socioecological conditions beyond simple predictions based on sex and age.

Supply of mates and mate choice criteria. In 1983 Guttentag and Secord published their classic synthesis of the effect of too many women (or too many men) on the shape of the marriage market and the relative status and freedom of women. At about the same time animal behaviorists began to discuss the supply of potential mates and the cost of search time, courtship, and defense of mates in a cost-benefit calculus for determining rates of polygyny and monogamy (Clutton-Brock and Harvey 1984; Dunbar 1984). Clearly the value of particular mates is partially defined by their scarcity, which may be due to variations in sex ratio resulting from differential mortality, to the monopolization of one sex by specific members of the other sex or to differences in quality so great that individuals in poor condition are effectively removed from the market. Such a skew of the sex ratio at mating leads to greater competition between members of the more common sex. For example, dowry as a transfer of wealth from the family of a woman to the family of a man at marriage historically replaced earlier forms of marriage payment transfers such as bride service and bride wealth, in which resources went to the family of the bride in exchange for access to her reproductive powers and for recognition of paternity (Dickemann 1981). As variance in male quality increased in the course of human history because reproductive resources became monopolizable, dowry (or groom price) developed as a form of competition between the families of brides for access to quality grooms.

Guttentag and Secord (1983) pointed to less sweeping historic trends in their review when they evaluated the shorter-term effect on marriage forms and sex roles of demographic fluctuations such as the baby boom and its effect on the supply of mates given the strong preference of women to marry men of older age (proven prospects)or superior status (James 1989). Women born early in the baby-boom generation found themselves in oversupply; men born at the end of the period find themselves either competing intensely for a much smaller cohort of younger women or else compromising their reproductive interests by marrying older women with reduced reproductive potential. Pedersen (1991) suggests that some of these overly abundant men may increase their individual value to women by offering them more egalitarian marriages and help in child care and housework. Similar patterns of male commitment to child care may be found among men whose employment is unpredictable, such as inner-city African-Americans (Sullivan 1989).

Men make other compromises in their reproductive fitness to gain access to reproducing women. Many agree to help a woman raise children she has borne for another man. In a study currently underway on the reproductive careers of a representative sample of nearly four thousand Anglo and Hispanic men in Albuquerque, New Mexico, Lancaster and Kaplan (1991) have found that 22 percent of the men acted for at least one year as a father to and raised one or more children whom they knew were not their own offspring. At first glance these seem to be truly generous, altruistic acts. When, however, the relationship of these children to the men was analyzed, 73 percent were the children or kin of the man's sexual partner. A further 16.2 percent of the children were kin to the man. In fact only 11 percent of the children were not directly related to the male as either his kin or the kin of his mate. It is interesting to recognize that, just as noted in the previous paragraph, human males often use parental investment in their own or even other men's children as a form of mating effort, a behavior correlated with the likelihood that they will be the father of a woman's next child. Although the offering of resources toward parental investment as a form of mating effort may reduce potential fertility, it also increases the likelihood of gaining access to women. Men least likely to raise the children of other men were those in the top income quartiles for both Anglo and Hispanic men. These men appear to be attractive enough to women on the basis of their resources that the men do not form alliances with women who are encumbered by previous children.

During this century in the United States we know that the completed fertility of individual men and women is predicted by many factors such as birth cohort, religion, education, employment, and ethnicity. Here I suggest that personal sexuality of both men and women may be similarly defined by the relative scarcity of one sex in a particular birth cohort independent of individual personal qualities. The very act of competition of one sex for access to scarce members of the other must favor feelings of sexual desirability and sexuality among members of the sought-after sex (Bowser, chap. 5, and Sterk-Elifson, chap. 4, this vol., for examples of how relative scarcity of suitable partners affects feelings of self-worth among young African-Americans).

Early versus Late Onset of Reproduction

The scheduling of reproduction in the life course is the other critical decision faced by all sexually reproducing organisms (Kirkwood and Rose 1991; Promislow and Harvey 1990; Wasser and Isenberg 1986). Predictions about the trade-offs involved in scheduling decisions, such as between growing more now or waiting until the resource context or personal physical condition improves, can best be understood by using the concept of reproductive value, first defined by Fisher (1958) and a key feature of life-history models. Reproductive value is the number of surviving offspring that an individual of a given age can expect to produce in the remaining years of its life, multiplied by the probability of surviving each of those remaining years. Reproductive value differs, then, between individuals of the same age but of differing conditions and is highly affected by mortality rates of both adults and juveniles. There are a number of situations that favor early reproduction: an environment that rewards short generation lengths, one with high adult mortality or rapidly deteriorating adult condition, or an environment with levels of resources to which quality offspring have no better access than less invested offspring. Delay in first reproduction is most common in saturated environments where adults must produce highly competitive offspring, and delay gives greater access to reproductive resources (Johnston 1982). Even under these conditions, however, the risk of juvenile morbidity and mortality always pushes toward reproduction as early as possible within the constraints of context.

Significant changes in the frequency of school-age pregnancy in modern industrialized societies is a useful case in point because ethnic and socioeconomic variability may be better explained by evolutionary biology and socioecological theory than by cultural preference. It is clear that there has been a secular trend in increasing risk of teenage childbearing during the past 150 years that was first noted in western Europe and is now a worldwide phenomenon (Eveleth 1986; Lancaster 1986). This secular trend began among relatively privileged social segments and then expanded to lower socioeconomic groups so that today there are a number of countries in western Europe, North America, and Asia in which there are no measurable socioeconomic status differences in age of menarche. This means that there are large areas of the world where the ancient biological constraints for the timing of first birth are now inoperable because even disadvantaged groups get enough fat and protein in their diets for environmental abundance to be perceived physiologically. However, teenage reproduction and parenthood are very unevenly distributed among these early maturers but are closely linked to ethnicity and socioeconomic status. It is likely that teenage reproduction can better be viewed as associated with the socioecological distribution of resources needed to raise children and with differential access to them for men and women.

Geronimus (1987, 1991, 1992) argues that the vast majority (98 percent) of teen mothers in U.S. society are not inexperienced babies having babies but rather women aged fifteen to nineteen, many of whom are underclass, who may well be optimizing the timing of reproduction in the life course in regard to maternal and child health, maternal fertility, and access to resources for the rearing of children. The familiar statistics that suggest the opposite (that delay in first reproduction to the ages of twenty-four or twenty-five promotes maternal and child health and maternal education and employment) come from comparisons with the life histories of middle-class women and not with the appropriate comparison, the teen mothers' sisters and peers who did not reproduce as teenagers. In contrast to most women in this country, the health and fertility of underclass women deteriorates very rapidly in the life course. For them, in fact, maternal fertility and infant survival peak nearly five years earlier than for middle-class women (Geronimus 1987), and access to family help is likely to be greater during the teenage years (Burton 1990; Geronimus and Korenman 1992). Furthermore, because in modern societies the cost of raising a child increases with each year of maturation (Espenshade 1984) (unlike the opposite condition in traditional societies), teen mothers are free to work in their later twenties to underwrite their children's development once they are in school. Access to quality male mates is not improved by waiting because of the high rates of male unemployment, incarceration, and death found in the underclasses of modern social systems (Mauer 1990; Wilson 1989).

According to Geronimus, underclass women make the best of a very bad lot by reproducing, often as single parents, while still in their teens. Such women will become grandmothers much earlier in life than do women who postpone their fertility to their mid-twenties or even mid-thirties, up to twenty years earlier in fact. Furthermore, active grandparenting in which daily investment of time and energy goes directly to grandchildren may be a major feature of family support systems that favor short generation length. We might predict that a fifty-year-old woman who has just completed an active phase of child rearing may have very different feelings about her sexuality than one of the same age who is a grandparent and perhaps even a great-grandparent. We might also expect that mother-daughter conflicts of interest will be greater when both are reproducing at the same time than when the mother has finished reproduction and assumes a supportive grandparental role toward her daughter's reproduction (see Burton and Bengtson [1985], for examples of on-time and off-time grandparenthood).

Cessation of Reproduction

Although the timing of the onset of reproduction is a critical factor in the completed fertility of women, the timing of its conclusion is a key feature of the adaptations of our species and appears to be less variable (Menken, Trussell, and Larsen 1986). Among noncontracepting women in natural fertility populations few women give birth after the age of forty and virtually none after forty-five. Unlike our closest living relatives, the great apes, human women cease reproduction long before other biological systems deteriorate (Hill and Hurtado 1991). This special feature of human reproduction has led to very different age-specific fertility rates for men and women. In keeping with female preference for males of proven quality and the slower physical and social maturation of males, an age difference between spouses of three to five years is common across cultures (James 1989). Although age-specific fertility of males is rarely given by demographers on the justification that women know who their children are but men can rarely be certain, what data have been published indicate a later onset of reproduction for men than women (Ellison 1990; Frisch 1978; Wood 1990). In traditional societies, however, men who survive to their middle and later years often increase their number of fertile wives through widow inheritance or through polygyny. Usually the age difference between each new wife and her spouse increases as the male ages. Research by James (1983) in contemporary marriages shows that the frequency of coitus in marriage is related to the age of the wife and not to the age of the husband or the length of the marriage. In other words male sexuality is most closely related to the fecundability of his sexual partner and not to her novelty or his age. Presumably similar processes should be at work on male virility in traditional societies. The combination of the biological phenomenon of menopause with marriage practices such as polygyny or serial monogamy have traditionally led to different age-specific fertility rates for men and women, with men actively reproducing well into their middle and even later years.

Grandparental investment. Until recently the evolution of menopause as a species-specific trait puzzled evolutionary biologists because it was hard to evaluate the adaptive value of not reproducing until death (as do the great apes) if there were any chance that the last born might survive the death of its mother. Parental investment theory has led to a new set of predictions about grandmothers and the opportunity costs of late reproduction versus nonreproduction and to a new series of empirical studies that attempt to quantify the value of specific sets of decisions (Clutton-Brock 1984; Hawkes, O'Connell, and Blurton Jones 1989; Hill and Hurtado 1991; Hurtado et al. 1992; Kaplan, forthcoming). Empirical studies in small-scale societies show that grandmothers do not retire but rather work very hard, even harder than younger, lactating women, in the provisioning of their grandchildren. Grandmothers, who do not bear the constraints of lactation or child care, are in a position to invest their energy most effectively in increasing the likelihood of survival of their grandchildren and actually may increase their productivity after menopause. If the results of these studies are borne out by further research in a wide variety of traditional societies, we might then ask how grandmotherhood and sexuality might interact in the life history of individual women. Might sexuality be different for women of the same age who are grandmothers versus those who are not? Does the presence rather than the existence of grandchildren make a difference in women's sexuality? Is the sexuality of women who are still cycling more influenced by grandmotherhood than those who have completed menopause? Because these questions have never been raised before, there are no data to reply to them. However, it is likely that a life-history perspective may inform much of the variability among women in their response to menopause and sexuality in their middle years.

Secular trends in the cost of children. One final consideration remains—historical trends in the cost of raising children. There is no question that the course of human history has witnessed a major shift in the cost to parents of raising children. There has been a secular trend in the cost of rearing children and patterns of parental investment that can best be illustrated by the differences between low-density and high-density social systems (Lancaster and Lancaster 1987), between societies of low variance in male quality and those with high (Lancaster and Kaplan 1991), and between natural fertility and limited fertility populations (Bulatao and Lee 1983; Draper 1989). These different labels all refer to the same historic factors. In low-density, low-male-variance, natural-fertility populations, parents try to raise as many healthy, fit children as possible. Control of fertility focuses on birth spacing to optimize the survivorship of children but not to limit the number of children a family produces. Under these conditions, fertility and sexual desire in women appear to be suppressed by lactation (Alder et al., 1986; Short 1987; Stern and Leiblum 1986), which in turn influences the length of interbirth spacing.

In contrast, high-density, high-male-variance, limited-fertility populations all have one factor in common. It is no longer enough for parents to rear healthy, fit children to sexual maturity. Reproductive unions are not a universal given and parents must be concerned about whether they are investing in sons and daughters who will not gain access to mates. The primary response of parents to this threat is to invest in children in ways that will raise their competitiveness on the mating market by endowing them with access to a treasured family estate to underwrite the costs of reproduction or by giving them access to specialized equipment, training, or education so they can create their own reproductive estate. The end result of these behavioral adaptations is a parental, ever-escalating arms race that not only increases the cost of each child but also changes the shape of the cost curve. In modern industrialized societies, each child increases in annual cost as it matures; in more traditional societies children begin to underwrite some of the cost of raising themselves by at least the age of five or six (Kaplen, forthcoming). Recent estimates for the United States by Espenshade (1984) indicate the total investment in a child up to the age of eighteen from a low-socioeconomic-status family under conditions of moderate inflation as $213,000 and from a family of high economic status as $282,000. Costs increase with the age of the child by a factor of four and further investment after age of seventeen can easily double the total amount.

It is informative to review the age-specific fertility of males under conditions of modern economies. Age-specific fertility for the men in our Albuquerque sample (fig. 2) and for men in another sample from Seattle, Washington (Lockard and Adams 1981), reveal curves that mirror that of women but delayed by about three years for both the beginning and the end of the reproductive span. The much-discussed potential for men to become fathers far into late age is rarely realized in modern societies in spite of serial monogamy, perhaps because of an interplay between the escalating cost of rearing children as they mature and the declining access to resources of most men at retirement.

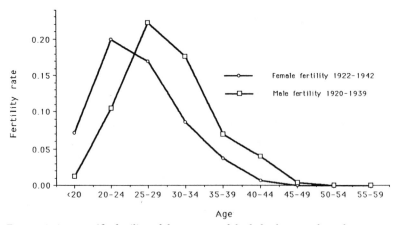

FIGURE 2 Age-specific fertility of the parents of the baby-boom cohort drawn from a sample of Anglo men and women living in Albuqerque, New Mexico.

Discussion

Life-history theory based on evolutionary biology and behavioral ecology provides us with a series of predictions about how individuals should allocate resources to optimize fitness. Because the primary function of sexuality has been as a proximate mechanism for reproduction, we can speculate as to how these two levels of causation, proximate and ultimate, might influence each other in the life course of an individual.

First and foremost, we can predict that, because fitness by definition depends on the relative performance of peers, self-image and self-esteem of individuals should be neither arbitrary nor unrealistic, and such comparative evaluations should guide the individual to pursue an optimal life-history strategy most suited to personal and socioecological condition. Sexuality, insofar as it is based on self-esteem, should be more vulnerable in individuals in poor condition or in oversupply based on the socioecological context in which individuals must compete for mates. In complex, stratified social systems, variability between individuals and subgroups predicts major differences beyond that of sex and age, because the socioecological opportunity structure presents itself so differently depending on how the individual is situated and the relative quality and scarcity of what the individual has to offer on the mating market.

Second, the role of past, present, and expected personal reproductive performance plays a major role in life-history strategies. Such factors as the presence or absence of grandchildren as alternative objects of parental investment or the availability of new, fertile mates affects the relative value of various trade-offs in life-history strategies. Accurate assessment of reproductive condition, access to fertile mates, access to reproductive resources, past reproductive performance, and future reproductive potential enable the individual to make informed choices about the costs and benefits of sexual activity during the life course. Individuals have been selected to be attuned to these sources of information and evaluation because they are so closely linked to decisions that optimize life-history strategies and reproductive success.

References

Alder, E., A. Cook, D. Davidson, C. West, and J. Bancroft. 1986. Hormones, mood, and sexuality in lactating women. *British Journal of Psychiatry* 148:74–79

Altmann, J. 1987. Lifespan aspects of reproduction and parental care in anthropoid primates. In *Parenting across the lifespan*, ed. J. Lancaster, J. Altmann, A. Rossi, and L. Sherrod, 15–29. New York: Aldine.

Belsky, J., L. Steinberg, and P. Draper. 1991. Childhood experience, interpersonal development, and reproductive strategy: An evolutionary theory of socialization. *Child Development* 62:647–70.

Betzig, L. L., M. Borgerhoff Mulder, and P. Turke, eds. 1988. *Human reproductive behaviour: A Darwinian perspective.* Cambridge: Cambridge Univ. Press.

Blurton Jones, M., W. McGrew, and M. McGuire, eds. 1990. Special issue on Darwinian anthropology and Darwinian psychology. *Ethology and Sociobiology* 11:239–463.

Borgerhoff Mulder, M. 1992. Reproductive decisions in ecological context. In *Ecology, evolution, and human behavior,* ed. E. Smith and B. Winterhalder, 339–74. Hawthorne, N.Y.: Aldine de Gruyter.

Bulatao, R. A., and R. D. Lee, eds. 1983. *Determinants of fertility in developing countries.* 2 vols. New York: Academic Press.

Burton, L. M. 1990. Teenage childbearing as an alternative life-course strategy in multigenerational black families. *Human Nature* 1:123–44.

Burton, L. M. and V. L. Bengtson. 1985. Black grandmothers: Issues of timing and meaning in roles. In *Grandparenthood: Research and policy perspectives,* ed. V. Bengtson and J. Robertson, 61–77. Beverly Hills, Calif.: Sage.

Buss, D. 1987. Sex differences in human mate selection criteria. In *Sociobiology and psychology,* ed. C. Crawford, M. Smith and D. Krebs, 335–51. Hillsdale, N.J.: Erlbaum.

————. 1988. The evolution of human intrasexual competition: Tactics of mate attraction. *Journal of Personality and Social Psychology* 54:616–28.

————. 1990. Sex differences in human mate preferences: Evolutionary hypotheses tested in 37 cultures. *Behavioral and Brain Sciences* 12:1–49.

Chagnon, N. 1988. Life histories, blood revenge, and warfare in a tribal population. *Science* 239:985–92.

Charlesworth, B. 1980. *Evolution in age-structured populations.* Cambridge: Cambridge Univ. Press.

Charnov, E. L. 1991. Evolution of life history variation among female mammals. *Proceedings of the National Academy of Science* 88:1134–37.

Clutton-Brock, T. H. 1984. Reproductive effort and terminal investment in iteroparous animals. *American Naturalist* 123:212–29.

————. 1991. *The evolution of parental care.* Princeton, N.J.: Princeton Univ. Press.

Clutton-Brock, T. H., and P. H. Harvey. 1978. Mammals, resources, and reproductive strategies. *Nature* 273:191–95.

Cohen, L. E., and R. Machalek. 1988. A general theory of expropriative crime: An evolutionary ecological approach. *American Journal of Sociology* 94:465–501.

Daly, M., and M. Wilson. 1988. *Homicide.* Hawthorne, N.Y.: Aldine de Gruyter.

————. 1990. Killing the competition: Female/female and male/male homicide. *Human Nature* 1:81–107.

Dickemann, M. 1981. Paternity confidence and dowry competition: A biocultural analysis of purdah. In *Natural selection and social behavior,* ed. R. Alexander and D. Tinkle, 417–38. New York: Cheiron.

Divale, W., and M. Harris. 1976. Population, warfare, and the male supremacist complex. *American Anthropologist* 78:520–38.

Draper, P. 1989. African marriage systems: Perspectives from evolutionary ecology. *Ethology and Sociobiology* 10:145–69.

Dunbar, R. 1984. *Reproductive decisions: An economic analysis of Gelada baboon social strategies.* Princeton, N.J.: Princeton Univ. Press.

———. 1988. *Primate social systems.* Ithaca, N.Y.: Cornell Univ. Press.

Ellison, P. T. 1990. Reproductive ecology and human fertility. In *Application of biological anthropology to human affairs,* ed. G. W. Lasker and C. G. N. Mascie-Taylor, 14–54. Cambridge: Cambridge Univ. Press.

Espenshade, T. J. 1984. *Investing in children: New estimates of parental expenditures.* Washington, D.C.: Urban Institute Press.

Eveleth, P. 1986. Timing of menarche: Secular trend and population differences. In *School-age pregnancy and parenthood: Biosocial dimension,* ed. J. Lancaster and B. Hamburg, 39–52. Hawthorne, N.Y.: Aldine de Gruyter.

Fisher, R. A. 1958. *The genetical theory of natural selection.* New York: Dover.

Frisch, R. E. 1978. Population, food intake, and fertility. *Science* 199:22–30.

Geronimus, A. T. 1987. On teenage childbearing and neonatal mortality in the United States. *Population and Development Review* 13:245–79.

———. 1991. Teenage childbearing and social and reproductive disadvantage: The evolution of complex questions and the demise of simple answers. *Family Relations* 40:463–71.

———. 1992. The weathering hypothesis and the health of African-American women and infants: Evidence and speculations. *Ethnicity and Disease* 2:207–21.

Geronimus, A. T., and S. Korenman. 1992. The socioeconomic consequences of teen childbearing reconsidered. *Quarterly Journal of Economics* 107:1187–1214.

Guttentag, M., and P. Secord. 1983. *Too many women?: The sex ratio question.* Beverly Hills, Calif.: Sage.

Harvey, P. H., L. Partridge, and T. R. E. Southwood, eds. 1991. *The evolution of reproductive strategies. Philosophical Transactions of the Royal Society of London,* ser. B, 332:1–104.

Hasher, L., and R. Zacks. 1984. Automatic processing of fundamental information: The case of frequency of occurrence. *American Psychologist* 39:1372–88.

Hawkes, K., J. F. O'Connell, and N. G. Blurton Jones. 1989. Hardworking Hadza grandmothers. In *Comparative Socioecology,* ed. V. Standen and R. Foley, 341–66. London: Blackwell.

Hill, K., and A. M. Hurtado. 1991. The evolution of premature reproductive senescence and menopause in human females: An evaluation of the "grandmother" hypothesis. *Human Nature* 2:313–50.

Hill, K., and H. Kaplan. 1988. Tradeoffs in male and female reproductive strategies among the Ache: Parts 1 and 2. In *Human reproductive behaviour: A Darwinian perspective,* ed. L. Betzig, M. Borgerhoff Mulder, and P. Turke, 277–90, 291–306. New York: Cambridge Univ. Press.

Hrdy, S. B. 1981. *The woman who never evolved.* Cambridge, Mass.: Harvard Univ. Press.

Hrdy, S. B., and G. C. Williams. 1983. Behavioral biology and the double standard. In *Social behavior of female vertebrates,* ed. S. K. Wasser, 3–18. New York: Academic Press.

Hurtado, M., K. R. Hill, H. Kaplan, and I. Hurtado. 1992. Trade-offs between food acquisition and child care among Hiwi and Ache foragers. *Human Nature* 3:185–216.

James, W. H. 1983. Decline in coital rates with spouses' ages and duration of marriage. *Journal of Biosocial Science* 13:83–87.

———. 1989. The norm for perceived husband superiority: A cause of human assortative marriage. *Social Biology* 36:271–78.

Johnston, T. D. 1982. Selective costs and benefits in the evolution of learning. *Advances in the Study of Behavior* 12:65–106.

Kaplan, H. Forthcoming. A test of two theories of fertility.

Kenrick, D. T., and M. R. Trost. 1987. A biosocial theory of heterosexual relationships. In *Females, males, and sexuality: Theories and research,* ed. K. Kelley, 59–100. Albany: State Univ. of New York Press.

Kirkwood, T. B. L., and M. R. Rose. 1991. Evolution of senescence: Late survival sacrificed for reproduction. In *The evolution of reproductive strategies,* ed. P. Harvey, L. Partridge, and T. R. E. Southwood. *Philosophical Transactions of the Royal Society London,* ser. B, 332:15–24.

Lancaster, J. B. 1986. Human adolescence and reproduction: An evolutionary perspective. In *School-age pregnancy and parenthood: Biosocial dimensions,* ed. J. Lancaster and B. Hamburg, 17–37. Hawthorne, N.Y.: Aldine de Gruyter.

———. 1989a. Evolutionary and cross-cultural perspectives on single-parenthood. In *Interfaces in Psychology: Sociobiology and the Social Sciences,* ed. R. Bell and N. Bell, 63–72. Lubbock: Texas Tech Univ. Press.

———. 1989b. Women in biosocial perspective. In *Gender and Anthropology,* ed. S. Morgan, 95–113. Washington, D.C.: American Anthropological Association.

Lancaster, J. B., and H. Kaplan 1991. The distribution of male parental investment between direct descendants, kin, and nonkin by Albuquerque men. Paper presented at the annual meetings of the American Association of Physical Anthropologists, April, Milwaukee, Wis.

———. 1992. Human mating and family formation strategies: The effects of variability among males in quality and of the allocation of mating effort and parental investment. In *Human origins.* Vol. 1 of Thirteenth Congress of the International Primatological Society, ed. T. Nishida, W. McGrew, P. Marler, M. Pickford, and F. de Waal, 21–33. Tokyo: Univ. of Tokyo Press.

Lancaster, J. B., and C. Lancaster. 1983. Parental investment: The hominid adaptation. In *How humans adapt: A biocultural odyssey,* ed. D. Ortner, 33–66. Washington, D.C.: Smithsonian Institution.

———. 1987. The watershed: Change in parental-investment and family-formation strategies in the course of human evolution. In *Parenting across the life span: Biosocial dimensions,* ed. J. Lancaster, J. Altmann, A. Rossi, and L. Sherrod, 187–205. Hawthorne, N.Y.: Aldine de Gruyter.

Lockard, J., and D. Adams. 1981. Human serial polygyny. *Ethology and Sociobiology* 2:177–86.

Mauer, M. 1990. *Young black men and the criminal justice system: A growing national problem.* Washington, D.C.: Sentencing Project.

Menken, J., J. Trussell, and U. Larsen. 1986. Age and infertility. *Science* 233:1389–94.

Partridge, L., and R. Sibley. 1991. Constraints in the evolution of life histories. In *The evolution of reproductive strategies,* ed. P. Harvey, L. Partridge, and T. R. E. Southwood. *Philosophical Transactions of the Royal Society London,* ser. B, 332:3–14.

Pedersen, F. A. 1991. Secular trends in human sex ratios: Their influence on individual and family behavior. *Human Nature* 2:271–91.

Promislow, D. E. L., and P. H. Harvey. 1990. Living fast and dying young: A comparative analysis of life-history variation among mammals. *Journal of the Zoological Society* (London) 220:417–37.

Rasa, A. E., C. Vogel, and E. Voland, eds. 1989. *The sociobiology of sexual and reproductive strategies.* London: Chapman & Hall.

Rogers, A. Forthcoming. The evolution of time preference.

Short, R. V. 1987. The biological basis for the contraceptive effects of breast feeding. *International Journal of Gynaecology and Obstetrics Supplement* 25:207–17.

Small, M. 1992. The evolution of female sexuality and mate selection in humans. *Human Nature* 3:133–56.

Smuts, B. 1992. Male aggression against women: An evolutionary perspective. *Human Nature* 3:1–44.

Standen, V., and R. A. Foley, eds. 1989. *Comparative socioecology.* Oxford: Blackwell.

Stearns, S. C. 1976. Life-history tactics: A review of the ideas. *Quarterly Review of Biology* 51:3–47.

Stearns, S. C., and J. C. Koella. 1986. The evolution of phenotypic plasticity in life-history traits: Predictions of reaction norms for age and size at maturity. *Evolution* 40:893–913.

Stern, J. M., and S. R. Leiblum. 1986. Postpartum sexual behavior of American women as a function of the absence or frequency of breast feeding: A preliminary communication. In *Primate ontogeny, cognition, and social behaviour,* ed. J. Else and P. Lee, 3:319–28. Cambridge: Cambridge Univ. Press.

Sullivan, M. L. 1989. Absent fathers in the inner city. In The ghetto underclass: Social science perspectives. *Annals of the American Academy of Political and Social Science* 501:48–59.

Tinbergen, N. 1963. On aims and methods of ethology. *Zeitschrift für Tierpsychologie* 20:410–33.

Trivers, R. 1972. Parental investment and sexual selection. In *Sexual selection and the descent of man: 1871–1971,* ed. B. Campbell, 136–79. Chicago: Aldine.

de Waal, F. B. M. 1987. Tension regulation and nonreproductive functions of sex in captive Bonobos (*Pan paniscus*). *National Geographic Research* 3:318–35.

Wasser, S. K., and D. Y. Isenberg. 1986. Reproductive suppression: Pathology or adaptation? *Journal of Psychosomatic Obstetrics and Gynecology* 5:153–75.

West-Eberhard, M. J. 1987. Flexible strategy and social evolution. In *Animal societies: Theories and facts,* ed. Y. Ito, J. Brown, and J. Kikawa, 35–51. Tokyo: Japan Scientific Society Press.

Williams, G. C. 1966. Natural selection, the costs of reproduction, and a refinement of Lack's principle. *American Naturalist* 100:687–90.

Wilson, M., and M. Daly. 1985. Competitiveness, risk taking, and violence: The young male syndrome. *Ethology and Sociobiology* 6:59–73.

Wilson, W. J., ed. 1989. The ghetto underclass: Social science perspectives. *Annals of the American Academy of Political and Social Science* 501:8–232.

Wittenberger, J. F., and R. L. Tilson. 1980. The evolution of monogamy: Hypotheses and evidence. *Annual Review of Ecological Systematics* 11:197–232.

Wood, J. W. 1990. Fertility in anthropological populations. *Annual Review of Anthropology* 19:211–42.

Wrangham, R. W. 1979. On the evolution of ape social systems. *Social Science Information* 13:335–68.

———. 1980. An ecological model of female-bonded primate groups. *Behaviour* 75:262–300.

ard Sexual Permissiveness: Trends, , and Behavioral Connections

Tom W. Smith

ᵗional wisdom, trends in sexual attitudes
ᵉe decades are captured by a pair of meta-
‑‑‑‑‑‑ ‑‑ ‑ sexual revolution in the 1960s that pre-
ᵉ counterrevolution of the 1980s. For example, *Time*,
ᵈlded the eruption of the sexual revolution on a cover in
ᵉd on another cover in 1984, "The revolution is over"

ᵡamines (1) recent trends in sexual attitudes toward
ᵡual activity—premarital, extramarital, and homosex-
how age, cohort, and period effects have shaped trends;
(ᵕ   ᵉs influence attitudes on sexual permissiveness in gen-
eraᵢ   ᵖremarital, extramarital, and homosexual relations in
partiᵥ   w attitudes about sexual behaviors relate to actual sexual beᵢ   ᵈ (5) when there is conflict between attitudes and
behaviᴄ   ; the impact on psychological well-being.

The ᵢ   yzed in this paper are from representative national
samples ᵕ ᵤdults living in the United States except as noted. Most data
come from the 1972–91 General Social Surveys (GSSs) conducted by the
National Opinion Research Center, University of Chicago. Full technical
details on the GSSs are available in Davis and Smith (1991). The remainder of the data comes from major public opinion firms such as
Gallup, Roper, and the *Los Angeles Times*.

TRENDS IN ATTITUDES TOWARD SEXUAL PERMISSIVENESS

Trends in Attitudes toward Premarital Sexual Relations

Before the 1970s evidence on trends in attitudes toward premarital
sexual relations is quite limited. There are few strictly comparable and
representative survey observations, but two broad generalizations seem
possible. First, the three short and/or sparse times series prior to 1960
show no evidence of any increase in approval of premarital sexual relations (table 1). Second, approval began to rise in the 1960s. Although

TABLE 1 Premarital Sexual Relations: Responses prior to 1960

A. ROPER: *Do you think it is all right for either or both parties to a marriage to have had previous sexual experience?*

Year	All Right (%)	All Right for Men Only (%)	Not All Right (%)	Don't Know (%)	Refused (%)
1937	22	7	55	14	2
1959	22	8	54	10	6

B. ROPER: *Do you consider it all right, unfortunate, or wicked when young men have sex relations before marriage?*

Year	All Right (%)	Unfortunate (%)	Wicked (%)	Don't Know (%)	N
1939 (women only)	9.7	35.4	47.3	7.6	. . .
1943 (women only)	5.3	43.2	45.9	5.6	2,632

C. NORC: *Please tell me whether you agree or disagree with this statement: No decent man can respect a woman who has had sexual relations before marriage.*

Year	Agree (%)	N
1950	29.4	1,135
1953	33.0	1,291

the lack of comparable data makes the timing and magnitude of the upswing uncertain, it appears to have been underway by the middle of the decade and from the mid-1960s to the mid-1970s approval increased by about 20–30 percentage points.[1] Evidence of an upswing is also provided by diverse college surveys (usually representing either single schools or just particular classes at one or more schools), which consistently show increased approval of premarital sexual relations during these years (Cannon and Long 1971; Clayton and Bokemeier 1980; DeLamater and MacCorquodale 1979; Robinson et al. 1991; Smith 1991b).

Since 1969 evidence on trends is more abundant (table 2). The increase in approval of premarital sexual relations that started in the 1960s continued until the early 1980s, but at a slower rate. The GSS time series indicates that the percentage saying premarital sexual relations were "not wrong at all" had a significant linear component of 1.0 percentage

TABLE 2 Premarital Relations: Responses since 1969

A. GALLUP: *There's a lot of discussion about the way morals and sex are changing in this country. Here is a question that is often discussed in women's magazines. What is your view on this—do you think it is wrong for a man and a woman to have sex relations before marriage, or not?*

Year	Wrong (%)	Not Wrong (%)	No Opinion (%)	N
1969	68.8	21.4	9.7	1,489
1973[a]	47.0	43.0	9.0	1,544

B. GALLUP: *There's a lot of discussion about the way morals and sexual attitudes are changing in this country. What is your opinion about this: do you think it is wrong for a man and a woman to have sex relations before marriage, or not?*

Year	Wrong (%)	Not Wrong (%)	No Opinion (%)	N
1985	39	52	9	1,525
1985[b]	36	61	3	1,003
1987	46	48	6	1,607
1990[c]	40	54	6	1,216

C. VIRGINIA SLIMS: *Now, turning to another subject, let me read you some statements. For each please tell me whether you tend to disagree or disagree: . . . Premarital sex is immoral.*

Year	Agree (%)	N
1970	59.5	3,984
1985	45.0	4,000

D. NORC-GSS: *There's been a lot of discussion about the way morals and attitudes about sex are changing in this country. If a man and a woman have sex relations before marriage, do you think it is always wrong, almost always wrong, wrong only sometimes, or not wrong at all?*

Year	Always Wrong (%)	Almost Always Wrong (%)	Wrong Only Sometimes (%)	Not Wrong At All (%)	N
1972	35.7	11.4	25.2	27.7	1,534
1974	33.4	12.9	23.9	29.8	1,430
1975	30.6	12.4	25.2	31.7	1,428
1977	30.8	9.9	23.0	36.3	1,479
1978	29.2	12.3	20.3	38.2	1,496
1982	28.2	8.9	21.8	41.1	1,457

(continued)

TABLE 2 *(continued)*

Year	Always Wrong (%)	Almost Always Wrong (%)	Wrong Only Sometimes (%)	Not Wrong At All (%)	N
1983	28.1	10.7	24.6	36.6	1,558
1985	28.1	9.0	20.0	43.0	1,485
1986	28.2	8.8	22.8	40.2	1,425
1987[d]	29.0	9.0	21.0	41.0	2,095
1988	26.2	10.2	22.2	41.4	952
1988[e]	35.0	13.0	28.0	24.0	2,556
1989	27.7	8.8	23.1	40.4	982
1990	24.7	11.3	24.5	39.5	905
1991	27.2	10.3	19.6	42.4	981

E. NORC-GSS: *What if they are in their early teens, say 14–16 years old? In that case, do you think sex relations before marriage are always wrong, almost always wrong, wrong only sometimes, or not wrong at all?*

Year	Always Wrong (%)	Almost Always Wrong (%)	Wrong Only Sometimes (%)	Not Wrong at All (%)	N
1986	67.1	18.9	10.9	3.1	1,443
1988	68.5	16.4	11.6	3.5	972
1989	70.2	16.5	9.2	4.1	1,001
1990	69.0	16.8	10.9	3.3	911
1991	68.0	19.1	8.9	4.0	983

F. MARK CLEMENTS RESEARCH: *I am going to read some statements to you. Please indicate whether you strongly agree, slightly agree, slightly disagree, or strongly disagree. . . . Sex before marriage is acceptable.*

	Women 18–65					
Year	Strongly Agree (%)	Slightly Agree (%)	Slightly Disagree (%)	Strongly Disagree (%)	Don't Know (%)	N
1982	20	27	14	36	2	1,000
1983	22	28	12	34	2	1,000
1984	18	31	13	34	4	1,000
1985	21	31	12	33	3	800
1986	23	32	12	29	4	800
1987	21	29	15	32	4	800

TABLE 2 *(continued)*

G. Los Angeles Times: *If a man and woman have sex relations before marriage, do you think that is always wrong, or sometimes wrong, or sometimes right, or always right?*

Year	Always Wrong (%)	Sometimes Wrong (%)	Sometimes Right (%)	Always Right (%)	Not Sure (%)	N
1989	25	24	35	9	7	2,095
1990	24	24	37	9	6	2,205

[a]Gallup: There's a lot of discussion about the way morals and sex are changing in this country. Here is a question that is often discussed in women's magazines. What are your views on this—do you think it is wrong for people to have sex relations before marriage, or not?

[b]Roper: A lot of people say sexual attitudes are changing in the U.S. What is your opinion about these issues—do you think it is wrong for a man and a woman to have sexual relations before marriage or not?

[c]Same as Gallup except "sexual relations" instead of "sex relations."

[d]Los Angeles Times.

[e]Gallup (Unchurched Americans Survey): What is your opinion about a man and a woman having sexual relations before marriage—do you think it is always wrong, almost always wrong, wrong only sometimes, or not wrong at all?

points per annum from 1972 to 1982.[2] Since 1982 approval of premarital sexual relations has been stable.

This stability in the 1980s is also shown on trends among women eighteen to sixty-five years old from 1982 to 1987 and in *Los Angeles Times* polls in 1989 and 1990. Similarly on the GSS from 1986 to 1991 approval of sexual relations between teenagers fourteen to sixteen years old did not change.

A similar Gallup series shows a 30–33 percentage points gain in approval of premarital sexual relations during the 1969–85 period.[3] Between 1969 and 1985 there is a significant linear component, with approval increasing by 1.6 percentage points per annum. The Gallup item shows no trend between 1985 and 1990 but does show increased disapproval in 1987, which is consistent with the GSS series and the other data.

Also of note is the fact that opinion on premarital sexual permissiveness tends to be bimodal. On the GSS item responses tend to cluster in the two extreme categories, "always wrong" and "not wrong at all" (table 2). The main shift in approval over time is a decline in "always wrong" and an increase in "not wrong at all," with the middle two categories showing little overall change. However, the *Los Angeles Times* question does not show this pattern. Responses are spread fairly evenly across the first three categories with "sometimes right" the modal category. The two modes shown on the GSS item thus are not polar-opposite camps that view premarital sexual relations as always wrong or evil versus always right or good, but those who think of it as inherently morally wrong versus those who see it as morally neutral. That is, although about 40 percent say it is "not wrong at all," only about a quarter of them (9–10 percent of all adults) believe it is "always right." The other three-quarters probably feel that there is nothing intrinsically wrong with premarital sexual relations but that only in particular circumstances are they right and advisable. The situational nature of approval is also shown by the much lower approval of teenage premarital sex (table 2) (See also Reiss [1967] and Klassen, Williams, and Levitt, [1989]).

Trends in Approval of Extramarital Sexual Relations

No trend data are available on approval of extramarital sexual relations prior to the 1973 GSS (table 3). From 1973 to 1987 there was no change in approval, with 72.6 percent saying that extramarital sexual relations were "always wrong." Then in the late 1980s disapproval increased slightly, averaging a constant 78.9 percent in 1988–91. The increase mostly occurred between 1987 and 1988. It is likely that this modest increase in disapproval was in reaction to the AIDS epidemic. Across all years (1973–91) disapproval increased at 0.47 percentage points per annum.

Trends in Approval of Homosexual Relations

Since 1973 attitudes regarding homosexual relations also show great stability, with a small shift toward disapproval (table 4). From 1973 to 1985 the percent saying homosexual relations were "always wrong" averaged a constant 73.6 percent; in 1987–1991 it was 76.7 percent. As with the increased disapproval of extramarital sex, this probably results from the outbreak of AIDS.

Although attitudes are heavily concentrated in the extreme "always wrong" category, the overall distribution is bimodal, with the other extreme "not wrong at all" forming a secondary peak of 12–15 percent and usually 10 percent or less in the two middle categories, "almost always wrong" and "wrong only sometimes."

TABLE 3 Extramarital Sexual Relations

NORC-GSS: *What is your opinion about a married person having sexual relations with someone other than the marriage partner—is it always wrong, almost always wrong, wrong only sometimes, or not wrong at all?*

Year	Always Wrong (%)	Almost Always Wrong (%)	Wrong Only Sometimes (%)	Not Wrong at All (%)	N
1973	69.8	14.8	11.7	3.8	1,491
1974	73.2	12.5	11.8	2.5	1,463
1976	68.7	16.5	10.7	4.0	1,479
1977	73.9	13.5	9.9	2.8	1,508
1980	71.0	16.4	9.6	3.0	1,446
1982	74.2	13.7	9.7	2.3	1,482
1984	71.5	18.0	8.7	1.8	1,450
1985[a]	72	16	10	2	1,003
1985	75.4	13.3	8.4	3.0	1,513
1987	74.3	16.2	7.4	2.1	1,446
1988	80.7	12.3	5.1	1.9	966
1989	78.5	12.3	7.5	1.6	1,026
1990	79.0	12.5	6.7	1.8	891
1991	77.2	13.5	6.2	3.0	965

[a]Roper: What do you think about a married person having sex with someone other than his or her spouse—is it always wrong, almost always wrong, wrong only sometimes, or not wrong at all?

A Gallup series on legalizing homosexual relations between consenting adults shows a more dramatic shift against homosexuality. There was a significant linear component increase in percent opposing the legalization of homosexuality of 1.1 percentage points per annum from 1977 to 1991. From 1977 to 1985 about 44 percent favored legalizing homosexual relations. Approval then dropped sharply in 1986 and averaged 34 percent from then until 1991. (We ignore the 1989 observation as either an error or outlier).

The sharper Gallup decline in approval might not show up in the GSS series if the shift occurred mostly among those who thought homosexual relations were always wrong. (Because these questions were not asked together, we cannot confirm this.) It might represent a decrease in tolerance of homosexuality; people who never approved of homosexuality may have become less willing to allow it to be legal. However, this

TABLE 4 Homosexual Sexual Relations

A. NORC-GSS: *What about sexual relations between two adults of the same sex—do you think it is always wrong, almost always wrong, wrong only sometimes, or not wrong at all?*

Year	Always Wrong (%)	Almost Always Wrong (%)	Wrong Only Sometimes (%)	Not Wrong at All (%)	Other (%)	N
1973	72.5	6.7	7.7	11.2	2.0	1,446
1974	69.4	5.6	8.5	12.9	3.5	1,413
1976	70.3	6.3	7.9	15.5	...	1,432
1977	72.9	5.8	7.5	13.7	...	1,457
1980	73.8	6.1	5.9	14.2	...	1,404
1982	74.3	5.0	6.5	14.1	...	1,438
1984	75.1	4.5	7.0	13.3	...	1,415
1985	75.7	4.2	7.0	13.1	...	1,487
1987	77.5	4.2	6.3	12.0	...	1,418
1988	77.4	4.4	5.5	12.7	...	945
1989	74.4	4.0	6.3	15.3	...	986
1990	76.5	5.0	5.8	12.8	...	867
1991	77.4	3.8	4.0	14.9	...	925

B. GALLUP: *Do you think homosexual relations between consenting adults should or should not be legal?*

Year	Legal (%)	Not Legal (%)	No Opinion (%)	N
1977	43	43	14	1,513
1981[a]	39	50	11	1,533
1982	45	39	16	1,531
1985	44	47	9	1,008
1986	32	57	11	1,539
1986	33	54	13	978
1987	33	55	11	1,015
1988	35	56	9	1,000
1989	47	36	17	1,227
1991	36	54	10	1,216

[a]ABC/WP.

interpretation is challenged by the fact that a GSS scale on civil liberties for homosexuals actually shows decreasing opposition to civil liberties for homosexuals in 1980s (table 5). Over the entire period intolerance decreased by −0.43 points and most of the decline happened in 1987–88. (−.06) and 1988–89 (−.20). Moreover, the decline in intolerance among those who thought that homosexuality was always wrong was even greater than among the general population (table 4). The opposite direction of the Gallup legalization and GSS civil liberties trends may

TABLE 5 Trends in Attitudes toward Civil Liberties of Homosexuals

	Intolerance Scale[a]		
Year	All (N)	People Saying Homosexual Relations Always Wrong (N)	Intolerance · Approval of Homosexual Relations (Pearson *r*)
1973	4.3 (1398)	4.7 (966)	−.46
1974	4.2 (1361)	4.6 (896)	−.45
1976	4.2 (1402)	4.6 (931)	−.44
1977	4.3 (1430)	4.7 (989)	−.46
1980	4.1 (1393)	4.5 (979)	−.42
1982	4.2 (1411)	4.5 (995)	−.43
1984	4.1 (1369)	4.4 (989)	−.40
1985	4.1 (1372)	4.5 (1060)	−.41
1987	4.1 (1450)	4.4 (1016)	−.40
1988	4.1 (901)	4.3 (669)	−.37
1989	3.9 (961)	4.1 (676)	−.29
1990	3.9 (851)	4.1 (622)	−.34
1991	3.9 (932)	4.1 (671)	−.34
Trend[b]	.0000	.0000	

[a]A three-item additive scale of the questions listed below. 3 = tolerant of all three activities; and 6 = intolerance of all three activities.
[b]Probability that scores differ from constant value.

NORC-GSS: And what about a man who admits that he is a homosexual? A. Suppose this admitted homosexual wanted to make a speech in your community. Should he be allowed to speak, or not? B. Should a such a person be allowed to teach in a college or university, or not? C, If some people in your community suggested that a book he wrote in favor of homosexuality should be taken out of your public library, would you favor removing this book, or not? An additive scale was created from these items such that a score of 3 meant allowing all three activities and a score of 6 meant opposing all three actions.

reflect an increased public desire to regulate homosexuality without restricting the nonsexual rights of homosexuals.

AGE-COHORT CHANGES IN ATTITUDES TOWARD
SEXUAL PERMISSIVENESS

One of the main mechanisms of social change is cohort turnover, the replacement of earlier birth cohorts by later cohorts that hold different views. Table 6 shows how attitudes toward premarital, extramarital, and homosexual relations changed over time within age groups and birth cohorts. For premarital sexual relations the first, third, and last columns show the percent saying premarital sexual relations are always wrong. By comparing each row of age groups, once can see how attitudes within age groups changed over time. The second and fourth columns show changes across time within birth cohorts. To compare how attitudes have changed within birth cohorts one compares along the diagonals. For example, among those who were eighteen to twenty-five in 1974–75 (born between 1949 and 1957) and twenty-six to thirty-three in 1982–83 disapproval increased by 5.2 percentage points.

Although the confounding of age, cohort, and period makes it impossible to untangle definitively the combination of effects that are going on, certain patterns are clear: for all three measures the difference between the youngest and oldest age groups are diminishing over time, as seen by the decline in the age-group differences in table 6. For premarital sexual relations it reduces from 51 percentage points to 35 percentage points, for extramarital from 35 to 10, and for homosexual from 35 to 17. For premarital sexual relations the decline comes from an increase in disapproval among the youngest age group (+6.1 percentage points from the 1970s to the 1990s) and a decrease in disapproval among the oldest age group (−9.6 from the 1970s to the 1990s). For extramarital and homosexual relations the reduced difference across age groups comes almost entirely from rising disapproval among the youngest age groups (+21 percentage points for extramarital and +17 for homosexual).

We believe this represents a narrowing of a generational gap that had been opening up prior to the 1970s. Although alternative explanations such as a decreasing age effect resulting from either changes in biological or in life-cycle factors would also fit the data, we believe a cohort difference followed by an antipermissive period shift is the most plausible. First, evidence from Klassen and his colleagues (Klassen, Williams, and Levitt 1989; Klassen et al. 1989) shows an increase in premarital

TABLE 6 Disapproval of Premarital, Extramarital, and Homosexual Sexual Relations by Age Groups and Year

A. Premarital Sexual Relations (% always wrong)

Age Groups	1974–75	Intracohort Change	1982–83	Intracohort Change	1990–91
18–25	12.0		14.0		18.1
		+5.2		+7.5	
26–33	17.1		17.2		21.5
		+6.3		+1.1	
34–41	35.2		23.4		18.3
		−5.0		+2.1	
42–49	33.9		30.2		25.5
		+1.0		−2.0	
50–57	40.0		34.9		28.2
		+3.3		−5.1	
58–65	44.5		43.3		29.8
		+1.5		+0.1	
66–73	54.2		46.0		43.4
		−0.9		+7.5	
74 and older	62.9		53.1		53.5
Total	32.0		28.1		26.2
Age-group difference	50.9		39.1		35.4
N	2,850		3,004		1,885

B. Extramarital Sexual Relations (% always wrong)

Age Groups	1973–74	Intracohort Change	1980–82	Intracohort Change	1987–90
18–25	56.0		67.7		77.4
		+6.7		+4.3	
26–33	63.3		62.7		72.0
		+5.5		+8.2	
34–41	70.3		68.8		70.9
		−1.7		+6.4	
42–49	73.7		68.6		75.2
		+3.5		+13.1	
50–57	80.1		77.2		81.7
		+0.9		+8.8	
58–65	78.2		82.0		86.0
		+8.6		+4.3	

(*continued*)

TABLE 6 *(continued)*

B. Extramarital Sexual Relations (% always wrong)

Age Groups	1973–74	Intracohort Change	1980–82	Intracohort Change	1987–90
66–73	85.2		86.8		86.3
		−4.2		+0.2	
74 and older	90.8		89.4		87.0
Total	71.4		72.6		77.7
Age-group difference	34.8		21.7		9.6
N	2,947		2,912		4,319

C. Homosexual Sexual Relations (% always wrong)

Age Groups	1973–74	Intracohort Change	1980–82	Intracohort Change	1987–90
18–25	56.0		65.2		73.3
		+8.5		+4.3	
26–33	61.7		64.5		69.5
		+8.7		+6.4	
34–41	76.9		69.4		70.9
		−2.5		+4.0	
42–49	70.3		74.4		73.4
		+9.5		+9.6	
50–57	82.4		79.8		84.0
		+2.0		+4.5	
58–65	85.0		84.4		84.3
		+3.2		+0.7	
66–73	89.8		88.2		85.1
		+1.9		+2.1	
74 and older	91.5		91.7		90.3
Total	71.0		72.6		76.5
Age-group difference	34.6		26.5		17.0
N	2,775		2,827		4,206

Source: NORC-GSS.

sexual activity across recent cohorts. Second, a study of aging and cohort effects over the last twenty years by Davis (1991) found this same model to apply to many nonsexual trends. For forty-some items ranging from civil liberties to race relations Davis found evidence of a conservative period effect in the 1980s offsetting a liberal cohort effect. Finally,

Cutler (1985) adopted a similar perspective to explain trends in sexual permissiveness up to the early 1980s.

On all three sexual attitude items the entering or new birth cohorts (those eighteen to twenty-five in the early 1980s or late 1980s and early 1990s) are less approving than their counterparts in the 1970s. We believe that the entering-cohort shifts and the within-cohort increases that show up within earlier cohorts reflect the impact of a disapproving period effect.

For premarital sexual relations the generational gap was especially large in the early 1970s (presumably a result of the large growth in approval during the so-called sexual revolution among entering cohorts) and the within-cohort, period shift was weak. This permitted attitudes to continue moving in an approving direction (but at a slowing rate) until the early 1980s. One way to show this is to look at what attitudes would have been in the early 1980s and 1990s if there had been no cohort turnover. The observed percentage saying premarital sex was always wrong was 32.0 percent in the 1970s, 28.1 percent in the early 1980s, and 26.2 percent in the early 1990s—a decline in disapproval of 5.8 percentage points. Fixing the birth-cohort structure in those latter years to match what it was in the 1970s changes the percentages to 33.6 percent in the 1980s and 34.0 percent in the early 1990s—an increase in disapproval of 2.0 percentage points. Thus, because of cohort turnover, disapproval of premarital sexual relations from the 1970s to the 1990s decreased rather than increased.

For extramarital and homosexual relations the generational gap was smaller (although still substantial) and the within-cohort period effect was larger and more consistent both in the 1970s and the 1980s. In each case cohort turnover dampened what would have been a more pronounced shift toward disapproval. For extramarital relations disapproval from the 1970s to the 1990s grew by 6.3 percentage points; without cohort turnover, it would have grown by 9.6 percentage points; for homosexual relations it rose by 3.5 percentage points and would have risen by 8.5 percentage points.

In brief, we interpret the age-cohort-period interaction on sexual permissiveness as showing a large cohort difference in the 1970s, with more recent cohorts being more permissive than earlier cohorts. This generation gap diminished over the next twenty years as a result of a period shift against permissiveness, which meant that new or entering cohorts were less permissive than their earlier counterparts. For approval of premarital sexual relations the cohort turnover's push toward permissiveness prevailed until the early 1980s, and since then the two have roughly balanced out. For extramarital and homosexual relations the cohort turnover and period shift initially balanced out, but by the mid-1980s, as the impact of cohort declined, there was a net swing toward less permissive attitudes.

Sexual Permissiveness Scale

Approval of premarital, extramarital, and homosexual relations form a general scale of approval of sexual permissiveness. They have moderately high inter-item correlations (Pearson r: premarital · extramarital = .37; premarital · homosexual = .38; extramarital · homosexual = .37) and a Cronbach's alpha of .62. In addition, they are generally associated with the same variables in the same way. The only exception is race. African-Americans are significantly more permissive than non-African-Americans on premarital and extramarital relations but less permissive than non-African-Americans toward homosexual relations.

This scale shows no statistically significant change from 1974 to 1991 (table 7). This stability comes from the offsetting shifts toward approval of premarital sexual relations and toward disapproval of extramarital and homosexual relations.

Most associates of permissiveness have also been stable across the last three decades. The overall stability of sexual permissiveness is reflected in a lack of change within most subgroups. The main exception is the age-cohort changes described above. Among those eighteen to

TABLE 7 Trends in Sexual Permissiveness

Year	Mean[a]	N
1974	5.6	1,320
1977	5.7	1,425
1982	5.8	1,388
1985	5.7	1,446
1988	5.6	459
1989	5.6	485
1990	5.5	439
1991	5.5	442

Source: NORC-GSS.

Note: Additive scale of approval of premarital, extramarital, and homosexual sexual relations. Ranges from low of 3 if all three are "always wrong" to 12 if all three are "not wrong at all."

[a]Probability = .077.

twenty-nine sexual permissiveness fell by 1.33 points from 1974 to 1991; for age groups from thirty to thirty-nine to seventy and above sexual permissiveness rose between .20 and .50. No other notable interactions occurred across time, although the edge in the permissiveness of metropolitan localities (central cities and suburbs) over small towns and rural areas and of the Northeast and West over the Midwest and South diminished somewhat over the period.

CORRELATES OF SEXUAL PERMISSIVENESS

Because there is little interaction across time (with the exception of age and cohort), we pooled all surveys to examine the correlates of sexual permissiveness (table 8). The existing literature has examined how various factors relate to approval of sexual permissiveness (Alston 1974; Alston and Tucker 1975; Anderson and Crane 1979; Bock, Beeghley, and Mixon 1983; Cutler 1985; DeLamater 1981; Harding 1988; Irwin and Thompson 1977; Klassen, Williams, and Levitt 1989; Mahoney 1978; Nyberg and Alston 1976–77; Reiss 1967; Reiss 1975; Reiss 1980; Reiss, Anderson, and Sponaugle 1980; Saunders and Edwards 1984; Schneider and Lewis 1984; Singh 1980; Singh, Adams, and Jorgenson 1981; Singh, Walton, and Williams 1976; Snyder and Spreitzer 1976; Stephan and McMullin 1982; Thornton 1989; Weis and Jurich 1985; and Wilson 1986). This research finds that sexual permissiveness is greater among the following groups and for the following reasons:[4]

1. More recent birth cohorts are more sexually permissive because society has moved away from a restrictive, puritanical sexual standard to a more open, modern standard.

2. The better educated are more permissive because education promotes liberality, progressive thinking, and a cosmopolitan worldview.

3. Those with a less religious upbringing and those currently less religious (in terms of affiliation, church attendance, beliefs, and theological orientation) are more permissive because Christian religions in general and conservative denominations in particular preach sexual regulation in general and the immorality of these behaviors in particular.

4. Men are more permissive than women because they have more of a biological and social imperative for maximizing their sexual relations while minimizing their responsibility for offspring and because the perception of less sexual need among women lowers this natural justification for sexual permissiveness and therefore makes female violation of traditional, sexual norms less acceptable.

5. African-Americans are more permissive because their family and

TABLE 8 Factors Associated with Approval of Sexual Permissiveness

Groups	Mean Score	r/probability[a]
Cohort (N = 7, 382):		
Born before 1910	4.21	
1910–19	4.63	
1920–29	5.07	
1930–39	5.38	.29***
1940–49	6.16	
1950–59	6.50	
1960+	6.05	
Current religion (N = 7,404):		
None	7.76	−.24***
Some affiliation	5.49	
Religion when growing up (N = 7,391):		
None	6.11	−.04**
Some affiliation	5.63	
Current religious orientation (N = 7,255):		
Fundamentalist	4.85	
Moderate	5.66	.29***
Liberal	6.75	
Religious orientation when growing up (N = 7,391)		
Fundamentalist	5.02	
Moderate	5.84	.18***
Liberal	6.17	
Church attendance (N = 7,364):		
Twice a year or less	6.63	
Almost weekly–several times per year	5.75	−.39***
Weekly	4.41	
Education (N = 7,386):		
Less than high school	5.02	
High school graduate	5.50	.25***
Some college	6.17	
College graduate	6.82	
Gender (N = 7,404):		
Men	5.84	−.08***
Women	5.47	
Race (N = 7,404)		
Non-African-American	5.62	.03**
African-American	5.84	

TABLE 8 *(continued)*

Groups	Mean Score	r/probability[a]
Household income (1986 dollars) (N = 6,744):		
0–9,999	5.28	
10,000–19,999	5.48	
20,000–29,999	5.64	
30,000–39,999	5.71	.13***
40,000–49,999	5.86	
50,000–74,999	6.08	
75,000+	6.37	
Current region (N = 7,404)		
Northeast	6.34	
Midwest	5.56	.18***
South	5.06	
West	6.06	
Region at age 16 (N = 7,404):		
Foreign	5.62	
Northeast	6.43	
Midwest	5.62	.19***
South	5.00	
West	6.03	
Current residence (N = 7,404):		
Central city	6.12	
Suburb	5.68	−.20***
Town	5.31	
Rural	4.88	
Residence at age 16 (N = 7,384):		
Central city/suburb	6.32	
Town	5.78	−.20***
Rural	4.92	
Marital status (N = 7,403):		
First marriage	5.33	
Remarried	5.76	−.18*** (Never
Widowed	4.48	married)
Divorced	6.53	−.11*** (Divorced
Separated	6.34	or separated)
Never married	6.54	

(continued)

TABLE 8 *(continued)*

Groups	Mean Score	r/probability[a]
Teenagers (N = 7,375):		
None	5.71	
1	5.45	
2	5.35	−.05***
3	5.30	
4	5.01	
Liberal self-identification (N = 7,386):		
Extremely liberal	7.41	
Liberal	6.86	
Slightly liberal	6.38	
Moderate/middle of the road	5.54	−.28***
Slightly conservative	5.33	
Conservative	4.74	
Extremely conservative	4.64	
Not rated	4.65	
General happiness (N = 7,391):		
Very happy	5.34	
Pretty happy	5.81	.08***
Not too happy	5.74	
Marital happiness (N = 4867):		
Very happy	5.26	
Pretty happy	5.61	.08***
Not too happy	5.90	
	(4,867)	

Source: NORC-GSS, combined years, 1977, 1982,1985, 1988–91.
** = $p < .01$ *** = $p < .001$
[a]Pearson's *r*'s are based on uncollapsed variables where appropriate (e.g., years of education and age). For nominal variables the following categorizations were used: Marital status = never married vs. other and divorced/separated vs. other; region-South vs. non-South.

social structures have contributed to early sexual initiation and a high rate of nonmarital births, which have since become established features of African-American society and perhaps because African-Americans never accepted as fully as whites Victorian and puritanical sexual norms.

6. The middle and upper classes are more permissive since they are more modern, cosmopolitan, and forward-looking. However, a counterhypothesis argues that the lower class will be more permissive because

it is less responsible, less likely to delay gratification, and less constrained by social conventions.

7. Current residents outside the South and those raised outside the South are more permissive because the South is more traditional in its social customs and more influenced by fundamentalism.

8. Residents of large metropolitan areas and those raised in such communities are more permissive because nonmetropolitan areas are more traditionally oriented.

9. (a) The never-married are more permissive because they have a self-interest in approving of premarital sexual relations and perhaps less personal commitment to the convention of marital fidelity. In addition, because of the prohibition on same-sex marriages, homosexuals are overrepresented in the never-married category (Smith 1991a). (b) The divorced and separated are more permissive because they, too, have a self-interest in nonmarital sexual relations and perhaps may be disillusioned about the norm of marital fidelity as a result of their own or their ex-spouse's sexual behavior.

10. Those without teenagers in the household are more permissive because the presence of teenagers might lead people to think about approval of teenage sexual behavior rather than adult sexual behavior. This would presumably apply mostly to premarital sexual permissiveness.

11. Liberals are more permissive than nonliberals because sexual permissiveness represents a modern and emergent orientation as opposed to traditional norms.

12. Those in unhappy marriages are more permissive because extramarital sexual relations might seem more justified. This would presumably apply only to extramarital sexual permissiveness.[5]

Table 8 shows that these hypotheses are in general well supported. In each case there are statistically significant and often substantial differences across subgroups in the anticipated direction. Sexual permissiveness is higher among those from more recent cohorts, the better educated, the less religious (those without a religious affiliation, with more theologically liberal affiliations, and attending church less frequently), men, African-Americans, higher-income earners, non-Southerners (currently and when growing up), metropolitan dwellers (currently and when growing up), the never married and currently divorced or separated, those without teenagers in their families, political liberals, and those unhappy with life in general and with their marriages in particular.

The multiple-regression analyses in table 9 show that most of these are independent predictors. Subcultural orientation (e.g., ethnicity, race, and region) in general and religion in particular has a pronounced impact on attitudes toward sexual permissiveness. Low church attendance and a liberal theological orientation (currently and to a modest extent when growing up) are associated with approval.[6]

Similarly, those raised in and currently living outside traditional regions (the South) and community types (nonmetropolitan areas) are more approving.

TABLE 9 Multiple-Regression Analysis of Sexual Permissiveness

Variables (high category)	Standardized Coefficient
Religion:	
Church attendance (weekly)	−.30***
Current religious orientation (liberal)	.10***
Current religion (some)	.03**
Religious orientation raised in (liberal)	.05***
Religion raised in (some)	.04***
Place:	
Current region (non-South)	.05**
Current residence (large central city)	.07***
Region raised in (non-South)	.04*
Residence when 16 (large central city)	.05***
Socioeconomic status:	
Education (20 or more years)	.12***
Family income in constant dollars (high)	.05***
Family:	
Never married versus other (other)	.03*
Divorced/single versus other (other)	−.07***
Teens in household (4 or more)	−.04***
Other:	
Race (African-American)	.07***
Birth cohort (more recent years)	.15***
Political ideology (extremely conservative)	−.17***
Sex (female)	−.01
R^2	.351
N	6,475

Source: NORC-GSS, combined years, 1974, 1977, 1982, 1985, 1988–91.
*$p < .05$.   **$p < .01$.   ***$p < .001$.

The effect of subculture is also shown by the greater approval of sexual permissiveness among African-Americans.

In the culture as a whole, the impact of changing sexual norms is indicated by the higher permissiveness among those raised in more recent cohorts.

Higher socioeconomic status (SES) is also related to more permissiveness. Both more education and higher family income are associated with more approval. Education, however, plays a much stronger role than income. This suggests that it is values assimilated via schooling (e.g., open-mindedness and cultural pluralism) rather than material conditions that promote permissiveness.

Family-status variables have modest relations in the predicted direction. Those who are divorced or separated or who have never married are more permissive than the currently married and widowed. The difference among the never-married is small and statistically marginal, however. Those having teens in the household are less permissive.

Political ideology is strongly associated with sexual permissiveness. This may indicate that those adopting a general liberal philosophy apply broad principles such as tolerance and individual choice to the sexual arena and that support for sexual freedom is directly seen as a liberal tenet. (In this latter case the causal ordering between liberalism and conservativism and sexual permissiveness becomes unclear because one might define oneself as a liberal or conservative because of one's stance on sexual permissiveness.)

We also find that gender has no association with overall sexual permissiveness. This results from two factors: First, the bivariate association between gender and permissiveness is accounted for by the fact that more women tend to survive from older cohorts and that women are more religious in general and in particular attend church more frequently than men do. Second, as indicated below, although men are more permissive toward premarital and extramarital sexual relations than women are, they are less approving than women of homosexual relations.

Finally, after allowing the above variables to enter the regression equation, we looked at whether marital happiness or general happiness were related to sexual permissiveness. Among the married, having an unhappy marriage was modestly but significantly associated with more approval of sexual permissiveness ($r = .045$/prob. $= .000$). Among everyone however, general happiness was not related to permissiveness ($r = .02$/prob. $= .117$).

Table 10 shows how the independent variables displayed in table 8 are related to each of the three separate components. Premarital sexual relations are explained to a greater extent by the independent variables than are attitudes toward homosexual and extramarital sexual relations as indicated by the R^2s in the three equations. Most associations are in the same direction, although their magnitude often varies. For three variables, however, there are statistically significant relations with oppo-

TABLE 10 Multiple-Regression Analysis of Attitudes toward Premarital, Extramarital, and Homosexual Relations (high = permissive)

Variables (high category)	Standardized Coefficient/Probabili		
	Premarital	Extramarital	Homos
Religion			
Church attendance (weekly)	−.32***	−.17***	−.16
Current religious orientation (liberal)	.11***	.05**	.06
Current religion (some)	.03*	−.09***	−.07
Past religious orientation (liberal)	.03*	.02	.05
Religion raised in (some)	.04***	.01	.01
Place:			
Current region (non-South)	.05**	−.00	.04
Current residence (large central city)	.05***	.05***	.06
Region raised in (non-South)	.05**	.01	.02
Residence when 16 (large central city)	.02	.04**	.05
Socioeconomic status:			
Education (20 or more years)	.04***	.09***	.15
Family income in constant dollars (high)	.03**	.04**	.05
Family:			
Never married versus other (other)	.03*	−.07***	−.05
Divorced/separated versus other (other)	−.05***	−.10***	−.04
Teens in household (4 or more)	−.06***	.02	−.03
Other:			
Race (African-American)	.10***	.09***	−.02
Birth cohort (more recent years)	.26***	−.02	.04
Political ideology (conservative)	−.14***	−.09***	−.16
Sex (female)	−.07***	−.05***	.08
R^2	.324	.137	.20
N	6,475	6,475	ε

Source: NORC-GSS, combined years, 1974, 1977, 1982, 1985, 1988–91.
*p = .05.   **p < .01.   ***p < .001.

site signs. First, men are more permissive than women (controlling for other variables) about premarital and extramarital relations but less permissive about homosexual relations. We speculate that homosexuality might be viewed either by people in general or men in particular as referring to man-with-man sex to a greater extent than woman-with-woman sex. Heterosexual men who are concerned about their sexual identity or who wish to signal that they are "straight" may therefore be more inclined to disapprove of homosexual relations.

Second, counter to our hypothesis, the never-married are marginally less approving than those with other marital statuses of premarital sexual relations, although they are more approving of extramarital and homosexual relations. Although there is a significant bivariate association between never having been married and approval of premarital sexual relations ($r = -.16$/prob. $= .000$), this is explained by cohort. The partial r between being never married and approval of premarital sexual relations controlling for cohort falls to $-.01$ and is not statistically significant (prob. $= .126$). The other control variables in table 10 further tip this weak relationship in the opposite direction. Extramarital and homosexual relations are not so reversed in large part because their association with cohort is weaker.

It is possible that the never-married are marginally less permissive (with controls) because this group includes a number of people with low sexual interest and those who are sexually repressed. These groups might select to remain unmarried and would offset the self-interest that most never-married adults would have in approving of premarital sex.

Third, those with no religious affiliation are, counter to the hypothesis, marginally less permissive than those with a religious affiliation toward premarital sexual relations, but, as predicted, the unaffiliated are more permissive toward extramarital and homosexual relations. The reversal of the hypothesized, bivariate relationship is accounted for by a combination of other religion variables (attendance and theology) and age.

Besides variables involving reversals, there are several instances in which relationships are not statistically significant for all three types of sexual permissiveness. As noted earlier, the cohort effect is much stronger for premarital sexual relations than for extramarital or homosexual relations. This probably reflects a much larger permissive period effect in the 1960s for premarital sexual relations than for extramarital and homosexual relations.

Similarly, as was also noted in the bivariate relationships, African-

Americans are more permissive toward premarital and extramarital sexual relations but less approving of homosexual relations. Racial differences in sexual behaviors (e.g., lower age of first intercourse, greater
teenage sexual activity, higher proportion of unmarried births, and
more marital instability among African-Americans than among whites)
are consistent with the greater permissiveness of African-Americans on
premarital and extramarital sex. This pattern may also in part result
from an imbalance in the effective African-American sex ratio. A short-
fall of suitable African-American male partners might encourage permissiveness because African-American males would have to expand
their mean number of partners to compensate for their lower numbers.
For women it would increase the sharing of male partners with other
women (Posner 1992; Bowser chap. 5, this vol.; Sterk-Elifson, chap. 4,
this vol.). The low sex ratio among African-Americans may also reduce
opportunistic homosexual behavior by males.

In addition, although having teenagers in the household is associated
with less sexual permissiveness (table 9), this comes largely from the
reduced approval of premarital sexual relations (table 10). Controlling
for marital status, gender, and age, we find that in twenty-five of the
thirty-one comparisons between households with and without teenagers approval is lower when a teenager is present (data not shown). It is
likely that concern about the sexual activity of their own teenage children reduces support for premarital sexual relations either by (a) making parents of teenagers think more about teenage sexual activity and
less about adult sexual activity and/or (b) by personalizing concerns
about teenage sexual activity. Some support for the latter idea comes
from examining the related question on sexual relations between
fourteen- and sixteen-year-olds (table 2). Because this item refers to
teenagers fourteen to sixteen years, attitudes toward adult premarital
sexual permissiveness are not relevant. Controlling for marital status,
gender, and age, households with teenagers are about 10 percentage
points more likely to say that teenage sexual relations are always wrong
than households without teenagers present (table 11).[7]

Likewise, greater extramarital sexual permissiveness occurs among
those in less happy marriages (regression coefficient = .093/prob. =
.000) and among those less happy with their lives in general (regression
coefficient = .061/prob. = .000), but neither marital nor general happiness are associated with permissiveness toward premarital or homosexual relations.

Finally, we examine one aspect of the role of marital status that was

TABLE 11 Disapproval of Teenage Sexual Relations by Marital Status, Controlling for Teenagers in the Household, Age, and Gender

	Age											
	Men						Women					
	34–41		42–49		50–57		34–41		42–49		50–57	
Marital Status	%	N	%	N	%	N	%	N	%	N	%	N
Married:												
First time:												
No teens	60.4	177	73.3	100	78.5	104	66.2	154	81.6	127	86.5	120
One or more teens	71.4	65	77.6	102	73.5	39	76.8	103	87.4	98	97.9	25
Remarried:												
No teens	56.0	64	62.4	39	62.7	32	58.5	71	68.5	41	81.0	46
One or more teens	56.0	27	79.3	30	...	15	69.7	43	...	19	...	4
Divorced or separated:												
No teens	47.9	50	55.3	40	53.4	29	65.0	55	63.5	59	82.1	37
One or more teens	...	7	...	4	...	1	74.8	39	77.9	43	...	5

Source: NORC-GSS, 1986, 1988–91.

Note: Other ages and marital statuses are excluded because there are too few cases for comparisons.

not covered in the initial hypotheses. Because the divorced and separated are more approving of both premarital and extramarital sexual relations as hypothesized, we wondered how the other postmarried group, the widowed, stood on sexual permissiveness. Traditionally the widowed are seen as asexual and/or prudish; divorced men and women are seen as sexually active and even morally loose. Clearly most of these differences in images comes from the fact that the widowed are typically thought of as old and female; the divorced are pictured as middle-aged and include both men and women. Controlling for both gender and age, we find that widows are in fact less approving of both premarital and extramarital relations (table 12). There are too few widowers to speak about with much confidence, but at least on premarital sexual relations they also appear less permissive. It may be that their state of bereavement or status as bereaved survivors lowers their interest in sexual relations and leads to less permissive attitudes. Similarly, idealization of their lost spouses or their marriages may increase support for marital fidelity among the widowed. Richard Green (chap. 13, this vol.) reports a special widower's syndrome familiar to sex therapists, men with sexual problems in late life, following the death of their wives.

TABLE 12 Disapproval of Premarital and Extramarital Sexual
Relations by Postmarital Status, Controlling for Gender and Age

	Postmarital Status							
	Men				Women			
	Widowed		Divorced or Separated		Widowed		Divorced or Separated	
Age	%	N	%	N	%	N	%	N
Premarital Sexual Relations (% always-sometimes wrong)								
42–49	...	7	31.0	97	63.0	48	51.5	198
50–57	...	16	44.1	73	70.3	99	69.3	118
58–65	81.5	25	57.0	45	79.4	178	76.2	90
66–73	66.8	53	57.0	26	85.8	235	70.0	51
74 and older	72.0	69	...	8	90.0	350	...	19
Extramarital Sexual Relations (% always wrong)								
34–41	...	5	50.0	118	69.0	21	58.1	221
42–49	...	7	58.1	96	80.1	45	65.9	204
50–57	...	17	59.2	73	86.4	94	72.3	113
58–65	65.0	33	63.4	51	86.3	165	68.1	87
66–73	70.5	56	78.6	28	88.4	256	93.5	54
74 and older	83.4	77	...	13	88.8	379	80.4	21

Source: NORC-GSS.
Note: Other age groups are not presented because there are too few cases for
comparisons.

SEXUAL ATTITUDES AND SEXUAL BEHAVIORS

There is a great deal of consistency between sexual attitudes and sexual behaviors (table 13). Those with more permissive attitudes toward
premarital, extramarital, and homosexual relations are more likely to
have engaged in the related behavior. For example, among those saying
that extramarital relations are always wrong 9.7 percent report ever having had a sexual partner other than their spouse while married; among
those saying extramarital relations are not wrong at all 75.8 percent report personal infidelity. This pattern occurs among both men and
women. (Data not shown.)

The general agreement between sexual attitudes and behaviors may
mean that people regulate their sexual behaviors to conform to their
personal norms or that people adopt norms that match their behaviors.
Probably both processes are at work.

ATTITUDINAL AND BEHAVIORAL CONFLICT AND
PSYCHOLOGICAL WELL-BEING

Although there is general consistency between sexual attitudes and behaviors, an appreciable number of people report sexual behaviors that are at odds with their expressed values. For example, although premari-

TABLE 13 Consistency between Attitudes toward Sexual
Permissiveness and Sexual Behaviors (%)

A. Premarital Sexual Attitudes and Behaviors

Attitudes toward Premarital Sexual Relations	Having Sexual Partner among the Never-Married	
	During Last Year	During Last 5 Years
Always wrong	31.5	38.6
Almost always wrong	68.2	61.1
Wrong only sometimes	74.1	82.8
Not wrong at all	85.5	95.2
N	729	173

B. Extramarital Sexual Attitudes and Behaviors

Attitudes toward Extramarital Sexual Relations	Having Sexual Partner Other than Spouse during Last Year (currently married)	Ever Having Sexual Partner Other than Spouse While Married (ever married)
Always wrong	2.4	9.7
Almost always wrong	8.5	30.7
Wrong only sometimes	12.4	37.9
Not wrong at all	18.3	75.8
N	2,076	631

C. Homosexual Attitudes and Behaviors

Attitude toward Homosexual Relations	Having Same-Gender Sexual Partner during Last Year
Always wrong	0.9
Almost always wrong	0.0
Wrong only sometimes	1.1
Not wrong at all	14.9
N	2,566

Source: GSS, 1988–91.

tal sexual activity is lowest among those saying such activity is always
wrong, 31.5 percent of the unmarried who disapprove of premarital
sexual activity still report having had a sexual partner within the last
year (table 13).

Table 14 examines how dissonance between attitudes toward premarital and extramarital sexual relations and corresponding behaviors
relates to psychological well-being. (There are insufficient homosexual
cases for a similar analysis.) Among the never-married, those saying that
premarital sexual relations are always wrong yet report having a sex
partner are less happy than those with similar attitudes and no sex partner. Among those saying that premarital sexual relations are *not* always
wrong (i.e., almost always wrong, wrong only sometimes, and not
wrong at all), there is no statistically significant relation between having

TABLE 14 Psychological Well-Being by Consistency between
Sexual Attitudes and Behaviors

Sexual Attitudes and Behaviors	Very Happy (%)	N
Premarital (Never married)		
Premarital sexual relations are always wrong:		
No sexual partner in last year	38.9	73**
Sexual partner in last year	8.3	36
No sexual partner in last 5 years	54.3	19*
Sexual partner in last 5 years	8.3	12
Premarital sexual relations are not always wrong:		
No sexual partner in last year	21.6	119
Sexual partner in last year	28.3	504
No sexual partner in last 5 years	18.5	14
Sexual partner in last 5 years	28.9	128
Extramarital (Married)		
Extramarital sexual relations are always wrong:		
No sexual partner other than spouse, last year	42.1	1,638*
Sexual partner other than spouse, last year	22.8	39
No sexual partner other than spouse, ever	34.5	443
Sexual partner other than spouse, ever	23.1	48
Extramarital sexual relations are not always wrong:		
No sexual partner other than spouse, last year	34.6	333***
Sexual partner other than spouse, last year	15.4	37
No sexual partner other than spouse, ever	14.3	52*
Sexual partner other than spouse, ever	35.8	84

*p = .05.   **p = .01.   ***p = .001.

a sex partner and personal happiness, but those with a sex partner tend to be happier. It thus appears that among the unmarried the conflict between nonpermissive attitudes and sexual activity is associated with a lower level of psychological well-being, presumably because of the conflict created by the discrepancy between attitudes and behaviors.

No similar pattern emerges for extramarital sexual attitudes and behaviors. Those reporting a sex partner besides their spouse are less happy (both in general and in terms of their marriages) than those with no other partners. However, this pattern occurs regardless of whether one says extramarital relations are always wrong or not always wrong.

The difference between these two cases may result from a different causal relation of happiness to sexual attitudes and behaviors. In the case of premarital sexual relations the conflict of attitudes and behaviors may be causing the unhappiness, but in the extramarital case, unhappiness may lead to changes in sexual attitudes and/or behaviors.

SUMMARY

The kernel of truth in the sexual revolution/counterrevolution metaphor is that approval of premarital sexual relations increased substantially from the 1960s to the early 1980s and then leveled off. But the counter revolution did not reverse the earlier gains in premarital sexual permissiveness. This trend fits a more general pattern that saw a number of liberal trends in such areas as civil liberties and abortion reach a liberal plateau in the later 1970s and 1980s (Davis 1991; Smith 1990b; Smith 1990c). This ending of liberal advance might reflect a homeostatic cycle of reform or a reaction to problems created by liberalism in general or sexual permissiveness in particular (e.g., increases in sexually transmitted diseases and nonmarital births, possibly a desire for commitment rather than casual, recreational sex, etc.)

Moreover, the revolutionary imagery is misleading because it does not clearly apply to sexual attitudes in general. At least since the early 1970s there has been no sign of a permissive trend, much less a sexual revolution, in regard to extramarital and homosexual relations.[8]

Nor are people particularly happy with the growth in permissiveness that has occurred. In 1974 and 1985 few men and women thought that increased acceptance of premarital sexual relations was a change for the better, and from 1978 to 1991 the percentage saying that they welcomed "more acceptance of sexual freedom" only varied between 22 and 29 percent (table 15).

For most people attitudes toward sexual permissiveness come from

TABLE 15 Attitudes Toward Increased Acceptance of Sexual Permissiveness (%)

A. ROPER: *All things considered, do you think society's more widespread acceptance of sexual freedom for people before marriage is a change for the better or a change for the worse, or do you have mixed feelings about it?*

| | 1974 | | 1985 | |
Response	Men	Women	Men	Women
Change for the better	19	12	19	15
Change for the worse	40	46	37	41
Mixed feelings	38	39	43	32
Don't know	3	3	2	2
N	958	2,922	1,000	3,000

B. GALLUP: *I'd like to ask about some changes that took place in the 60s and 70s. Please tell me whether you feel each was a good thing or a bad thing for our society. More acceptance of premarital sex.*

Response	1991
Good thing	38
Bad thing	56
Don't know	6
N	1,216

C. GALLUP: *Here are some social changes which might occur in coming years. Would you welcome these or not welcome them? More acceptance of sexual freedom.*

Response	1978	1981	1988	1991
Welcome	29	25	22	29
Not welcome	62	67	68	66
Don't know	9	8	10	5
N	1,523	1,483	2,556	1,216

moral standards that are notably shaped by religious practice and orientation and by other subcultural influences, such as community standards and racial norms. The religious and moral dimension is evident in a follow-up to the 1991 Gallup item on approval of premarital sexual relations. When those saying that it was wrong (40 percent) were asked why they felt this way, 77 percent mentioned moral and religious grounds, 4 percent stated that women should be virgins before marriage, 25 percent mentioned risk of pregnancy, 14 percent mentioned risk of disease, and 1 percent mentioned something else. In 1987 in response to a similar follow-up question the moral and religious dimension was even more pronounced: 83 percent mentioned moral and religious grounds, 9 percent mentioned virginity, 13 percent mentioned pregnancy, 20 percent mentioned risk of diseases, and 5 percent mentioned other reasons. (Percentages add to more than 100 percent because of multiple mentions.) Similarly, a random-probe study on the 1984 GSS found that religious mentions followed by references to immorality and sin were the most common factors cited when people were asked to elaborate on their attitudes toward extramarital sexual relations (Smith 1989a).

At least in regard to premarital sexual relations these moral strictures were changing across generations that increased approval of sexual permissiveness among more recent cohorts. The permissive period and cohort effects began to reverse by the 1980s however. Although the threat of AIDS might be offered as an explanation for this reversal, this connection is questionable. There appears to have been a period effect against approval of homosexual relations in the 1970s and this effect did not increase in the mid-1980s after knowledge of AIDS became widespread.

The SES variables play a secondary role, with more income and especially more education leading to increased sexual permissiveness.

Family and gender variables have less impact than often supposed. Divorced or separated adults are more permissive than the currently married or widowed, but being never married is associated only with permissiveness toward extramarital and homosexual relations and not toward premarital sexual relations. Similarly, gender itself has no simple, overall association with sexual permissiveness. Women are less approving of premarital and extramarital relations but more approving of homosexual relations. Finally, having a teenager in the household reduces approval of sexual permissiveness but this mostly applies to less approval of premarital sexual relations.

Finally, a liberal political orientation is associated with more permissiveness.

Moreover, sexual attitudes not only are important in their own right but are closely related to sexual behaviors. More permissive attitudes are associated with more permissive behaviors. This relationship is probably reciprocal, with permissive attitudes leading to permissive behaviors and permissive behaviors often leading to permissive attitudes.

When premarital sexual attitudes and behaviors are in conflict, psychological well-being is affected. Among the never-married with nonpermissive attitudes, those who are sexually active are less happy than those who are sexually inactive. But among the never married with more permissive attitudes, sexual activity is not related to happiness. This relation does not occur for extramarital sexual attitudes and behaviors, however.

Sexual attitudes are strongly influenced by subcultural norms in general and religion in particular, by sociopolitical ideology, SES, and, to a lesser extent, gender, and family structure. These attitudes in turn are closely (but not perfectly) related to sexual behaviors. When the two are in conflict, they create a dissonance that at least in the case of premarital sexual relations is associated with and probably leads to lower levels of psychological well-being.

Notes

1. For a full analysis of the trends in the 1960s, see appendix 1 in Smith (1992).

2. We fit time-series models to this and various other trends. Four models are used: (1) constant—no trend, (2) significant linear component—some trend, but with significant variation, (3) significant linear trend—simple, straight-line trend, and (4) nonconstant, nonlinear—varies over time but no simple trend. For details see Taylor (1980).

3. Because of wording differences and possible house effects (i.e., artifactual differences between data collectors), the 1985 Gallup question rather than the 1985 Roper item should be the better comparison point in 1985. The women's magazines clause may have lowered approval in 1969 and 1973 and thus exaggerated the gain in approval from then to 1985.

4. The following hypotheses and explanations derive from the previously cited research. They are based on hypothesized direct and independent effects, not effects operating through related or intervening variables. In testing these hypotheses we can generally determine whether a relation exists but not whether the particular proposed explanations for the relation are correct.

5. General happiness is also examined as a surrogate for marital happiness because to use marital happiness would restrict analysis just to the currently married. On the general relation between sexual activity, sexual satisfaction, and general and marital happiness see Smith (1990a), and Edwards and Booth (1976).

6. But having no religious preference and being raised in a nonreligious home are modestly related to less permissive attitudes, counter to both the theory and the bivariate results. In part this reversal is due to the structural relation that exists between having some religious affiliation and one's theological orientation. People without an affiliation are classified as having a liberal orientation. Thus with orientation as a control, we are in effect comparing the permissiveness of members of liberal denominations to those with no religion. Looking only at these two variables

we see that there is no difference in permissiveness between those raised in no religion (6.1) and those raised in a liberal denomination (6.2). However, for current status those with no religion are significantly more permissive than those in a liberal denomination (7.8 vs. 6.3).

7. Because having teenagers may in part shift attitudes because it redefines the meaning of man and woman, it might be useful to compare adults from specific age groups. In addition, it would be useful to have an item about nonmarital sex between people who are widowed or divorced.

8. For evidence on how sexual attitudes have changed on pornography, sex education, and other sexual matters among both adults and youths, see Smith (1990c).

References

Alston, J. P. 1974. Attitudes toward extramarital and homosexual relations. *Journal for the Scientific Study of Religion* 13:479–81.

Alston, J. P. and F. Tucker. 1975. The myth of sexual permissiveness. In *Intimate life styles: Marriage and its alternatives,* ed. J. R. DeLora and J. S. DeLora. Pacific Palisades, Calif.: Goodyear.

Anderson, M. T., and J. L. Crane. 1979. Adult homosexuality: A case of American tolerance. Paper presented to the Southwestern Sociological Association, Fort Worth, Texas.

Bachrach, C. A., and M. C. Horn. 1987. Married and unmarried couples. *Vital and Health Statistics,* series 23, no. 15, 1–52.

Bock, E. W., L. Beeghley, and A. J. Mixon. 1983. Religion, socioeconomic status, and sexual morality: An application of reference group theory. *Sociological Quarterly* 24:545–59.

Cannon, K. L., and R. Long, 1971. Premarital sexual behavior in the sixties. *Journal of Marriage and the Family* 33:36–49.

Clayton, R. R., and J. L. Bokemeier. 1980. Premarital sex in the seventies. *Journal of Marriage and the Family* 42:759–75.

Cutler, S. J., 1985. Ageing and attitudes about sexual morality. *Ageing and Society* 5:161–73.

Davis, J. A. 1991. Changeable weather in a cooling climate atop the liberal plateau: Conversion and replacement in 42 GSS items. Paper presented to the American Association for Public Opinion Research, Phoenix, Ariz., May.

Davis, J. A., and T. W. Smith. 1991. *General Social Surveys, 1972–1991: Cumulative Codebook.* Chicago: National Opinion Research Center.

DeBouno, B. A., S. H. Zinnerm, M. Daamen, and W. M. McCormack. 1990. Sexual behavior of college women in 1975, 1986, and 1989. *New England Journal of Medicine* 322:821–25.

DeLamater, J. 1981. The social control of sexuality. *Annual Review of Sociology* 7:263–90.

DeLamater, J., and P. MacCorquodale. 1979. *Premarital sexuality: Attitudes, relationships, behavior.* Madison: Univ. of Wisconsin Press.

Edwards, J. N., and A. Booth. 1976. *The cessation of marital intercourse* 133:1333–36.

Ehrmann, W. 1961. Changing sexual mores. In *Values and ideals of American youth,* ed. E. Ginzberg. New York: Columbia Univ. Press.

Harding, S. 1988. Trends in permissiveness. In *British social attitudes: The 5th report,* R. Jowell, S. Witherspoon, and L. Brook. Hants: Gower.

Irwin, P., and N. L. Thompson. 1977. Acceptance of the rights of homosexuals: A social profile. *Journal of Homosexuality* 3:107–21.

James, W. H. 1983. Decline in coital rates with spouses' ages and duration of marriage. *Journal of Biosociological Science* 15:83–87.

Jasso, G. 1985. Marital coital frequency and the passage of time: Estimating the separate effects of spouses' ages and marital duration, birth and marriage cohorts, and period influences. *American Sociological Review* 50:224–41.

———. 1986. Is it outliers deletion or is it sample truncation? Notes on science and sexuality. *American Sociological Review* 51:738–42.

Kahn, J. R., W. D. Kalsbeek, and S. L. Hofferth. 1988. National estimates of teenage sexual activity: Evaluating the comparability of three national estimates. *Demography* 25:189–204.

Kahn, J. R., and J. R. Udry. 1986. Marital coital frequency: unnoticed outliers and unspecified interactions. *American Sociological Review* 51:734–37.

Klassen, A. D., C. J. Williams, E. E. Levitt. 1989. *Sex and morality in the U.S.: An empirical enquiry under the auspices of the Kinsey Institute.* Middletown, Conn.: Wesleyan Univ. Press.

Klassen, A. D., C. J. Williams, E. E. Levitt, L. Rudkin-Miniot, H. G. Miller, and S. Gunjal. 1989. Trends in premarital sexual behavior. In *AIDS: Sexual behavior and intravenous drug use,* ed. C. F. Turner, H. G. Miller, and L. E. Moses, 500–536. Washington, D.C.: National Academy Press.

Mahoney, E. R. 1978. Age differences in attitude change toward premarital coitus. *Archives of Sexual Behavior* 7:493–501.

Nyberg, K. L., and J. P. Alston. 1976–77. Analysis of public attitudes toward homosexual behavior. *Journal of Homosexuality* 2:99–107.

Posner, Richard. 1992. *Sex and reason.* Cambridge, Mass.: Harvard Univ. Press.

Reiss, I. L. 1967. *The social context of premarital sexual permissiveness.* New York: Holt, Rinehart & Winston.

———. 1975. How and why America's sex standards are changing. In *Intimate life styles: Marriage and its alternatives,* ed. J. R. DeLora and J. S. DeLora. Pacific Palisades, Calif.: Goodyear.

———. 1980. Some observations on ideology and sexuality in America. *Journal of Marriage and the Family* 43:271–83.

Reiss, I. L., R. E Anderson, and G. C. Sponaugle. 1980. A multivariate model of the determinants of extramarital sexual permissiveness. *Journal of Marriage and the Family* 42:395–411.

Robinson, I., K. Ziss, B. Ganza, S. Katz, and E. Robinson. 1991. Twenty years of the sexual revolution, 1965–1985: An update. *Journal of Marriage and the Family* 53:216–20.

Saunders, J. M., and J. N. Edwards. 1984. Extramarital sexuality: A predictive model of permissive attitudes. *Journal of Marriage and the Family* 46:825–35.

Schneider, W., and I. A. Lewis. 1984. The straight story on homosexuality and gay rights. *Public Opinion* 7:16–20,60.

Singh, B. K. 1980. Trends in attitudes towards premarital sexual relations. *Journal of Marriage and the Family* 36:387–93.

Singh, B. K., L. D. Adams, and D. E. Jorgenson. 1981. Factors associated with general sexual permissiveness. *Sociological Spectrum* 1:145–57.

Singh, B. K., B. L. Walton, and J. S. Williams. 1976. Extramarital sexual permissiveness: Conditions and contingencies. *Journal of Marriage and the Family* 38:701–12.

Smith, T. W. 1989. Random probes of GSS questions. *International Journal of Public Opinion Research* 1:305–25.

―――. 1990a. Adult sexual behavior in 1989: Number of partners, frequency, and risk. Paper presented to the American Academy of the Advancement of Science, New Orleans, La., February.

―――. 1990b. Liberal and conservative trends in the United States since World War II. *Public Opinion Quarterly* 54:479–507.

―――. 1990c. The sexual revolution? *Public Opinion Quarterly* 54:415–35.

―――. 1991a. Adult sexual behavior in 1989: Number of partners, frequency of intercourse, and risk of AIDS. *Family Planning Perspectives* 23:102–7.

―――. 1991b. A comment on "Twenty years of the sexual revolution." Unpublished NORC report.

―――. 1992. Attitudes towards sexual permissiveness: Trends and correlates. GSS Social Change Report no. 35. Chicago: National Opinion Research Center.

Snyder, E. E., and E. Spreitzer. 1976. Attitudes of the aged toward nontraditional sexual behavior. *Archives of Sexual Behavior* 5:249–54.

Stephan, G. E., and D. R. McMullin. 1982. Tolerance of sexual nonconformity: City size as a situational and early learning determinant. *American Sociological Review* 47:411–15.

Taylor, D. G. 1980. Procedures for evaluating trends in public opinion. *Public Opinion Quarterly* 44:86–100.

Thornton, A. 1989. Changing attitudes toward family issues in the United States. *Journal of Marriage and the Family* 51:873–93.

Turner, C. F., H. G. Miller, and L. E. Moses, eds. 1989. *AIDS: Sexual behavior and intravenous drug use.* Washington, D.C.: National Academy Press.

Weis, D. L., and J. Jurich. 1985. Size of community of residence as a predictor of attitudes toward extramarital sexual relations. *Journal of Marriage and the Family* 47:173–77.

Wilson, T. C. 1986. Community population size and social heterogeneity: An empirical test. *American Journal of Sociology* 91:1154–69.

Sexuality among African-American Women

Claire Sterk-Elifson

Human sexuality has intrigued social scientists for many years, and its complexity has led scientists to employ a variety of different theoretical frameworks. These include the biological, the social psychological, the sociological, and the sociobiological perspectives. Each theoretical framework emphasizes different aspects of sexuality. Whereas, for example, the focus of biological studies tends to be on the effect of biological factors on mating strategies and reproductive capacities (Daly and Wilson 1979), the emphasis of social-psychological studies is on cognitive factors (Murstein 1971). Sociologists and anthropologists accentuate the sociocultural context in which sexual behavior occurs (Schwarz and Gilmore 1990), and sociobiological researchers combine aspects of all these perspectives (Kenrick and Trost 1987; Udry 1985). Recently sexuality has received more attention as a result of its link with health issues such as sexually transmitted diseases (STD), including human immunodeficiency virus (HIV) infection, the virus causing acquired immunodeficiency syndrome (AIDS) (see, e.g., Wasserheit, Aral, and Holmes [1991]).

Sexuality cannot be studied in a vacuum. It is, like other human behaviors, influenced by the sociocultural context in which the behaviors occur, structural factors such as the age-specific sex ratio, and individual characteristics including physical attractiveness and personality.

For most people, sexuality is a salient issue. Although one function of engaging in sexual activities is reproduction, there are also other motivations, such as physical pleasure, intimacy, emotional commitment, and love. The functions of individual sexuality are related to group norms, values, and beliefs. In other words, sexual behaviors occur and are shaped within a larger cultural context. Several demographic characteristics such as gender, race, social class, and age influence sexuality. For example, the ways in which partners are recruited tend to vary by

This manuscript would not have been possible without the help of Jacqueline Boles, Kirk Elifson, Gail Myers, Tanya Telfair Frazier, Susan Pettit, and all the women who were willing to share their stories.

gender (Aral et al. 1991; Maccoby 1988); women take a more selective approach as opposed to the more nondiscriminating approach among men. Men are also more inclined to have more sex partners than women.

Differences also occur because each racial or ethnic group has some distinctive attitudes, norms, beliefs, and values regarding behaviors, including sexuality. Traditionally, the majority of studies on sexuality have focused on whites, the dominant racial group in the United States (Mason, Czajka, and Arber 1976). Several other studies concentrated on differences between white and black Americans (Aguirre and Parr 1982; Ransford and Miller 1983). The relatively limited number of studies including heterosexual, African-American women frequently were limited to fertility issues such as teenage pregnancy (Furstenberg 1971; Pope 1967) or out-of-wedlock births (Aug and Bright 1970). Other aspects of sexuality were neglected. Studies among women who attended STD clinics indicate that African-American women might be younger when they first engage in sex and have a relative higher average rate and variability of new partners than do their white counterparts (Aral et al. 1991).

Martin Weinberg and Colin Williams (1980) examined the relation between social class and sexual behavior and reported that social class is an important determinant of sexual behavior. They challenge the embourgeoisement thesis that the sexual behavior of the different social classes has become blurred. Studies linking sexuality to the life course (Ehrhardt and Wasserheit 1991; Osmond and Martin 1975; Rand and Krecker 1990; Rubin 1990) identified that the frequency of sexual activity varies inversely with age.

Demographic characteristics, however, do not provide an exclusive explanation for human behavior in general. Specific characteristics of different racial and ethnic groups and their development over time should also be taken into consideration. The historical background of African-Americans differs from that of other racial and ethnic groups and might have led to the development of attitudes, norms, values, and beliefs that differ from those of other groups. The African-American historical context includes the preslavery period and the slavery period. For example, in the African preslavery period, premarital virginity was not an important value; during slavery sexual exploitation of women occurred frequently, and this made the women feel they had no control over their body, which in turn reduced the importance of virginity. Racism and economic exploitation continued once slavery ended (Hooks 1981; Staples 1973, 1978; Wilson 1986).

Robert Staples (1973) pointed out that African-Americans' sexual behavior is influenced by their current social status; many African-Americans live under high-density housing conditions that hamper the parents' privacy when engaging in sex. The children's early introduction to sex might lead them to become sexually active at a relatively young age. Pamela Wilson (1986) writes that the prevalence of female single-headed families largely influenced the gender and sex roles of African-American women: men are often characterized as no good, and girls are socialized to become independent of men.

The focus of this chapter is on sexuality among a sample of African-American women in Atlanta, Georgia. The chapter seeks answers to several empirical questions including ways in which partners are selected, contacts are established, and sexual activities develop. In addition, it discusses the effect of the AIDS epidemic on sexuality.

METHODS

This chapter is based on in-depth interviews conducted with thirty-three heterosexual, African-American women who live in the Atlanta metropolitan area. The total population of the Atlanta metropolitan area continues to increase, primarily because of migration from other parts of the United States. African-Americans account for 28 percent of the total population in the Atlanta metropolitan area. In particular among African-Americans, the area has the reputation of providing opportunities for upward social mobility. For example, between 1980 and 1990 the metropolitan area registered net gains of 516,000 jobs, mainly in the service sector—this is almost one new job for every person added to the metropolitan area population (Atlanta Regional Commission 1992). Of the thirty-three respondents, fifteen women moved as (young) adults to Atlanta from different locations including metropolitan and urban areas in California, Illinois, Pennsylvania, and New Jersey; ten women moved to Atlanta with their parents when they were younger than sixteen years old, and three of these women moved from rural areas in the southeastern United States; three other women were born in Atlanta; however, their parents grew up in other urban parts of the country—namely Charlotte, North Carolina, Washington, D.C., and Chicago. Five women were born into families who had been living in Atlanta for multiple generations. Although the respondents were recruited in one major U.S. metropolitan area, their social roots were in many other parts of the country. The geographical mobility patterns among the respondents helps to counterbalance the regionality of the sample.

Respondents were recruited into the study using chain referral or snowball sampling (Kaplan, Korf, and Sterk, 1987; Watters and Biernacki 1989). This technique, developed by Goodman (1961), allows for comparing data emerging from exploratory or qualitative studies with theoretical categories (Glaser 1978). Women selected in the zero stage of the chain consisted of a convenience sample and were identified using methods varying from contacting service providers or colleagues to directly approaching women in public settings. Chains were started in at least five different networks; weak social ties existed between the members of each chain. Because one of the major drawbacks of the snowball-sampling or chain-referral technique is selection bias, stratified quota sampling was introduced as a means to reduce this bias. The study was designed to reach a cross section of women of different ages and social classes in order to enhance the representativeness of the sample. The chain-referral procedure was introduced after completion of each interview, and the women in the zero stage of the chain were asked for references to potential respondents belonging to a specified age category and social class. The recruitment procedure became more purposive as more interviews were conducted. Three women were unable to list another woman; two women felt uncomfortable with the referral procedure.

The analysis contrasts those women younger than twenty years with those twenty-one through forty-four years old, and with those forty-five years or older. Variations within each of these categories are highlighted in the analysis. The respondents' ages ranged from eighteen to sixty-two years. Social class was operationalized using the respondents' reported gross income. Respondents whose incomes were $20,000 or less were compared with those whose income exceeded this figure. These categories were mediated by educational level and number of dependents.

The interviews were conducted at a setting selected by the respondents. The most common interview site was the respondent's home. Prior to the interview, each respondent provided written consent. No personal identifiers were recorded. The first part of the interview focused on demographic characteristics, followed by open-ended questions covering issues such as sexual and relational history, ideal relationship and partner, physical attractiveness, and opinions regarding sexuality issues. These topics were selected after a limited number of pilot interviews were conducted, and their importance was also verified by a number of African-American women who did not participate in the study.

The respondents willingly participated in the study because sexuality was a salient issue about which they considered themselves to be knowledgeable. Rapport between the respondent and the interviewer is a key issue to the success of in-depth interviews (Kirk and Miller 1986). Building rapport was facilitated because the interviews were conducted in a setting selected by the respondents and by the referral procedure. With the exception of two situations, the respondents themselves contacted a referral and asked whether the person was interested. A positive response was followed by a phone call from the interviewer during which the potential respondent was invited to participate.

Cooperation also increased because the respondents were not pressured to answer any queries with which they felt uncomfortable. None of the women, however, refused to answer any questions, and they all talked freely about a variety of intimate topics. The validity of the data was enhanced by the rapport established between the interviewer and the respondents, the confidentiality of the interviews, and the utilization of multiple measurements. As is typical for qualitative data, the validity is high; however, their reliability is relatively low (Kirk and Miller 1986).

The interviews ranged from one to four hours. On completion of an interview the interviewer immediately recorded her impressions regarding the interview and the respondent. Following grounded theory (Glaser and Strauss 1970), data collection and analysis occurred simultaneously. Codes were based on issues that appeared salient, and coding allowed for identifying general as opposed to individual patterns.

Although it is unclear to what extent the respondents are representative of African-American women in general, the findings provide insight into an area that has been neglected and offer baseline knowledge for hypotheses to be tested with a larger sample.

General Sample Characteristics

The use of a stratified sampling frame assured that the women represented a cross section of age categories and social classes. Their weekly income ranged from $80 to $1,250; most women held full-time jobs, varying from a lower service position to secretarial and professional work. Other sources of income included welfare payments, unemployment compensation, and financial support from relatives. Most women grew up in lower-class (frequently single-parent) households, and eleven of them subsequently have been upwardly mobile. Only five women were raised in families with incomes that would put them into the middle class. Ten women, most of whom were younger, lived in racially mixed neighborhoods. (See table 1.)

The educational background of the women varied from high school

TABLE 1 General Sample Characteristics

Category	Distribution
Age:	
20 or younger	7
21–30	8
31–44	8
45–59	8
Older than 59	2
Income level:	
Less than $20,000 per year	17
$20,000 or higher per year	16
Income source:	
Full-time job	21
Part-time job	8
Other	4
Marital status:	
Married	6
Living with steady partner	3
Not living with steady partner	2
Single, never married with steady partner	5
Single, divorced, or widowed	17
Educational background:	
Less than high school	7
High school or equivalent	13
Some college	5
College	5
Postcollege	3
Religious affiliation:	
Baptist	13
African Episcopal Church	11
Other	5
None	4
N	33

short of graduation to some college, college graduation, and postcollege studies. Fourteen women mentioned that their financial situation required that they truncate their education to work or take care of siblings. Overall, the respondents' positions in the labor market did not achieve parity with their educational background. Particularly women who had a high school diploma or several years of college held jobs for which they were overqualified. These jobs often were in the food preparation or the domestic service sector or involved low-paying and low-status administrative jobs. African-American women have traditionally had lower occupational status than their education would warrant (Allen and Britt 1983; Simmons 1979).

It is uncommon for African-American women to be upwardly mobile through marriage (Wilson 1986). Norval Glenn and his colleagues (1979) challenge the myth of mobility through marriage as opposed to mobility through personal attainment. They show that women's upward mobility through marriage is overestimated. Three-fourths of the respondents were or had been married, but only eight of them married a man of socioeconomic status higher than their own. African-American women often are intermittently married (Brown and Gary 1985).

Fifty-five percent of the women in this study were single at the time of the interview. The main reason mentioned for being single was the perceived unavailability of suitable male partners. This same explanation also has been reported by others (Brown and Gary 1985; Gump 1975; Wilson 1986). African-American women significantly outnumber available African-American males. The fetal and infant mortality rate among African-American males is higher than among whites as a result of the lack of prenatal care. In addition, the mortality rate among males tends to be higher than among females because of the fact that male infants are more vulnerable than females. Among adolescents the rate of casualties to health and life among African-American males is higher than among their white or female counterparts. Structural factors such as the high incarceration and unemployment rates among adult African-American males further contribute to the lack of suitable male partners (Posner 1992). The recent census data support the perceived lack of available African-American male partners for female African-Americans; the reported sex ratio in 1986 for African-Americans between the ages of twenty-five and forty-four was .87 (U.S. Bureau of Census 1987).

African-American males are often perceived as more promiscuous than white males because the sex ratio causes them to be more likely to have multiple female sex partners. In addition, they are more likely to father illegitimate children from more than one partner (Smith, chap. 3, this vol.) and to start engaging in sex at an earlier age as a result of both their early maturation and the less age-graded interaction between the sexes (Bowser, chap. 5, this vol.; Posner 1992). This causes many of the African-American women to be single parents (Brown, Perry, and Harburg 1977; Mays 1985). Three-fourths of the respondents had children from multiple male partners (range 0–4; mean 3); the children's ages varied depending on the respondent's age. Six women also reported that they took care of their grandchildren who lived with them.

The respondents' religious affiliation was primarily with the Baptist or the African Methodist Episcopal church. Most of the women considered religion to be very important and stated that religion gave meaning to life and assisted in keeping faith and in coping with life. Older, lower-class women also mentioned the importance of social support offered by church members.

DATING

The respondents defined dating as going out. This included going out one or more times to have dinner, to see a movie, or to attend another social activity together. The women remarked that dating very often resulted in sexual activity. Particularly for the lower-class women, this activity frequently included sexual intercourse. Dating was important for two reasons: to have a good time, and to identify a partner for a long-term, steady relationship. The women also commented that it is acceptable for a man to date more than one woman, although proscriptions against women simultaneously dating several men were apparent. The expectation is that a man pays for a date. This unilateral gift puts the women in a subordinate position. Mauss (1925) was one of the first scholars to show how unilateral gifts symbolize the giver's superiority and the receiver's inferiority. Dating is clearly linked to partner selection and making contact with potential partners.

Partner Selection and Physical Attractiveness

The availability of potential male partners influences the process of partner selection. The lack of available men (see, e.g., Brown and Gary [1985]) increases the importance of the females' physical attractiveness. Vickie Mays (1985) described that at times African-American women might not invite a girlfriend they perceive to be beautiful to a party if they expect that her presence could decrease their chances of attracting a good or suitable partner themselves. Similar incidents were described by the respondents in this study. They defined a suitable partner as a man who has the same racial background, is of the same age or older, is good-looking, passionate, and romantic, and who has a high-status, well-paying job.

The majority (63 percent) of cross-racial intermarriages involve marriages between an African-American male and a white female (Posner 1992). This further reduces the effective sex ratio among potential mates for African-American women. No data are available on the number of black American males whom the respondents considered to be suitable but who were involved with a white female. The women were asked, however, about their own experiences with interracial relationships. With the exception of four women, all middle class and under thirty years old, the respondents had not been involved in interracial relationships. The women noted that partners with the same racial background share greater empathy, act more similarly, and are more accepted by relatives and friends. One-third of the respondents also mentioned the importance of having pure-black children to ensure the survival of the race. The four women who had relationships with men from other racial and ethnic groups told stories about the conflict this caused with their relatives and their partner's relatives, friends, and colleagues. Only one woman was involved in an interracial relationship at the time of the interview.

The majority of the women considered themselves physically attractive and emphasized the importance of weight, face, hair, bust, and hips. They revealed that body weight was important; however, being slim was not perceived as positive and was regarded as a white value. "White men go after skinny chicks. . . . Black men like to be able to hold a lady." Several respondents also questioned why some African-American women straightened their hair. They considered this another sign of trying to conform to dominant, white values. Several times the respondents joked about how black women tried to imitate white women and vice versa because they expected this would make them more attractive to males. A frequently heard example was that of African-American women who straighten their hair because they think men like straight hair better; white women perm their hair because they think men like curly hair better.

The respondents emphasized that a woman should not be taller than her male partner. The women did not consider skin color to be an important indicator of physical attractiveness. Sometimes the women would hint at differences between fair or dark skin and one woman mentioned that "skin color has become a political issue that is being introduced by whites as a means to divide blacks." Three women referred to a recent movie, *Jungle Fever*, and pointed out that they wished the director, Spike Lee, had not emphasized skin color because this could create tension among African-American women.

Most respondents assumed physical attractiveness to be more significant for women than for men; one-third of the respondents mentioned that it was equally important for men and women to be physically attractive. Approximately one-half of the respondents associated aging with becoming more attractive. The remainder stated that older women were differently or less attractive. This view on aging seems to differ from the white pattern (Patzer 1985; Rossi, chap. 1, this vol.).

The women's opinions varied on whether being physically attractive enhances one's chances of finding a suitable partner. The following quotes from two women who described themselves as physically attractive capture their differences in opinion:

> It is harder to find a partner because being attractive makes people feel insecure. . . . It makes people think the person is not approachable. . . . People assume you already have enough candidates.

> It is easier to find a partner because you have a choice . . . because you get immediate attention . . . but the guys want to show you off and are not serious about the relationship. . . . It is harder to hold on to a partner.

The first quotation reflects the opinion of others; the second quotation is from an ego's perspective. Attractive individuals were assumed to have less difficulty dating because they more naturally draw attention from men. In addition, these attractive women could be more selective because they would have more men interested in them. As illustrated in the quotations above, the respondents were also aware of the negative consequences of being attractive. For example, a good-looking woman might make a man feel so insecure that he would feel uncomfortable approaching her. The respondents frequently mentioned that very attractive women are more likely to be used by men to show off to their friends. They suspected that being with an attractive woman increases a man's status in his friends' eyes.

Making Contact

Although the women remarked that physical attractiveness influences the chances of having a date, they added that personality traits became more relevant once two people agreed to a date. The most common ways to meet men were through friends, jobs, church, or the neighborhood. Younger and divorced women were most likely to encounter their dates at bars or nightclubs. The lower-class women mentioned their neighborhood as a potential recruitment site, and the middle-class women often met a date through their job.

Findings on sex-role socialization of African-American women are inconsistent. Women sometimes are viewed as self-sufficient, independent, and resourceful (Stack 1974); others state that African-American women are socialized to accept a traditional female role (Gurin and Gaylord 1976). This contradiction is reflected in the respondents' opinion regarding a woman's role in making contact with a man. Several respondents asserted that, once a woman identified a potential date, she should wait for him to take action, but others said the woman should herself make a move. Taking initiative includes giving nonverbal messages such as smiling, making eye contact, or moving closer. The extent to which a woman should approach a man varies by the situation; the respondents warned that a woman should know how far she can go before being labeled as seductive or flirtatious. The lower-class women acknowledged and endorsed the importance of women's assertiveness in approaching men more than their middle-class counterparts did. A similar class distinction is reported by Victoria Binion (1990) in her study of African-American women.

The respondents cautioned that a woman who takes too much initiative might have difficulty establishing limits on sexual activity. Several respondents used the illustration of a woman who had initiated a date and had been dancing with her partner. This scenario was perceived as problematic because the woman might not want to go beyond dancing, kissing, and hugging. The man, on the other hand, could conclude incorrectly that she wished to have sex. Many respondents emphasized that, if a woman approaches a man, she is not suggesting a sexual interest, and, as one woman stated, "There is a big gap between dancing and screwing."

Sexual Activity

Individuals who date may or may not intend to become sexually involved. The women under twenty were more likely than their older counterparts to engage in sex after one or two evenings with the same date. For many of them this was their first sexual experience, and they reported that they did not feel prepared for this first time and that they were getting involved without knowing what was going on. For a number of them, particularly the lower-class women, this experience included sexual intercourse. As one eighteen-year-old woman mentioned, "I was fifteen. I thought kissing was cool, but before I knew it he was trying to get my panties off."

The women over forty-five indicated that their main reason for dating was to meet people and to identify a male companion. Sexual expectations were secondary and sometimes nonexistent. Having a date or boyfriend, independent of his social class, was associated with a higher status position among the lower-class women. As one forty-seven-year-old woman joked, "A woman must have something special if she can get a man and hold on to him."

First Sexual Experience

Sexual behavior, including the first sexual experience, depends on an individual's biological development as well as on the sociocultural context (Schwarz and Gilmore 1990). The respondents considered the first menstrual period an important turning point in a woman's life (Thompson, chap. 8, this vol.); "It marks the transition from being a girl to becoming a woman." They reported that their first menstrual period occurred between the ages of eleven and sixteen (mean age 12.5 years), and, besides the memory of feeling like a "real" woman, they remember the monthly cramps and being inhibited from engaging in physical activities.

Previous studies indicate that African-American adolescent girls are sexually active at a relatively younger age than white adolescents (Johnson 1974; Staples 1973; Weinberg and Williams 1980; Zelnik and Kantner 1980). There appeared to be a relationship in this study between the women's social class and the age of their first sexual experience (Zelnik, Kantner, and Ford 1981). The middle-class respondents were likely to be eighteen or older (average is 20.2 years) when first engaging in sex, as opposed to the average age of 14.5 years among the lower-class women. The lower-class women frequently reported that their first sexual encounter included sexual intercourse. This might be due to the lower level of sexual knowledge among lower-class adolescents (Fine 1988). For the middle-class women, currently and when they were younger, intercourse did not occur until after several dates. Their initial sexual activities included kissing, petting, and sometimes oral sex.

Sharon Thompson (1990) wrote in her study of African-American adolescents that most girls would discuss their first experience with their friends without sharing intimate details. The respondents also reported that they primarily talked with their friends about the romantic aspects of relationships, about "doing it" and the physical hurt of the first experience. They would, however, not discuss details regarding the actual act, the circumstances under which this occurred, or their true feelings.

Most women indicated that their friends were their primary information source but that they did not know what to expect until they actually engaged in sex. Ruby, a twenty-three-year-old single mother of three children, described her first experience:

> We [black women] do not talk much about those things. Your mother might mention something. . . . You share with your friends, but you don't talk about details. It is important to be able to say you did it and with whom you did it, but you don't give your true feelings away. . . . You learn from doing it. I always was with guys who knew what to do. . . . At schools and in health centers they mainly tell kids not to get pregnant but there is more to sex than that.

Reflecting on their first sexual intercourse, none of the women remembered having experienced an orgasm. Almost all women recalled being disappointed because their first intercourse hurt, occurred too quickly, and was not romantic. Those women who had their first sexual experience at an older age did not feel better prepared than their younger counterparts; however, they did feel more assertive and in control. "I could have done it earlier, but I waited until I was ready for it." They had given sex more thought, and they were more likely to take oral contraceptives or to have condoms available.

Engaging in sex acts other than vaginal intercourse is less accepted among African-Americans (Staples 1973; Wilson 1986). These unacceptable sexual activities include oral and anal sex and masturbation. A forty-three-year-old social worker who lives with two of her daughters and three grandchildren explains why she finds sex acts other than intercourse inappropriate.

> Those kinds of sex are wrong. Human beings are not cre-
> ated to do those kind of things. It is evil and disgusting. . . .
> Anal sex got gay men in trouble. . . . Oral sex should make
> people vomit. It is sex invented by whites. . . . Prostitutes
> are willing to do that and that causes major relational prob-
> lems. . . . Masturbation is also wrong. You are not supposed
> to touch your body. . . . I would accept it from a boy, but
> there is no need for girls to touch themselves at those
> places.

Two-thirds of the respondents would concur with the above quote. The remaining respondents declared that each individual should decide for herself or himself what to do. Only a few women, all under thirty and primarily middle-class, considered masturbation an appropriate way for a woman to get to know her body and would engage in oral sex as long as the man washed himself before engaging in this act.

Later Sexual Experiences

The respondents unanimously agreed that their later sexual experi-ences differed markedly from their first; they felt more prepared and knew better what to expect. One-third of the women, mainly middle-class and under thirty years, also explained that with experience they have become more actively involved in the sex act. They might, for ex-ample, tell their partner that they preferred some clitoral stimulation, and they learned how to feel more satisfied and reached orgasm. The respondents who were under thirty assumed that the sexual experience would change over time, particularly as they aged. They believed that women whose reproductive years were over would become less inter-ested in sex and would decrease their sexual activity. The women in their thirties were frustrated more than the other women because "young chicks were taking their men."

Approximately half of the ten respondents over forty-five years old, especially the three women who experienced their menopause as nega-tive, stated that they were less interested in sex. Four other women had hysterectomies for medical reasons. They feared that they would not be seen as competent sexual partners (Bernard 1985). On the other hand, three of the older women remarked that they enjoyed sex more now that they mainly had sex for pleasure and did not have to be concerned about pregnancy.

Independent of age and social class, the respondents anticipated positive outcomes such as love, affection, good feelings, understanding, and respect in return for sex. Two women limited their expectations to having a good time. Younger and middle-class women had relatively higher expectations than their older, lower-class counterparts. They expected a long-term commitment from their sexual partner. Although the other women valued this commitment as important, they describe the expectations as an illusion.

Two-thirds of the women felt that good sex was a requirement for a good relationship. All respondents included the following in their definition of good sex: sex with which both partners feel good; gentle sex with time for foreplay; and sex that allows both partners to experience an orgasm. Good sex was considered important for an ideal relationship. Other aspects of an ideal relationship include faithfulness, good communication, and financial security. With the exception of three women, the respondents did not consider their current or most recent relationship as ideal. Four single, middle-class women over thirty years often referred to the fact that at times they felt used in sexual relationships. Gloria, who is a divorced executive at a large company, states, "I am not going to be pushed around at my job nor in my bed." Although the older women mainly complained about men wanting them to engage in sex acts they did not want, the younger women, independent of social class, feared that their partner would leave them if they would not cooperate. Pam, one of these younger women, explains:

> The guys push you around. They know it is important for a girl to hold on to a guy.... They use you and then tell you that some other bitch is better. I understand a man wants to be in control, but there are limits.... Jay, my boyfriend, tells me he can get at least ten other women and that I should feel good he chose me.... He tries to get his way by telling me he'll leave for whoever.... I don't want to get pregnant and one time I mentioned condoms to him.... He went off and told me that was my problem. I love him and he takes good care of me. He is very gentle and always wants me to come.... Sometimes, I fake an orgasm because he would feel bad.... I should leave him, but he is so great. He is especially good after we have had an argu-

ment and he wants to make up for it. . . . I know several other girls who are flirting with him all the time. They don't care he already has a woman.

This statement suggests that Pam is willing to engage in sex in order to maintain a relationship. Over two-thirds of the women referred to sex as an act of forgiveness that symbolized a new start. The remaining respondents, all of whom were older middle-class women, felt that sex could not guarantee a good, long-term relationship. Similar findings have been reported in studies on sex and marital happiness (Glenn 1979).

Pam also revealed that at times she would fake an orgasm to please her boyfriend. This type of deception also was reported by three-fourths of the women, especially the younger women. Although the women viewed physical and emotional satisfaction as equally important for both partners, they frequently would act satisfied without experiencing complete satisfaction. A woman in her mid-thirties, who has been dating the same man for seven months, shared her explanation: "A guy would not feel a feel a real man if he can't get his lady to come. A woman doesn't lose anything if she fakes it."

Contraceptives, Pregnancies, and Children

The availability of modern contraceptives increased the control women have over their fertility (Gerrard 1987). Until contraceptives such as the pill, diaphragm, IUD, and condom were available, women had to rely on methods such as rhythm, the calendar, or the basal body-temperature technique. The women who knew about contraceptives and saw their use as positive were more likely to use contraceptives than women who lacked knowledge or who saw their use as negative or as interfering with nature. The majority of the women over forty mentioned that they did not know about contraceptives when they became sexually active. The younger respondents had more knowledge but often did not know where to purchase condoms or how to suggest their use to their partners. The youngest women were most knowledgeable and associated condom use with the prevention of pregnancies and STDs, including AIDS.

About half the respondents mentioned that, when they became sexually active, they believed they could not get pregnant if the sex act was not romantic or passionate or if they did not have an orgasm. For three women this lack of knowledge resulted in an unplanned pregnancy

(Mosher 1979; Mosher and Cross 1971). Irrational beliefs and fears about negative side effects of contraceptives are related to the misconceptions (Gerrard, McCann, and Fortini 1983; Horowitz 1980). Tashia, a nineteen-year-old single mother of a two-year-old son, touched on many issues that are relevant in a discussion about contraceptives:

> I would not dare to ask my mother about contraceptives. . . . She wouldn't know much about it and always told us that those were developed by whites to stop black folks from reproducing. When I asked her, she also told me the pill caused cancer. . . . I could have talked with my friends . . . girls who used something were seen as bad (promiscuous). The boys don't like it either. . . . I didn't think I would get pregnant because for me it wasn't anything sexual or romantic. . . . I thought about an abortion but didn't know where to go. . . . I went in for prenatal care, and they told me I could have had an abortion if I hadn't waited that long.

Tashia's mother told her she could get cancer from using the pill. Other women revealed that they associated infertility with contraceptive use. Linda is in her early thirties and has used the pill and a diaphragm for many years. She has been trying to get pregnant for four years and is convinced that she might have problems conceiving because of years of contraceptive use. A minority of the women, particularly older women, mentioned that contraceptives were a form of genocide promoted by whites. Other studies support this belief (Mays and Cochran 1988; Wilson 1986).

Two theoretical frameworks, the theory of reasoned action (Fishbein and Azjen 1975) and the health-belief model (Rosenstock, Strecher, and Becker 1988), can provide insight into decision making about the use of contraceptives. The following process was observed among the respondents. Initially, they contemplated their own attitudes and beliefs about contraceptives—for example, "Using a contraceptive is good because it prevents pregnancies." In addition, they often took their beliefs about expectations of others into consideration—for example, "My partner will think I am sexually active; otherwise I would not be using a contraceptive." Next the women asked themselves how important it was to comply with the perceived expectations of others. An example of this step is "If he is going to think about me as a slut because I use contraceptives, I'm better off not using any or not telling him about it." In other words the respondents' behavior is guided by the expected outcomes of the action. Another woman in her late twenties reacted as follows: "He might think I am an easy catch because I take the pill and try to put me down, but I'm the one who is not going to get pregnant."

These theoretical frameworks merely focus on rational decision making; they do not provide a complete explanation for why women continue to engage in sex without using contraceptives and have unplanned pregnancies. Factors that are not rational influence the women's decisions (Luker 1975). For example, actions might be primarily based on group norms that conflict with individual knowledge. For instance, several women mentioned that they knew the use of contraceptives would prevent them from getting pregnant; however, they might not use contraceptives because this is considered immoral among many of their friends. Half the respondents considered the use of contraceptives a sin prohibited by their church. Knowledge is mainly relevant and effective when the actions derived from this knowledge correspond with the norms. One respondent revealed, "People will not use condoms as long as it is seen as a sign of distrusting a partner, being sexually active, and a barrier for good sex." Some of the younger, lower-class women also mentioned that they heard their mothers tell stories about getting pregnant at a young age. Their socialization reinforced pregnancies at a young age. Three-fourths of the respondents noted that their own sexuality was closely linked to their mother's sexuality in terms of the age at which they started engaging in sex and the age of pregnancy.

The younger and middle-class women would discuss contraceptives with their peers; the older, lower-class respondents remarked that, although they discussed many topics with their friends, they were very unlikely to discuss contraceptives. The younger women were uncomfortable discussing contraceptives with their mothers. More than half the women reported actually using or having used contraceptives, primarily the pill or condoms. The use of the pill was strongly related to the extent of sexual activity; condom use was primarily linked to the sexual partner's preference. Only a minority of the women believed that it was time for men to start taking some initiative instead of complaining about the fact that condoms did not feel good. Most respondents asserted that it was a woman's responsibility to use contraceptives if she decided to have sex without intending to become pregnant.

Three-fourths of the respondents reported a pregnancy (range 0–3; mean 1.9), approximately half of which were planned. One woman had a miscarriage and two women had an abortion. One of these women felt this allowed her to finish school; the other woman felt guilty about her abortion. Overall, the respondents' opinions about abortions varied from very negative, for example, "It means killing a child to be born; doctors who perform abortion should be put in jail," to a more tolerant stance such as "To each its own; I wouldn't do it but I understand that some women would, especially if they were raped." The older, single mothers seemed to be the most tolerant, possibly because of their personal experience.

The single mothers, of planned or unplanned children, tended to describe their situation as a hard life, although at times as better than with a man who doesn't care. Several of them revealed that they became pregnant in the hope that their partners, sometimes their husbands, would stay with them. The younger single mothers described their situation differently in that they emphasized aspects such as becoming a real woman or having a family without having to deal with a man. Despite the impression that they chose to have a child as a single person, they also hinted that they hoped a pregnancy would make their partner feel more committed to the relationship. For the younger lower-class women, having children was seen as a way to escape home, start a happy life, and have something to care for and love. The middle-class women expressed concerns that children might restrain their career.

Sexuality during the AIDS Era

Infection with HIV, the virus causing AIDS, has become the major public health concern of the twentieth century. The main routes of transmission of the virus are through homosexual contact and intravenous drug use, followed by heterosexual contact (Centers for Disease Control and Prevention 1992). The number of AIDS cases resulting from heterosexual transmission of the virus is the fastest-growing category (Burnham and Ronald 1991). In addition, African-Americans are disproportionately represented among persons infected with HIV (see, e.g., Centers for Disease Control and Prevention [1986]; Selik, Castro, and Pappaioanou [1988]). This implies that AIDS, which first was seen as a disease of white, middle-class gay men, also has become an African-American disease. The high incidence among African-Americans, as among gay men, is attributed to behavioral and environmental factors and not related to genetic characteristics (Selik, Castro, and Pappaioanou 1988).

Women in general are at risk for HIV infection through their own high-risk drug-using behaviors or indirectly through sexual activity with high-risk partners. None of the respondents reported that they were HIV positive. Two women mentioned that they had been crack-cocaine users in the past but never were tested for HIV. Three other women engaged in sexual intercourse without the use of a condom with a male, intravenous drug user. They were tested for HIV during the last year and were HIV negative. Only one of these women knew at the time she had sex that her partner was an intravenous drug user.

An extensive discussion including all aspects of the AIDS epidemic would go beyond the scope of this chapter. It seems important, however, to discuss the effect of the AIDS epidemic on the sexuality of African-Americans, especially women. Several specific HIV risks for African-Americans are related to the low sex ratio and the related problems in maintaining relationships; to the stigma attached to condom use (e.g., condom use is a sign of promiscuity); to the belief that the use of contraceptives, including condoms, limits the reproduction of African-Americans and thus is a form of genocide (Osmond et al. forthcoming); and to the religious norms and values that inhibit the use of contraceptives (Cochran, Mays, and Roberts 1988). Although these risks exist both for men and women, gender distinctions related to power differences occur (Collins 1990; Hooks 1990). The women revealed, for instance, that they preferred to ask a partner questions about his sexual history. At the same time, however, they might never pose these questions out of fear that "the men will get upset and walk away." They were concerned that a tough stand would cause men to seek another relationship and that they would lose the support, both tangible and emotional, provided by the relationship.

The respondents knew that no AIDS cure was available, were familiar with the various routes of transmission, and mentioned several ways in which they could protect themselves—for example, have first sex at an older age, abstain from having sex, or have safer sex. They admitted that it had become more difficult to find a male partner. In particular, the older and the middle-class women stated that they had become more selective. Two women, both of whom knew someone who died of AIDS, abstained from sex. The youngest women and the middle-class women indicated that, although they were worried, they did not think that many, if any, of their male partners were at risk. "I can tell if a guy is a sleaze, and I don't hang out with trash." These women, more than their older, lower-class peers, assumed that they could look at someone and discern whether the person was healthy and free of the virus.

In order to deal effectively with the AIDS epidemic, the African-American community as a whole has taken an initiative (see, e.g., Bakeman, Lumb, and Smith [1986], Farley and Allen [1987], and Friedman et al. [1987], Mays and Cochran [1988]). Despite the fact that the respondents had knowledge regarding AIDS, a substantial number continued to put themselves at risk for HIV by having sexual partners whose risk status was unknown and by not using condoms. The main reasons for this are that their social norms and beliefs do not support such behavior. The cultural context prompts the women to engage in high-risk sex despite their knowledge (Kane 1990). Community organizations and African-American churches have started responding to the AIDS epidemic and are taking a more active role (Mays and Cochran 1988). This has facilitated more open discussion of sexual matters. As women start feeling more comfortable discussing sexual issues, including discussion with their male partners, they will also develop the necessary negotiation skills and more consistently be able to protect themselves. Men, on the other hand, will also become more aware of the importance of protecting themselves as well as their female partners. Michelle Fine (1988) discussed the importance of providing sexuality education to adolescent females, particularly to those girls who are vulnerable.

Summary

Our knowledge of female sexuality is largely limited to white women. Studies including African-American women primarily have focused on fertility patterns and not on the sexuality underlying these patterns (see, e.g., Furstenberg [1971] and Johnson [1974]). Women's sexual behaviors are internalized through the process of sex-role socialization, and one should be aware that the socialization varies by racial and ethnic groups. This chapter is based on an in-depth, ethnographic study of African-American women of different ages and socioeconomic backgrounds and their views of sexuality.

The findings support the literature on the effect of age (Ehrhardt and Wasserheit 1991; Osmond and Martin 1975; Rubin 1990) and social class (Weinberg and Williams 1980) on sexuality. For the younger women in this study, dating connoted status, and one of the primary expected outcomes was sexual activity. For the older women, dating was mainly a means to meet people and possibly a lifetime companion. Thus, dating has different meanings that are age related. The lower-class women considered it acceptable for a woman to approach a man directly. The middle-class women, however, were inclined to label all behaviors other than making eye contact as flirtatious.

The settings in which the respondents met their potential dates varied. Lower-class women under the age of twenty primarily met their dates in their neighborhood, through friends or the church, or in bars and clubs. Women in their late thirties mainly mention church-related social activities; four women in their thirties and early forties who recently divorced reported frequenting bars and clubs. Almost none of the lower-class women mentioned their job as a potential meeting place; however, this was an important site for the middle-class women. Work settings especially were mentioned by the older women whose careers had been established. None of the middle-class women mentioned their neighborhood as a possible meeting site.

All respondents expressed the feeling that "deep inside" they longed for a steady, male lifetime companion. Six of the nine women who were married or were engaged in a long-term relationship at the time of the interview indicated that they did not know whether their marriage would last throughout their lifetime. The other three women had been married for over ten years and did not fear their relationships would end. The younger women tended to cope more easily with disappointing dates that did not lead to a steady relationship. Their older counterparts reacted more bitterly and reported that they felt they were running out of time. Those older women (over forty-five) who were anxious about finding a steady partner appeared more than the others to be involved in relationships in which they felt unsatisfied. It appeared that a number of these women, most of whom had low incomes, were engaging in relationships for the sake of relationships. Middle-class women considered having a steady relationship less relevant than other aspects of their lives such as having a well-paying job and a nice house. They also admitted that at times they felt frustrated by the lack of "classy" men, or, as one woman noted, "If a black woman wants a man, she probably ends up with a guy who is less successful than she is." Wilson (1986) writes that African-American men see successful African-American women as competitors who take their jobs, money, and power. A forty-two-year-old respondent who works in a management position and whose salary is above $65,000 a year angrily remarked, "Those men can't stand black women who have their act together. If you look around you'll see that most of them try to find some white chick."

Although their socialization taught the women that sex and love need to be linked, it appeared that, particularly among the older single women, sexual and interpersonal relationships were not necessarily related. The meaning of the sex act was not necessarily tied in with a good relationship, and the quality of their sexual relationship was not an indicator of the quality of their relationship.

Despite the widespread assumption that female sexuality primarily is influenced by males, it appears that among the respondents the role of other women might be equally or even more relevant. Sex primarily takes place in heterosexual relationships; bonding tends to occur with other women (Lorde 1978). Others (Allen and Britt 1983; Mays 1985; Wilson 1986) also stress the importance of interpersonal ties between African-American women. These intimate ties often include mother-daughter relationships (Binion 1990; Chodorow 1978). The importance of these relationships is shown by the fact that the respondents' attitudes toward sexuality tended to correspond with their mothers' attitudes.

The role of sex also changed throughout the life course. The women in their late teens and early twenties would at times engage in sex if they perceived this as a way to hold on to a partner. The women of reproductive age primarily engaged in sex for pleasure and reproduction; the older women either lost interest or enjoyed not having to be concerned about becoming pregnant. The younger respondents were more familiar with contraceptives and were more likely to be using them than the older women. The latter were sometimes misinformed about contraceptives and tended to hold negative associations with contraceptive use (e.g., sexual promiscuity). In addition, compared with the middle-class women, those of the lower-class were more likely to experience their first sexual encounter, frequently including unprotected vaginal intercourse, at a relative younger age. This might provide a potential explanation for the relatively high pregnancy rate among lower-class, African-American adolescents. The middle-class adolescents often delay their first sexual experience, which tends to include kissing, petting, and oral sex but not intercourse. Overall, the middle-class women were more assertive toward their partners than their lower-class peers and therefore report relatively higher rates of condom use. The middle-class women had marginally entered the masculine world—for example, they supervised others at the job. In their relationships, however, they were expected to remain feminine, causing internal conflict for these women.

The dynamics of the African-American women's relationships are very complex. The women in this study desired a steady relationship, mainly because they will then be viewed as real women. Because of the perceived lack of male partners, the women compete with each other and are more willing to forgive their partners than they would otherwise. Such an attitude upholds the symbolic power of men. The older women particularly redefine being real women as independent of a relationship with a man.

The AIDS epidemic among African-American women is a major concern (Centers for Disease Control and Prevention 1992). Considering that AIDS is an STD, one can expect that this epidemic will have an effect on the women's sexuality and that new patterns of sexual behavior will emerge. Several changes in sexual norms and behaviors are already apparent. For example, the importance of the use of condoms is being highlighted, and the negative associations with condom use are being replaced by more positive statements. The respondents commented that they are becoming more critical of their sexual partner's history and are willing to chance alienating him with their interrogation.

Although further studies among a larger sample of African-American women are needed, the data presented here underscore the importance of distinguishing African-American sexuality from sexuality among other racial and ethnic groups. African-American women also should not be seen as a homogeneous group. The data also indicate the influence of individual, social, and structural factors on sexuality. In addition, there is a need to study sexuality, and not merely fertility patterns, among other groups such as Hispanic (Latino) women and to do so with a multidisciplinary perspective.

References

Aguirre, B., and W. Parr. 1982. Husbands' marriage order and the stability of first and second marriages among white and black women. *Journal of Marriage and the Family* 44:605–20.

Allen, L., and D. Britt. 1983. Black women in American society: A resource development perspective. *Issues in Mental Health Nursing* 5:61–79.

Aral, S., R. Fullilove, R. Coutinho, and A. van der Hoek. 1991. Demographic and societal factors influencing risk behaviors. In *Research issues in human behavior and sexually transmitted diseases in the AIDS era*, ed. J. Wasserheit, S. Aral, and K. Holmes, 161–76. Washington, D.C.: American Society for Microbiology.

Atlanta Regional Commission. 1992. *Atlanta region outlook*. Atlanta: Atlanta Regional Commission.

Aug, R., and T. Bright. 1970. A Study of wed and unwed motherhood in adolescents and young adults. *Journal of American Child Psychiatry* 9:577–94.

Bakeman, R., J. Lumb, and D. Smith. 1986. AIDS statistics and the risk for minorities. *AIDS Research* 2:249–52.

Bernard, L. 1985. Black women's concerns about sexuality and hysterectomy. *Sage* 2:25–27.

Binion, V. 1990. Psychosocial androgyny: A black female perspective. *Sex Roles* 22:487–507.

Brown, D., and L. Gary. 1985. Social support network differentials among married and non-married black females. *Psychology of Women Quarterly* 9:229–41.

Brown, P., L. Perry, and E. Harburg. 1977. Sex role attitudes and psychological outcomes for black and white women experiencing marital dissolution. *Journal of Marriage and the Family* 39:549–61.

Burnham, R., and A. Ronald. 1991. Epidemiology of sexually transmitted diseases in developing countries. In *Research issues in human behavior and sexually transmitted diseases in the AIDS era,* ed. J. Wasserheit, S. Aral, and K. Holmes, 61–81. Washington, D.C.: American Society for Microbiology.

Centers for Disease Control and Prevention. 1986. AIDS among blacks and hispanics. *Morbidity and Mortality Weekly* 35:655–58, 663–66.

————. 1992. *HIV Update.* Atlanta: Centers for Disease Control and Prevention.

Chodorow, N. 1978. *The reproduction of mothering: psychoanalysis and the sociology of gender.* Berkeley: Univ. of California Press.

Cochran, S., V. Mays, and V. Roberts. 1988. Ethnic minorities and AIDS/ARC. In *Nursing care of patients with AIDS/ARC,* ed. A. Lewis, 17–24. Rockville, Md.: Aspen.

Collins, P. 1990. *Black feminist thought.* Boston: Unwin Hyman.

Daly, M., and M. Wilson. 1979. *Sex, evolution, and behavior.* North Scituate, Mass.: Duxbury.

Ehrhardt, A., and J. Wasserheit. 1991. Age, gender, and sexual behaviors for sexually transmitted diseases in the United States. In *Research issues in human behavior and sexually transmitted diseases in the AIDS era,* ed. J. Wasserheit, S. Aral, and K. Holmes, 83–96. Washington, D.C.: American Society for Microbiology.

Farley, R., and W. Allen. 1987. *The color line and the quality of life in America.* New York: Russell Sage.

Fine, M. 1988. Sexuality, schooling, and adolescent females: The missing discourse of desire. *Harvard Educational Review* 58:29–53.

Fishbein, M., and I. Azjen. 1975. *Belief, attitude, intention, and behavior: An introduction to theory and research.* Reading, Mass.: Addison-Wesley.

Friedman, S., J. Sotheran, A. Abdul-Quadar, S. Tross, and D. Des Jarbis. 1987. The AIDS epidemic among blacks and hispanics. *Milbank Memorial Quarterly* 65:455–99.

Furstenberg, F. 1971. Birth control experience among pregnant adolescents: The process of unplanned parenthood. *Social Problems* 19:192–203.

Gerrard, M. 1987. Emotional and cognitive barriers of effective contraception: Are males and females really different? In *Females, males, and sexuality,* ed. K. Kelley, 141–74. Albany: State Univ. of New York Press.

Gerrard, M., I. McCann, and M. Fortini. 1983. Prevention of unwanted pregnancy. *American Journal of Community Psychology* 11:153–68.

Glaser, B. 1978. *Theoretical sensitivity.* Mill Valley, Calif.: Sociological Press.

Glaser, B., and A. Strauss. 1970. *The discovery of grounded theory: Strategies for qualitative research.* Chicago: Aldine.

Glenn, N., and C. Weaver. 1979. A note on family situation and global happiness. *Social Forces* 57:960–67.

Goodman, L. 1961. Snowball sampling. *Annals of Mathematical Statistics* 32:148–70.

Gump, J. 1975. Comparative analysis of black women's and white women's sex-role attitudes. *Journal of Consulting and Clinical Psychology* 43:858–63.

Gurin, P., and C. Gaylord. 1976. Educational and occupational goals of men and women at black colleges. *Monthly Labor Review* 6:10–16.

Hooks, B. 1981. *Ain't I a woman: Black women and feminism.* Boston: South End.

———. 1990. *Yearning: Race, gender, and cultural politics.* Boston: South End.

Horowitz, N. 1980. Contraceptive practices of young women with two adolescent pregnancies. In *Teenage pregnancy: research related to clients and services,* ed. J. Bedger. Springfield, Ill.: Thomas.

Johnson, C. 1974. Attitudes toward premarital sex and family-planning for single-never-pregnant teenage girls. *Adolescence* 34:255–62.

Kane, S. 1990. AIDS, addiction, and condom use: Sources of sexual risk for heterosexual women. *Journal of Sex Research* 27:427–44.

Kaplan, C., D. Korf, and C. Sterk. 1987. Temporal and social contexts of heroin using populations: Illustration of the snowball sampling technique. *Journal of Nervous and Mental Diseases* 175:566–74.

Kenrick, D., and M. Trost. 1987. A biosocial theory of heterosexual relationships. In *Females, males, and sexuality,* ed. K. Kelley. Albany: State Univ. of New York Press.

Kirk, J., and M. Miller. 1986. *Reliability and validity in qualitative research.* Beverly Hills, Calif.: Sage.

Lorde, A. 1978. Scratching the surface: Some notes on the barriers to women and loving. *Black Scholar* 9:31–35.

Luker, K. 1975. *Taking chances: Abortion and the decision not to contracept.* Berkeley: Univ. of California Press.

Maccoby, E. 1988. Gender as a social category. *Development Psychology* 24:755–65.

Mason, K., J. Czajka, and S. Arber. 1976. Change in U.S. women's sex-role attitudes, 1964–1974. *American Sociological Review* 41:573–96.

Mauss, M. 1925. *The gift.* Glencoe, Ill.: Free Press.

Mays, V. 1985. Black women working together: Diversity in same sex relationships. *Women's Studies International Forum* 8:67–71.

Mays, V., and S. Cochran. 1988. Issues in the perception of AIDS risk and risk reduction activities by black and hispanic/latino women. *American Psychologist* 41:949–57.

Mosher, D. 1979. Sex guilt and sex myths in college men and women. *Journal of Sex Research* 15:224–34.

Mosher, D., and H. Cross. 1971. Sex guilt and premarital sexual experience of college students. *Journal of Consulting and Clinical Psychology* 36:27–32.

Murstein, B. 1971. *The bases of human sexual attraction.* London: Academic Press.

Osmond, M., and P. Martin. 1975. Sex and sexism: A comparison of male and female sex-role attitudes. *Journal of Marriage and Family* 36:744–58.

————. 1983. Women, work, and welfare: A comparison of black and white female heads of households. *International Journal of Sociology of the Family* 13:37–56.

Osmond, M., K. Wambach, D. Harrison, P. Levine, A. Imershein, D. Quadagno, and J. Byers. Forthcoming. The multiple jeopardy of race, class, and gender for AIDS risk among women.

Patzer, G. 1985. *The physical attractiveness phenomena.* New York: Plenum.

Pope, H. 1967. Unwed mothers and their sex partners. *Journal of Marriage and Family* 29:555–67.

Posner, R. 1992. *Sex and reason.* Cambridge, Mass.: Harvard Univ. Press.

Rand, A., and M. Krecker. 1990. Concepts of the life cycle: Their history, meanings, and uses in the social sciences. *Annual Review of Sociology* 16:241–62.

Ransford, H., and J. Miller. 1983. Race, sex, and feminist outlooks. *American Sociological Review* 48:46–59.

Rosenstock, I., V. Strecher, and M. Becker. 1988. Social learning theory and the health belief model. *Health Education Quarterly* 15:175–83.

Rubin, L. 1990. *Erotic wars: What ever happened to the sexual revolution?* New York: Farrar, Straus & Giroux.

Schwarz, P., and M. Gilmore. 1990. Sociological perspectives on human sexuality. In *Sexually transmitted diseases,* ed. K. Holmes, P. Mardh, P. Sparling, P. Wiesner, and W. Cates, 45–53. 2d ed. New York: McGraw-Hill.

Selik, R., K. Castro, and M. Pappaioanou. 1988. Racial/ethnic differences in risk of AIDS in the United States. *American Journal of Public Health* 78:1539–45.

Simmons, J. 1979. The black women's burden. *Black Enterprise* 10:57–60.

Stack, C. 1974. *Strategies for survival in a black community.* New York: Harper & Row.

Staples, R. 1973. *The black women in America: Sex, marriage, and the family.* Chicago: Nelson Hall.

————. 1978. The myth of black sexual superiority: A reexamination. *The Black Scholar* 9:16–22.

Thompson, S. 1990. Putting a big thing into a little hole: Teenage girls' accounts of sexual initiation. *Journal of Sex Research* 27:341–61.

Udry, J. R. 1985. Biological predispositions and social control in adolescent sexual behavior. *American Sociological Review* 53:709–22.

U.S. Bureau of Census. 1987. *Population profile of the United States.* Washington, D.C.: Government Printing Office.

Wasserheit, J., S. Aral, and K. Holmes, eds. 1991. *Research issues in human behavior and sexually transmitted diseases in the AIDS era.* Washington, D.C.: American Society for Microbiology.

Watters, J., and P. Biernacki. 1989. Targeted sampling: Options for the study of hidden populations. *Social Problems* 36:416–30.

Weinberg, M., and C. Williams. 1980. Sexual embourgeoisement? Social class and sexual activity: 1938–1970. *American Sociological Review* 45:33–48.

Wilson, P. 1986. Black culture and sexuality. *Journal of Social Work and Human Sexuality* 4:29–46.

Zelnik, M., and J. Kantner. 1980. Sexual activity, contraceptive use, and pregnancy among metropolitan area teenagers: 1971–1979. *Family Planning Perspectives* 12:69–76.

Zelnik, M., J. Kantner, and K. Ford. 1981. *Sex and pregnancy in adolescence.* Beverly Hills, Calif.: Sage.

African-American Male Sexuality through the Early Life Course

Benjamin P. Bowser

> So after years of trying to adopt the opinions of others I finally rebelled. I am an invisible man. Thus I have come a long way and returned and boomeranged a long way from the point in society toward which I originally aspired . . . So I took to the cellar. I hibernate. I got away from it all. (Ellison 1947, 496)

Forty-five years ago, Ralph Ellison's novel, *Invisible Man,* was hailed as a work of art and a first resolutely honest look into the minds and hearts of African-American men and women. What was not apparent then was that *Invisible Man* was even more so a specific metaphor about black men and about their sexuality. Ellison described the saga of how a young man's attempts at conformity and, later, self-definition were ultimately defeated by many in the larger society who believed in black inferiority and the necessity to control and minimize black men. The invisible man said, "When they approach me, they see only my sur-roundings, themselves, or fragments of their imagination—indeed, everything and anything except me" (Ellison 1947, 7).

It was Ellison's thesis that whites thought they knew who and what black men were, when in fact they really did not know black men. The reason was quite simple. Most whites were historically conditioned to fear and misperceive black people in general and black men in particu-lar. A large part of the emotional content and motivation for rendering black men invisible and powerless had to do with sexuality. The prob-lem was not black men's sexuality or that it needed to be controlled; rather the real problem was the larger society's denial of its own sexual-ity. The most frightening and violent scene in *Invisible Man* involved white men who thought the protagonist was taking an interest in a white woman. He was severely beaten. Even more revealing was that the reader was allowed to witness all but one of the invisible man's own emotions

This study was supported in part by grant no. R89BPF002 from the University of California universitywide AIDS Research Program, Berkeley, California.

and feelings. The one life dimension that was invisible even to the invisible man was his own sexuality.

Ellison's *Invisible Man* provides the central theme of this chapter. Black men are familiar social actors and are thought to be known social entities, when in fact they are not. Furthermore, if black men are essentially invisible, then their sexuality is also invisible. Within this theme, the central thesis is the following: American black men's sexuality is varied and socially defined. It is varied by social class, but, more important, its varied expression is conditioned over the life course and by the extent to which black men participate in the economic mainstream of American society.

This central theme and thesis is discussed in four parts. First, there is a brief review of the historic assumptions of black male sexuality. The historic assumptions are compared to the characterizations of black male sexuality in recent social science literature. The historic images and social scientific characterizations have points in common; both are distorted. Second, there is a review of who are black men. In American society a male's visibility, self-definition, and manhood are heavily dependent on meaningful participation in the economy. This point might be true even more for black men than for whites and, when ignored, is key to how black men are rendered invisible. Third, contemporary working- and lower-class black male sexuality is outlined based on in-depth interviews of adolescents and from focus groups with adult men. Here is evidence of variations in sexuality across the life course and of the effect of varied economic participation on sexual attitudes and practices. Finally, the implications of the evidence are discussed for future research on black male sexuality in the context of life course theory and research.

IMAGES OF BLACK MALE SEXUALITY

One of the English slave traders' earliest written comments was about African sexual behaviors (Jordan 1968; Okoye 1971). In comparison with seventeenth-century Englishmen, Africans expressed their sexuality openly and placed little value on modesty or secrecy. It was also assumed that Africans had no prohibitions against premarital or extramarital sex and that African men had tremendous sexual appetites. In the English view, polygamy was clear evidence that African males could not be sexually satisfied. In addition, African men's genitalia were enlarged and "got in the way" when they walked (Jordan 1968, 158; Okoye 1971, 28–29).

These observations were gross distortions. Indeed, sexuality among Africans was not a secret and was expressed openly. Boastfulness was a part of African oral cultures, and men were expected to exaggerate their sexual powers verbally (Blassingame 1972, 85). But what these English observers did not perceive was that, despite African openness regarding sex, Africans, like Englishmen, had variations in how premarital and extramarital sex were valued and practiced. High-status persons in stratified African societies placed high value on virginity and chastity (Dickemann 1981; Goody 1976). Few men had more than one wife, and, when they did, the senior wife ran the household and regulated his relations with subsequent wives. In contrast, people at the bottom of the stratification system never placed high value on controlling sexuality. Africans, like Englishmen, practiced a double standard, and virginity and chastity were never valued male characteristics (Caldwell and Caldwell 1983; Draper 1989).

The English slave traders set the stage for American and English familiarity with African men. The initial distortions were expanded and codified into the American culture and even became topics of scientific inquiry by the nineteenth century (Stanton 1960). Many slave owners justified slavery by claiming that Africans were repressed savages who could be bought and sold (Gutman 1976, 291). Eventually, this categorical belief was modified. If slaves were human, they were clearly not as evolved as whites (Englishmen) and could not be successfully constrained by higher civilization or contribute to it. Out of the basic assumption that slaves lacked humanity came a series of racist beliefs regarding sexuality that are with us in fact and symbol to this day (Stember 1976). These distortions, when used in reference to black men, are particularly resistant to change.

The first observation was that black men and women had smaller brains than whites and that black men, in particular, were more muscular and had denser body mass (Stanton 1960, 35–36). There was even so-called scientific evidence of this fact. As a result, blacks were considered innately less intelligent than whites and could work harder, longer, and under more physically adverse conditions. A belief that persists to this day is that black men's body density makes them poor swimmers. Third, it was believed that black women could never get enough sex and that black men were unable to control their sexual desire and were by nature rapists (Jordan 1968, 151). Black men in particular were thought to have an uncontrollable desire for white women and, unlike black women, were, therefore, a direct threat to the white race. Fourth, it was believed that blacks were incapable of higher human emotions, altruistic motivations, or adhering to moral conventions (Jordan 1968, 304–11). The final belief was that blacks in general and black men in particular were incapable of caring about their children and families (Genovese 1976, 495–99). Virtually all the nineteenth-century white racial beliefs were attempts to affirm that black people, and especially black men, had innate, unchangeable and inferior natures. It was therefore not only justified but absolutely necessary to exploit blacks and to rigidly control black men.

Images of Black Men in the Social Sciences

Certainly modern social scientific studies and evidence are more valid than nineteenth-century ideation. There have been approximately three hundred studies of some aspect of black sexual behavior published between 1964 and 1989 in the social and behavioral science journals (Weinstein et al. 1990). Some 191 are devoted specifically to black "sex, sexuality, sexual attitudes, sexual practices, drugs and sex, homosexuality, sex education, and contraception." Of the studies that focus on men or women, 83 percent concern black women. Forty-two percent of all the studies focused on black preteens and teens. The most typical study of black sexual behavior is conducted in a family-planning clinic and consists of closed-end questions asking female adolescents about frequency of intercourse, contraception, and pregnancy. There are very few studies on black male adolescents or adults, black drug users (mostly males again), and black married couples.

The few studies that obtained information from black males inform us repeatedly that in comparison with their white peers black males begin having sex at an earlier age, have sex more often, have more sexual partners, are less likely to use condoms, and practice a double standard with reference to their female partners (Fullilove et al. 1990). What is remarkable about these studies is that there is virtually no discussion, analysis, or even speculation about the causes of these behaviors among black men. In addition, there is little attention to the extent to which these behaviors are common among all black men. The one study that attempts to look at black male sexual behaviors across social class found that even black middle-class adolescents were partly but properly described above (Weinberg and Williams 1988).

Is there any relation between nineteenth-century racial beliefs and contemporary social scientific studies of black male sexuality? Do we have any better knowledge or insights today about black male sexuality than we had at the turn of the century? One could argue that contemporary studies are not identical to the beliefs of the prior century and that the social and behavioral scientific work is empirically grounded and, therefore, more accurate. Alternatively, one could also conclude that recent social and behavioral scientific findings have not informed us very well about black male sexuality. This apparent enigma can be explained.

The problem is not in the science. Rather, the problem is in what has been systematically omitted from study and how the little information we get is used. The essence of distortion is to take evidence of some real event or phenomenon and to either overgeneralize or minimize it for some self-serving purpose. The attempt of nineteenth-century scholars to write the contributions to civilization and the influences of Africans and Africa out of history was precisely this kind of distortion (Bernal 1987; James 1954). So, on the surface, when an observation or information is distorted, there is some truth, but the inferences and conclusions drawn tend to render the subjects less visible and comprehensible. The first problem with contemporary studies of black sexuality is that male subjects are consistently drawn from lower-class adolescents and young men. There are well-known variations in attitudes (Centers 1961; Kohn 1969) and in sexuality (Cuber and Harroff 1966; Rainwater 1960) by social class. But even if social class is properly considered, results from lower-class respondents cannot be generalized across all black males in the lower class. More often, black male respondents are purposefully recruited into the study because their sexual behavior has called them to the attention of some social service and health agency. Not one of the studies of black male sexual behavior published since 1964 had a representative sample of black males from any social class.

The second problem with contemporary studies of black sexuality is in their purpose: they are all descriptive. Not one empirical study was found that attempted to explain or understand the consistent findings about black male sexual behavior—early sex activity, more frequent sex, more partners, and the double standard. If these behaviors are accurate and found consistently, then the most important question is, Why do they exist? There was not a single study that examined these findings with any sensitivity to culture or social structure. The third problem gets to the heart of the matter. A review of the literature on black sexuality does not contain a single study that hypothesizes that black male sexual behavior varies in any way, has any sort of dynamic, or is even malleable.

The final problem is that black sexuality in empirical studies is defined as comparative behavior. It has no empirical reality apart from mainstream white sexuality. Comparative studies of white and black sample populations are notorious for ignoring the social and economic class differences between the races. Researchers who are unfamiliar with black social class history and structure continue to assume that black and white respondents with the same income, education, and approximate occupations are in the same social class (Landry 1987). They ignore racial differences in class longevity, personal wealth, extended family resources, social class of friends, and ethnic background. Even age differences are not consistently controlled for. Ethnic and racial subcultural backgrounds open the door to a wide range of attitudes, beliefs, and values that may dispose people in the same social class to have significant differences.

The bottom line is that, if a slave trader or slave master had hibernated over the past century, awoke, and then read contemporary studies of black male sexuality, he would find little to disturb him. He would see that black men still have sex earlier. There would be little to dissuade his belief that all black men have little control over their sexuality once it begins. By omission, there would be little empirical evidence that would suggest or even hint that black male sexuality varied in any way or was anything other than innately driven. Given the invisibility of black men and black male sexuality in the empirical literature, who then is the black man?

WHO ARE BLACK MEN?

Patriarchy, primogeniture, and patrilineage are English traditions that have shaped American sex roles (Houlbrooke 1984, 18). Black men are the only group of men in American history who have been restricted through law and custom from fulfilling adult sex roles as heads of families and communities for more than three consecutive age cohorts. During slavery, black marriages were not legally recognized and slaves could not own property (Blassingame 1972, 78). Black men were heads of households only at the pleasure of their masters. After the Civil War and the Emancipation, the efforts of black men to head and protect families, own property, and participate in the economy as equals were met with violence (Gutman 1976, 433–42). By 1890 that violence and subsequent subordinate status was codified into Jim Crow laws and etiquette where blacks were officially subordinated to whites in every aspect of life (Woodward 1966). This system was in place until the 1964 Civil Rights Act. The past twenty-seven years is only the second brief period in the past two hundred and fifty years when racial subordination was not formally written into law.

Black men are the only group of men in American history who have been restricted for more than three age cohorts through laws or customs from participation in the American industrial economy as any other than the last hired and first fired (Harris 1982; Jaynes and Williams 1989, 271–77). Historically, black men were hired into well-paying city jobs only as long as there were no new European immigrants available (Lieberson 1980). But as soon as new immigrants arrived, black men were displaced and pushed back in the job queue or out of work entirely. This history has had a devastating long-term effect on black men's efforts to form and head families, accumulate resources for subsequent generations, and fully participate in the mainstream of American life. This point is clearly evident in African-Americans' lack of wealth in comparison to whites (Jaynes and Williams 1989, 291–94).

It is one thing to be relegated to the bottom of the economy because of one's race. But it is quite another thing to find oneself out of the economy entirely. The past decade has been unique for African-Americans. There has always been some kind of work. But this past decade was the first decade where there is clear evidence that growing numbers of black Americans have no useful role to play in declining urban and domestic economies (Jaynes and Williams 1989, 296–97). This process began with black youth after 1970 and has continued for subsequent cohorts of blacks who wish to enter the job market (Bowser 1989; Glasgow 1981). It is one thing to be discriminated against in one's participation in the workforce. It is quite another thing for the bottom sectors of the labor force to have fewer jobs than prospective workers. Unskilled and semiskilled jobs have disappeared from urban centers and have gone overseas or into the outer suburbs and rural areas (Bluestone and Harrison 1982). The long-term effects are declining black urban communities, deteriorating family life, children supported by the state, and the fact that black men, who in past decades would have headed families and held jobs, have been unemployed so long that many of them are no longer counted in monthly unemployment rates.

The economic transitions now apparent make prophetic Sidney Willhelm's 1971 book, *Who Needs the Negro?* From the beginning of American slavery the argument has been made that either slavery or racially restrictive laws or customs were needed and justified because of blacks' innate physical or moral inferiority. Now the racially restrictive laws are gone and even the fact of continued racial discrimination can be denied as a primary cause of inequality and the deteriorating status of black Americans (Wilson 1978). The more recent transitions in the economy have potentially locked up to one-third of all blacks into a semipermanent underclass (Jaynes and Williams 1989, 277–83). Here it can be claimed that economic class and race to a lesser extent are now the primary barriers to upward mobility. But ironically, whether these barriers are economic or continued racial discrimination or both, the people at the bottom continue to be held largely responsible for their plight.

Now distorted white perception and racial discrimination have economic transitions as an additional, new, and powerful force in pushing black men toward even greater invisibility. Not only is black male economic invisibility a historic metaphor; it can actually be measured across each cohort of black men by comparing them with their white male peers. If invisibility is operationalized in terms of labor-force participation rates, then table 1 gives some indication of trends in black male economic invisibility.

Three trends are apparent in black male labor-force participation rates across the cohorts shown in Table 1. From 1939 until 1969, each successive age cohort of black men has had progressively fewer men enter the work force (3.0 percent, 6.6 percent, 7.2 percent, 13.1 percent) in comparison to white men of the same age and at the same time of entry into the labor force. The most recent cohort of black men who began work in 1969 had the largest difference (13.1 percent) in white-black entry into the labor force of any prior age group. The second trend

TABLE 1 1980 Percent Differences in Labor-Force Participation Rates for African-American and White Men Who Entered the Labor Force, 1939–69 (%)

	Age Cohort in 1980			
Decade of Entry	65+	55–64	45–54	35–44
1939	3.0	. . .	. . .	. . .
1949	4.4	6.6	. . .	. . .
1959	6.4	6.5	7.2	. . .
1969	8.9	8.2	8.4	13.1
1979	. . .	9.9	10.3	10.8

Source: U.S. Bureau of the Census 1983.

is that black men are leaving the workforce in progressively higher proportions the younger the cohort and at earlier points in their work careers. These trends suggest the following: despite legal desegregation,
the brief economic gains of the 1960s and higher educational attainment across cohorts, black men are entering the labor force in progressively lower proportions in each younger cohort. In addition, they are
leaving the labor force sooner and in higher numbers.

If labor-force entry is a proxy for the economic transition from invisibility to visibility, then each younger cohort of black men is progressively more invisible. These trends in labor-force participation are powerful contexts that shape black men's life course development and
sexuality. Others have pointed out some of the consequences of long-
term isolation from participation in the economy. William Moore
(1969) described these men as having "masculinity without status," and,
more recently, Elijah Anderson (1990) pointed out that relationships
between men and women become games as substitutes for more traditional presentations of manhood. With economic status eliminated as a
basis of manhood, dress, hairstyle, language, and dance ability take on
greater meaning and importance as the basis for status and competition.

BLACK MALE SEXUALITY IN EARLY PHASES OF THE LIFE COURSE
Early Sex

> When I was about 9, I got caught up under my porch trying
> to have sex with a girl. I got my ass kicked. So that kinda
> puts a fear into you. . . . [Later] I was trying out for football
> and basketball, so I really didn't have time to get into it
> (sex). . . . (BVHP-BMS, 12)

The speaker was a forty-year-old black man who grew up during the
1950s in what is now the largest black community in San Francisco. One
of six other black men, all between thirty and forty-five years old, he
was part of a focus group on black men and sexuality conducted in
1989.[1] The men were outreach staff and clients at a health-care agency
in the community. Their experiences were in direct contrast to those of
twenty-four black male adolescents from thirteen to nineteen who have
grown up in the same community in the 1980s and were interviewed
one-on-one in 1990.[2] The younger men were interviewed on two occasions six months apart by youth outreach workers at the same community health center. After a series of background and rapport-setting

questions, the young men were asked to tell the age and circumstance of their first sexual experiences. The youngest age reported of first sex was nine and the oldest was sixteen.

Interviewer: How old were you when you started [having sex]?
Answer: Ten . . . actually nine and a half.
Interviewer: Where did you meet this person?
Answer: At—ah—[the local high school] in school. No. From the
    neighborhood.
Interviewer: Where did you have sex at ?
Answer: At her house.
(CU-NARG 49:3–4)

The respondent was eighteen years old and went on to describe a series of casual sexual encounters with a number of other young women since his first. He had also been arrested for auto theft, had sold drugs, been shot, and had contracted gonorrhea. All but one of the young men had had sex and had similar experiences. Their interviews contrasted with those of the older men. Every single adolescent respondent reported having his first sexual encounter either in his own or the girl's home. In most cases, these encounters went on for months and were never discovered by parents or siblings and were never punished. The young men were also asked about after-school activities. Most had played some sports in junior high school, but, by the time they reached high school, many had to financially support themselves. Work excluded the opportunity to play sports but left them with free time to be at home alone and in the streets.

What had happened in the thirty years between the older and younger men's experiences? First of all, a comparison of the two experiences suggest that parents have virtually disappeared as socializing agents regarding sexuality and as barriers to early male sexual exploration. All the older men had a parent, grandparent, or some other older relative at home after school. But none of the younger men had anyone at home regardless of their family household composition. All their parents either worked or had to be away from home for regular periods during the day. The younger men grew up in households where they were regularly alone at home for some period during the day. The second thing the two sets of interviews revealed was that the younger men had no memory of preadolescent sex play prior to their first intercourse. One of the older men reported, "I got caught playing doctor with a girl under the kitchen table. I was about eleven years old and my stepfather actually laughed at me. Mom, she beat me, you know, but my stepfather pulled me aside . . ." (BVHP-BMS 13). The younger men had no memory of early sex play. Shortly after they began to take a serious interest in girls, they had their first intercourse. There was no playing up to it. Their attitude toward having sex was very straightforward. It was simply something they wanted to do, and they did it. There was no moralizing, and it required very little effort. Same-age or older partners were readily available. There were no concerns about finding compliant partners as with the women interviewed by Claire Sterk-Elifson (chap. 4, this vol.). One young man claimed to have begun his sexual career with his babysitter when he was thirteen years old.

Multiple Partners

The young men were asked about their second and subsequent sexual partners. Their responses revealed an interesting pattern. Those who claimed to have had preadolescent sex (prior to twelve years old) had as much as two years between their first and second partners. But by sixteen all the young men began to have either a series of steady girlfriends or a number of casual sexual partners. The onset of intercourse also appears to coincide with the onset of drug use. Although all but one was sexually active, there were two distinct patterns: In the first, the young men had steady girlfriends whom they tended to express some love for. We asked the young men, When was the first time you fell in love? Unlike the teenage girls described by Sharon Thompson (chap. 8, this vol.), these young men had little use for romance and had no problem establishing relationships. Most of these young men with steady girlfriends maintained their relationships from six months to a year.[3] They would break up and were soon into new relationships for another six months to a year.

In the second pattern, the majority of the young men had a series of casual partners and claimed they never fell in love. There was nothing romantic about their intent. The core of this second group were young men who were financially on their own from the time that they could legally work—since they were fifteen to sixteen years old. *On their own* meant being in their parents' minds old enough to be responsible for their own food, clothes, expenses, and in extreme cases their own shelter whether or not they had jobs. There appears to be a close relation between being on their own and a rapid increase in casual sexual partners, drug use, and drug selling. Only one young man reported that, because of behavioral problems, he had been put out by his parents. The following are excerpts from an interview with an eighteen-year-old who first had sex at fifteen, dropped out of school at sixteen to support himself, drifted away from home and family, and was living with his girlfriend.

Interviewer: Has anyone moved out since the time of the last interview?

Answer: I kicked her ass out. [She] wasn't supportive. Didn't bring me no money. . . . I live by myself; I can do better by myself.

Interviewer: Who is currently supporting you?

Answer: I support myself. . . . I hustle. And, I do odd jobs.

Interviewer: Have you been sexually active over the past six months?

Answer: Every day.

Interviewer: How many partners have you had in the past six months?

Answer: Past six months it's been . . . seventeen.

Interviewer: . . . You stay with all of them . . . ?

Answer: They're friends. . . . Well, I put it like this: I be here for them so sex is what they need; I try to be more than just a friend.

Interviewer: How do you meet these people . . . ?

Answer: Old friends from school.

(CU-NARG 1:3–5)

This is not a young man who is attractive to young women because of a bright future. He is attractive precisely because he has nothing, is young and no threat, can make no status demands, and works at being a good lover. After separating from his live-in girlfriend, he now essentially provides sexual service to a network of young working women who occasionally want to have sex but without the hassles of a relationship. He reported that they are up to twenty-four years old and are former schoolmates who trust him and his discretion. Is this young man an isolated case? He is certainly the most extreme in claiming seventeen partners. But to a lesser extent, all the young men who are on their own and self-supporting at sixteen to eighteen years are involved in fragmented, provisional, and casual sexual relations. As young men, they may think of themselves as sexually successful, but they are also hunted, sought out, and exploited. One of the other young men who was also eighteen, had dropped out of school, hustles, and was self-supporting when interviewed:

Interviewer: How old are your sexual partners?

Answer: Older. They're all older. One is twenty-five. One was thirty-eight, and one was thirty-six.

(Six months later.)

Interviewer: How many different partners have you had over the past six months?

Answer: About three.

Interviewer: How old are they?

Answer: Going on twenty . . . And other one is twenty-five . . . And the other, she is twenty-seven.

Interviewer: How did you meet these people?

Answer: Met [the twenty-year-old] at a party.

Interviewer: How long did you know this person before having sex with her?

Answer: A couple of hours.

Interviewer: Where did you have sex with these people?

Answer: Hotels . . . say about three, four times in one night.

Interviewer: What goals and dreams do you have for your life?

Answer: To have a lot of money; be a jig.

(CU-NARG 45:8–11)

Double Standard

There are two components of the male double standard: The first component is that it is normal and expected for young men to be sexually adventurous and to have sexual experiences before they settle down. In contrast, young women bring scandal and disgrace to themselves by being sexually adventuresome and by having experiences that compromise their virginity (D'Emilio and Freedman 1988, 86–87). The second component of the double standard is to be in a supposedly monogamous relationship and to occasionally have sex on the side. Again, men may take this liberty, but women may not. The contrast between our older and younger black men suggests that the male double standard might not have been all that it was claimed to be. But whatever it is, the practice has undergone a radical transition. The focus group leader asked the older men where they learned about sex:

> Out on the street. I'll tell you where you really learn it. Somebody else sayin' how good "Sally" was. Oh, is she easy. And that's the first thing they go for—Sally. Sally may not be (giving up anything), but he gonna try to make himself look good. And he ain't doin' nothin'. And when he come back with a black eye, you know he just seen Sally, right? That's where, you know, fellas get to talk and lying. (BVHP-BMS 7)

The great male sexual adventures may not be as extensive or as universal as they were claimed to be. But there appeared to be universal agreement on how girls were classified into those whom one could or could not approach sexually. The focus group leader asked if they had made distinctions between "the girls that you could do it with and (the) ones that you couldn't?" The responses were as follows:

Respondent 1: Oh, definitely.

Respondent 2: Yeah, I did. I did, I know I did. I dated all sorts of girls. [The most popular] didn't appeal to me. . . . Everybody was going after them.

Respondent 3: One of them was popular. But she wasn't doing anything everybody said she was doing, but everybody—all the fellas—liked her.

(BVHP-BMS 11)

In contrast, the young men did not have any particular knowledge of their current steady or casual partner's reputation or of their prior partners' reputations, either. There was no longer a community of knowledge or of reputations about individuals in the community to draw on. People simply did not know one another. Also the young men assumed that the women were out getting sex whenever they could, just like the fellas—a quarter of the young men had gotten a venereal disease as evidence. Sex was engaged in so casually that it could not be any other way. For the young men, it appears that both components of the double standard now apply to women as well. In their case, it is no longer a *double* standard.

Black Men Do Not Use Condoms

According to the comparative literature on sexuality, black men use condoms less frequently than do white men. Aggregated survey data obscure underlying complexity and realities. The older men were introduced to condoms on the streets, by older brothers, and by their fathers. Initially, they used them infrequently. But then,

Respondent 1: As far as right now, I use it.

Respondent 2: I'm scared, too, man.

Respondent 3: She gave me the clap. I tried to keep it a secret. My wife wasn't around at the time. I'd never leave home without [a condom]. Don't leave without one now.

Respondent 4: My father always stressed, if you gonna do it, hey man, you gotta take care of yourself.

Respondent 2: Your old man sounds like mine.

Respondent 5: So much is going on now, today, that you need to have
that raincoat. And that ain't gonna protect you too much,
either. . . .

(BVHP-BMS 14)

The young men did not use condoms initially, either. One claims to
have used a condom during his first intercourse, but none of the others
did. Only after they became very sexually active did condom use begin,
and even then condoms were used only occasionally. The most consistent condom users had experienced having a sexually transmitted disease and wanted to avoid another such experience. Those who were the
least consistent in condom usage had steady sexual partners. In comparison to the older men, the younger men as a group seemed ambivalent
about condoms. One of these young men illustrates this ambivalence
despite being AIDS conscious and being very careful about selecting his
sexual partners. He was eighteen, raised in foster homes, did not complete the eleventh grade, and supported himself by going around wash-
ing people's windows unsolicited and hoping they would pay him and
by helping pump gas—again unsolicited and in the self-service isle.

Interviewer: Did you have sex with anybody [in the past six months]?

Answer: Say ten. I couldn't exactly say.

Interviewer: [Of your most current partners] how often do you have
sex with M?

Answer: Two times [in the last six months]. . . . Yeah, I didn't want to
take too many chances of catching AIDS and her getting AIDS.

(CU-NARG 10:7–9)

In response to the interviewer asking him why he knew the second
woman nine months before having sex with her, he responded, "I
wanted to get [to know] a person a little better before I had any kind of
sex or anything like that with them. I really get to know a person real
well before I ask them over for a nightcap" (CU-NARG 10:13). The interviewer asked him whether he had ever gotten a girl pregnant. His
response put his AIDS awareness, yet inconsistent condom use into perspective. "I would like to (get a girl pregnant), though. To have my own
kid. To have my own child in the world. Someone can live out my name
when I pass on" (CU-NARG 10:15). I do not think that his desire is an
isolated one. Several of the other young men had gotten girls pregnant
and had children. One young man had gotten three girls pregnant five

times—all but one of the pregnancies were aborted. It appears that the clearer it is that their lives are at a dead end despite their young age, the more casual the sex and, possibly, the more they want to have children. Jane Lancaster (chap. 2, this vol.) provides a context to suggest that wanting children under their social circumstances may be a reasonable and even natural response.

Changes in Community

The older black men's sexuality was contextualized by the community in which they lived. Despite racial segregation, and relatively low incomes in comparison to whites, there was a community in which their fathers or their friends and neighbors' fathers headed families. Their families were extended. All the adults in the household and in the community were expected to socialize young people. There was a consensus in the community on what constituted appropriate sexual behavior among young adults, and every adult member of the community was expected to enforce those standards for their own as well as their neighbors' children. One of the older men reported,

> When I was growing up, it seemed like I could walk out of my house and I could just leave the door open. Walk around the corner and do whatever. You can't do that these days.... Even the physical appearance of the neighborhood. You know, beer cans, a problem with youth drinking and sex for drugs and all that. Just the whole community has changed and I feel like it's just the beginning. (BVHP-BMS 3–4)

There may be a tendency to exaggerate the 1950s and 1960s, but community change for the worse is undeniable. Once the struggle was to get the city to build a swimming pool in the community. Now people—who can—are selling their property and moving out because of drug trafficking, drug use, and drive-by shootings. Another older man pointed out,

> ... A lot of people would not even walk up to the store. My mother is one.... Everyone is crying uncle instead of brother. People don't believe in helping their neighbor go through rough times.... We need more jobs. I don't mean no MacDonald jobs. I'm talking about something a young

person can get into and, you know, seriously pay the rent [and a] car note. (BVHP-BMS 3)

The young men's sexuality was also contextualized by community— or rather the lack of it. The young men have had few positive experiences with community. To them community is something you survive. It is a place that is dangerous and that they hope one day to get away from. A community consensus of what is and is not appropriate behavior no longer operates on the streets. The community they know has not been able to shape or even restrain their sexuality. These young men have no vision of playing any useful or productive roles in society. Selling drugs is the most immediate way to make money and to work toward gaining some measure of independence. Most have been arrested. Half have been in jail. Ironically, all have been employed at least during the summer, either full- or part-time. But none of their job experiences inspired or motivated them to raise their aspirations. In response to the question of what is going on in his environment, one young man summarized what the other young men said. He also echoed the old men's observations. He responded, ". . . Everybody is doing their own thing. If you are selling [drugs], you are selling; if you're going to work, you're going to work. . . . It's like everybody's cool. Most people down there [wouldn't] stop [selling drugs]" (CU-NARG 2:16).

THE MYTH OF BLACK SEXUAL SUPERIORITY

There is another factor associated with black sexuality that has a known dynamic and goes beyond the negative view that most of the public has of these men and the decline of community in their neighborhoods. A very specific message in the negative generalized other that these black men have incorporated into themselves is the myth of black sexual superiority (Staples 1978). The myth is possibly the intervening variable between both the experience and perception of economic marginality and hypersexuality. The myth of black sexual superiority provides a cultural context for sexual exploitation among blacks and between blacks and others. The social network of working women who used the young man in the second example in this study were white and Filipino. Everything that made him socially subordinate to them (being a high school dropout, having a poor or no future) also made him sexually attractive. The lower his social status, the more he fulfilled their belief in black hypersexuality. But the problem is not primarily white sexual exploitation of blacks. The main problem is that blacks believe the myth of their alleged sexual superiority. The older black men talked about "the rumor":

Respondent 1: I found they were more attracted to us. You know, my buddy, we played on the basketball team. And he had [a white partner]. She would go back and tell her friends about her sexual encounter with my buddy. Her friend became interested. So we used to go over his house every night. So I made it with her.

Respondent 2: I agree with that totally.

Respondent 3: I've been approached by several different races.

Respondent 4: If you ask me, I think it's true. . . . I think it's true, you know, the rumor about black people being more athletic. You know, bigger sexually and having more drive. You know, I have been approached and asked by, you know, another race, more than one time. . . . I feel that it's me in a way being attracted to them just, you know, to obtain a piece of pussy, but it's more them approaching me. Definitely more.

(BVHP-BMS 15–16)

Some women of other races were attracted to these men because of curiosity about black sexual superiority. Experience and maturity had not dissuaded these older black men from belief in the myth themselves. The problem is that the belief calls for superior sexual performance, in which case greater effort then produces sexual experiences that reaffirm the myth as a self-fulfilling prophecy. If the older men believe the myth and have experiences that suggest that the myth is true, the younger men face an even greater challenge. What happens to the young person who is sexually inexperienced, becomes aware of the myth, and is expected to be immediately a superior lover because of some innate ability? This is the one thing society's generalized other expects him to be good at. This young person then has tremendous motivation to become experienced as soon as possible and to prove to himself and to his partners that he is indeed sexually superior. Break the belief in the myth of black sexual superiority and the cultural imperative to define oneself through sexual performance, and black male hypersexuality may be considerably diminished.

Implications for Sex and Life Course Research

Both the older and younger black men in this study could have been asked closed-end questions about their sexual behavior and their responses could have been compared with those of their white social class peers. The aggregate results would have undoubtedly been another confirmation that black men have their first intercourse earlier, have sex more often and with more partners, and use condoms less frequently. But what these interviews and focus groups revealed is that underneath the aggregate statistics there are variations in these men's sexuality. The variability is both across and within age cohorts. The interviews also suggested that the men have phases of sexual activity and inactivity as well as the ability to direct and control their behavior. The variability in black male sexuality suggested in these interviews is all the more significant because these men are from the same community health center, recruited from the same lower-class to working-class population that has been used to characterize black male sexuality in prior studies.

Clearly, these black men have a complex, highly conditional and socially defined sexuality. The intergenerational comparisons suggest that black male sexuality has changed along with transformations in the community and family household composition. This means that there is a social context to black male sexuality. Certainly, changes in black male sexuality did not change the community, but rather changes in community led to changes in cohorts of younger men. The aggregate and comparative descriptions of black male sexuality have missed both the effect of community on sexuality and the basis of the changes in black male sexuality across age cohorts. It appears that between two age cohorts black male sexuality has gone from being a community sexuality, where sexuality was highly contextualized in social relationships that were heavily influenced by family, neighbors, and community, to an anomic sexuality, where sexuality was isolated from family and community constraints and almost entirely individual and personal.

There is a critical need to precede formal studies of black sexuality with open-ended questions, focus groups, and a willingness to listen. Researchers need to learn more of what goes on in the lives of these men and what explanations they provide for their behaviors. The social context of their behavior is also crucial. The end result will be grounded questions and interpretations of data.

Black men represent a special challenge to life course research precisely because of their historic and continued invisibility. Life course analysis of white and black matching age cohorts may show not only what is similar to both races in each cohort but also what distinct effect social change has had on each racial group's perception of one another (Blauner 1989). Lawrence Gary's *Black Men* (1981) was the first social science reader devoted to black men that attempted to provide a comprehensive view. Reginald Jones's *Black Adult Development and Aging* (1989) was the first reader to explore the effects of black Americans' racial culture and the circumstances on their life course development. There are two chapters devoted specifically to black men that summarize the existing literature on black men's life course (Bowman 1989; Gooden 1989), a literature that is otherwise virtually nonexistent.

Sex-Ratio Imbalance?

Finally, to what extent were the patterns of sexual behaviors and attitudes exhibited by both young and older black men outcomes from imbalanced sex ratios? Because of poor pre- and postnatal health care, fewer black males survive through infancy. Among males who survive infancy, more die as a result of murder, accident, and poor health during adolescence. Then, as adults, more black males are imprisoned and enter cross-racial marriages than black women. The imbalance in sex ratio then could account for lower homosexuality among black men, starting sex earlier, informal polygamy, and shifting the burden of contraception to women (Posner 1992). Bayview Hunter's Point is no exception to these national trends; the community has an imbalanced sex ratio. Certainly the imbalanced sex ratio provided more opportunities for both younger and older black men to have relationships with black women than for black women to have relationships with black men. But there is no evidence from the interviews that these men directly and consciously exploit the imbalance in the sex ratio as suggested by the women in Sterk-Elifson's interviews (chap. 4, this vol.).

The interviews and focus groups did not address a concern in sex-ratio research regarding the basis of gender preference. It is not clear that the younger black men are even aware that they have a sex-ratio advantage when they begin their sexual careers. The younger men who had multiple partners saw themselves engaging in mutual polygamy—the women had multiple partners as well. The older men, whether or not they were in monogamous relationships, claim that AIDS and other sexually transmitted diseases had tempered their interest in sex with casual partners and that they had settled down. None of the men consistently used contraceptives, which is consistent with the sex-ratio effect thesis. But neither did their partners. The motive for this omission among the men was not because they did not have to or because they could always go to someone else. The more closed the life-choice opportunities before them, the stronger was the drive to have children and the more conflict they had about using condoms. For these men, the imbalance in sex ratio is more of a structural than social-psychological or situational variable.

CONCLUSION

Sexuality is socially conditioned and then becomes expressed in individual behaviors. In other words, sexuality is a product of psychobiological readiness, historic conditioning, circumstance (social context), self-identity, and generalized others' definition of self. If the distorted images of black men and the barriers to economic and social participation disappeared tomorrow, black male sexuality would still be qualitatively distinct from white males. The historically conditioned habits and self-perceptions would still be unchanged at least for another generation. This does not suggest that black males would continue to begin sex earlier, have sex more often, have more partners, and use condoms less frequently. If black males in the aggregate began sex at the same age as white males, had sex as often, and had the same number of partners, black male sexuality would still not be the same as that of white males. For black male sexuality to be the same as white male sexuality, black men would have to have at least the same cultural conditioning and social circumstances as white men. A comparative study of black middle-class male sexuality with white middle-class male sexuality would demonstrate this point, provided that the real bases of each class were considered.

Black male hypersexuality is also socially conditioned. In addition to being social class specific, black male hypersexuality is a product of limited life prospects, failed legitimate economic mobility, an exploitive generalized other self-definition, and belief in the myth of black sexual superiority. The acquisition of the hypersexual role is particularly tragic for black male adolescents. The hypersexual dynamic is that, the greater the exposure to the generalized other's cultural expectation of hypersexuality and the greater the sense of failure and limitations, the greater is the motivation toward hypersexuality. This is the one area that a stigmatized black male can succeed in. With age and experience, the hold of the hypersexual role that motivates early, frequent, and multipartner sexual behavior diminishes. But the key elements of the social conditioning remain in place through the black male's life course and must be dealt with.

Ultimately the generalized other's culturally conditioned expectation of black hypersexuality as well as blacks' belief in the myth of black sexual superiority must be challenged. To effectively challenge the myth will take renewed economic opportunities, a change in the larger society's generalized view of black males, and blacks themselves to challenge their own beliefs in sexual superiority. Then the black invisible man can step forward, come out of hibernation, and cease to be invisible.

NOTES

1. The focus group was conducted in 1989 at the Bayview Hunter's Point (BVHP) Foundation in San Francisco, California, and the transcript is unpublished. The transcript is referred to as the black male sexuality focus group or BVHP-BMS, with reference to the transcript page number.

2. Quotes are taken from the transcripts of twenty-four male adolescents interviewed at the Bayview Hunter's Point Foundation in 1990. The study title, "Crack Users: The New AIDS Risk Group," is referred to as CU-NARG. The numbers that follow are the case number and transcript pages. There were also twenty-nine female adolescents interviewed in addition to the males for a total of fifty-four cases. The purpose of the study was to gain insight into the relation between drug use, sexuality, and HIV high-risk behaviors by comparing adolescent crack cocaine users with their peers who were nonusers.

3. All three of the young men in dual-parent households reported that they had "fallen in love" and had steady girlfriends. This finding suggests only that family household composition or some quality of the parents' relation with their sons and with one another may influence the quality of relations their sons develop with young women. Further research would have to establish how and to what extent the young men's sexuality and relationships are influenced by parents.

REFERENCES

Anderson, E. 1990. *Streetwise: Race, class, and change in an Urban community.* Chicago: Univ. of Chicago Press.

Bernal, M. 1987. *Black Athena: The Afroasiatic roots of classical civilization.* London: Free Association.

Blassingame, J. 1972. *The slave community: Plantation life in the antebellum South.* New York: Oxford Univ. Press.

Blauner, R. 1989. *Black lives, white lives.* Berkeley: Univ. of California Press.

Bluestone, B., and B. Harrison. 1982. *The deindustrialization of America.* New York: Basic.

Bowman, P. 1989. Research perspectives on black men: Role strain and adaptation across the black adult male life cycle. In *Black adult development and aging,* ed. R. Jones, 117–50. Berkeley, Calif.: Cobbs & Henry.

Bowser, B. 1989. Generational effects: The impact of culture, economy, and community across the generations. In *Black adult development and aging,* ed. R. Jones, 3–30. Berkeley, Calif.: Cobbs & Henry.

Caldwell, J. C., and P. Caldwell. 1983. The demographic evidence for the incidence and cause of abnormally low fertility in tropical Africa. *World Health Statistics Quarterly* 36:2–34.

Centers, R. 1961. *The psychology of social class.* New York: Russell & Russell.

Crack users: The new AIDS high risk group, interviews (CU-NARG). 1991. Bayview Hunter's Point Foundation, San Francisco. Unpublished.

Cuber, J. F., and P. Harroff. 1966. *Sex and the significant Americans: A study of sexual behavior among the affluent.* Baltimore: Penguin.

D'Emilio, J., and E. Freedman. 1988. *Intimate matters: A history of sexuality in America.* New York: Harper & Row.

Dickemann, M. 1981. Paternity confidence and dowry competition: A biocultural analysis of purdah. In *Natural selection and social behavior,* ed. R. Alexander and D. Tinkle, 417–38. New York: Cheiron.

Draper, P. 1989. African marriage systems: Perspectives from evolutionary ecology. *Ethology and Sociobiology* 10:145–69.

Ellison, R. 1947. *The invisible man.* New York: Signet.

Focus Group on Black Male's Sexuality (BVHP-BMS). 1989. Bayview Hunter's Point Foundation, San Francisco. Unpublished.

Fullilove, M. T., M. Weinstein, R. Fullilove, E. Crayton, R. Goodjoin, B. Bowser, and S. Gross. 1990. Race/gender issues in the sexual transmission of AIDS. In *Clinical Review 1990,* ed. P. Volberding and M. Jacobson, 25–62. New York: Dekker.

Gary, L., ed. 1981. *Black men.* Beverly Hills, Calif.: Sage.

Genovese, E. 1976. *Roll, Jordan, roll: The world the slaves made.* New York: Vintage.

Glasgow, D. 1981. *The black underclass: Poverty, unemployment and entrapment of ghetto youth.* New York: Vintage.

Gooden, W. 1989. Development of black men in early development. In *Black adult development and aging,* ed. R. Jones, 63–90. Berkeley, Calif.: Cobbs & Henry.

Goody, J. 1976. *Production and reproduction.* Cambridge: Cambridge Univ. Press.

Gutman, H. G. 1976. *The black family in slavery and freedom, 1750–1925.* New York: Pantheon.

Harris, W. 1982. *The harder we run: Black workers since the Civil War.* New York: Oxford Univ. Press.

Houlbrooke, R. 1984. *The English family, 1450–1700.* London: Longman.

James, G. 1954. *Stolen legacy.* New York: Philosophical Library.

Jaynes, G., and R. Williams, Jr. 1989. *A common destiny: Blacks and American society.* Washington, D.C.: National Research Council.

Jones, R., ed. 1989. *Black adult development and aging.* Berkeley, Calif.: Cobb & Henry.

Jordan, W. 1968. *White over black: American attitudes toward the Negro, 1550–1812.* Chapel Hill: Univ. of North Carolina Press.

Kohn, M. 1969. *Class and conformity: A study in values.* Homewood, Ill.: Dorsey.

Landry, B. 1987. *The new black middle class.* Berkeley: Univ. of California Press.

Lieberson, S. 1980. *A piece of the pie: Blacks and white immigrants since 1880.* Berkeley: Univ. of California Press.

Moore, W. 1969. *The vertical ghetto: Everyday life in an urban project.* New York: Random House.

Okoye, F. 1971. *The American image of Africa: Myth and reality.* Buffalo, N.Y.: Black Academy.

Posner, R. 1992. *Sex and reason.* Cambridge: Harvard Univ. Press.

Rainwater, L. 1960. *And the poor get children.* Chicago: Quadrangle.

Stanton, W. 1960. *The leopard's spots: Scientific attitudes toward race in America, 1815–1859.* Chicago: Univ. of Chicago Press.

Staples, R. 1978. The myth of black sexual superiority: A reexamination. *The Black Scholar* 9:16–22.

Stember, C. 1976. *Sexual racism: The emotion barrier to an integrated society.* New York: Elsevier.

U.S. Bureau of the Census. 1983. Labor force by age, race and sex: 1940 to 1980. *1980 census of population and housing: General social and economic characteristics.* Washington, D.C.: Government Printing Office.

Weinberg, M., and C. Williams. 1988. Black sexuality: A test of two theories. *Journal of Sex Research* 25:197–218.

Weinstein, M., R. Goodjoin, E. Crayton, and C. Lawson. 1990. Black sexuality: A bibliography. *Sage Race Relations Abstracts* 15:3–4.

Willhelm, S. 1971. *Who needs the Negro?* Garden City, N.J.: Anchor.

Wilson, W. J. 1978. *The declining significance of race: Blacks and changing American institutions.* Chicago: Univ. of Chicago Press.

Woodward, C. V. 1966. *The strange career of Jim Crow.* New York: Oxford Univ. Press.

SIX

Single Worlds and Homosexual Lifestyles: Patterns of Sexuality and Intimacy

Martha R. Fowlkes

This chapter offers an extensive interpretive review of the major social science literature pertaining to the affective and companionate features, as well as to the patterns of sexual behavior, that characterize the
lives of voluntarily single adults and lesbian women and gay men. Particular attention will be paid to the differences between men and women
in the meaning and enactment of both intimacy and sexuality and the
mesh or separation of the two (as the case may be). Whenever a deep
emotional attachment develops between two persons, there exists also
the potential for its sensual and sexual expression, and the reverse holds
true as well—that is, wherever intimacy is an organizing theme, within
either a same-sex or cross-sex relationship, it is not unreasonable to
search for a physical component. Similarly sexual relationships give rise
to the possibility of emotional meaning and commitment. The absence
of sex, of course, does not imply the absence of love, just as the presence
of sex does not in itself imply the presence of love.

The discussion that follows is of populations who, by living some or
all their adult lives outside the framework of marriage, draw our attention to some of the possibilities for variability and change in sexual relationships and close partnerships in adult life. At the same time the diversity of sexuality and intimacy under discussion here is not socially
unbounded. The imprints are clear of prevailing structures of family
and work roles and of cultural norms of masculinity and femininity.

THE MARITAL IDEAL OF INTIMACY AND SEXUALITY

It is the American way to treat adult intimacy as synonymous with
marriage, and marriage, in turn, as synonymous with sexuality. Despite,
or perhaps because of, the extent to which ours is a highly sexualized
society (D'Emilio and Freedman 1988; and Ehrenreich, Hess, and Jacobs
1986) and also a society that provides both opportunities and needs for
intimacy that may not be encompassed by marriage and family (Fowlkes
1990), as a public we nonetheless continue to impose marriage as the

standard by which all sexual and intimate relationships are evaluated. Even as social scientists who are aware of the often-vast discrepancies between what people say and what they actually do, particularly in the realm of sexual behavior, we more often than not posit the institution of marriage and the family as both the singularly real and ideal repository of intimacy and sexuality. Moreover, so strongly has the quest for a particularly feminized version of intimacy (cf. Cancian 1986) taken hold in present-day American society that virtually all our personal, popular, and professional thinking is shaped by the largely taken-for-granted conviction that the intensely emotionally examined, expressed, and heterosexually married life is the sine qua non of adulthood.

To be sure, the study of marriage and family now quite routinely includes consideration of premarital and extramarital relationships, as well as of alternative lifestyles, the accepted euphemism both for homosexual and unmarried heterosexual relationships. But, by definition premarital, cohabiting, and extramarital relationships are viewed as important only in reference to marriage, as pathways either toward or away from marriage respectively. The notion of alternative lifestyles prompts the question, Alternative to what? "Because any alternative must be alternative *to* something, this formulation presumes a central paradigm of family shared by most people in a society" (Weston 1991, 6).

Certain styles of interpersonal relationships and committed partnerships, both sexual and nonsexual, are more appropriately construed quite simply as *nonmarital.* That is, they exist independently of marriage and are not best or fully understood in terms of family or kin ties but deserve recognition and legitimation in their own right. What follows is intended as an introduction to the study of nonmarital intimacy and sexuality in the dual context of gender and the life course. The categories of relationships I have selected for discussion—the socioemotional and sexual engagements of the voluntarily unmarried and gay and lesbian relationships—are not exhaustive or definitive of the topic. Nor, as is obvious, are these categories themselves mutually exclusive. One may overlap with or contain the other, depending on the perspective employed. Yet there are distinctions between the categories that warrant their separate investigation and, when summarized together, permit a solid introduction to what we know of the similarities and differences between men and women whose social, emotional and sexual lives are centered or come to be centered in nonmarital worlds.

SINGLE LIVES

There are many different ways of being single and, consequently, many different ways to depict the experience of singlehood. In the broadest sense, the term *single* refers to all unmarried adults—a total, in 1979, of approximately fifty-five million Americans over the age of eighteen. This population represents wide-ranging demographic diversity with respect to age, race, ethnicity, education, occupation, income, religion, and parental status. It is similarly heterogeneous in its connection to the institution of formal, legal marriage, including as it does those who have never married, together with the divorced, the separated, and the widowed. Peter Stein (1981, 10) offers a typology of singlehood based on whether an individual's single status is voluntary or involuntary, stable or temporary. Of particular interest here are those described by Stein as voluntary stable singles—"those who have never married and are satisfied with that choice; those who have been married but do not want to remarry; cohabitors who do not intend to marry; and those whose lifestyles preclude the possibility of marriage (e.g., priests and nuns)" (Stein 1981, 10). These are nonmarital singles, persons for whom marriage either never has been or is no longer a salient or sought-after status.

Census data reveal only what an individual's life situation is, not why it is what it is. For that reason it is impossible to assess precisely what proportion of the total population of single adults would be properly categorized as nonmarital or voluntary stable singles. Not only are the choices that shape relationship status obscured by descriptive survey categories, but those choices are susceptible to change at different points in the life span in response to circumstance and experience. Drawing on 1979 census data, Stein (1981) summarizes the life cycle of single adults. By the time people reached their mid-thirties (in 1979) only 15 percent of men and 10 percent of women had never married. Among those in the age range of thirty-five to forty-four, 8.3 percent of men and 5.9 percent of women had never married in 1979. The numbers of never-married decline to 6.9 percent for men and 4.4 percent for women by the time they reach the age group of forty-five to fifty-four (Stein 1981, 12–15).

At the same point in the life course that the numbers of never-marrieds begins to shrink, the ranks of singles swell as a result of divorce. Fully 41 percent of all people now of marriageable age are expected to experience a divorce, and the greatest increase in the rate of divorce occurs among couples who are between twenty-five and thirty-nine years old (Blumstein and Schwartz 1983, 34). Previously married women, especially divorced women, are less likely than men to remarry and, apparently, less likely to *want* to remarry than men (Bernard 1972; Glick and Lin 1986, 1987; Riessman 1990). The marital choices of women following divorce, though, are indisputably entangled with de-mographic realities. Philip Blumstein and Pepper Schwartz (1983) note that, as people enter their forties, there are 233 unattached women for every one hundred men, and in 1980, fully 94 percent of all men aged fifty or older were married (Blumstein and Schwartz 1983, 32). Among persons sixty-five and older, men are a minority and unmarried men are a minority within that minority, although in the specifically never-married population men outnumber women until the age of sixty-five. In the *total* elderly singles population, comprising the widowed and di-vorced together with the never-married, unmarried women begin to outnumber men by the age of thirty-five. The proportion increases steadily through the life course, and by age sixty-five the 1979 census reported that the singles population was made up of 56 percent more women than men (Stein 1981, 359). Although more women than men marry, women are more likely than men to be alone for some or all of their lives from their middle years on.

Because some 95 percent of all adults eventually marry, a discussion of nonmarital singles encompasses many more persons, particularly women, with a personal history of marriage than not. In this connection we need to bear in mind that some unknown number of never-married men and women may be presumed to be lifelong homosexuals whose lives, therefore, are not informative of the lifestyles of heterosexuals who choose either not to marry or, more often, not to remarry. This is not to say that all homosexuals experience their sexual preference as fixed and invariant from a very young age—homosexuality is not convinc-ingly linked to a common or innate cause, nor does the organization of homosexual object choice follow a singular developmental course—but that those who do will certainly account for some fixed number of the never-marrieds. Homosexual persons and their relationships are the subject of separate examination in this chapter.

The available knowledge base about the lives and life course of men and women who choose either not to marry at all or, once having been married, not to remarry, is strikingly sparse. The relative lack of atten-tion to this group is an indication of the lack of serious regard extended to this group compared to the married, the widowed, and the remarried, whose blended family relationships have received considerable attention in recent marriage and family literature. These latter groups are all typically understood with reference to their ties or, in the case of the widowed, to the involuntary loss of ties, to the institution of marriage. The voluntarily unmarried, whether previously married or not, stand entirely outside that framework and, on that account, have been rendered both invisible and irrelevant. Yet the little information that does exist is revealing of some important differences between men and women and the needs that are met (or not met) in the choice to remain single.

Single Men

Never-married men outnumber never-married women, and some bachelors, such as former New York City mayor Ed Koch and 1992's presidential hopeful Jerry Brown are prominently in the public eye. But compared to never-married women, who have attracted some sociological attention, never-married men have attracted almost none—possibly because bachelorhood, with its connotations of independence and freewheeling sexuality, is consonant with the normatively acceptable male role. For that reason it is not seen as a problem to be explained compared to the spinster who is viewed as an incomplete and pitiable person. Still it is astonishing that Robert Rubinstein's profile (1986) of a mere eleven never-married men within his total sample of forty-seven "old men living alone" seems to constitute the *only* systematic study, if indeed that term is even applicable to such a tiny data base, of voluntarily unmarried men. Rubinstein (1986) does not find these men to be "lifelong isolates" (cf. Gubrium 1975) so much as poorly individualized. Throughout their young and middle-adult years their primary emotional ties, and usually their residential base, were with members of their family of origin, either parents or siblings. Their lives, then, have not been devoid of meaningful close relationships, but these relationships have reinforced dependent childhood roles rather than individuated adult roles. After the death of key family members, which, for most, was a major bereavement experience, they continued on alone. Of the eleven men interviewed by Rubinstein, the majority are described either as "the socialized isolates"—those with a strong preference not to be attached to others—or "the outsiders"—those whose relationships with people are more instrumental than affective. Aside from the two "sophisticates"—worldly, sociable, and involved with girlfriends—Rubinstein concludes that this older generation of never-married men "shows a good deal of unhappiness, stress, conflict and ambiguity" (Rubinstein 1986, 142).

Stein's (1976) study casts singles generally in a more favorable light, but he is not attentive to gender differences in any detail. He suggests that male singles (both never married and previously married) reject the limited number of roles available to them in marriage in favor of the more varied experiences open to them as singles. The men quoted by Stein are openly uncomfortable with the responsibilities expected of them in marriage, and their words lend support to Ehrenreich's (1983) argument that many American men are in a "flight from commitment." The singles' bar scene is largely male. The sex ratio tends to be about two-thirds men and one-third women (Allon and Fishel 1981). Men most often come to these bars by themselves to relieve boredom and isolation, in search of momentary sociability and companionship. They are looking to meet women to date for the short-term rather than as possible marriage partners. Following divorce both men and women typically use brief relationships for sexual outlets, but women tire of these relationships sooner because they are clear in their own minds about the loneliness they experience in continuing isolated sexual encounters without intimacy. "Men, on the other hand, are often confused and frightened by their reaction. They do not understand the rising needs for tenderness and intimacy that come with their middle years, and they tend to classify these feelings as weak and unmanly" (Cleveland 1981, 124).

It is difficult to know whether and to what extent single men use friendship as a source of support in their lives because friendship has not been studied specifically in the context of single manhood. According to Stein (1976) opposite-sex friendships do not occur easily or frequently for single men or women at any age. It may also be telling that Stein quotes mostly from women respondents about the general importance of friendship in their lives. Based on Stein's few examples, single men, like all men, are oriented toward doing—shared activities and mutual help-giving or assistance—rather than expressiveness in their male friendships. The literature on friendship now spans some twenty years and has been remarkably consistent in the finding that women are the experts in intimacy and self-disclosure and, far more than men, develop deep, trusting, confiding friendships (See, e.g., Cozby 1973; Hess 1972; Jourard 1971; Pleck 1974; and Rubin 1983). This pattern, in turn, has been consistently associated with early socialization experiences that are linked to the preservation of male power and dominance in the public world (Maccoby and Jacklin 1974; Sattel 1976). Most commonly men rely on women and on marriage to provide them with socioemotional security, and, when divorce occurs, it "creates expressive hardships for men that it does not create for women" (Riessman 1990, 209). After divorce men are at greater risk of emotional disorder. They also remarry more quickly and more frequently than women, lending credence to Pleck's observation of "[men's] dependence on women's power to express men's emotions and to validate men's masculinity" (Pleck 1974, 22).

All of what we know about the lifestyles and values of single men add up to strong—albeit inferential—evidence that the man who remains voluntarily unmarried also remains voluntarily at some remove from companionate relationships of any duration or depth. Heterosexual men do not appear to fashion "threads of connectedness" outside of marriage to others or to another in the manner described by Lofland (1982). On the other hand, marriage is more than an emotional arrangement; it is a set of roles. And for some subset of men, the costs of the marital breadwinner role may outweigh the much advertised benefits of settled commitment. Jessie Bernard (1981) reminds us that there have always been defectors from the good-provider role. In today's urbanized, occupationally standardized and domestically driven society, scarcely a niche remains in which a man may live as the lone ranger, the prospector, the sailor, or the hobo of yesteryear in a society based on a principle of same-sex companionship.

Of course, it is possible that cohabitation, as distinct from marriage, exists as a viable setting for lasting intimacy among the voluntarily unmarried, both male and female. Unfortunately, though, there is scant literature on cohabitation other than to note its dramatic increase in the past two decades (Clayton and Voss 1977; Glick and Spanier 1980; and Macklin 1972). Also according to Glick and Spanier, this increase is accounted for primarily by young couples without children. Altogether, couples living together without children present constituted 72 percent of the total cohabiting couples population in 1981. Of men who are cohabitors, about one-half have been previously married; for women the number is somewhat higher, about 60 percent.

But this knowledge of the marital and parental status of cohabiting couples provides virtually no insight into the properties of the cohabiting partnership itself. That is, we have no basis for distinguishing and thereby comparing the nature of the relationship in those couples for whom cohabitation is a temporary premarital experience, a trial marriage, or a stable nonmarital alternative. The Clayton and Voss (1977) study found that the majority of men who were cohabiting had been married at least once, but the majority of men also did not plan to, and in fact did not, marry their present partner.

The most in-depth look at cohabitation is supplied by Philip Blumstein and Pepper Schwartz's (1983) study of American couples. "Other research on cohabitation has in general confirmed our own findings: At present, cohabitation for most couples is not a lifetime commitment or one that is uniquely set apart from marriage" (Blumstein and Schwartz 1983, 37). Cohabitation is an ambiguous arrangement, often lacking in predictability and clear understanding between partners as to their hopes, expectations, and role definitions for the relationship. Cohabitation, furthermore, does not build on trust or mutual cooperation that is the basis for future planning, and the disproportionate emphasis on the present in the relationship does not ground it for long-term growth. Those couples who do forge a meaningful and functional interdependence between them tend to marry. Most do not accomplish this, and they break up.

A careful reading of the Blumstein and Schwartz (1983) study strongly suggests that the values and traits described earlier as characteristic of nonmarital men are the very ones that predominate in the relationships of cohabiting couples and are the main source of the tensions that lead to their impermanence. By all accounts, cohabiting men are not more relationship focused and less work focused than married men. They have happily cast off the responsibility for the provider role but not their ambition to achieve. Their excessive commitment to work, however, is rooted far more in self-interest than in a more selfless sense of responsibility for the material support of a relationship unit. Nor have cohabiting men reorganized their expectations of male privilege with respect to their attitudes toward participation in housework and the priority of their sexual needs and desires in shaping the sex life of the couple. "The assumption that they should be indulged shapes the lives of heterosexual men, both married and cohabitors" (Blumstein and Schwartz 1983, 326). This assumption works against the development of equitable intimacy and taps one of the reasons why unmarried women, historically and in the present, choose not to marry.

Single Women

Unmarried women apparently remain outside of marriage in different ways and for different reasons than men do; permanently single men give every indication of living out socially and emotionally underdeveloped lives compared to their married counterparts, according to both Margaret Adams (1976) and Stein (1981). Women who remain single identify the advantages of preserving and fully developing their personal and social autonomy by not accommodating to the secondary status of the traditional wife role. Indeed, Lawson (1988) observes that many married women discover that extramarital affairs afford them degrees of freedom, pleasure, and independence unknown and unavailable to them in marriage. Barbara Simon's study, *Never Married Women,* reveals that of her fifty elderly respondents, thirty-eight, or 76 percent, actively chose singlehood. Although citing individually variable reasons for their choice, "the theme of freedom, freedom from the demands embedded in the institution of a wife's role, emerged over and over again in the interviews as a major reason to remain single" (Simon 1987, 42). The freedom valued by these women, though, is not comparable to the relatively antisocial freedom sought by unmarried men. Simon found that, contrary to popular stereotypes, these women lived in larger worlds than women whose lives are marriage and family based. Typically, the women had been actively engaged in volunteer service, and during their employed years they were deeply committed to the value of work for its personal and social rewards.

Historically the women interviewed by Simon came of age between the First World War and the Great Depression, and they speak of "feeling a pressure within themselves to choose between meaningful work and marriage and an external pressure of an informal kind from suitors and bosses to view marriage and paid work as mutually exclusive" (Simon 1987, 43). Largely as a consequence of the modern women's movement, educational and employment opportunities for women have expanded mightily in the very decades since these now-elderly women have retired. At the same time an ideology of equality between men and women in work and family spheres has taken hold, especially among the middle classes. Today's young career women do not face the same obviously stark choice between marriage and work as the one that faced women two generations their senior. Yet there is strong evidence that the choice remains, disguised in more subtle form, particularly among women at the top, or heading for the top, of the occupational hierarchy. Kanter (1977) has persuasively documented the conflicting definitions and demands of womanhood to which high-level-career aspirants are subjected in the corporate world. Among lay college presidents 93 percent of the men, but only 49 percent of the women, are married (Green

1988, 8), data suggestive of an enduring incompatibility between marriage and top career success for women. Although potential conflict persists between professional commitment and family life, it is not well spelled out for women in any way that would permit them to see and evaluate it ahead of time.

Although most women seek and expect to find work as well as marriage in their futures, the percentage of American women remaining single is steadily increasing. Fully 22 percent of college-educated women born in the mid-1950s (now in their mid- to late thirties) will never marry, compared to just 9 percent of college-educated women born two decades earlier (Greer 1986, 48). Unlike their predecessors, this is not a choice that contemporary women self-consciously make at the point of entry into the world of work. Rather it appears to be a choice that emerges from a combination of attitudinal and structural factors they encounter in the course of pursuing their career goals. Christine Doudna and Fern McBride describe the phenomenon of the "opposite marriage gradient: Educated professional men marry earlier and stay married longer than other men, while their female peers marry later and have a higher probability of divorce than other women. . . . The female elite have become demographic losers; they've priced themselves out of the market" (Doudna and McBride 1981, 22). Andrew Hacker observes "that as women enter positions once held by men they become either less attracted to marriage or less attractive as marriage partners. Nor is it clear that even open-minded husbands want wives with attainments approaching their own" (Stein 1981, 23). Within marriage, Rossi (1992) cites recent evidence of the higher risk of divorce in couples where a wife earns as much or more than her husband. The world, in other words, has changed for women and women have changed in it, but men have not. Under these conditions it is not surprising that women may come to prefer the increased professional, financial, sexual, and personal freedoms available to them as single women to the more limited and subordinate marital options.

A sizable number of today's educated women will move from a self-identification of voluntarily but temporarily single to a definition of themselves as stable singles. In marriage women are reported to be more dissatisfied than men (Bernard 1972; Kelly 1982) and are far more likely to be the initiators of divorce than men (Wallerstein and Blakeslee 1989). Women who stay single now or who become single through divorce and remain single into the future frequently come to that choice reactively rather than proactively and by default rather than determination. As a result, they are probably more likely than the unmarried women who came before them to experience feelings of disappointment and failure. Because marriage is now less clearly recognized as an impediment to the development of women's aspirations and sense of individual worth, the contemporary single woman, it may be argued, is actually more susceptible to social devaluation than in the past (Adams 1976).

In this regard the older women of Simon's study (1987) are exemplary because they chose singlehood precisely for its assets and are affirmative of its sources of personal intimacy and fulfillment. Most of Simon's subjects dated men and were serious candidates for marriage during their young adulthood. By the time they reached thirty, they had decided that life was more satisfying and less compromising of selfhood outside the wife role than within it. Having decided not to marry, they found validation and companionship among other unmarried female friends. The importance of long-standing intimate friendships that enhanced a sense of personal wholeness was a recurrent theme in the life-history narratives of the women Simon interviewed. A dyadic bond with another single woman was the most common and meaningful form of friendship to these women, and many of them lived together in the mode of the so-called Boston marriage that had been a rather commonplace and socially acceptable arrangement between educated women in the late nineteenth century (Faderman 1981). Early in her study Simon was forced by her respondents' antagonism to the subject to bypass questions about sexuality in these female friendships, but the intensity of their attachments is undeniable, even between women who did not cohabit. Numerous women, although not the majority, admitted that friendships had been far more sustaining to them than kinship.

Unmarried, childless women studied by Allen (1989), who focused their lives on family caregiving reported feeling devalued by their single status. In contrast the women interviewed by Simon remained close to family members but did not live with them through adulthood. In general they received encouragement from relatives to live separately and to form independent identities and turned most to family members in their old age, following retirement, when friends had begun to die and the needs for mutual assistance and economizing had escalated. In addition to their ongoing close relationships in friendship dyads and their extended families, the majority of these women were well integrated into friendship groups drawn largely from colleagueships in occupationally segregated female work settings and their volunteer associates.

Based on interviews with thirty-one never-married, older childless women, Rubinstein (1991) summarizes three major categories of primary relationship engagement: blood ties of the coresident daughter or aunt roles and collateral family ties; constructed kinlike ties of affiliation with nonkin families, quasi-parental relations with younger nonrelatives and same-sex companionate relationships; and close personal friendships. Taken together, these data sturdily support Simon's conclusion that the single women in her study fashioned lives of relational depth and breadth.

In the late twentieth century, however, it is doubtful whether the majority of women who are more or less voluntarily single, either as never-married or unremarried women, will so readily build on the rewards of female friendship as a fulfilling dimension of singlehood, or even as an alternative to marriage, in the ways that now elderly women once did. Since the 1980s feminists and career-committed women have become widely stigmatized as antifamily and antimale to such a degree that less than a third of all American women are willing to identify themselves as feminists despite their support for equal opportunity (Faludi 1991, ix–xxiii). Analyzing the backlash against women, Susan Faludi (1991) argues that the women's movement is now commonly portrayed as having weakened the traditional family structure and damaged the lives of children by its emphasis on women's equality and personal and sexual freedom. In their quest for women's liberation, women themselves have been cast as the losers both by the popular culture of film, press, and television and by what Faludi calls the "backlash braintrust," including Betty Friedan, whose book *The Feminine Mystique* (1963) was a major force in launching the contemporary women's movement. More recently Friedan has helped to construct the image of the unmarried career-directed woman as a pathetic, lonely, and sexless outcast (Friedan 1981).

It has been estimated that fully three-quarters of single women subscribe to feminist principles (Simenauer and Carroll 1982), but successful, as contrasted with suspect, feminism now bears the imprint of male dominance and exerts on women a renewed pull toward "compulsory heterosexuality" (Rich 1980). The unmarried woman who does not demonstrate her heterosexuality through marriage is under great pressure, nonetheless, to demonstrate that she is heterosexually as well as professionally active and accomplished. Ironically, the sexual revolution, which "discovered" the extent of women's sexual appetites and recast sexual norms to permit the casual indulgence of them, also carries with it the expectation that women should be freely sexually available to men as an assertion of female power (Ehrenreich, Hess, and Jacobs 1986). Laurel Richardson (1985) locates the dual ambitions of contemporary single women in their conviction that career efficacy and success will naturally carry over into a similar self-determination in their relationships with men.

In writing of the phenomenon of the "new other woman"—that is, the single woman engaged in an affair with a married man—Richardson interprets this as a distinctly modern product of structured tensions and contradictions in women's lives rather than as an expression of characterological deviance. "In a world where there are not enough men, but where a persistent cultural imperative demands that women be heterosexually coupled to feel good about themselves, and in a world where women are restricted by the demands of social convention and pulled by new opportunities, being with a married man seems to be a genuine solution" (Richardson 1985, 12). Moreover the life course of women is marked by more and different kinds of role transitions and shifts in identity than ever before, and these increase the likelihood of meeting, working with, and becoming sexually involved with married men. Although the women Richardson studied did not set out to have liaisons with married men, once these became established, many women initially viewed them as offering the best of all possible worlds—intimate communication and sexual and romantic pleasure wrapped in a cocoon of secrecy that seems also to preserve the freedom and autonomy of each partner. In the end, though, these relationships end, and their breakdown is revealing of how profoundly these alliances disadvantage women and how very much at odds they are with the fundamental tenets of feminism. The arrangement of the single woman involved with a married man provides the unmarried woman with only illusory freedom from male control. In reality it leaves men with control over two worlds and two women; it divides women against one another and reinforces male privilege and the sexual exploitation of women. Ironically the adulterous married woman may fare better insofar as the extramarital liaison—regardless of its fate—reveals to her the imbalance of power to which she is subjected in marriage and opens up possibilities for reordering her life to gain more control and space for herself (Lawson 1988).

Although professional women find their same-sex friendships to be more intimate, enjoyable, and nurturing than those with men (Sapadin 1988), the neotraditionalism that has inserted itself into feminism will

assuredly discourage women from assigning full value to their friendships with other women. The politics of professionalism remain the politics of male power and, by extension, of heterosexuality, which posits
an inextricable linkage between only that sexuality and intimacy. And
insofar as feminism has come to bear the taint of lesbianism, so female
homosociality has come to bear the taint of homosexuality.

HOMOSEXUAL RELATIONSHIPS

Oddly, Faludi (1991) makes no mention of the contribution of homophobia to the backlash against feminism. Compared to the feminist
movement of a hundred years earlier, the feminism of the 1970s produced a comprehensive social analysis of the interrelationship of the
personal and the political, of the inequality "built in" to heterosexual
relationships, and of the part played by women in their traditional unemployed roles as wives and mothers to the preservation of male dominance in both the private and public spheres (cf. Fowlkes 1980). In the
view of radical feminists, especially, relationships with men were seen
as the bedrock of the subordination of women. Woman-to-woman relationships were extolled as a superior, even utopian, alternative to conventional heterosexual relationships. Although many mainstream feminists were wary of having their cause contaminated by a lesbian
presence, a 1971 resolution of the National Organization for Women
"acknowledged the inherent feminism of lesbianism and the anti-
feminism of lesbian persecution" (Faderman 1991, 212).

Lesbian feminism and the gay rights movement that gathered momentum after the Stonewall rebellion of 1969 converged, with the result that for the first time in Western history homosexuals have designated themselves and achieved recognition as a distinct social group
(D'Emilio and Freedman 1990). This has worked both to their advantage and disadvantage. On the one hand homosexual persons, both gay
men and lesbians, may find and claim membership in a visible, well-
defined community with a highly elaborated culture of its own. No
longer closeted or hidden from view, those inside the community find
validation and support for their minority sexual preference to a degree
that has never before existed. On the other hand, the straight world is
now sharply demarcated from that of gays and lesbians, and the recognition that heterosexuals have perforce extended to homosexuals is not
to be confused with acceptance. Data from the *General Social Surveys,
1972–1987* (Davis and Smith 1987) show that the gay liberation movement has had no success in reducing generalized prejudice toward ho-

mosexuals. In 1987, as in 1973, nearly three-quarters of all Americans believed that homosexual behavior is always wrong. (Davis and Smith 1987). In 1987–91, the percent rose to 76.7 percent, a small upward shift in disapproval (see Smith, chap. 3, this vol.). In an apparent paradox, support for the civil liberties of homosexuals has also increased along with intolerance. Tom Smith interprets these opposing trends as reflecting public support for the regulation of homosexuality as *sexual* behavior without restricting the nonsexual rights of homosexuals.

The uneasy public awareness of the widespread existence of a homosexual way of life, combined with a raised consciousness and accompanying eagerness among gays themselves to secure a legitimate homosexual identity, have resulted in the production of a voluminous literature by and about homosexuals in an effort to explain this newly visible phenomenon. Preoccupation with etiology and ideology prevail. The debate rages between essentialists and social constructionists, between those who are concerned to identify biological or core determinants of sexual attraction and behaviors and those who emphasize the power of social naming and context to influence sexuality. (For an overview of this debate see McWhirter, Sanders, and Reinisch [1990]; Weeks [1986]). Each of these paradigms, in turn, is associated with a politics— the former with possibilities for intervention with and control of pathological or dysfunctional biological predispositions or, alternatively, with the defense of minority status as a unique and inescapable condition; the latter with the normalization of homosexual behaviors together with the subversion of sexual orthodoxy and the idealization of homosexual lifestyles.

From a sociological perspective, excessive concern with causation imposes an undue and unproductive emphasis on categorical and dichotomous distinctions and in so doing obscures the great variety in the types of homosexual experience that occur among men and among women, the types of persons who have homosexual experience, the possibilities for individuals to change their gender preferences in erotic and intimate relationships across the life course, and the salience of individuals' own perceptions of themselves and their social worlds—their identity formation—to the development of sexual and emotional preference (Cass 1990, 242). All etiological research, whether biomedical or social constructionist in focus, runs the risk of reductionism and of misguided attention to genital sexual activity alone, to the exclusion of considerations of affection and affiliation (Hansen and Evans 1985, 2).

Accordingly, the discussion that follows is meant to dispel the narrow definition of sexuality, by moving away from the usual emphasis on heterosexual coitus not only to encompass a diversity of sexual orientations but also to consider the intimate dimensions of various sexual orientations. The focus here is not on homosexual behaviors per se but on the emergence of sexual preference and the characteristics of nonmarital lesbian and gay relationships, of which sexual activity is but one feature. It is inappropriate and constricting to allow the homosexual's object choice alone to assume an overwhelming significance, something we do not do when our interest is focused on the heterosexual (Gagnon and Simon 1973, 137).

SEXUAL AND PARTNER PREFERENCE OVER THE LIFE COURSE

Neither patterns of sexual behavior nor activities that supply sexual comfort and pleasure necessarily remain habitual and unchanged over a lifetime. Just as it is possible for an individual heterosexual to engage in a wide array of sexual experiences and to undergo numerous changes in the form and content of sexuality over the life course, so it is perfectly possible for an exclusively heterosexual pattern of behavior to be exchanged for an exclusively homosexual one (Kinsey, Pomeroy, and Martin 1948; Kinsey et al. 1953). Indeed bisexuality, or the capacity for both heterosexual and homosexual engagement and attachment, beginning with Freud and into the present, has been widely regarded as the natural condition of humanity (Money and Tucker 1975; Paul et al. 1982; Stoller 1972). On the basis of what we know of how people form and change their sexual preference, there is strong reason to believe that desire emerges from circumstances and available interpretations of such circumstances. If one is open to the possibility that partners may be of either sex, a relationship contains an added fluidity with the option to include physical contact when affection is the starting point or to build from physical contact to affection (DeCecco and Shiveley 1984, 19). Of course social structures and values also influence the very processes and pathways through which preferences emerge.

Surely the malleability of sexuality and the fluidity of sexual choice account as much, if not more, than social prejudice for the difficulties in identifying and counting a definitive homosexual population. Although we continue to rely on the Kinsey estimates, there is no reason to believe that those estimates are valid today because of enormous changes in gay self-identification following from the gay rights movement that began in the 1970s and continues in the present. Same-gender erotic desire is now well established in the public consciousness. Opportunities for anticipatory socialization and same-sex erotic experimentation are widespread, and being gay or lesbian presents itself as a reasonable possibility, offering a positive alternative to heterosexuality. The audience for homosexuality is wider now than ever before (Gagnon 1990, 197).

Unfortunately there are no studies that systematically inquire into the factors that shape sexual preference change in adult life, although there is ample indication that such change—especially in the direction from heterosexual to homosexual—is sufficiently frequent (and likely to become more so) to warrant such research. As early as 1978 Alan Bell and Martin Weinberg documented that 20 percent of their white male homosexual sample and a somewhat lower percentage of black males had been previously married. One-third of the white homosexual females and almost half of black homosexual women had been married at least once. In the same study they estimated that 20 percent of gay men had fathered a child or children and that the number of lesbians who had given birth to children in a heterosexual relationship was 40 percent.

There is general agreement that social forces very probably affect men and women differently when it comes to sexual-preference change in adulthood. For women born before 1950, the feminist movement was undoubtedly an important influence (Faderman 1991). Though the voice of radical feminism is now somewhat subdued, it has bequeathed to women a legacy of options not previously available or recognizable as such. Beyond the political movement that fostered a high status for women's sexual and emotional associations with other women, there are some enduring continuities in the socialization of women that have paved a distinctively female pathway that women tend to travel in changing from a heterosexual to a homosexual relationship preference.

Compared to boys, young girls do not engage in an upsurge of experimental, impersonal, and autoerotic sexual activity during adolescence. More than girls, boys arrive at a non-relationship-based experience of sexual feelings and encounters. Females live primarily in homosocial worlds in which adult women reinforce the girl's future status as wife and mother. Women tend not to seek sex for its own sake, and, far more than men, they establish their sexuality through a relationship. The young black women studied by Claire Sterk-Elifson (chap. 4, this vol.) exhibit a variation on this theme. So keenly do they value partnership that they will frequently use sex as a means to obtain and hold onto a relationship, allowing black men in turn to be sexual adventurers who are able to find and have sex with readily available girls and women. The result is a high level of sexual activity among black teens, but the motivation for this is quite different for boys than it is for girls (see Bowser, chap. 5, this vol.).

A recent survey of teen attitudes toward sex, published in *Seventeen*, finds that four out of five girls indicate a preference for dating one person exclusively. More than 80 percent of the girls who had intercourse stress the importance of love as a precondition for sex (Pesman 1991, 64). Sharon Thompson (chap. 8, this vol.) suggests that for a small but growing number of teenage girls the conventional script of staking everything on love (and losing) is being rewritten as a strategic romantic comedy. In this sexual script girls remain active and able to add sexual expression to an already affectionate friendship rather than passively anxious and consumed by the fusion of love and sex. But, in Thompson's words, these are both "majoritarian" stories because they are stories of heterosexual preoccupation, which, for most girls, is the initial preoccupation. It is not surprising, then, that a considerably higher proportion of homosexual women than men have been previously married or that their behaviors and fantasies prior to marriage were almost exclusively heterosexual (Coleman 1985). It is a rare lesbian of any age who does not have a substantial history of heterosexual involvement. For women emotional attraction, notwithstanding some decline in the emphasis on romantic melodrama, is the catalyst for physical attraction.

Just as emotional attraction serves as the organizing framework for women's heterosexual feelings, it functions similarly to organize their homosexual feelings. Whether married or unmarried, women have a long history of acculturation into a sphere of intense attachments to other women (Faderman 1981; and Smith-Rosenberg 1975). Many women, married and unmarried, have found in their same-sex friendships a fuller, more respectful, and more egalitarian companionship than in marriage (Nichols 1990). Women are frequently able to maintain commitments to marriage alongside their passionate investments in their friendships with women, and of course marriage and children exert a greater pull on women's lives than on men's. Women have greater freedom than men (possibly because women are more devalued than men and their sexual labels less loaded) to form close same-sex emotional ties without stigma. Women do not necessarily see affectionate behaviors directed toward women as having implications for their sexuality.

John Gagnon and William Simon (1973) refer to the "romantic drift" into sexual behavior, meaning that even when women's sexual feelings are aroused by emotional intimacy, there is often a long period when sexual activity does not include genital contact (Blumstein and Schwartz 1977). These are probably the major reasons why changes in erotic gender preference have historically occurred later in the lives of women than of men. "The disappointments of other-gender relations . . . as well as the attractions of women's emotional and interpersonal company have always been the grounds for women to change their gender commitments" (Gagnon 1990). Victoria Vetere's study (1982) confirms that most lesbians have their first homosexual experience in the context of friendship.

Women are less likely than men to be traumatized by their first homosexual experience and find it less disruptive to personal self-concept to see themselves as homosexual in one relationship and heterosexual in another (Blumstein and Schwartz 1977). There is a noteworthy absence of scholarly discussion or study of the flexibility of gender preference in men; in part because gay men find their way to a homosexual identification through autonomous sexual activity first and secondarily through a pair bond or relationship attachment. Sexual behavior in itself, therefore, looms larger for men than for women in the consolidation of a homosexual gender preference. The greater sexual freedom and experience permitted to young boys means that for males gender instability may be particularly prevalent in adolescence rather than in later years, because their first experiences with same-sex sexual activity happen when they are younger rather than older. Ethel Spector Person has written of "the curious phenomenon by which sexuality consolidates and confirms gender in men, while it is a variable feature in women" (1980, 629). Similarly Gagnon (1990) observes that men have traditionally viewed sexual preference in terms of its fixity. Young men, especially, are so intensely sexually isolated, no doubt because they are intensely interpersonally isolated, that a single sexual experience may indeed a sexual preference make.

Then, too, the few small-scale biomedical studies that are even tentatively suggestive of the presence of genetic and related determinants of sexual preference have focused almost entirely on men and encouraged them to think of their homosexuality as predisposed. Gay men themselves, however, have a strong vested interest in adhering to an essentialist view of sexual preference because of the structures of sexism and male power in society. For women to choose a same-sex relationship is to choose to remain or to step outside of the socioemotional sphere of male dominance. "By contrast, it would represent a loss of power and an acceptance of oppression for a heterosexual man to look at his life and say 'I think I'll become gay'" (D'Emilio and Freedman 1990, 185). In our culture masculinity and male identity are achieved by fending off threats to it, and this entails both the rejection of femininity and homosexuality. The rigid classification of acceptable real male behaviors and the greater stigma and anxiety attached to sissy-boy behaviors compared to tomboy girl behaviors do much to explain Richard Green's preoccupation with the study of sissy boys and the equation of their behaviors with gender dysfunction (Green 1987). Simply put, a same-sex gender choice is imbued with a different meaning for men and women; the woman who chooses lesbianism can be seen as becoming more than, or self-actualized, and the man who chooses homosexuality is perceived as less than, or weakened by that choice.

There is a subtle and often not-so-subtle bias about male sexuality regardless of object preference to the effect that men are controlled by, rather than control, their sexuality and that the erect penis has a life of its own. Even Kinsey, who is regarded as the archetypal sexual liberationist, supported women's premarital sexual activity on the basis of the traditional sexual double standard. Kinsey saw premarital sexual activity as a useful socializing agent for women in their relationships with men and encouraged women to engage in premarital sexual activity primarily to satisfy the male need for physiological release (Miller and Fowlkes 1980, 785).

This same view of men helplessly driven by their sexuality colors the little research that has been conducted on the topic of gay men in marriages. The very titles are revealing: *Uncommon Lives: Gay Men and Straight Women* (Whitney 1991) and *Married Homosexual Men* (Ross 1983). Both of these works could have been more appropriately titled to indicate that their true subject matter is heterosexual men (or bisexual) in homosexual affairs. Instead they begin and end with the unquestioned premise that these men are really gay and have chosen nonetheless to be married. By casting these men and their relationships in this way, the authors portray them as acted on rather than acting. They are not adulterers but victims, not men who hide their extramarital liaisons from their wives, but turn to them for forbearance, sympathy, and support. The men in Ross's study (1983) are by and large too fearful of social condemnation to choose a life that is openly gay. Whitney's more recent study (1991) is of men more frankly unwilling to forsake either the gains of familied heterosexual privilege or the pleasures and freedom of nonmonogamous sex with men. The majority of these men had a history of both heterosexual and homosexual relationships prior to marriage and found that, although relationships with men offered exciting sex, it did not provide them with the friendship and emotional closeness that women offered. This is not surprising because the role of women as emotional caretakers is strongly embedded in the American culture of both masculinity and femininity. In her study of friendship and gender, Sapadin (1988) found that both men and women described their friendships with women as more nurturing than their friendships with men.

The men in Whitney's study live with the peculiar contradiction that they have purposefully chosen a marital partnership with a woman and at the same time define themselves as unable to choose *not* to have sex with men. Even when their marriages break up, they rarely view themselves as formerly heterosexual men who have actively chosen to be gay but as overpowered by a sexual orientation toward other men. In part, though, the bifurcated lives of these men have their roots in persistent binary thinking about sexuality that withholds recognition of the normalcy of bisexuality. The gay rights movement has further discredited bisexuality by labeling it as politically incorrect.

We need to bear in mind that homosexuality is a social role as well as a sexual preference. Homosexual desire is one thing; the lived homosexual preference quite another. The homosexual lifestyle, as it has come to be called, is not merely a matter of same-sex genital activity. It is a culture with identifiable norms and values about the interrelationship of sexuality and intimacy. As a culture of same-sex eroticism it appears, at first glance, to be clearly marked off and set apart from the majority heterosexual culture. In reality, though, it is a culture profoundly reactive to and conditioned by the customs and mores of present-day American heterosexuality.

Gay and Lesbian Relationships

Interest in the interpersonal relationships of homosexual men and women is a fairly recent development in research on homosexuality and very likely reflects the overall societal preoccupation with individual fulfillment, personal growth, and the search for intimacy. The body of scholarly literature on gay relationships is actually still rather slight and in most instances is founded on small-scale studies lacking in breadth of sociocultural diversity. (Major reviews of this literature are by Blumstein and Schwartz [1983], Harry [1983], Larson [1982],

McWhirter and Mattison [1984], Peplau [1982], Peplau and Amaro [1982], and Peplau and Gordon [1983].) Mary Hotvedt's succinct statement stands as the best general summary about the qualities of the so-called lifestyles of gay men and lesbian women: "To simplify, men are like men and women are like women despite differences in sexual orientation" (Hotvedt 1982, 288–89).

Contrary to popular stereotypes and historical thinking, homosexuals are not inverts of heterosexuals (Ellis [1897] 1936), and the familiar depiction of lesbians as predominantly masculine women and gay men as effeminate is not accurate. Lesbians and heterosexual women are more alike than different, as are gay and heterosexual men. Like most of their American heterosexual counterparts, large numbers of lesbians and gay men assign a high priority to forming lasting close relationships. But in the values and behaviors that link love and sex, lesbians and gay men seem to cluster at the extreme ends of the continuum of normative femininity and masculinity, respectively.

Notwithstanding the many variations of homosexual lifestyles, there are readily identifiable gender-typed commonalities among gay men and lesbians that distinguish and separate them. In the search for emotional partners gay men search first for sexual partners in a highly predatory macho community of public meeting places—bars, baths, and sexually explicit newspaper advertisements. Casual and impersonal sexual encounters are prized and have long been a hallmark of gay male life. Male pornography, strip shows, and burlesque are popular forms of erotic entertainment. In the context of the gay rights movement gay men have reacted to the feminine image of male homosexuality by creating hypermasculinized gay ghettos where much of public life is a sexual playground (Fitzgerald 1986; Kinsman 1987; White 1980). Initially the appearance of the AIDS epidemic put a damper on unbounded sexual experimentation among gay men and the unabashed glorification of pleasure for its own sake (Ehrhardt and Wasserheit 1991). Gay men do not readily endure a climate of relative sexual aridity, and there is strong anecdotal evidence of a gradual return to the "cult masculinity" (Silverstein 1990) that for a full generation now has replaced femininity as the desirable social behavior of gay men. Anke Ehrhardt (1992) is of the opinion that what currently passes for sexual constraint among gay men consists less in minimizing sexual contacts than in maximizing their safety and protection.

Long-lived partnerships between gay men are not uncommon, but neither are they typical. The percentage of gay men between the ages of thirty and fifty who are in coupled relationships is about forty percent, or less than half the percentage (85 percent) of heterosexual men who are married in the same age group. Among gay men, furthermore, "the percentages currently coupled become smaller as the additional criteria of co-habitation and length of relationship are introduced" (Harry 1984, 90). It is estimated that only about half of gay male couples actually live together (Harry 1983, 225). Sexual frequency is higher in same-sex male couples than married couples (among couples who have been together from one to ten years), and gay couples "have evolved a norm of having relationships that allow either occasional or a great deal of sex with persons other than one's partner" (Blumstein and Schwartz 1990, 317). Blumstein and Schwartz further note that, although coupled heterosexual men, either married or cohabiting, would like their relationships to include permission for recreational sex, the great majority live by the rule of monogamy. Homosexual men have altered that rule of acceptability and 79 percent of coupled gay men in the Blumstein and Schwartz study (1983) reported at least one instance of sex outside the relationship in the past year. A psychoanalytic interpretation would view this pattern as a compulsive search for affirmation of an internalized sense of deficient masculinity (Bieber et al. 1962). A more sociological interpretation would underscore the socialization of all males to value sexuality in its own right, both inside and outside of relationships and the freedom of homosexual men to act on that value.

Sexual exclusiveness or nonexclusiveness itself does not present a problem to the homosexual couple, but lack of agreement about sex outside the relationship does. The masculine approach to sexuality poses far less of a threat to the stability of gay relationships than the masculine approach to intimacy. Weston (1991) found that "some gay men considered their relationships especially susceptible to dissolution because they believed men do not learn to nurture" (Weston 1991, 142). Charles Silverstein (1990) is also persuaded that gay men have a phobia about closeness and as males have serious difficulties initiating and sustaining intimacy.

Cultural femininity is analogously manifest in the lesbian expression of attraction. The majority of lesbians attach a very high priority to permanent living-together partnerships (Bell and Weinberg 1978), and more lesbians than gay men are in committed relationships at any given time (Weston 1991, 140). Most studies have found that the proportion of lesbians in a coupled relationship is close to 75 percent (Peplau and Cochran 1990). Lesbian relationships, however, break up with greater frequency than any other kind of partnership, either heterosexual or homosexual. As a result, lesbians spend most of their adult lives in relationships in a pattern of serial monogamy. Susan Johnson (1991) does not read into this pattern any inherent instability either of individual lesbians or of lesbian relationships. On the contrary, it is probably best understood as a consequence of what might be termed an overeager search for stability. Lesbians, Johnson argues, confuse dating and commitment and are quick to live together based on an initial attraction. As women, lesbians are not well versed in initiating and managing protracted dating relationships, and they also are negatively predisposed toward casual sex and playing the field. Lacking well-defined conventions for dating, lesbians tend to move in together and try out the relationship in that context.

Certainly the stability of the old Boston marriage does not predominate, probably because lesbian relationships now take many more forms, and women begin to experiment with same-sex partnerships at a younger age and for a different set of reasons than those that drew older women together in the past. Lesbianism does not seem to flow from an overriding single-focus attraction and thus does not have the same intensely sexualized meaning to women as homosexuality does to men. Like heterosexual women, lesbians rank sharing of affection and intimate feelings and the ability to laugh together as the most important features of a relationship (Peplau et al. 1978; Peplau and Cochran 1990; Ramsey, Latham, and Lindquist 1978). Gay men stress personal and sexual independence; lesbians are often less individually differentiated, and sexuality is not a matter of isolated genital activity alone.

Much has been made of the findings from the Blumstein and Schwartz (1983) study of the low frequency of sex in lesbian couples compared to any other type of couple. More than one quarter of their lesbian respondents who had been coupled from two to ten years reported they had sex once a month or less. It is very difficult to know what this means or even whether it means anything. It is not clear that lesbians themselves are particularly disturbed by the relatively low levels of sexual activity in their relationships. Lesbians indicate high levels of sexual satisfaction and are less likely than heterosexual women to have difficulty achieving orgasm. In a study by Schaefer (1976), lesbians said that compared to sex with men, sex with women was more tender, considerate, partner related, excitingly diversified, and less aggressive. Margaret Nichols (1990) reminds us that all surveys of sexual behavior show women, overall, to be less active sexually than men. Without men to insist on and initiate sex, it is possible that lesbian women more accurately represent the level of women's sexual desires than heterosexual women do. Blumstein and Schwartz (1983) have offered this as one possible explanation for their findings. Among the long-term lesbian couples studied by Johnson (1990), age rather than duration of the relationship was more strongly correlated with sexual frequency: as lesbians age they are less likely to have sex.

Lesbian relationships are often suffused with sensuality of which sexuality is but one dimension. Displays of physical affection such as hugging, caressing, and holding are forms of endearment that lesbians prize as ends in themselves and not merely the means to the end of genital stimulation and orgasm. Lesbians also tend to be extremely close in all areas of their lives and more than other types of couples live a shared rather than separate existence. Some clinicians (Kaufman, Harrison, and Hyde 1984) have identified this pattern as one of fusing and have criticized it as inimical to individuation and productive of tensions that may result in the avoidance of intimate sexual contact (Nichols 1990, 362). This immersion in the dyad, however, can also be construed differently and more positively as a source of comfort, understanding, and mutuality that extends the expression of sensuality and lessens the need for overt sexual activity to reinforce intimacy (Johnson 1991; Weston 1991, chap. 6). The monogamous lesbian couple whose passion is composed of emotional attachment as much, if not more, than sexual attachment "represent[s] an extreme version of the kind of closeness and intimacy in which all women are trained so well. In one sense lesbians achieve what many other women idealize" (Nichols 1990, 361).

There can be no question of the continuity between the prevailing sociosexual scripts for maleness and prototypical male homosexuality and femaleness with prototypical lesbianism. But these comparisons to the conventional gender-linked attitudes and behaviors of the heterosexual world must not be overdrawn or misconstrued as an attempt to imitate or recreate that world in a same-sex married format. For, although the imprint of conventional masculinity and femininity on homosexual styles is obvious, actual relationships are organized along distinctly nonmarital lines. The relational and social worlds of homosexual men and women constitute major and intentional departures from the structures and expectations of heterosexual marriage. Homosexuals are marital nonconformists and are best understood in that framework.

Where homosexual men are concerned, Harry (1984) states that the rather high proportion of gays who are uncoupled should not provoke a judgment but is merely indicative that not everyone is suited for on-going stable relationships. There are some sizable numbers of men who do not prefer intimacy and are not comfortable with the constraints of a relationship. These are Silverstein's (1981) "excitement seekers" who find their enjoyment in the present and seek gratifications outside of relationships. John DeCecco is adamant in his opposition to the nor-malization of homosexual behavior, lest it lose its status as a critique of heterosexual monogamy. He locates the appeal of homosexuality pre-cisely in its nonmarital features: pleasurable sex with many partners, the absence of children and domestic trappings, and personal freedom with its attendant emotional, social, and physical options (DeCecco 1990, 146).

Lesbians live in a world as free as possible from male influence, and their lesbianism is frequently derived from or combined with a commit-ment to feminism and the absence of marital constraints on women's intellectual and professional development and opportunities for per-sonal independence and self-determination. Feminists of the 1970s cele-brated women alone, women unfettered by marital roles both of wife-hood *and* motherhood. In that period feminism "tried to take on the issue of motherhood seriously, to criticize the institution, explore the actual experience, theorize the social and psychological implications" (Snitow 1992, 3). In the climate of today's pronatalism, feminists, in-cluding lesbians, are no longer willing to endorse the attractions of the child-free life. Lesbian feminists now rush to embrace parenting, albeit with the conviction that as women together they can forge more flex-ible and mutual models of parenting than the motherhood role within marriage.

Blumstein and Schwartz (1983) found that married couples are most likely to have one partner who is relationship centered and one who is not. Their study also found that couples in which both partners are relationship centered are the happiest and most committed. More than any other type of couple, lesbians tend to be equally relationship cen-tered and seem to have solved the problems that continue to plague married couples concerning the balance between work and family. "The only work-centered women who can easily find partners who will dedi-cate themselves to the emotional well-being of the relationship are lesbi-ans" (Blumstein and Schwartz 1983, 187). Their point is well taken, but it stops short of the main point about the interrelationship of the per-sonal and the professional in lesbian relationships. A good part of being successfully relationship centered consists of integrating full recognition of the place of work in a partner's life. The successful career woman has achieved more visibility than tolerance in any number of occupational fields that continue to be intensely male dominated numerically and culturally. The work-centered woman, therefore, is likely to receive the most respect and appreciation for her professional commitments from other women, who for all of those reasons are also prospectively desirable emotional partners. Tending to the emotional well-being of a relationship includes full acceptance of and support for a partner's work-related activities and goals. Women do this for men, but most men, either as colleagues or as spouses, do this less well for women than other women do.

Where leisure time is concerned, marriage tends to separate partners because men and women are often drawn to different interests and activities. The companionate marriage does not easily come into existence as a reality because men and women rarely feel the same affinity for the opposite sex as they do for their own sex. Marriage, then, acts to erect barriers between friendship and romantic love that are generally not present in the nonmarital relationships of homosexuals. Both gay men and lesbians enjoy a high degree of companionship together because they tend to enjoy the same activities. Homosexual couples combine love and friendship, and they spend more time together, which deepens intimacy, and enhances relationship satisfaction (Blumstein and Schwartz 1983).

Additionally, homosexual relationships, by virtue of ideology as well as certain features inherent to same-sex couples, are more predisposed to equality than marital relationships. Although gender role-playing is sometimes present in homosexual relationships, it is less common than in married heterosexual relationships (Marecek, Finn, and Cardell 1982). Among both lesbians and gay men there is a strong emphasis on economic self-sufficiency. Consequently the traditional dependency of women on a male breadwinner disappears as does the male-provider role itself. Many contemporary lesbians and gay men actively strive to achieve an equal balance of power and shared decision making in their relationships. When questioned about their ideal for the balance of power in their current relationship, 92 percent of gay men and 97 percent of lesbians responded that it should be exactly equal (Peplau and Cochran 1990, 339). However, women, both heterosexual and homosexual, put a greater premium on equal power than men of either sexual orientation. Although the great majority (65 percent) of homosexual men say they share decision making equally, in those relationships where there are inequalities of income and age, inequality of decision making is also present (Harry 1984). In homosexual couples, the division of labor is worked out through a process of trial and error based on tastes and talents (Blumstein and Schwartz 1983). It is more difficult for heterosexual couples to negotiate a gender-free division of labor because of the power of early socialization. When traditional gender roles are present in a same-sex couple, they are a feature of the individual relationship, which neither reflects nor predicts a pattern of role allocation across couples.

In short, homosexual men behave within a framework of cultural masculinity and lesbian women within a framework of cultural femininity. But homosexual couples, male or female, do not behave like married couples and would be unlikely to do so even if their unions were formally and legally recognized.

Conclusions

This chapter is not intended to argue the social or individual superiority or inferiority of a marital as distinct from a nonmarital orientation toward intimacy and sexuality. It is, however, meant to highlight the existence of well-elaborated, distinctive nonmarital lives that are not merely residual categories unaccounted for by marriage whose participants are merely the amorphously unmarried. What stands out very clearly in this overview of the socioemotional and sexual worlds of the never-married, the voluntarily unremarried, and gay men and lesbians is that there are certain persons or groups of persons for whom marriage is not, or proves not to be, a good fit. The reasons for this may change or evolve over the life course or through historic time, and they often vary along gender lines in accordance with prevailing definitions of male and female roles.

Unmarried men, both homosexual and heterosexual, place a high priority on access to sexual freedom along with freedom from the male-provider role of marriage. And some sizable portion of men appear to be genuine loners, a preference that is often assumed to reflect personal pathology in a society so committed to commitment. Rather than stigmatize those who distance themselves from intimacy, it would be far more productive to conduct further research into the personal and social characteristics of men who make this choice. Similarly, we know little about the role of personality traits, life transitions, socioeconomic factors, and community contexts as they influence gay men toward or away from a preference for long term relationships.

Women remain outside of marriage most commonly to avoid wifely subordination to men. Among women there does not seem to be a counterpart of the male loner. Both never-married women and lesbian women are heavily invested in dyadic same-sex attachments and larger friendship networks. Neither unmarried heterosexual nor homosexual women are lacking intimacy in their lives, and it would appear that they experience their same-sex relationships as more companionate and egalitarian than their relationships with men. Lesbian sex is experienced as more satisfying and mutually attentive than heterosexual sex, despite the lower frequency of sex in lesbian relationships.

As professionally ambitious women encounter the work-relationship strains still widely inherent in marriage (Goode 1982; Hochschild 1990), lesbian partnerships might well pose an attractive alternative. Similarly, divorced women, disillusioned with marriage, might logically look to a same-sex relationship as the foundation for intimacy and shared domesticity. On the other hand, now that the "love that dare not speak its name" between women does have a name, the very label (and all that it implies) *lesbianism* may deter formerly married and career women, especially, from making lives together or more probably from being openly public about their lives together compared to never-married or less upwardly mobile lesbians. The Boston marriage was quite a matter-of-fact and un-self-conscious arrangement. The lesbian relationship of today has social and political conditions that have led to gains in gay rights but, at the same time, may have reduced the freedom of individual women to construct their relationships as they choose. There are great pressures nowadays that make it difficult for the personal to remain personal. Nonetheless, a large proportion of high-ranking professional women are unmarried, and many divorced women choose not to remarry. Studies of the configuration of their personal and social lives would certainly be illuminating of patterns of nonmarital intimacy and sexuality.

Finally, we know very little about the circumstances surrounding a change in gender preference over the life course. We are also lacking in understanding of whether previously married or heterosexual persons enter into and live in homosexual relationships with significantly different expectations and values from those whose lives have been invariantly homosexual. That such changes occur is indisputable. But there is a need for narrative research on the meaning and timing of life events and the processes by which a new sexual self-identity emerges and settles that will articulate how and why some persons depart from the conventional avenues of marital intimacy and sexuality to arrive at a nonmarital destination.

References

Adams, M. 1976. *Single blessedness.* New York: Basic.

Allen, K. R. 1989. *Single women/family ties: Life histories of older women.* Beverly Hills, Calif.: Sage.

Allon, N., and D. Fishel. 1981. Singles' bars: Examples of urban courting patterns. In *Single life: Unmarried adults in social context,* ed. P. Stein, 115–120. New York: St. Martin's.

Bell, A. P., and M. S. Weinberg. 1978. *Homosexualities: A study of diversity among men and women.* New York: Simon & Schuster.

Bernard, J. 1972. *The future of marriage.* New York: World.

———. 1981. The good provider role: Its rise and fall. *American Psychologist* 36(1):1–12.

Bieber, I., H. J. Dain, P. R. Dince, M. G. Drellich, H. G. Grand, R. H. Gundlach, M. W. Kremer, A. H. Rifkin, C. B. Wilber, and T. B. Bieber. 1962. *Homosexuality: A psychoanalytic study.* New York: Basic.

Blumstein, P., and P. Schwartz. 1977. Bisexuality: Some social psychological issues. *Journal of Social Issues* 33(2): 30–45.

———. 1983. *American couples: Money, work, sex.* New York: Morrow.

———. 1990. Intimate relationships and the creation of sexuality. In *Homosexuality/heterosexuality: Concepts of sexual orientation,* ed. P. McWhirter, S. Sanders, and J. Reinisch, 307–20. Vol. 2 of the Kinsey Institute Series. New York and Oxford: Oxford Univ. Press.

Cancian, F. M. 1986. The feminization of love. *Signs: Journal of Women in Culture and Society* 11(4):692–709.

Cass, V. C. 1990. The implications of homosexual identity formation for the Kinsey model and scale of sexual preference. In *Homosexuality/heterosexuality: Concepts of sexual orientation,* ed. D. McWhirter, S. Sanders, and J. Reinisch, 239–66. Vol. 2 of the Kinsey Institute Series. New York and Oxford: Oxford Univ. Press.

Clayton, R. R., and H. L. Voss. 1977. Shacking up: Cohabitation in the 1970s. *Journal of Marriage and the Family* 39(2): 273–83.

Cleveland, M. 1981. Sexuality in the middle years. In *Single life: Unmarried adults in social context,* ed. P. Stein ,121–27. New York: St. Martin's.

Coleman, E. 1985. Bisexual women in marriages. In *Bisexualities: Theory and research,* ed. F. Klein and T. Wolf, 87–99. Vol. 11 of Research on Homosexuality. New York and London: Haworth.

Cozby, P. C. 1973. Self disclosure: A literature review. *Psychological Review* 79: 73–91.

Davis, J. A., and T. Smith. 1987. *General social surveys, 1972–1987: Cumulative data.* Storrs, Conn.: Roper Center for Public Research, Univ. of Connecticut.

DeCecco, J. 1990. The homosexual as acts or persons: A conversation with John DeCecco. In *Homosexuality as behavior and identity.* Vol. 2 of *Dialogues of the sexual revolution,* ed. L. D. Mass, 132–69. Binghamton, N.Y.: Harrington Park.

DeCecco, J., and M. D. Shively. 1984. *Bisexual and homosexual identities: Critical theoretical issues.* Vol. 8 of Research on Homosexuality. New York: Haworth.

D'Emilio, J., and E. Freedman. 1988. *Intimate matters: History of sexuality in America.* New York: Harper & Row.

———. 1990. Dialogues of the sexual revolutions: A conversation with John D'Emilio and Estelle Freedman. In *Homosexuality as behavior and identity.* Vol. 2 of *Dialogues of the sexual revolution,* ed. L. D. Mass. Binghamton, N.Y.: Harrington Park.

Doudna, C., and F. McBride. 1981. Where are the men for the women at the top? In *Single Life: Unmarried adults in social context,* ed. P. J. Stein, 21–33. New York: St. Martin's.

Ehrenreich, B. 1983. *The hearts of men: American dreams and the flight from commitment.* New York: Anchor, Doubleday.

Ehrenreich, B., E. Hess, and G. Jacobs. 1986. *Re-making love: The feminization of sex.* New York: Anchor, Doubleday.

Ehrhardt, A. 1992. Personal communication to the author.

Ehrhardt, A. A., and J. N. Wasserheit. 1991. Age, gender, and sexual risk behaviors for sexually transmitted diseases in the United States. In *Research issues in human behavior and sexually transmitted diseases in the AIDS era,* ed. J. Wasserheit, S. Aral, K. Holmes, and P. Hitchcock, 97–121. Washington, D.C.: American Society for Microbiology.

Ellis, H. [1897] 1936. *Studies in the psychology of sex.* New York: Random House.

Faderman, L. 1981. *Surpassing the love of men: Romantic friendship and love between women from the Renaissance to the present.* New York: Morrow.

———. 1991. *Odd girls and twilight lovers: A history of lesbian life in twentieth century America.* New York: Columbia Univ. Press.

Faludi, S. 1991. *Backlash: The undeclared war against American women.* New York: Crown.

Fitzgerald, F. 1986. *Cities on a hill: A journey through contemporary American cultures.* New York: Simon & Schuster.

Fowlkes, M. R. 1980. *Behind every successful man: Wives of medicine and academe.* New York: Columbia Univ. Press.

———. 1990. The social regulation of grief. *Sociological Forum* 5(4):635–50.

Friedan, B. 1963. *The feminine mystique.* New York: Dell.

———. 1981. *The second stage.* New York: Summit.

Gagnon, J. H. 1990. Gender preference in erotic relations: The Kinsey scale in sexual scripts. In *Homosexuality/heterosexuality: Concepts of sexual orientation,* ed. D. McWhirter, S. A. Sanders, and J. Reinisch, 177–207. Vol. 2 of the Kinsey Institute Series, New York and Oxford: Oxford Univ. Press.

Gagnon, J., and W. Simon. 1973. *Sexual conduct: The social sources of human sexuality.* Chicago: Aldine.

Glick, P. C., and G. B. Spanier. 1980. Cohabitation in the United States. *Journal of Marriage and the Family* 42 (February): 19–30.

Glick, P., and S. Lin. 1986. Recent changes in divorce and remarriage. *Journal of Marriage and the Family* 48 (November): 737–47.

———. 1987. Remarriage after divorce: Recent changes and demographic variations. *Sociological Perspectives* 30(2):162–79.

Goode, W. J. 1982. Why men resist. In *Rethinking the family*, ed. B. Thorne and M. Yalom, 131–47. New York: Longman.

Green, M. F. 1988. *The American college president: A contemporary profile*. Washington, D.C.: American Council on Education.

Green, R. 1987. *The "sissy boy" syndrome and the development of homosexuality*. New Haven, Conn.: Yale Univ. Press.

Greer, W. R. 1986. The changing women's marriage market. *New York Times*, 22 February, 48.

Gubrium, J. 1975. Being single in old age. *Aging and Human Development* 6:29–41.

Hansen, C. E., and A. Evans. 1985. Bisexuality reconsidered: An idea in pursuit of a definition. In *Bisexualities: Theory and research*, ed. F. Klein and T. J. Wolf. Vol. 2 of Research on Homosexuality. New York and London: Haworth.

Harry, J. 1983. Gay male and lesbian relationships. In *Contemporary families and alternative lifestyles: Handbook on research and theory*, ed. E. Macklin and R. Rubin, 216–34. Beverly Hills, Calif.: Sage.

———. 1984. *Gay couples*. New York: Praeger.

Hess, B. B. 1972. Friendship. In *Aging and society*, ed. M. W. Riley, M. Johnson, and A. Foner. Vol. 3 of *A sociology of age stratification*, 357–93. New York: Russell Sage.

Hochschild, A. 1990. *The second shift*. New York: Avon.

Hotvedt, M. E. 1982. Life adaptations: Summary and conclusions. In *Homosexuality: Social, psychological, and biological issues*, ed. W. Paul, J. Weinrich, J. C. Gonsiorek, and M. E. Hotvedt, 288–89. Beverly Hills, Calif.: Sage.

Johnson, S. E. 1991. *Staying power: Long term lesbian couples*. Tallahassee, Fla.: Naiad.

Jourard, S. M. 1971. *Self-disclosure: An experimental analysis of the transparent self*. New York: Wiley-Interscience.

Kanter, R. M. 1977. *Men and women of the corporation*. New York: Basic.

Kaufman, P., E. Harrison, and M. Hyde. 1984. Distancing for intimacy in lesbian relationships. *American Journal of Psychiatry* 14: 530–33.

Kelly, J. B. 1982. Divorce: the adult perspective. In *Families in transition*, ed. A. S. and J. H. Skolnick, 304–37. 5th ed. Boston: Little, Brown.

Kinsey, A. C., W. Pomeroy and C. E. Martin. 1948. *Sexual behavior in the human male*. Philadelphia: Saunders.

Kinsey, A. C., W. Pomeroy, C. E. Martin and P. H. Gebhard. 1953. *Sexual behavior in the human female*. Philadelphia: Saunders.

Kinsman, G. 1987. Men loving men: The challenge of gay liberation. In *Beyond patriarchy: Essays by men on pleasure, power, and change*, ed. M. Kaufman, 103–19. Toronto: Oxford Univ. Press.

Larson, P. C. 1982. Gay male relationships. In *Homosexuality: Social, psychological and biological issues*, ed. W. Paul, J. D. Weinrich, J. C. Gonsoriek, and M. E. Hotvedt, 219–32. Beverly Hills, Calif.: Sage.

Lawson, A. 1988. *Adultery: An analysis of love and betrayal*. New York: Basic.

Lofland, L. H. 1982. Loss and human connection: An exploration into the nature of the social bond. In *Personality, roles and social behavior*, ed. W. Ickes and E. Knowles. New York: Springer-Verlag.

Maccoby, E. E., and C. N. Jacklin. 1974. *The psychology of sex differences.* Stanford, Calif.: Stanford Univ. Press.

Macklin, E. D. 1972. Cohabiting college students. *The Family Coordinator,* October, 463–71. Reprinted in Stein (1981, 210–20).

Marecek, J., S. E. Finn, and M. Cardell. 1982. Gender role in the relationships of lesbians and gay men. *Journal of Homosexuality* 8(2):45–50.

McWhirter, D., and A. M. Mattison. 1984. *The male couple.* Englewood Cliffs, N.J.: Prentice-Hall.

McWhirter, D. P., S. A. Sanders, and J. M. Reinisch. 1990. *Homosexuality/heterosexuality: Concepts of sexual orientation.* Vol. 2 of the Kinsey Institute Series. New York and Oxford: Oxford Univ. Press.

Miller, P. Y., and M. R. Fowlkes. 1980. Social and behavioral constructions of female sexuality. *Signs: Journal of Women in Culture and Society* 5(4):783–800.

Money, J., and P. Tucker. 1975. *Sexual signatures: On being a man or a woman.* Boston: Little, Brown.

Nichols, M. 1990. Lesbian relationships: Implications for the study of sexuality and gender. In *Homosexuality/heterosexuality: Concepts of sexual orientation,* ed. D. McWhirter, S. Sanders, and J. Reinisch. Vol. 2 of the Kinsey Institute Series. New York and Oxford: Oxford Univ. Press.

Paul, W., J. D. Weinrich, J. C. Gonsiorek, and M. E. Hotvedt. 1982. *Homosexuality: Social, psychological, and biological issues.* Beverly Hills, Calif.: Sage.

Peplau, L. A. 1982. Research on homosexual couples. An overview. *Journal of Homosexuality* 8(2):3–7.

Peplau, L. A., and H. Amaro. 1982. Understanding lesbian relationships. In *Homosexuality: Social, psychological, and biological issues,* ed. W. Paul, J. P. Weinrich, J. C. Gonsiorek, and M. E. Hotvedt. Beverly Hills, Calif.: Sage.

Peplau, L. A., and S. D. Cochran. 1990. A relational perspective on homosexuality. In *Homosexuality/heterosexuality: Concepts of sexual orientation,* ed. P. McWhirter, S. Sanders, and J. Reinisch, 321–49. Vol. 2 of the Kinsey Institute Series. New York and Oxford: Oxford Univ. Press.

Peplau, L., and S. L. Gordon. 1983. The intimate relationships of lesbians and gay men. In *The changing boundaries: Gender roles and social behavior,* ed. E. R. Allgeier and N. B. McCormick, 226–44. Palo Alto, Calif.: Mayfield.

Peplau, L. A., S. Cochran, K. Rook, and C. Padesky. 1978. Loving women: Attachment and autonomy in lesbian relationships. *Journal of Social Issues* 34(3):7–27.

Person, E. S. 1980. Sexuality as the mainstay of identity: Psychoanalytic perspectives. *Signs: A Journal of Women in Culture and Society* 5(4):620–30.

Pesman, C. 1991. Love and sex in the 90s. *Seventeen,* November, 63–68.

Pleck, J. H. [1974] 1992. Men's power with women, other men and society: A men's movement analysis. In *Men's Wives,* ed. M. S. Kimmel and M. A. Messner. New York: Macmillan.

Ramsey, J., J. D. Latham, and C. L. Lindquist. 1978. Long-term same-sex relationships: Correlates of adjustment. Paper presented at the Annual Meeting of the American Psychological Society, Toronto, Canada, August.

Rich, A. 1980. Compulsory heterosexuality and lesbian existence. *Signs: A Journal of Women in Culture and Society* 5(4):631–60.

Richardson, L. 1985. *The new other woman: Contemporary single women in affairs with married men.* New York: Free Press.

Riessman, C. K. 1990. *Divorce talk: Women and men make sense of personal relationships.* New Brunswick, N.J.: Rutgers Univ. Press.

Ross, M. W. 1983. *The married homosexual man: A psychological study.* London: Routledge & Kegan Paul.

Rossi, A. S. 1993. The future in the making: Recent trends in the family/work interface. *American Journal of Orthopsychiatry,* 63:166–76.

Rubin, L. B. 1983. *Intimate strangers: Men and women together.* New York: Harper & Row.

Rubinstein, R. L. 1986. *Singular paths: Old men living alone.* New York: Columbia Univ. Press.

Rubinstein, R. L., D. B. Alexander, M. Goodman, and M. Luborsky. 1991. Key relationships of never married, childless older women: A cultural analysis. *Journal of Gerontology: Social Sciences* 46(5):S270–77.

Sapadin, L. A. 1988. Friendship and gender: perspectives of professional men and women. *Journal of Social and Personal Relationships* 5:387–403.

Sattel, J. W. 1976. The inexpressive male: Tragedy or sexual politics? *Social Problems* 26(4):469–77.

Schaefer, S. 1976. Sexual and social problems of lesbians. *Journal of Sex Research* 12:50–69.

Silverstein, C. 1990. Male couples: A conversation with Charles Silverstein. In *Homosexuality and sexuality.* Vol. 1 of *Dialogues of the sexual revolution,* ed. L. D. Mass. Binghampton, N.Y.: Harrington Park.

Simenauer, J., and D. Carroll. 1982. *Singles: The new Americans.* New York: New American Library.

Simon, B. L. 1987. *Never married women.* Philadelphia: Temple Univ. Press.

Smith-Rosenberg, C. 1975. The female world of love and ritual: Relations between women in nineteenth century America. *Signs: Journal of Women in Culture and Society* 1(1):1–29.

Snitow, A. 1992. What feminism has said about motherhood. *Feminist Review* 40 (in press).

Stein, P. J. 1976. *Singles.* Englewood Cliffs, N.J.: Prentice-Hall.

———. 1981. *Single life: Unmarried adults in social context.* New York: St. Martin's.

Stoller, R. J. 1972. The "bedrock" of masculinity and femininity: Bisexuality. *Archives of General Psychiatry* 26: 207–12.

Vetere, V. A. 1982. The role of friendship in the development and maintenance of lesbian love relationships. *Journal of Homosexuality* 2 (winter): 51–66.

Wallerstein, J. S., and S. Blakeslee. 1989. *Second chances: Men, women, and children a decade after divorce.* New York: Tichnor & Fields.

Weeks, J. 1986. *Sexuality.* London: Horword, Tavistock.

Weston, K. 1991. *Families we choose: Lesbians, gays, kinship.* New York: Columbia Univ. Press.

White, E. 1980. *States of desire: Travels in gay America.* New York: Dutton.

Whitney, C. 1991. *Uncommon lives: Gay men and straight women.* New York: Plume, Penguin.

III Sexuality at Selected Phases of the Life Course

SEVEN

Getting Started on Sexual Behavior

J. Richard Udry and Benjamin C. Campbell

Sexual behavior plays a more important part in the lives of some people than in the lives of others. Alfred Kinsey was the first to call our attention to the enormous diversity of sexual motivation and behavior in the general population. He also highlighted the fact that these differences in sexual behavior exhibit continuity across the life course. Thus individuals who experience sexual behavior early have a higher frequency of sex and more sexual partners, experience a wider variety of sexual behavior, have more continuity, and continue sex later into old age. So it should be clear that, when we learn something about the timing of the onset of sexual behavior, we are also learning something about sexual behavior over the rest of the life span.

ONSET OF SEXUAL BEHAVIOR

When we talk about the beginnings of sexual behavior, it is important to establish exactly what behaviors we mean. We do not mean early sexual abuse. Although most people have sexual feelings, sexual thoughts, some autoinduced sexual experience, and some range of nongenital erotic body contact before experiencing coitus, coitus is a simple identification of starting. Maybe we start here because, as Ira Reiss says, Western sex is coitus centered, as contrasted to some imaginary society that is centered on something else.

For the purpose of this chapter, we also deal only with the initiation of heterosexual sex and omit the initiation of homosexual experience, even though some of the sexual experience of those who are primarily heterosexual is homosexual. We do this only for the purpose of focusing our discourse narrowly enough to fit into one chapter, not because we think the beginnings of homosexual behavior require a different theo-

This work was partially supported by research grants HD12806 and HD25 and National Research Service Award HDO7816 from the National Institute of Child Health and Development (NICHD), center grants from NICHD to the Laboratories of Reproductive Biology (HD18969) and the Carolina Population Center (HD05798) and a Clinical Research Unit Grant (RR00046) from the National Institutes of Health.

retical model. In fact, an understanding of homosexual behavior may provide an important insight into the biological foundation of all human sexual experience, which we consider later.

In most discussions, sexual initiation is associated with adolescence. It is true that in many societies females are not considered eligible sexual participants until a certain stage of puberty has been reached (generally menarche, although breast development is sometimes also considered). However, the fact that adolescents may be considered culturally eligible for sexual experience should not blind us to the fact that only some individuals actually avail themselves of the opportunity.

Even today in our own society, when there is a widespread impression that the majority of adolescents are sexually active, a substantial portion of women may not experience intercourse until their twenties. We have just finished interviews on a moderately representative sample of 350 white women born in California from 1960 to 1963, who are thus around thirty years old at interview. The earliest age at first coitus reported was eleven, the median was 17.5, and at interview seven of these women had not experienced coitus. First coitus is spread over a twenty-year age span, less than half of which is in adolescence. Any theory that relates simply to adolescence can tell only part of the story. Fortunately, both Jessor et al. (1983) and Udry (unpublished data) have separately found that the same explanatory models that discriminate among early starters also hold for late starters. This is an important finding whose importance—that similar processes are involved in sexual initiation, regardless of age—has been overlooked.

When we talk about sexual initiation, it has become customary to use the term *sexually active* to describe the sexually initiated, irrespective of their current activity. It is as though, once begun, sex inevitably continues. This certainly does not describe the experience of early adolescence in which the first act of coitus may be widely separated in time from those that follow it (Hofferth 1987). Nonetheless, unpublished analysis indicates that the same factors that predict starting also predict continuing once started. Thus we may still concentrate on first coitus as the beginning because it is almost never also the end.

THEORETICAL PERSPECTIVES

We are going to limit our consideration to explanations of individual differences in timing of sexual initiation. We are not going to discuss, except in passing, theories that explain secular social change in the timing of initiation. Contrary to common patterns of discourse, these two types of theories have no necessary relationship to one another. The variables that explain variance in a cohort need not be the same variables that explain secular change in a society. Thus, for example, although girls from single-parent families may exhibit an earlier age at sexual initiation (Inazu and Fox 1980; Newcomer and Udry 1984), an increasing number of single-parent families does not necessarily explain decreasing age at first intercourse.

We will divide the discussion of the factors underlying the initiation of sex according to the perspectives that give the factors general meaning. Three perspectives lead us in three different directions: The sociological perspective directs us to examine the current social environment of individuals and groups for norms, peer association patterns, and family influences. The biological perspective leads us to look for biological processes that shape behavior. The perspective of developmental psychology directs us to look for characteristics of individuals that emerge early in life that shape later behavior.

Social Environment

Of these three approaches, almost all the available research is guided by sociological theory. We are also including under sociological theory, primarily for convenience, all psychological and social-psychological theories that emphasize the current state or the current environment of the sexual actor, where those theories account for the current state of the individual at least implicitly by sociological explanations. For example, we include here all subjective expected utility theories. Under this rubric falls almost everything that is known about the timing of sexual initiation.

Unfortunately, we do not know as much about the role of the social environment in the onset of sexual behavior as we think we do. Without trying to be exhaustive, let us take a few examples of things we think we know. All studies agree that African-Americans start earlier than whites (Furstenberg et al. 1987; Hofferth, Kahn, and Baldwin 1987; Kantner and Zelnick 1972), with many African-American males starting before puberty (Clark, Zabin, and Hardy 1984; Finkel and Finkel 1975; Zabin et al. 1986). All studies agree that adolescents with high church attendance or religiosity start later (Devaney and Hubley 1981; Zelnik, Kantner, and Ford 1981). Most studies find that those with better-educated parents start later (Forste and Heaton 1988; Thornton and Camburn 1987; Zelnick, Kantner, and Ford 1981). Most studies find that adolescents from mother-only households start earlier (Hogan and

Kitagawa 1985; Inazu and Fox 1980; Miller and Bingham 1989; Newcomer and Udry 1984). Most studies find that early starters have low grades in school, but these studies cannot determine which causes which (McAnarney and Schreider 1984).

Most studies find that adolescents who have sexually active friends are more likely to be sexually active (Miller and Moore 1990). But these studies are nearly all based on cross-sectional data and cannot separate friendship selection and deselection from friends' influence. Nearly all are based on respondents' reports of their friends' sexual activity. In the one study in which these methodological problems are solved, friendship influence is found for white girls but not white boys or African-American girls (Billy and Udry 1987).

Beyond these few consistent findings is a tangle of inconsistent results or single-study findings of dubious replicability. The number of studies in which the predictive characteristics are measured at a time prior to the sexual behavior is so small as to preclude much confidence in what we think we know. Given the funding climate over the last decade for sexual research, future progress is likely to be slow.

Biological Processes

Biological studies on the beginnings of sexual behavior at adolescence are based on both behavior-genetic and endocrine-behavior relationships. So far as we can determine, the only published genetic study of adolescent sexual behavior is by Martin, Eaves, and Eysenck (1977). It shows (for too small a sample) a genetic influence for age at first intercourse, but it has never been replicated. It is the senior author's ambition to replicate it in the future.

The only studies of human adolescent sexuality based on an endocrine-behavior theory have been done by Udry. The theory derives from animal literature and is supported by a number of studies on human adults. The adult studies generally agree that testosterone is necessary for the maintenance of sexual interest in both males and females. In males it has been demonstrated experimentally that exogenous testosterone (T) administered to hypogonadal males (males with abnormally low levels of T) increases sexual interest and behavior (Kwan et al. 1983; Skakkebaek et al. 1981). One study shows increased sexual functioning with exogenous T for a sample of males with normal T complaining of lack of sexual interest (O'Carroll and Bancroft 1984). However, attempts to demonstrate that among normal adult males differences in endogenous T are associated systematically with sexual interest or behavior have not been successful (Brown, Monti, and Corriveau 1978; Persky et al. 1978). The favorite reconciliation of the results for normal men with the experimental findings is that there is a threshold range for T effects, followed by an asymptote, and that most normal adults were beyond the asymptotic level.

For normal females, there is also evidence from experimental studies to show that exogenous testosterone increases sexual interest and awareness (Burger et al. 1984; Burger et al. 1987; Sherwin and Gelfand 1987; Sherwin, Gelfand, and Brender 1985). In addition, naturally occurring variation has been related to differences in both sexual behavior (Morris et al. 1987; Persky et al. 1978) and motivation (Alder et al. 1986), although it is clear that changes in sexual behavior are also dependent on the behavior of male partners (Sherwin and Gelfand 1987).

Research on boys. Folk lore has held that adolescent sexual interest is stimulated by the increased levels of hormones associated with puberty, especially among males. In planning our adolescent work, we thought of the preadolescent as a hypogonadal adult. We knew that, if adults had the level of T that preadolescents had, the adults would display very little interest in sex. We thought of puberty as the endogenous treatment for their hypogonadal state. We thought that, as they entered the threshold range, we would find a relationship between their T levels and the beginning of sexual behavior. Because previous studies had found that testosterone levels among boys went from prepubertal to minimum adult levels in a year or less, we thought that the effects would be confined to a relatively short time period and easy to find. The case for the girls was less clear because by the time they reach menarche girls' hormone levels are increasing much less dramatically than the boys' levels. In fact, some girls might exhibit a decrease in testosterone levels during this time period. Nonetheless, the basic conceptual model still holds. Changes in sexual motivation and behavior at puberty could be expected to be related to changes in T.

Our first study, and the first attempt to empirically examine the relation between hormones and sexual behavior among adolescents in a nonclinical population, was a sample of one hundred white boys and one hundred white girls, recruited randomly from a list of pupils in grades 8, 9, and 10, and ranging in age from twelve to sixteen. We gave them a questionnaire and took their blood. (The details are provided in Udry et al. 1985; and Udry, Talbert, and Morris 1986).

For the boys we found whopping T effects on a series of measures of sexual motivation and behavior ranging from thinking about sex to noncoital sexual experience to intercourse. The effects of testosterone were present even when entered into a multivariate model with self-ratings of pubertal development and age. Thus we could conclude that the testosterone effects represented direct effects on motivation rather than indirect effects acting through pubertal development.

Few of our girls had coitus, but we found hormone effects, particularly of androgens, on noncoital sexual behavior ranging from kissing to heavy petting, and motivation. These findings are consistent with studies of adult women indicating that, although testosterone affects sexual motivation, the expression of this motivation as behavior may depend on the circumstances. For adolescents, those circumstances would be social controls specifically on intercourse.

The findings of a cross-sectional relation between hormones and sexual behavior among adolescents suggested but could not prove an important role for testosterone and other androgens in the initiation of sexual behavior. Confirmation required more complicated panel studies whose goals were to examine the behavior consequences of hormone change and to identify the lag time between increases in hormones and changes in behavior. By following our respondents intensively over a critical period of two to three years, beginning at about age 13, we thought we would be able to observe changes in sexual behavior and see whether those changes could be identified as responses to either absolute hormone levels or changes in hormone levels.

We followed one sample of over one hundred white boys from about age 13 to about age 16. The sample was drawn randomly from a list of pupils enrolled in a North Carolina city near us. The boys were interviewed, and afternoon blood samples were obtained in month 0, 6, 12, 18, 24, and 36 of the study. The plasma was prepared and stored. Final assays were done with all samples from a single boy in the same assay batch to protect within-subject changes from between-batch shifts in assay materials and technicians. Samples were assayed for T, sex-hormone-binding globulin (SHBG), and other hormones by radioimmunoassay. Interviews were done in the boy's home. The boys were also visited once a week by the interviewer to collect saliva samples and weekly behavior checklists. Subjects were told that biological specimens were obtained in order to measure hormones levels.

Initial statistical analysis showed significant correlations between the month 0 testosterone and all subsequent rounds of sexual behavior. The month 36 behavior correlated with the month 0 testosterone as well as behavior from earlier rounds. But testosterone from other than the first round did not correlate with behavior at all. Furthermore, careful measures of pubertal development did not correlate with sexual behavior for the sample as a whole. We did extensive change analyses using various lag periods and lag times of varying duration. Neither changes in hormones nor changes in pubertal development were related to changes in sexual behavior.

Figure 1 shows that we did find interesting hormone-behavior relationships. This graph shows the level of progression in sexual experience (a sum of items ranging from heavy petting to intercourse) among our boys over three years, based on two independent variables (testosterone and church attendance) measured at time 1. Both independent variables were dichotomized, and cross-classified to create four groups. At time 1, all groups are clearly differentiated with high T–low church boys clearly more active, low T–high church boys least active and high T–high church and low T–low church boys intermediate, as expected. Over time this pattern is maintained with low T–low church and high T–high church groups converging, so that by the end of the study the two are

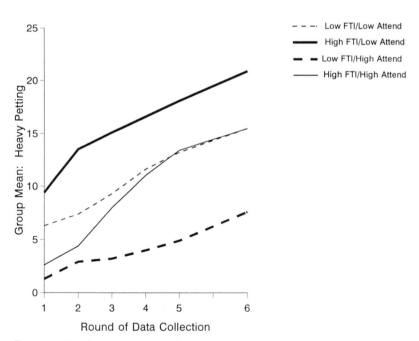

FIGURE 1. Boys' sexual experience by round 1 testosterone, round 1 church attendance.

identical. Repeated-measures analysis of variance (ANOVA) shows a round by group interaction that is statistically significant. Both church and T effects are very easy to discern, and the differences by group in sexual behavior are large. But when round two independent measures are used, the pattern begins to disintegrate, and, when round three independent measures are used, the pattern dissolves completely.

On the basis of these observations, we concluded that we could not identify true hormone effects. Rather we identified the testosterone at round 0 as a proxy for early timing of puberty. This is apparent when the sample is divided on the basis of pubertal development at round 1 into earlier or later maturers. Table 1 shows that pubertal development has a significant positive effect on noncoital sexual experience (a sum of items from kissing and holding hands to heavy petting) among the earlier maturers but not among the later maturers, using either concurrent measures or those with a six-month lag.

Our favorite hypothesis now is that early high testosterone is a marker for a growth and development trajectory that we may be able to identify before puberty. It is this growth trajectory, and not pubertal hormones, that is associated with early sexual behavior. The way in which this growth trajectory is related to sexual behavior is unknown,

TABLE 1 Effect of Pubertal Development on Noncoital Sexual Experience among Boys, Using Repeated-Measures ANOVA

Relation of Measures	Later Maturers	Earlier Maturers
Concurrent:		
Time	$p = .000$	$p = .000$
Pubertal	NS (+)	$p = .009$ (+)
Time * pubertal	NS	NS
Six-month lag:		
Time	$p = .000$	$p = .02$
Pubertal	$p = .002$ (−)	$p = .03$ (+)
Time * pubertal	NS	NS
One-year lag:		
Time	$p = .000$	$p = .000$
Pubertal	NS (+)	NS (+)
Time * pubertal	NS	NS

Note: The term *sexual experience* indicates the sum of sexual behavior items ranging from holding hands and kissing to heavy petting (does not include intercourse). NS indicates "not significant."

although it might act through physical characteristics or through the peer group. This is a matter of speculation at this point.

Research on girls. We have recently completed a two-year panel study of one hundred white and one hundred African-American postmenarcheal girls of about age 13, drawn from the same schools as the boys' sample. The girls were interviewed semiannually for five rounds. Interviews were scheduled during a narrow window in the early follicular phase of the menstrual cycle to control for menstrual variation in hormone levels, and interviews were conducted at home in the late afternoon. Blood samples were obtained at the time of interview. Girls were also visited once a menstrual cycle, at which time other data were collected. Final interviews and blood draws were completed at the Clinical Research Unit at North Carolina Memorial Hospital in Chapel Hill.

Blood samples were prepared and frozen for later analysis and assayed for testosterone, SHBG, estradiol, androstenedione, and progesterone. Various comparisons of hormones and behavior were made, including cross-sectional, lagged, and change models. We have just completed the last round of data collection, and it is therefore not yet analyzed. In the first four rounds, the pattern of relationships between hormones and sexual behavior and motivation is essentially random. Occasional significant correlations are observed, but they are not consistent from round to round, or from lag to lag, and the signs are as often as not counter to theoretical expectations.

Contrary to the boys' study, we did find significant effects of level of pubertal development on girls' sexual behavior. Pubertal development was a significant predictor of both coital and noncoital sexual behavior among African-American and white girls, although the timing in the role of pubertal development appears to differ between the two groups. Pubertal development was a significant predictor of sexual behavior for African-Americans in rounds 1 and 2, while for whites it became important in rounds 3 and 4 (table 2). This difference in timing parallels differences in the timing of pubertal development among the two groups as shown in figure 2. We interpret these results as suggesting that a particular stage of female pubertal development may play a role in the initiation of sexual activity.

The lack of significant hormone-behavior relationships among our findings precludes the possibility that the role of pubertal development represents hormone effects on behavior. Instead they should be interpreted as attractiveness effects—that is, the more pubertally developed a girl is, the more likely she is to attract sexual attention from males. In

J. Richard Udry and Benjamin C. Campbell

TABLE 2 Pubertal Development and Sexual Behavior among
Adolescent Females (standardized regression coefficients)

Variable	Round			
	1	2	3	4
	Whites			
Intercourse:				
Pubertal development	.12	.01	.16[+]	.19[+]
Age	.02	.19[+]	.13	.10
Sexual experience:				
Pubertal development	.08	.18[+]	.13	.20[*]
Age	.15	.19[+]	.22[**]	.18[+]
	African-Americans			
Intercourse:				
Pubertal development	.21[*]	.20[*]	.17[+]	.13
Age	.09	.18[*]	.10	.22[*]
Sexual experience:				
Pubertal development	.40[***]	.17[+]	.16[+]	.08
Age	.20[*]	.33[**]	.19[*]	.29[**]

[+]$p < .1$
[*]$p < .05$
[**]$p < .01$
[***]$p < .001$

previous studies we have shown that pubertal development is a significant predictor of subsequent sexual behavior for girls (Udry and Billy 1987). The pubertal development effects cannot be interpreted as merely the identification of early developers as being different from late developers, but rather pubertal development has an effect on sexual behavior at the age at which it occurs.

The panel studies we have described are elaborate and expensive. They cover a stage during which both sexual behavior and hormone levels are changing at a fairly rapid rate. If there is any important direct causal relationship between hormones and behavior in early adolescence, our study design should have identified it. Thus our failure to identify testosterone relationships to adolescent sexual behavior is hard to reconcile with the idea that testosterone is the foundation of sexual motivation among adults. Is it true that the relationship is not there during adolescence? Or is the mechanism more complicated than our models?

We were sobered by reading a recent article on the sexual behavior

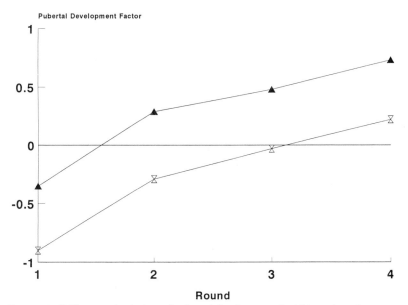

FIGURE 2. Differences in timing of pubertal development in African-American (▲) and white (⨯) girls.

of the red-sided garter snake (Crews 1991). Recent studies have uncovered a relation between testosterone and male sexual behavior in this snake after earlier attempts had concluded that courtship behavior in males was not hormone dependent (Crews et al. 1984). In fact, it turns out that the male's readiness to court in the spring is related to the seasonal peak in androgens during the *previous* summer. And then only if the snake undergoes hibernation in the intervening eight months (Crews 1991). Clearly, the relation between testosterone and sexual behavior in this species is sufficiently complex that it would never have been discovered without starting with the conviction that there must be testosterone effects.

We are not suggesting the red-sided garter snake as an analogue for testosterone effects on sexual behavior among human adolescents. But can we assume that human mating behavior and its underlying hormonal foundations is simpler than that of the red-sided garter snake? Although our current results fail to support an important role for testosterone, it is important not to conclude that we are at the end of the line with respect to unraveling the hormone-behavior relations involved in adolescent sexuality. The failure of simple models should not discourage us but should compel us to develop more sophisticated ones.

Childhood Precursors of Age at First Sex

The final theoretical perspective we examine is from developmental psychology. This perspective says that we can learn what kind of adults people will be by finding out what kind of children they were. We assume that basic behavior patterns emerge during childhood, either from socialization experiences or from genetic foundations. These basic behavior patterns indicate enduring behavior predispositions that lead individuals in adolescence and adulthood to selected environments that provide opportunities for preferred behaviors and opportunities to avoid other behaviors. This theory is the complement of the sociological theories that focus on the effect of differential environments rather than on the characteristics of individuals. The burden of the developmental model is that it requires long-term longitudinal studies beginning early in childhood. Because we rarely know how early in the childhood of individuals we should look for the predictive patterns, we should start at the beginning of life. Then we must follow the same individuals until the adult behavior of interest is fully manifest. In the case of first intercourse, an ideal study would follow individuals until they were all sexually experienced. This would require a thirty-year study.

Fortunately, early developmentalists have left a legacy of longitudinal studies on which we can capitalize. We capitalized on the Child Health and Development Study (CHDS) begun by Yerushalmy in cooperation with Kaiser Plan hospitals in the California bay area in 1960 (See van den Berg, Christianson, and Oechsli [1988] for a full description). Women presenting for prenatal care were entered into the study, and for the early cohorts, data were collected on them and their offspring at the child's ages 5, 9–11, and 15–17. For purposes much broader than the present paper, we were able to follow up a sample of 350 female offspring born into the CHDS from 1960 to 1963. The follow-up was done in 1990–91, when the women were twenty-seven to thirty years old. At follow-up, women were asked their age at first intercourse, as a part of a set of self-administered questionnaires.

From the childhood data available, we excluded information collected at ages 15–17 and used data that were collected before any woman's age at first sex. The data were collected during the mother's pregnancy, at the daughter's age 5, and at ages 9–11. Three general categories of variables were identified: early family characteristics, early behavioral characteristics of the child, and temperamental characteristics of the child at ages 9–11, as described by the mother in questionnaire responses. Temperamental characteristics of the child were considered separately from behavioral characteristics because they were based on a separate set of mothers' yes-or-no response to one hundred terms describing the child's personality. We used these variables to build regression models predicting age at first sex.

In this sample of women, seven had not yet had first sex at the time of interview. As mentioned at the beginning of this chapter, age at first sex varied from eleven to thirty, with a median of 17.5, which is about the same figure shown in national samples of the same birth cohorts.

Table 3 shows that early family characteristics alone explained about 8 percent of the variance. This included whether the family attends church together (at age 9), mother's education (at pregnancy), number of siblings (at age 5)—all of which predicted later age at first sex—and whether mother smoked (at pregnancy), which predicted early age at first sex. Characteristics of the child at age 5 explained 11 percent of the

TABLE 3 Early Predictors of Age at First Intercourse for Females

Variable Name	Direction of Effect
Early family characteristics ($R^2 = .08$; N = 262):	
Family attends church together at age 9	+
Mother's education at pregnancy	+
Number of siblings at age 5	+
Mother smokes at pregnancy	−
Early characteristics of the child ($R^2 = .11$; N = 262):	
Motor skills at age 5	−
Has nightmares at age 5	−
Wets bed at age 5	−
Temperament of the child ($R^2 = .14$; N = 297):	
Often seems tired	−
Shy, bashful	+
Domineering factor	−
Mature factor	−
Combined model ($R^2 = .25$; N = 222):	
Family attends church ($F = 4.74$)	+
Motor skills ($F = 8.13$)	−
Nightmares ($F = 9.35$)	−
Wets bed ($F = 4.03$)	−
Too generous ($F = 5.28$)	−
Domineering factor ($F = 13.39$)	−
Mature factor ($F = 8.02$)	−

variance in age at first intercourse. This included a motor skills test, whether the child has nightmares, and whether the child wets the bed, all of which predicted early age at first sex.

Temperamental characteristics of the child at age 9 predicted 14 percent of the variance. These included two single items—whether the child is shy or bashful (late) and whether the child often seems tired (early)—and two groups of items combined into factor scores—whether the child is domineering (early), which included such items as whether the child never minds without a fuss, always wants the biggest piece, and bosses others and similar items; and social maturity (early), which included such items as whether the child makes friends easily, prefers to play with older children, and acts older than she is, and whether older children follow her lead. A joint model stripped down to significant variables explained 25 percent of the variance in age at first sex. The most predictive items were motor skills, nightmares, domineering behavior, and social maturity. (See Thompson, chap. 8, this vol., for another perspective on how temperamental characteristics are related to sexual behavior among adolescent girls).

Some of these predictors fall into existing conceptual models and are easily interpreted. Early family characteristics represent socialization processes. Whether the family attends church together and the mother's education are also predictors when measured at adolescence so it is not a surprise that they should be predictors when measured prior to adolescence as well. Presumably the number of siblings and whether the mother smoked are other indicators of these same processes. The predictive temperamental variables are also easily related to sexual behavior. Shy individuals are less likely to engage in social interactions leading up to sex; the opposite surely holds for those who are socially mature and might be true for a domineering personality as well. Why the variable *often seems tired* predicts early age at sexual onset is less clear.

Other predictors, however, such as motor skills and whether the child has nightmares or wets the bed do not have an immediately obvious connection to sexual behavior. It is most likely that they are indications of something else that does have an influence on sexual behavior. This something else need not represent the effects of socialization. Both bed-wetting (Bakwin 1973; Fergusson, Horwood, and Shannon 1986) and the having of nightmares (Hartmann 1984) have significant genetic components. The temperamental factors may also have genetic components. Whether the predictors are socialization or genetic in origin, the models demonstrate that one can predict age at first sex from before adolescence as well or better than by using adolescent situational variables. And you know you have the causal order correct.

Implications for Sexuality at Midlife

What can research about getting started on sex tell us about sex at midlife? The answer at this point must necessarily be speculative, but we can make some general points: Because sexual behavior is not an autonomous and separate behavior but is an integral part of the individual, we can expect a large measure of continuity in sexual behavior from adolescence to midlife. However, exactly what shape that continuity takes is unclear. It would be useful to follow up the California sample of women in twenty more years. We know a lot about their love lives from adolescence to age 30. It seems likely that the childhood factors that predict age at first sex will also tell us things about sex in midlife. Women who have first sex at age 30 will not have a middle age dominated by their sex lives. Women who started their sex lives early will stay with them later.

Underlying speculations about the continuity of sexual behavior from its beginning in adolescence to middle age (and beyond) are questions about the biological foundation of sexuality that we are only beginning to understand. Our picture of the role played by differences in hormones in the sexual behavior of normal men and women in midlife is no clearer than it is for adolescents (See McKinlay and Feldman chap. 10, this vol.). Nor has the role of genetic factors in adult sexuality received substantially more attention than it has among adolescents. Adolescence, where dramatic changes in hormones and sexual behavior should make it easier to identify any relation between the two, will, we hope, give us clues as to how to tackle these same issues among adults.

However, we want to emphasize that in our view the importance of adolescent sexuality to an understanding of adult sexuality comes not because adolescent sexuality is causal to adult sexuality but because both reflect the same underlying biogenetic and early developmental influences. The finding that among boys the timing of pubertal development, and not hormone levels, predicts sexual behavior points toward differences in developmental trajectories that may start even before birth. We already know that biological predictors of adolescent sexual behavior that have been identified, such as age at menarche, represent developmental processes that have a strong genetic component (Damon et al. 1969). When we eventually unravel the hormone effects of puberty on sexual behavior, because hormone increases are part and parcel of pubertal development, they will necessarily reflect the same biogenetic processes.

To make this argument more concrete we can follow its logic for the role of hormones in male sexual behavior. Even if we find that T turns on sexual behavior at adolescence, current evidence has been unable to establish that normal variation in T is related to sexual behavior among adult males. Thus the continuity in T levels from adolescence to adulthood suggested by genetic studies (Meikle et al. 1988) cannot underlie continuity in sexual behavior. Instead the association between starting early and being more sexually active in adulthood that Kinsey noted must reflect some other process that underlies both adolescent and adult sexual behavior. The findings among the CHDS females suggest temperament, which may have genetic components, as one possibility.

Given the emphasis on biogenetic and developmental factors in both adolescent and adult sexuality, we feel that an important part of future research on the biological foundations of sexual behavior will be centered around the investigation of the effects of prenatal hormones on adolescent and later sexual behavior. Research among primates has shown that the same hormones that affect sexually dimorphic behavior in humans and other primates also affect sexual behavior throughout life (Pomerantz, Goy, and Roy 1986; Pomerantz, Roy, and Goy 1988), through the effects of prenatal androgens on neural structure (Bonsall, Zumpe, and Michael 1990).

Although experimental manipulation of the prenatal hormone environment has convincingly established the role of prenatal androgens in primates, similar experiments are not possible with humans. As a result the evidence of prenatal androgen effects is sparser. However, so-called natural experiments have produced support for the effects of prenatal androgens on both childhood characteristics and adult sexual behavior. A number of studies have documented the effects of extremely high levels of androgenic hormones, resulting from either metabolic defects or endogenous administration, on behavior during childhood (Ehrhardt and Money 1967; Money and Ehrhardt 1972; Reinisch 1981). Continuing follow-ups on women with congenital adrenal hyperplasia have now demonstrated that prenatal androgens also have effects on sex of sex-partner preferences in women (Dittmann, Kappes, and Kappes 1991; Money, Schwartz, and Lewis 1984).

The evidence for prenatal hormone effects on sexual orientation among males is less clear and more controversial. LeVay (1991) has reported differences between heterosexual and homosexual men in the size of hypothalamic structures known to be related to sexual behavior. Because the area of the hypothalamus in question is presumed to be subject to the effects of prenatal androgens, LeVay's results strengthen earlier suggestions that the biological foundations for homosexual-heterosexual preference in males lie in the hormone experiences of the prenatal period. However, no clear link between levels of prenatal hormonal exposure and sexual preference has yet been demonstrated among men.

Sex-of-partner preference is an easily identifiable but relatively undifferentiated component of sexual behavior. There is no reason to assume that it is fundamentally divorced from other aspects of sexuality. Rather it can be seen as representing an extreme outcome on a continuum of sexual behavior related to the effects of prenatal androgen exposure. More subtle effects on sexual behavior may exist in the range of normal variation in prenatal androgen exposure. Because our understanding of prenatal effects suggests that the brain becomes masculinized by exposure to androgens, to uncover these prenatal hormone effects we need to clearly specify components of sexual behavior related to male-female differences in sexual behavior, such as the initiation of sexual encounters, and concentrate on them. Furthermore, because prenatal hormone influences work through predispositions and any sexual behavior must ultimately be learned, we have to be aware of how these dispositions interact with social environment to produce the observed sexual behavior.

When we do get around to doing prenatal hormone and behavior-genetic studies of sexual behavior on dimensions beyond sex preference, we will eventually identify genetic effects on many aspects of sex, some of which may work through prenatal hormone exposure. The important point is not that there are genetic or hormonal effects on human sexual behavior; we regard this as the inevitable outcome of the fact that sexual behavior is performed by biological organisms. What is important is that, although some of these effects emerge at adolescence, others are not apparent until midlife. We should not mistake the continuity of sexual behavior from adolescence to midlife as representing a causal relationship but rather as different expressions of the same underlying processes.

REFERENCES

Alder, E. M., A. Cook, D. Davidson, C. West, and J. Bancroft. 1986. Hormones, mood, and sexuality in lactating women. *British Journal of Psychiatry* 148:74–79.

Bakwin, H. 1973. The genetics of enuresis. In *Bladder control and enuresis,* ed. I. Kolvin, R. C. MacKeith, and S. R. Meadow, 73–77. London: Heinemann Medical.

Billy, J. O. G., and J. R. Udry. 1987. The influence of male and female best friends on adolescent sexual behavior. *Adolescence* 20:21–31.

Bonsall, R. W., D. Zumpe, and R. P. Michael. 1990. Comparisons of the nuclear uptake of [^{3}H]-testosterone and its metabolites by the brains of male and female macaque fetuses at 122 days of gestation. *Neuroendocrinology* 51:474–80.

Brown, W. A., P. M. Monti, and D. P. Corriveau. 1978. Serum testosterone and sexual activity and interest in men. *Archives of Sexual Behavior* 7:97–103.

Burger, H. G., J. Hailes, M. Menelaus, J. Nelson, B. Hudson, and N. Balazs. 1984. The management of persistent menopausal symptoms with oestradiol-testosterone implants: clinical, lipid, and hormonal results. *Maturitas* 6:351–58.

Burger, H. G., J. Hailes, J. Nelson, and M. Menelaus. 1987. Effect of combined implants of oestradiol and testosterone on libido in postmenopausal women. *Lancet* 284:936–37.

Clark, S. D., Jr., L. S. Zabin, and J. B. Hardy. 1984. Sex, contraception, and parenthood: Experience and attitudes of urban black young men. *Family Planning Perspectives* 16:77–82.

Crews, D. 1991. Trans-seasonal action of androgen in the control of spring courtship behavior in male red-sided garter snakes. *Proceedings of the National Academy of Sciences* 88:3545–48.

Crews, D., B. Camazine, M. Diamond, R. Mason, R. R. Tokrz, and W. R. Garstka. 1984. Hormonal independence of courtship behavior in the male garter snake. *Hormones and Behavior* 18:29–41.

Damon, A., S. T. Damon, R. B. Reed, and I. Valadian. 1969. Age at menarche of mothers and daughters, with a note on accuracy of recall. *Human Biology* 41:161–75.

Devaney, B. L., and K. S. Hubley. 1981. *The determinants of adolescent pregnancy and childbearing.* Final report to the National Institutes of Child Health and Human Development. Washington, D.C.: Mathematica Policy Research.

Dittmann, R. W., M. E. Kappes, and M. H. Kappes. 1991. Congenital adrenal hyperplasia (CAH) in females: Do prenatal hormones affect adolescent and adult sexual behavior and sexual orientation? Paper presented at the tenth World Congress for Sexology, Amsterdam, June.

Ehrhardt, A. A., and J. Money. 1967. Progestin-induced hermaphroditism: IQ and psychosexual identity in a study of ten girls. *Journal of Sex Research* 3:83–100.

Fergusson, D. M., L. J. Horwood, and F. T. Shannon. 1986. Factors related to the age of attainment of nocturnal bladder control: An 8-year longitudinal study. *Pediatrics* 78:884.

Finkel, M., and D. J. Finkel. 1975. Sexual and contraceptive knowledge, attitudes, and behavior of male adolescents. *Family Planning Perspectives* 7:256–60.

Forste, R. T., and T. B. Heaton. 1988. Initiation of sexual activity among female adolescents. *Youth and Society* 19:250–68.

Furstenberg, F. F., S. P. Morgan, K. A. Moore, and J. L. Peterson. 1987. Race differences in the timing of adolescent intercourse. *American Sociological Review* 52:511–18.

Hartmann, E. 1984. *The nightmare.* New York: Basic.

Hofferth, S. L. 1987. Factors affecting initiation of sexual behavior. In *Risking the future: Adolescent sexuality, pregnancy, and childbearing,* vol. 2, ed. S. L. Hofferth and C. D. Hayes, 7–35. Washington, D.C.: National Academy Press.

Hofferth, S. L., J. R. Kahn, and W. Baldwin. 1987. Premarital sexual activity among U.S. teenage women over the past three decades. *Family Planning Perspectives* 19:46–53.

Hogan, D., and E. Kitagawa. 1985. The impact of social status, family structure, and neighborhood on the fertility of black adolescents. *American Journal of Sociology* 90:825–55.

Inazu, J. K., and G. L. Fox. 1980. Maternal influence on the sexual behavior of teenage daughters. *Journal of Family Issues* 1:81–102.

Jessor, R., F. Costa, S. L. Jessor, and J. E. Donovan. 1983. Time of first intercourse: A prospective study. *Journal of Personality and Social Psychology* 44:608–26.

Kantner, J. F., and M. Zelnik. 1972. Sexual experience of young unmarried women in the United States. *Family Planning Perspectives* 4:9–18.

Kwan, M., W. J. Greenleaf, J. Mann, L. Crapo, and J. M. Davidson. 1983. The nature of androgen action on male sexuality: A combined laboratory and self-report study in hypogonadal men. *Journal of Clinical Endocrinology and Metabolism* 57:557–62.

LeVay, S. 1991. A difference in hypothalamic structure between heterosexual and homosexual men. *Science* 253:1034–37.

Martin, N. G., L. J. Eaves, and H. J. Eysenck. 1977. Genetical, environmental, and personality factors influencing the age of first sexual intercourse in twins. *Journal of Biosocial Science* 9:91–97.

McAnarney, E. R., and C. Schreider. 1984. *Identifying social and psychological antecedents of adolescent pregnancy.* New York: Grant Foundation.

Meikle, A. W., J. D. Stringham, D. T. Bishop, and D. W. West. 1988. Quantitating genetic and non-genetic factors influencing androgen production and clearance rates in men. *Journal of Clinical Endocrinology and Metabolism* 67:104–9.

Miller, B. C., and C. R. Bingham. 1989. Family configuration in relation to the sexual behavior of female adolescents. *Journal of Marriage and the Family* 51:499–506.

Miller, B. C., and K. Moore. 1990. Adolescent sexual behavior, pregnancy and parenting: Research through the 1980s. *Journal of Marriage and the Family* 52:1025–44.

Money, J., and A. A. Ehrhardt. 1972. *Man and woman, boy and girl: The differentiation and dimorphism of gender identity from conception to maturity.* Baltimore: Johns Hopkins Univ. Press.

Money, J., M. Schwartz, and V. G. Lewis. 1984. Adult erotosexual status and fetal hormonal masculinization and demasculinization: 46,XX congenital virilizing adrenal hyperplasia and 46,XY androgen-insensitivity syndrome compared. *Psychoneuroendocrinology* 9:405–14.

Morris, N. M., J. R. Udry, F. Khan-Dawood, and M. Y. Dawood. 1987. Marital sex frequency and midcycle female testosterone. *Archives of Sexual Behavior* 16:27–37.

Newcomer, S. F., and J. R. Udry. 1984. Mother's influence on the sexual behavior of their teenage children. *Journal of Marriage and the Family* 46:477–85.

O'Carroll, R., and J. Bancroft. 1984. Testosterone therapy for low sexual interest and erectile dysfunction in men: a controlled study. *British Journal of Psychiatry* 145:146–51.

Persky, H., H. I. Lief, D. Strauss, W. R. Miller, and C. P. O'Brien. 1978. Plasma testosterone level and sexual behavior of couples. *Archives of Sexual Behavior* 7:157–73.

Pomerantz, S. M., R. W. Goy, & M. M. Roy. 1986. Expression of male-typical sexual behavior in adult pseudohermaphroditic rhesus: Comparisons with normal males and neonatally gonadectomized males and females. *Hormones and Behavior* 20:483–500.

Pomerantz, S. M., M. M. Roy and R. W. Goy. 1988. Social and hormonal influences on behavior of adult male, female, and pseudohermaphroditic rhesus monkeys. *Hormones and Behavior* 22:219–30.

Reinisch, J. M. 1981. Prenatal exposure to synthetic progestins increases potential for aggression in humans. *Science* 211:1171–73.

Sherwin, B. B., and M. M. Gelfand. 1987. The role of androgen in the maintenance of sexual functioning in oophorectomized women. *Psychosomatic Medicine* 49:397–409.

Sherwin, B. B., M. M. Gelfand, and W. Brender. 1985. Androgen enhances sexual motivation in females: a prospective cross-over study of sex steroid administration in the surgical menopause. *Psychosomatic Medicine* 7:339–51.

Skakkebaek, N. E., J. Bancroft, D. W. Davidson, and P. Warner. 1981. Androgen replacement with oral testosterone undecanoate in hypogonadal men: A double-blind controlled study. *Clinical Endocrinology and Metabolism* 14:49–61.

Thornton, A., and D. Camburn. 1987. The influence of the family on premarital sexual attitude and behavior. *Demography* 24:323–40.

Udry, J. R., and J. O. G. Billy. 1987. Initiation of coitus in early adolescence. *American Sociological Review* 52:841–55.

Udry, J. R., J. O. G. Billy, N. M. Morris, T. Groff, and M. Raj. 1985. Serum androgenic hormones motivate sexual behavior in adolescent boys. *Fertility and Sterility* 43:90–94.

Udry, J. R., L. M. Talbert, and N. M. Morris. 1986. Biosocial foundations for adolescent female sexuality. *Demography* 23:217–30.

van den Berg, B. J., R. E. Christianson, and F. W. Oechsli. 1988. The California Child Health and Development Studies of the School of Public Health, University of California at Berkeley. *Pediatric and Perinatal Epidemiology* 2:265–82.

Zabin, L. S., E. A. Smith, M. B. Hirsch, and J. B. Shah. 1986. Ages of physical maturation and first intercourse in black teenage males and females. *Demography* 23:595–606.

Zelnik, M., J. F. Kantner, and K. Ford. 1981. *Sex and pregnancy in adolescence.* Beverly Hills, Calif.: Sage.

Changing Lives, Changing Genres: Teenage Girls' Narratives about Sex and Romance, 1978–1986

Sharon Thompson

Finally, stories are all that we come up with when we ask others questions, and these stories change over time. Although we can check the distance between fact and report, moment and biology, with statistical maneuvers, there's no sure way around this. We can mark the distance and go on, or we can attend to it, but it's always there—a sharp question slicing right through the social sciences and journalism, a mockery, a doubt, a possibility.

The most common solution—peppering everything with variations on the word *said*—is a reasonably good defense, but it does not begin to answer the question of what lies between report and reality. Retrospectively, psychoanalysis fills in the distortions of infancy and the family romance, transference and projection. A great deal of work has drawn liberally and often brilliantly on this approach, but there are other kinds of distortions in texts, and texts have more immediate purposes than those of interest to psychoanalysis.

In arguing for narratology and against psychoanalysis, Mikhail Bakhtin, an early twentieth-century Russian scholar who broadly limned the maze between genre and speech, experience and fabrication, observed that narrative analysis deals with consciousness and the other (what we can, at least, articulate and what is social) rather than repression of the id (what we cannot remember or collectivize) (Todorov 1984, 32). It is not an entirely fair observation. The unconscious is reasonably at issue in textual analysis; psychoanalysis deals bountifully with consciousness and leads to expression; a fictional other is often not an other at all; and there's room for both disciplines within scholarship; but, as a matter of emphasis, Bakhtin's remark holds.

Since Bakhtin, the term *narrative analysis* has come to include the very psychoanalytic practices he deplored, some new ones that focus entirely on what has *never* been said, and an increasingly popular variety of criticism that derogates texts (but not criticism) as unconscious ideology (Derrida 1980; Scott 1991, 279). In this paper, the term means something more practical and limited: treating testimony or texts (by which I mean virtually everything from inquiry and reports to fictions and criticism) in part as narrative forms with histories, strategies, structures, techniques, and purposes. This kind of narrative analysis may draw on psychoanalysis, but it puts appreciation before problematization and history before judgment, and embraces surveys and journalistic reports alike as collective stories told at certain times for particular reasons. The question is not, Is a particular story true? but, What's the tradition here? What have been its uses? Why now? What's the strategy? What questions and concerns does the story answer?

Testimony has at least two histories: that of the conditions that generate it and that of its own tradition—in effect, of its genre. (For my purposes here, it is sufficient to think of genre roughly in terms of standard garden-variety popular forms of long standing—mystery, melodrama, romantic comedy, electoral poll, and so forth.) Bakhtin proposed that the relation between narrative tradition and contemporary expression and experience is dialogical—part of a conversation between the past and the future. This expansive approach understands narrative traditions—genres like the mystery or the multiple-choice questionnaire—as parts of speech that color, even help to make, our experiences, perceptions, and understanding as we use and change them. In this vein, over the last decade or so, feminist critics have taken up the dialogue between gender and genre. The richest criticism has dealt with genres previously reviled for sentimentalism and eroticizing victimization—for example, melodrama—and with the relation between romance reading and becoming a woman. The bildungsroman (story of development) has proved harder to elaborate on, perhaps because there is a notable lack of persuasive female examples before the late twentieth century (Abel, Hirsch, and Langland 1983; Brownstein 1982; Burke [1941] 1957, 262; DuPlessis 1985; Modleski 1984; Snitow 1979; Spacks 1975).

Recently, Carolyn Heilbrun proposed that women's laughter is "the revealing sign, the spontaneous recognition of love and freedom," but the narrative tradition of that kind of radical laughter remains largely unreported (Heilbrun 1988, 129). Feminist critics who have begun to work on comedy have so far concentrated on the history of domestic and radical feminist comedy—both artifacts of single-sex society—and on women comics and cartoonists (Barreca 1991; Sochen 1991; Walker 1988). Linda Bamber's study of gender and genre in Shakespeare, *Comic Women, Tragic Men,* sets a standard in describing a relation between comedy and the conditions of female existence and suggests the productive tack of contrasting genres that I will take up here (Bamber 1982).

This paper reads teenage girls' accounts of sexual and romantic experience in the combined terms of feminist and genre analysis, as it moves back and forth between life and genre, romance, melodrama, and comedy. It draws on a 1978–86 narrative study of four hundred teenage girls' sexual, romantic, and reproductive histories in the wake of the series of legislative, juridical, and social changes that made it feasible to separate coitus from its usual coordinates—marriage and reproduction—and include it in adolescence.

One hundred and fifty interviews took place between 1978 and 1983, and another two hundred and fifty between 1983 and 1986. About a third of the first one hundred and fifty were puberty interviews, and just under half of those were done in groups. The 1983–86 interviews were all carried out with teenage girls over thirteen and under twenty. About ten took place in pairs; none in groups. Three-quarters of all the narrators had had sexual intercourse; about a quarter were teenage mothers. Ten percent identified themselves as lesbian; a few more had had sexual experiences with girls but did not identify as lesbian. Interviews took place in the Northeast, Midwest, and Southwest, mainly in large and midsize cities, although I also interviewed in a small agricultural center and two suburbs. About equal proportions of poor, working-class, and middle-class teenagers are represented, about 15 percent African-American, another 15 percent Puerto Rican, Cuban, or Chicana. I interviewed some girls several times.

Throughout, I relied on a snowball technique: Beginning with narrators met through friends, teachers, and counselors or by introducing myself in teenage hangouts (shopping malls, roller rinks, and pizza parlors, as well as social service settings), I went on to interview as many of their friends as possible. During the later period (1983–86), I actively looked for stories that represented racial, ethnic, and sexual minorities as well as uncommon sexual and romantic points of view.

By and large, girls enthusiastically referred a *few* of their friends. "You have to talk to her!" was a common refrain but only one or two made a project out of referral, and few crossed clique, class, sexual status, or race. No one who was not pregnant or a teenage mother referred a pregnant teenager or teenage mother. The racial gap in the referral chain was passed over in silence; clique and class gaps were articulated through the discourse of "other girls"—disapproving talk about girls who are "worse" in some way than the speaker. Although many narrators clearly had close acquaintanceships with the other girls who figured prominently in their narratives, they never gave an other a chance to air her presumably opposing view of good and bad femininity. I had to start a lot of snowballs in order to obtain a range of girls' opinions and experiences, but, the more I found difference, the more important it seemed and the more I sought it.

Adolescence is usually treated as one, or at most two, stories, distinguished by period, gender, race, class, and subculture. This study adds the dimensions of narrative and sex. In her study of twentieth-century women writers' literary strategies, critic Rachel DuPlessis observed that romantic conventions are tropes for the sex-gender system. (DuPlessis 1985, ix). Girls' narrations, and the increasing appreciation of difference, require multiplying this understanding, adding variation and progression, and reading other genres as tropes for systems that, in part, generate them (DuPlessis 1985, ix; Stack 1990). Toward that end, this study turns on a concept of the sex-gender variations—that is, different relations between such factors as puberty and reproduction, sex and love, gender and sexuality, love and monogamy, and age (Rubin 1975; Vance 1984). In full, the study divides girls' accounts according to sex-gender variations that ten or more girls described or assumed—and explores the extent to which these variations give rise to the genres that girls drew on to express and interpret their experience and to very different life courses. It also considers the histories and uses of the genres involved.

This chapter focuses on two variations, contrasting a collective story I heard most often from heterosexual teenage girls, a melodrama about staking everything on love and losing, with a group of heterosexual romantic comedies. It begins to show the usefulness for girls of maintaining a connection between preadolescent and adolescent perspectives while keeping a strategic distance from love, and it explores the play between genre and experience. The larger study includes lesbian and bisexual accounts in their own right and within several collective stories that also represent heterosexual experience and also gives an equal voice to other minority stories (Thompson 1986, 1987, 1990). Because I've written about the first story (melodrama) at length before, it is treated more cursorily than the second (romantic comedy) in this chapter (Thompson 1984). Names have been changed for confidentiality.

BROKEN-HEART STORIES: FROM ROMANCE TO MELODRAMA

Like the heroines of romance novels, the first group of narrators made their own virginity a pivot of their stories (Snitow 1979). They saw their virginity as a particularly rare attribute in their generation. In the recent past, they thought, most girls were virgins before marriage. Now most took intercourse lightly:

> See, the reason they can't really understand why a girl says no is because so many girls say yes. 'Cause where I live there are so many girls that just say, "Oh, sure, come on, let's go."

They, in contrast, said, Wait a minute. I want to be sure you care. Sooner or later they would "give in," they thought (many had given in by the time of the interview), but they wanted to wait until they were sure that first sex would be something "to feel good about." They wanted it to be special and they wanted it to bode well. Mainly white and working-class, they expected to work on and off during their lives—when they had to—but they did not foresee much meaning or richness to come from work. If they were going to have a good life, love was going to be a big part of it, and sex was the foundation of adult love, as they understood it. A first lover who "cared enough" and did not just "run out" foretold a daydream of esteem, caresses, and, later, two good incomes. They wished to avoid a callous lover who never called again—the frantic nightmare of single motherhood, low wages, and maternal sublimation that more and more women were waking up to, or a treadmill of bars, clubs, dating services, several-night stands—lovers who vanished with dawn's early light. There were more women than men, the magazines said. If you could not catch one early when you had the advantage not just of youth but of virginity, how would you ever catch one late in the game (Faludi 1991)?

Above all, these narrators said that they feared being dropped after first intercourse. They told dozens of stories illustrating this likelihood. Tracy, for example, worried about how she would take a loss she had seen a younger girl endure:

> I know a girl—fifteen years old . . . and she was seeing this guy for about six or seven months. She thought he was just seeing her and nobody else because they were supposedly going steady. But he was seeing all these girls behind her back, and she didn't even know it. She got pregnant and he left her. Fifteen years old. That's bad. . . . She's going to be hurt for a long time because she really fell in love with this guy. . . . I guess that's what I'm afraid of.

Seduced and abandoned—designed both to elicit pity for girls who give into male persuasion and to justify resistance, it's an old, old story in the annals of femininity. But Tracy's story also diverged from the standard. She did not imply, for example, as a nineteenth-century reformer or melodramatist probably would have, that the fifteen-year-old girl's life was over. She didn't think, as most 1950s teenage girls might have, that the two should have gotten married. Rather, the fifteen-year-old "was going to be hurt for a long time" because (1) she was so young when it all happened and (2) "she really fell in love with this guy." She had been ruined, that is, not by sex or pregnancy but by love in combination with youth. The damage was not to her hymen or her marital chances but to her sense of self. Her "ruin" was psychological, not physical or economic. She had been old enough for sex but underage for the emotional distress of acting on love, having intercourse, and getting dumped.

In romance novels, delay produces undying love but Tracy's first boyfriend got tired of waiting and stopped calling. Perhaps because she had retained her virginity—her chance to exchange innocence for love—she did not narrate minding that much, but she evidently took a lesson from the experience and "gave in" to her second important boyfriend before she lost him to someone who would.

Despite all the time she had spent worrying over whether to have sex, she said she "didn't use any birth control because it was a spontaneous thing"—a common account. She "hadn't expected it to happen." He was "gentle" with her, and "it was beautiful" because she "loved him so much," but it hurt. He didn't drop her *right* after first intercourse, but it wasn't long before he chafed at the bit. Tracy hinted that his interest may have waned because she avoided frequent intercourse, which she still did not enjoy, but she said he said that he wanted to go out with his friends more—to return to the party and the crowd. Ultimately he returned to the girl he had been with before he was with Tracy—a girl she derided for being "possessive—really kiss ass" and for doing "oral sex and stuff like that."

Tracy was devastated. When I interviewed her several months after the breakup, she had gained an enormous amount of weight, a fact she mentioned immediately. Her bleached hair was losing ground to shadowy roots, and she could not stop talking about what had happened to her:

> It's really had an effect on me. I've become very quiet. That
> is not me. I am not a quiet girl. I go to parties and I'll go

out. But I find that I can't talk to guys. I'll sit there and I
won't say a word. . . . I'll laugh with my friends a little
maybe. But I am not the same person. . . . That's only little
parts of it. I can't even begin to explain how I feel inside. I
almost killed myself over him.

This part of the experience, this misery, was what her whole account
had led up to—its point, what she wanted to warn other girls against.

These were not romances at all. They were melodramas.

There has been a tendency in historical work on melodrama to
blame the genre for the problem it represents: female victimization, unhappy endings, foreclosed possibilities. It is true that the genre is implicated historically in some egregious instances of political mystification.
In the nineteenth century, for example, social purity melodramas en-
abled the passage of highly repressive legislation (Gorham 1982; Walkowitz 1980). But melodramas are typically about women's trials and
sorrow, and some of the derogation of melodrama is misplaced and
misogynist. Although melodrama can be a narrative trap, it is also a
profoundly appropriate form—in fact, *the* genre—for telling certain
kinds of experiences, the traditional expressive form for accounts of
spoilage and awakening, for example, and for accounts of ruinous love.
Melodrama is also the form for the stories about thwarted fusions of
sex and love or meaning, and it is produced in the course of these attempts. To be melodramatic is to tell such a story as it is traditionally
told—expressively, dramatically.

These stories are often repressed or diminished, and melodrama is,
as Peter Brooks has called it, "a victory over repression." That further
explains their overblown quality (Brooks 1985, xii, 28–29, 32, 41). Finally, melodramas express profound inner disturbances about subjects
that have no general validity: I really needed him to love me. My life,
my hope, my sense of self depended on it. It was my only hope. Now I
don't have any hope at all. I can't stand school. I don't anticipate a great
career. What is going to make this life worth living?

Only love.

In the view of narrators like Tracy, the mistake was to have stopped
waiting and delaying, to have had sex before they were absolutely sure.
Now what they had to do was cancel out what had already happened
and start over. They did everything they could to reconstruct a world of
limits and permissions, taboos and guarantees, even to reconstruct the

body, and their accounts mainly ended with that staple of the genre of melodrama that these accounts honorably belong within: virtue restored (Brooks 1985, 32). Tracy, for example, decided that her first coitus really did not count because her boyfriend hardly got inside her. She went on to reconstruct her previously held declaration of sexual limits:

> No one's ever going to hurt me that way again and I'll make sure of it. I'm not saying I'll never be hurt again, but I'll try my hardest to avoid it. My idea right now is that I don't think I'm ever going to let a guy touch me again until I'm engaged or married. Until I'm sure that guy means it. I'm not saying that he's going to stay with me for the rest of his life, but until I'm sure that relationship means as much to him as it does to me and until I'm positively proven that it does, there's going to be no way that guy is going to lay a hand on me. That's my attitude right now and that's the way it's going to stay.

(But it didn't.) And another:

> I guess we had the right love at the wrong time. . . . I won't let no one else touch me. Never again. It's either Lenny or nobody.

What followed was a waiting period not for marriage but for desire or for a better boyfriend or for the renewal of a good reputation, but sooner or later second intercourse occurred. Often hearts were broken once more, and the whole process began again. For some, heartbreak became a pattern, a way of romantic life, but most gradually adjusted. As they did, virginity was no longer spoken about as a vulnerable protected condition; prudes became objects of contempt; contraception—an acceptable subject and practice. But momentum had been lost and there remained a residue of doubt and fear—a bad feeling about the self.

If the narrators above had it all to do over again, they would have done more of the same, they said—they would have waited longer before they had intercourse; they would have tested love harder. Had they spent the time they would have gained on learning, developing a sense of vocation, securing manifold social relations, rooting the sense of self in enterprises other than love, delay might have generated resources with which to decenter love. But were they to spend a long hiatus between puberty and love as they spent the time they *had* had, it would not have served them well. Although many teenage mothers narrated having spent all of childhood rehearsing their weddings and marriages, these narrators reported much wider preadolescent experience—having been tomboys, gotten A's, been committed to a talent. But thrilled at adolescence's well-advertised possibilities for fun and romance, they had given up almost every avocation of preadolescence just after puberty in order to concentrate first on beauty and then on the search for love. It was not that they needed to work so hard on beauty; they had it naturally, it seemed to me, but they had put everything they had into turning themselves into the blond bombshells whom they believed had the best chances at love.

The broken-heart narrators could not imagine another way to go at love. Theirs was the only love story they seemed to know, and in the first years of this study it was practically the only story I heard. As time passed, however, and I reached beyond my original largely white working-class sample, I heard an increasing number of alternative stories. Those with established preexisting traditions—substituting pregnancy for love, for example, or choosing someone other than a male peer as a sexual partner (another girl or a woman or a man)—I probably had not heard often before because I interviewed few top students or teenage mothers before 1983. But others represented teenage girls' increasing adroitness at handling the coitalization of adolescent sexuality—a development that shows up beyond the narratives in statistics showing teenage coital and pregnancy rates leveled off substantially during the period for girls over fifteen (Hofferth, Kahn, and Baldwin 1987). Here I want to present one such story, told by a small, remarkable group of narrators who took a strategic view of sex and gender. The sample is very small—eleven—although there are many more examples *within* other histories and from all the groups represented in this study. The narrators were literally the daughters of second-wave feminism: their mothers worked, exercised economic power within their families, and believed in gender equality. In this respect, like the heroines of the movies of the 1930s (whose invisible mothers were the feminists of the early twentieth century), these narrators came to equality as if to inherited wealth but denied the influence (Cavell 1981, 16).

Playing the Game of Love: From Romance to Comedy

> One tries, as far as possible, to develop a strategy whereby one can't lose.
>
> —Kenneth Burke

Conventionally, as Carol Gilligan observed, even upper-middle-class girls put preadolescent initiatives and skills behind them in the transition from childhood to adolescence. In the process, they lose moral clarity and academic force, as Gilligan complained (Gilligan 1990, 10). Her solution is to elongate preadolescence. A longer preadolescence would offer more time to develop identity in the context of friendship and play before entering the lists of love. But how would we construct it? Is it more feasible to delay puberty or separate it further from sexuality? Is either one a good idea?

Puberty has come earlier and earlier in recent years. We could, presumably, push it back by taking hormones out of the diets of the animals most girls eat and making marathon exercise programs compulsory, as op-ed pieces and letters to the editors of daily newspapers occasionally recommend. It sounds healthy enough but impractically dictatorial, and it is odd to encourage boys to strengthen and mature but girls to lighten up and extend their youth. (Why not retard boys' puberty? In most cases, they initiate intercourse, and they have the physical edge that gives them power.)

More seriously, girls whose exercise and diet regimens delay puberty—gymnasts, for example—lose an important chance to absorb calcium and build bone. As a result, they run an increased risk of fractures in the short run and osteoporosis in the long run. Besides, despite the long-standing belief that the hormonal fluctuations of puberty produce the problems of adolescence, there's no evidence that girls' sexuality is hormone driven. On the contrary, the evidence suggests that girls are so influenced by social factors that there's no observable synchrony between hormones and sexual initiation (Udry and Campbell, chap. 7, this vol.). If girls' sexuality is already a product of socialization rather than biology, would a simple change in the developmental schema—for example, extending preadolescence to sixteen or promoting latency on MTV as the coolest of all the life stages—not do the job? A longer preadolescence would further delay entry into the job market and adolescence is so much superstructure anyway, but there's little material reason for the young to accept such a change. Preadolescence is a colonial state. Adolescence, in contrast, is halfway to independence; and teenage sex—indeed, all the quasi-rebellions of adolescence—mainly takes place in the liberated zone: the automobile, the time between school letting out and dinner, Saturday night, the 7-Eleven parking lot. It would be quite a fight to take this all away.

In addition, like reinstituting separate schools for separate genders (a requirement, I would say, for rolling back adolescence), lengthening preadolescence would decrease the time that girls have to practice managing sex and gender. As I read teenage girls' situation, they need more practice not less. Ultimately, it is better, surely, to go through the blur of love and romance than to remain forever latent; it is far better to learn to balance love and work before one's livelihood and happiness depend on not dropping either ball. For all these reasons, it seems preferable to encourage girls to take preadolescent skills along into adolescence and into romance, adding love to the mix of life. Some of the narrators in this chapter described doing exactly that, and, as they told it, the approach transformed teen romance into a comedy.

Anja and Ginger were best friends, and they both related playing run-catch-kiss avidly in elementary school. Anja even narrated a girls' revolt in the face of a school directive to give the game up. In high school, Anja began to accumulate sexual and romantic experience earlier than Ginger, but neither had as much experience as they hoped for by junior year when the boys in their school started playing an invitational game of opposing pairs. The game was called "doubles killer." In the first round, each pair was assigned to shoot an opposing pair with a tracer gun—an inexpensive toy that shoots flat plastic disks 10–15 feet. If only one member of a pair was shot, that pair remained in the game next round. If both were shot, they were out.

Doubles killer was already in progress when the game's organizer, James, told Anja the boys were placing bets on fooling with girls. Her competitive spirit whet, she bet she would sleep with Sam before March. About the same time, she and Ginger talked James into letting them play doubles killer. At first the other boys were furious: "All the other guys got on James' case. 'Why did you let a couple of girls in? Girls aren't going to take it seriously. . . .' It was a men's club. And Ginger and I got really mad and we were like 'Well, we're going to show them. . . .'"

Now Anja and Ginger were in two games at once—killer and chase. First, she and Ginger went up against Artie and Sam. (Artie, whom Ginger had her eyes on, had a minor leg injury, which gave the girls a slight advantage.) The opening night of play, the boys let the air out of the girls' bicycle tires. Anja and Ginger responded by taking the rivets out of Artie's crutches. Later that night they waited for Sam to come home. He saw them first but expressed respect for their "great plan" and aggression. "And we were like, 'Cool, cool.'"

Similarly impressed with their seriousness, James gave them a chance at "wild-card spots" in the next round.

At first they played "really well," "like really aggressive," but, when Ginger got shot, Anja found herself playing a passive game to avoid also being shot. "I began to live my life by this game and like never go out of the house."

Meanwhile, her crush on Sam increased. To move things forward on that score, she turned her situation into no lose by making a bet on the outcome of the round: loser buys dinner:

> I was trying to play it up like I was really confident even though I was pretty sure I was going to lose because there was two of them and one of me. But everyone was telling me they were so stupid because it had been like a week, and they hadn't gotten me, and it was just me and two of them. They just looked so bad, you know—which was really fun. I had such a good time. . . . There was supposed to be a mixed doubles killer next, like boy-girl pairs, and everyone was asking me to be their partner. And I was like, 'Well— you know, I don't know. I'll have to think about it.' You know.

Getting "so sick of the game," Anja challenged Sam to a shoot-out. When he refused, she forced his hand by going out into the street. He came running after her. "I got behind a car and we shot, and so he got me. But it was honorable, you know, because I stayed in for a week and a half—just me against the two men."

She began negotiating over dinner. "So I said, 'Well, I don't think I should have to take Bart out for dinner. He didn't even get me.' And he said, 'Well, I don't know.'"

She won. She was nervous about dinner, but she managed to confirm with Bacallian suavity: "He recognized my voice. And he said, 'Sure, we're still going out.' So I said, 'Well, come over here.'"

She took him to a Mexican restaurant. "It was a very platonic evening." She "really didn't know what he was thinking" until the week when he claimed that her taking him out gave him the right to take her out. She agreed and they decided to watch the finals of "Jeopardy," during which she initiated petting: "And I said, Well, maybe he's just scared.

He's not sure if I want him, too. So I was being cute and like cuddling next to him. . . . Finally, I just sort of leaned over and when I leaned over, he kissed me. And then so we were, uh, there for a while."

In joining doubles killer, Anja and Ginger added gender difference to a homosocial game. Even as a mere claim, this is impressive. In addition, by joining a teenage boys' game, they found a way to bridge preadolescent and adolescent romantic experience and enter the arena of teen romance with preadolescent skills, especially boldness, initiative, and a sense of play. As with any other game, so with teen romance, these girls realized, it takes at least two to play. When Ginger was not as fast off the romantic mark as Anja, for example, she looked for someone she thought might also be looking for her. Tom came to mind. She liked him, and they had danced at parties, but he had never made a move. Ginger knew she could not override his passivity entirely on her own. She did confront him, though:

> And I'm saying how he drives me crazy because I don't know if he likes me and stuff like that. And he's just sitting there and he goes, "Yeah, well, ditto," he goes. And I go, "Ditto!?" And he's like, "Yeah, you know, same thing," like he had a crush on me last year and duhduhduhduh. That kind of thing. And I'm like, "You can't just say ditto, Tom. You have to tell me something back." And he's like, "No, I mean, I know what you're talking about. I get your drift." And I'm like, "Nonono, no no, you have to say it to me." And he won't tell me he likes me. He just can't say it. He said, "Ginger, you can say things like that to people. I can't say things like that to people." And I'm like, "You have to like give me a message or something." And he's like, "I can't do these things. I can't talk to girls like this. I can't. I'm not into it. That's why I don't ask out girls. I can't do this stuff," you know, so he keeps telling me, "I can't do it." And I'm like, "Tom, I can't do everything," you know.

Finally, he spoke up.

These narrators couched their sense of self and other in romantic experience differently than did the broken-heart narrators, positioning themselves as active, able, optimistic, romantic strategists rather than passive and anxious victims. In addition, they took themselves humorously, something the broken-heart narrators never did. Treating the self humorously is, of course, a tendency that can cut in a number of ways: self-deprecation is a standard variety of joke. It is funny; it vents humiliation and anger, and it is restorative to some extent, but in women's traditional humor it also often totally undercuts the teller's entitlement to pain or pleasure. The humorousness of these narrators derived, rather, from a sense of proportion and realism about identity and innocence. Like siblings in a large family, they did not disown or sublimate their first-person interests; but they did not totally isolate them, either. This lightened the load of expectations they brought to bear on the self and the future, and that, in turn, lightened everything.

They also treated the other differently. Broken-heart narrators treated the other mainly as a credential to be or means to an end (albeit love). Romantic strategists, in contrast, never acknowledged giving an other the power to affirm or destroy them, and they did not go in much for understanding. They had a sense of the bodies and characters with which they were dealing. They included graphic physical descriptions; they referred to topics of conversation—sports, politics, school, professional hopes. They had a comparative sense: "He's a little bit more confident, and he's fooled around with so many girls."

But although their perspective cut the other down to their size, it also kept his reality in view. Because they realized there was someone on the other side of their daydream, they were more likely to notice upfront when they were dealing with a louse or putting themselves in a position to be stepped all over: "He says, 'Uhm, I'm cleaning my house. You can come over and clean my house if you want.' I'm like, 'Okay.' I mean, I went all the way [there]. I mean it was like ridiculous."

At the same time, they recognized that as subjects—equals—they ran the risk of exploiting boys. This came through in statements like, "I feel badly about experimenting at someone else's expense" (from a narrator who had done just that).

The Meaning of Youth

Broken-heart narrators represented youth, like innocence, as their one chance. To romantic strategists, in contrast, youth and innocence represented a pleasure, a *bon chance* they were having the good fortune to enjoy. Youth also offered perspective, in their rendition of the life course. They might make a mistake today—go with the wrong guy, get dumped when they weren't quite ready. But there was always tomorrow—another day, another chance. This further lightened the weight romance had to bear. At the same time, they treated youth as a humorous situation that often generated funny—that is, awkward or comically original—trains of thought or experience, a Chaplinesque condition. If they were bumbly, they were nonetheless sympathetic characters to themselves, the objects of affectionate delight rather than the butts of ridicule.

From Friendship to Love

Friendship was described as primary in this group of histories—a first cause, the beginning, a condition that made romance feasible and kept it light and comedic. Anja and Ginger were partners in the game of chase. Stacey told of an affair her friend Gigi helped her begin. Stacey's family had just moved to a new city. Before that she lived in towns with very small African-American populations. Summers she spent in the rural south on her grandparents' farm. There she had African-American friends, but in the cities where her parents were employed, most of her friends were white. The new town had a substantial African-American middle class, but African-American and white high school students did not mix much. It took Stacey a while—and a lot of help from Gigi "the first person I ever met"—to reorient.

Broken-heart narrators portrayed friends as dividers, regulators, and warners. Groups of friends made and repeated the rules of good girlship according to which all the members of the clique were both better and more vulnerable: special, sensitive, living examples of what girls should be. They stigmatized girls who did not follow the rules. They warned each other to be careful: not to give it up to just anyone, not to get hurt. Their first job was to keep each other from making a variety of mistakes—from going too far to picking the wrong guy to wearing the wrong style. Their second job was to commiserate when, after all, things went wrong: to build their friends' courage, resolve, and sense of self back up again.

The narrators of these romantic comedies, in contrast, talked a lot about each other but little about their differences from other girls or the difference between the good kind of girl and the bad. They represented friends as partners in the game of love. Instead of warning each other off, these friends evidently egged each other on. Stacey, on the subject of Gigi, says, "She's a fun outgoing type person. And so I was like 'cool.' And that day she asked me, Did I want to go to lunch? So I went to lunch with her. And Arthur—we met up with Arthur in the hall. I was like, 'Oh, he's so cute,' you know, and everything."

Gigi introduced Stacey to Arthur and asked him to come along with them to MacDonald's. "And I was like, 'Oh, god, why did you ask him that,' you know? And he was like, 'Yeah, sure.'"

She and Gigi plotted bedding Arthur as conspiratorially as Anja and Ginger played doubles killer. They started with contraception. Gigi accompanied Stacey to Planned Parenthood. "She told me, 'You should always be safe' because she is—Gigi is just the most crazy person and she talks about everything and nothing is taboo for her, you know. She'll just pop right out of the clear blue sky, 'So are you on the pill?'"

Once on the pill, with Gigi for moral support, Stacey was ready to make a sexual move. She went to Arthur's house one afternoon when his parents were not home. He was "nervous." She was forthright. He asked whether she wanted to watch TV:

> And I was like, "No, I want you to show me your bedroom."
> And he was like, "You want me to what?" And I said, "Well,
> you never gave me a tour of your whole house." . . . So he
> finally took me upstairs . . . and he was like, "Well, this is
> my room, you know, look at it." And I was like, "Well, aren't
> we gonna go in?" And he said, "Well, no, there's no reason,
> you know, to go in." And I was like, "Child, you know,
> what's the matter with you? Don't you—?" And he's like,
> you know, "I guess," and everything. And then he was so
> shy. . . .

For Stacey, the feeling of knowing much more than he did about sex was as erotic as age difference was to those who narrated volitional affairs with men.

Romantic Tactics

Even narrators who represented themselves almost totally as passive victims revealed a strategic component to their romantic thinking. Tracy, for example, pondered long and hard about how to get her boyfriend "wrapped" before she committed herself to sex, but she relied on an unrealistic notion of love itself as a lasso that would give her control of his attention once she got it around his neck. Romantic strategists had a very different sense of romantic power, realizing that even the most tender or committed gender relations include power differentials. They admitted a degree of cool calculation in romantic encounters that never came out in the true-love narratives: "I was playing with him a little bit." "It was a little bit of a power play."

When they played with the masculine ego or entered the more seri-ous game of romance, they played to win. For them being a competitor rather than a victim was represented as exciting, and they described knowing exactly what they were doing: "That was my tactic and it hap-pened to work."

The practice of noting exactly what was happening moment by mo-ment in the course of each romantic exchange continued as they ap-proached narrating coitus itself, and this practice seemed to keep them on the realistic side of romantic planning. Although broken-heart nar-rators narrated spending thousands of hours planning for the first sex, they forgot contraception, caught up instead in the problem of exchang-ing sex for love. Romantic strategists, in contrast, put contraception just under desire (which never came up in the broken-heart narratives) at the top of a list of coital preconditions: Anja, for example, refused to sleep with the first boy she was sexually moved by because he seemed oblivious to the risk she would run. She was more certain from the start that she would sleep with her next boyfriend. When he, too, seemed oblivious, she put him off without saying anything. At length, he asked her straight out whether she wanted to sleep with him. She shrugged, "Aren't you forgetting something?" He did not ask what she meant, and he did not mention contraception the next time they got together. He just tried making moves. She turned him down flat again. On their next encounter, he showed that he had gotten the hint:

> So then there was a party . . . after like an achievement test. So we went to the party and—
>
> Q: Oh my god, in the midst of all this you were taking an achievement test?
>
> A: Yeah, well, this was junior year, so we had a lot of work to do. Yeah.

She and a few friends had access to an empty apartment for a week-end. This time Monty gave her notice he had gotten the picture. "So, uh, Monty said to me, 'You know, we're stopping at a drug store on the way down.' And I was like, Oh. Monty was pretty macho but I really thought it was very cute. So I was like, 'Okay.'"

Sex and Strategy

Seeming to draw a parallel between the hymen and the mind, broken-heart narrators posited first sex as a major trauma that left girls tender and vulnerable to romantic injury. If they did not get caring love (nursing?) from their first lovers, they would never get over it. Romantic strategists represented first coitus very differently. Instead of making an issue out of first sex, they treated it as ordinary, every day—one of many experiences. Anja listed her postcoital feelings as if she were going to score the experience at the end. She felt "good" because (1) "I liked Monty. I did like him a lot" (this answer took a common old-fashioned girl response, "I felt good because I loved him," down a peg but it came to basically the same thing. She was only beginning her response, however); (2) "I was very attracted to him"; (3) "I was like it was another thing I could get out of the way"; and (4) "It felt like the right time." For all these reasons, she concluded that it was "fun." As if to emphasize the relative unimportance of the event, she and Monty went out to get Chinese food afterward. Later when Monty referred cryptically to "last night," she rose to the occasion with comic panache:

> I said, "What are you talking about? Last night. I don't re-
> member anything about last night." And he was like, "Very
> funny." And I was like, "Really. I remember like we smoked
> a little bit and walked toward the master bedroom and then
> everything's a blur. I just can't remember anything else."
> And he said, "Very funny." And I said, "What did we do
> last night, Monty?" And he said, "We had incredible sex last
> night." And I said, "Oh, really?" I said, "I remember sex,
> now that you mention it. I don't remember anything in-
> credible. But I remember sex."

She was only being honest, she protested when I laughed. The sex had not been much that time but the next time, she said, she "really began to enjoy it."

After You

Nevertheless, soon, they began to argue. Anja did not describe this as Tracy had, as all *his* doing. Rather, she said, it was *their* doing. They just did not get along that well. She might have held on for longer but suddenly she felt "he was going to say, 'Let's break up.'" Instead of fighting off a break up or descending into self-pity, she thought it over: "And I sort of felt like, Oh no, because I felt really bad because I really did like him. But then I said, He's right, he's right, he's right." When he did not say it, she called him to beat him to the punch. He said he was about to call her to say the same thing.

In the wake of a break up, broken-heart narrators blamed their lovers for everything. If they could not have love, they insisted on innocence—goodness, victimhood. Anja, in contrast, construed taking blame as taking power. When Monty tried it, she responded with fury, explaining that his formulation—she was wonderful, he was a louse—implied that even though she had been wonderful, he had the power to dismiss her. The arbitrary nature of his desire was frightening and so was his assumption of power. "I was like, Great! You know, here, I've been wonderful. That leaves me like with nothing. It leaves me feeling like I just tried and tried and I just couldn't get—you know, it sort of made me feel like no matter how hard I tried, I wasn't good enough, and sort of like he had all the power."

She did not let on that she felt that way. She did not complain or implore him to see her. She took it like an equal. That was it then—the end. They did not talk for the rest of the summer. The relationship had failed; they had gotten sick of each other; she had not maintained the balance of power. Looking for a point of view that fit her image of herself and made acceptable sense of what had transpired, she concluded it was "an experience, you know, and it was important to have." Time helped, and so did the fact that she had not let her studies, friendships, or other interests fall by the wayside at puberty or when she and Monty got involved. When school started, it had all "sort of faded" and her feelings toward him resolved into a vague friendliness.

Like Anja, all the romantic strategists consciously refused melodrama at the end of their relationships, taking instead a narrative perspective that salvaged their pride and their ability to look forward to the next romance. "At that point, it was a lot easier to decide that I hated him than that I hated most men, so I decided the guy was a real schmo. Well, interesting experience."

This was possible partly because they had kept their eyes open all along. Talking with each other and to themselves, they had consistently recognized the risk of romantic loss. Acting on serial expectations really helped, they said. "I have this opinion, too. . . . You can't get over somebody until there's somebody that gets it over." A few like Anja went on to indulge in a few acts of revenge that twisted gender conventions. When one guy started pestering her in the wake of a petting party interlude, for example, she confronted him with her right to kiss and forget: "I said, 'I just want you to know that I don't owe you anything.' And he said, 'I know, I know.' And I said, 'Well, I just get the feeling that you think I do.' And he said, 'No, no, no. Forget it.'" She took some satisfaction in these small gender twists for a while, but ultimately romantic inclinations tempered bitterness, and she decided to wait—not, like the broken-heart narrators, for a good bet, but until she was really interested in someone before she tried sex or romance again. If she had begun with the sense that love was a game, she ended with a heightened sense of the difficulty of sex and romance and a sharpened commitment to equality.

It is a mistake to read the romantic strategists as wholly lacking not only *caritas* but *eros*. Theirs are the adolescent stories of girls with no expectation of having to depend on love for the meaning of adult lives for years to come. Unlike the broken-heart narrators, they did not anticipate settling down—making a home, for example—for a very long time. Rather they would spend well over a decade getting an education and developing vocations beyond marriage and family. Yet if they did not have the broken-heart narrators' desperate need for love, they had a zest for it, and there is no textual reason to believe that their insistence on maintaining a balance in erotic power would not lead, finally, to passion and care. In fact, it is possible to read them as more interested in love and more caring than the broken-heart narrators by interpreting their coolness and calculation as we read Tracy's delays—as defenses against being fools for love and ways to get a bead on whom they were dealing with: what was this boy, what were boys like? and to find lovers worthy of their attention. These objectives are very different from the broken-heart narrators' quest for recognition and safety, but they reach nonetheless for love.

Romances for Living

As long as it remains possible to separate sex from reproduction and to balance an interest in love with other intrigues and ambitions, we can expect teenage romance to shift increasingly from tragedy and melodrama to comedy as teenage girls become more savvy about power, gender, and the mechanics of sex and reproduction, more able to reasonably construct themselves as subjects—in short, more equal.

Unfortunately, at present the factors that incline teenage girls toward romantic comedy instead of tragedy or melodrama—high economic and vocational expectations, access to confidential reproductive services and information, even sexual optimism—are in jeopardy. While the battle goes on, so will teenage lives, and it may be important to approach adolescence from angles other than sexuality and reproduction. These histories suggest that work on the intersection between preadolescence and adolescence might be as productive as Gilligan has previously suggested (Gilligan 1990).

At the same time, the histories are a reminder of how important the popular culture of romance is to the construction of adolescence for girls. The parallels between these histories and the literature of romance suggests that working on that literature (novels, films, and teenage periodicals) is one feasible way to strengthen teenage girls' hand. This isn't a new idea. In the 1970s, writers like Judy Blume, Andrea Eagan, and Norma Klein directly addressed teenage girls' sexual and romantic concerns with novels and advice books that dealt forthrightly and strategically with the facts of young lives, importing realism into the marketplace of teenage romances and young adult novels generally. It was a brilliant and essential move, but, under attack from the fundamentalist right wing, realistic young adult novels have been increasingly dropped from school library and reading lists. Teenage romance novels, in contrast, have been liberally distributed and promoted in public schools as if they contained essential life lessons, particularly to girls with low reading skills. As a result, industrywide sales approached twenty million dollars in the 1980s and the current editor of *BP Report* guesstimated that they reached sixty to seventy million dollars by mid-1992 (Million 1992; "Teen Romance" 1983).

It is worth asking, then, What is in this stuff? What does it teach? A study by Linda K. Christian-Smith indicates that in the 1980s young adult publishing enterprises transposed the Harlequin Romance formula to teenage novels. Even Scholastic Books, which distributes through schools, developed a romance line, the Wildfire series. These romances construct female adolescence as a personal, heterosexual "transforming experience" that gives "meaning to girls' lives," endowing girls "with prestige and importance" through their subordination to males (Christian-Smith 1988, 81). The books are filled with experiences that were notably absent in accounts like Tracy's—kisses, embraces, tenderness—and their heroines succeed where so many teenage girls fail. They get caring and recognition from first love. This is probably enough to explain their popularity, but feminist critics offer some provocative additional explanations. In explaining the female compulsion to read romances, Ann Snitow, for example, has described the genre as "pornography for women" (Snitow 1979). Tania Modleski observed that most romances narrate girls' giving up identification with the male in favor of erotic attachment, "via a regression to an infantile fantasy." An aspect of the narrative pleasure women enjoy from reading romances, Modleski suggests, is a "revenge fantasy" in which erotic passion brings men to their knees before women (Modleski 1984, 45). Extending Modleski's train of thought, the fantasy of the groveling lover may entice girls to give up their identification with masculinity and lose their best chance at equality in a world in which femininity entails subordination.

In the literature on romance as in that of psychoanalysis and the broken-heart narratives themselves, there is a compulsory quality to this script. It's been hard to imagine a way out—a path toward a heterosexual erotic adulthood that does not require giving up identification with power. For this reason, many feminist critics have recommended expunging romance altogether (or at least heterosexual romance). It is a pipe dream, and just as well. In working through hostility and contextualizing desire, romance does a job that probably does not become unnecessary with the millenium of gender equality. The romantic strategists' accounts suggest a credible alternative that at once decenters romance and makes perhaps the best of it in making it a comedy. The accounts did not accept masculine dominance at all. The narrators appeared neither passive nor subordinate. They displayed initiative in every sphere, including sex, romance, and friendship, and they were as responsible as they were strategic. They decentered not only romance but everything; every interest and impulse had a counterpoise. They thought about birth control in the heat of desire, crammed for tests and fulfilled all their academic responsibilities in the midst of romantic negotiations, held onto a sense of self at the nadir of romantic loss. At the same time, they remained deliciously romantic and underneath their romantic strategies lay a fine ideal: a model in which affection, recognition, and equality, not blind neediness and desperation, would generate the centripal force of love. They were not there yet, and they could not do it alone, but they were not ruined by love, either.

Why should not the novelists of teenage romance pass the experience of romantic strategists on as "equipment for living," as literary critic Kenneth Burke called the genres? A genre cannot change the material conditions of existence. A comic view, for example, does not eliminate tragedy; it simply adds another excruciating twist. But genres can, as feminist critic Elizabeth Bruss observed, help "to define what is possible" (Bruss 1976, 7). If the teenage romances of the 1950s could reasonably point high school girls away from the job market and toward the altar, those of the 1990s can surely define other possibilities for balancing love, work, and sociability through late adolescence and young adulthood. The romantic comedies above suggest one approach. If they are only stories, at least they are about equality, love, and freedom, rather than misery, subordination, and obsession, and they are stories that girls are already telling. Spreading them is one way to make them come true.

References

Abel, E., M. Hirsch, and E. Langland. 1983. *The voyage in: Fictions of female development.* Hanover, N.H., and London: Dartmouth College, Univ. Press of New England.

Bamber, L. 1982. *Comic women, tragic men: A study of gender and genre in Shakespeare.* Stanford, Calif.: Stanford Univ. Press.

Barreca, R. 1991. *They used to call me Snow White . . . but I drifted: Women's strategic use of humor.* New York and London: Viking, Penguin.

Brooks, P. 1985. *The melodramatic imagination: Balzac, Henry James, melodrama, and the mode of excess.* New York: Columbia Univ. Press.

Brownstein, R. 1982. *Becoming a heroine: Reading about women in novels.* New York: Viking.

Bruss, E. 1976. *Autobiographical acts.* Baltimore: Johns Hopkins Univ. Press.

Burke, K. [1941] 1957. *Philosophy of literary forms.* New York: Vintage, Random House.

Cavell, S. 1981. *Pursuits of happiness: The Hollywood comedy of remarriage.* Cambridge, Mass., and London: Harvard Univ. Press.

Christian-Smith, L. 1988. Romancing the girl: Adolescent romance novels and the construction of femininity. In *Becoming feminine,* ed. L. G. Roman, L. K. Christian-Smith, and E. Ellsworth. Philadelphia: Falmer.

Derrida, J. 1987. *The post card: From Socrates to Freud and beyond,* trans. Alan Bass. Chicago: Univ. of Chicago Press.

DuPlessis, R. 1985. *Writing beyond the ending: Narrative strategies of twentieth-century women writers.* Bloomington: Indiana Univ. Press.

Faludi, S. 1991. *Backlash.* New York: Crown.

Gilligan, C. 1990. Preface to *Making connections: The relational worlds of adolescent girls at the Emma Willard School,* ed. C. Gilligan, N. P. Lyons, and T. J. Hanmer, 6–29. Cambridge, Mass., and London: Harvard Univ. Press.

Gorham, D. 1982. *The Victorian girl and the feminine ideal.* Bloomington: Indiana Univ. Press.

Heilbrun, C. G. 1988. *Writing a woman's life.* New York and London: Norton.

Hofferth, S. L., J. R. Kahn, and W. Baldwin. 1987. Premarital sexual activity among U.S. teenage women over the past three decades. *Family Planning Perspectives* 19:46–53.

Million, Jim. 1992. Private conversation, February.

Modleski, T. 1984. *Loving with a vengeance: Mass-produced fantasies for women.* New York and London: Methuen.

Rubin, G. 1975. The traffic in women. In *Toward an Anthropology of women,* ed. R. Reiter, 157–210. New York: Monthly Review Press.

Scott, J. 1991. The evidence of experience. *Critical Inquiry* 17:773–97.

Snitow, A. 1979. Mass market romance: Pornography for women is different. *Radical History Review* 20:141–61. Republished in A. Snitow, C. Stansell, and S. Thompson, eds. *Powers of desire: The politics of sexuality,* 245–63. New York: Monthly Review Press.

Sochen, J., ed. 1991. *Women's comic visions.* Detroit: Wayne State Univ. Press.

Spacks, P. M. 1975. *The female imagination.* New York: Avon.

Stack, C. 1990. Different voices, different visions: Gender, culture, and moral reasoning. In *Uncertain terms,* ed. F. Ginsburg and A. L. Tsing, Boston: Beacon.

Teen romance market estimated at $15-$20 million. 1983. *BP Report.* 2 May, 1, 6–7.

Thompson, S. 1984. Search for tomorrow: On feminism and the reconstruction of teen romance. In *Pleasure and danger,* ed. C. S. Vance, 360–84. Boston: Routledge & Kegan Paul.

———. 1986. Pregnant on purpose: Choosing teen motherhood. *Village Voice,* 23 December, 1, 31–34, 36–37.

———. S. 1987. Now you see her, now you don't: The lesbian teenage mother. In *Homosexuality, which homosexuality? Current Issues.* Conference Papers, International Scientific Conference on Gay and Lesbian Studies. Amsterdam: Free Univ.

———. 1990. Drastic entertainments. In *Uncertain terms,* ed. F. Ginsburg and A. L. Tsing, 269–81. Boston: Beacon.

Todorov, T. 1984. *Mikhail Bakhtin: The dialogical principle,* trans. Wlad Godzich. Minneapolis: Univ. of Minnesota Press.

Vance, Carole S. 1984. *Pleasure and danger: Exploring female sexuality.* Boston: Routledge & Kegan Paul.

Walker, N. 1988. *A very serious thing: Women's humor and American culture.* Minneapolis: Univ. of Minnesota Press.

Walkowitz, J. R. 1980. *Prostitution and Victorian society: Women, class, and the state.* Cambridge: Cambridge Univ. Press.

Sexuality, Marriage, and Well-Being: The Middle Years

John N. Edwards and Alan Booth

Cultures vary enormously in the emphasis given to the expressive nature of the conjugal relationship. For societies in which expressiveness has preeminence over the instrumental aspects of marriage, sexual expression is the sine qua non of intimacy. Compared to other societies, American society represents an extreme case of the extent to which the expressive character of marriage is emphasized and to which sexuality is seen as the wellspring of intimacy and well-being.

As a sign of this emphasis, perhaps in no other place in the world do we find the acceptance and enthusiasm for marrying for love as we do in the United States. When people are in love, they think they should marry (Simpson, Campbell, and Bercheid 1986). Even in spite of recent demographic indications of the deferral of marriage (Bumpass 1990), there continues to be strong evidence that unmarrieds seek highly expressive relationships. Sexuality in such circumstances and as the sine qua non of close relationships is not only permissible; it is obligatory.

Our interest here is to provide a broad overview of the connection between sexual expression and various indicators of the well-being of married people in the middle years of life. We first sketch a historical background to serve as a baseline from which we can assess change, for those individuals who are currently in their middle years (thirty-five to sixty years old) have been exposed to very different sexual climates that might affect their sexual expressions. Second, we assess existing research literature on the connection between different dimensions of sex and the well-being experienced by married couples. Various interpretations of this interrelationship are evaluated, including the role played by sociological factors versus those of a biological nature. As a final step, we consider the extramarital component of sexuality in the middle years and attempt to weigh its effects on the well-being of those individuals who are sexually active outside of their marriages.

We must recognize at the outset that, in general, studies of marital

We thank Laurie Janajreh for research assistance.

sexuality suffer from several generic problems: (1) the sampling frames used (self-selection or nonrandom samples, small size, undersampling of minorities); (2) cross-sectional designs; (3) a limited focus (frequency of intercourse or orgasm, ignoring of other forms of sexual expression and outlets); (4) measurement deficiencies (limited indicators of well-being, single-item indicators, global indicators); and (5) a lack of controls for theoretically significant variables (health, psychosocial problems, alcohol and drug use, presence of children, etc.). Especially surveys based on magazine readership may contain unintentional biases. Compared to the number of studies on the young—or the elderly, for that matter—we have only a modest storehouse of knowledge on the sexuality of married people in the middle years and obviously flawed knowledge at that. We have confined our review to the better-designed studies, although they, too, are not immune to some of the forementioned problems.

A Brief Historical Panorama

As a backdrop for historical comparison, Kinsey's findings (Kinsey, Pomeroy, and Martin 1948; Kinsey et al. 1953) provide us with a baseline of the sexuality of the parents and grandparents of those now in the middle years. In looking at the findings in relation to marital duration, Kinsey and his associates found that the incidences and frequencies of marital coitus reached their peaks in the first or second years of marriage. From that juncture, they noted, "There is no other type of sexuality activity . . . which shows such a steady decline with advancing age" (Kinsey et al. 1953, 348). Particularly after the mid-thirties, active incidence began to decline. The decline reported by married men was less steep than that for females. The reported figures were very comparable to those in still earlier studies (Terman et al. 1938).

Kinsey observed, however, that there was considerable individual variation in coital frequency, which he attributed to the difference in the interests and capabilities of individuals and their spouses (Kinsey et al. 1953, 350). In all age groups, the maximum frequencies extended substantially beyond the median and modal values, with some individuals reporting having intercourse twenty or more times per week; others reported near zero. Even so, in comparing different age groups, Kinsey found that maximum frequencies steadily declined with age.

In the four decades of birth represented in the female sample, Kinsey (Kinsey et al. 1953) observed a steady but distinct increase in the number and incidence of orgasms among married women. This, he concluded, was largely the result of changing attitudes about sex and a greater openness in discussing it. Kinsey further indicated, "While orgasm is not the final test of the effectiveness of a sexual relationship, and while there may be considerable significance and satisfaction in coital relationships which do not lead to orgasm, the female's failure to respond to orgasm in her sexual relationships is, nonetheless, one of the most frequent sources of dissatisfaction in marriage, and it is not infrequently the source of other types of conflict which may lead to the dissolution of a marriage" (Kinsey et al. 1953, 358).

As another facet of sexuality, the accumulative incidence of extramarital experience for females, Kinsey found, was 26 percent, almost half that for married men (50 percent). This incidence peaked at about the age of forty but persisted in accumulating up to age 60 (Kinsey et al. 1953). The active incidence of extramarital coitus, of course, was considerably lower, the highest being for those in their thirties. After the early forties, the rate fell off. Average coital frequency in extramarital relationships followed a similar pattern, reaching a maximum for women in their late thirties and early forties. But as Kinsey pointed out, his data suggest that there are few sexual activities that are more sporadic than extramarital intercourse, and average frequencies, therefore, may be misleading (Kinsey et al. 1953, 420). Once more, a great deal of individual variation was noted.

Interestingly, Kinsey and his colleagues found that the rates of orgasm as a proportion of total contacts were higher in extramarital relationships than in marriage. The majority of women (81 percent), they further indicate, had had five or fewer partners, half that majority having confined their experience to one partner. The largest percentage had limited their extramarital experience to a single year or less, but about one-third had four or more years of experience, including some who sustained relationships for more than ten years and, in a few cases, for more than twenty years.

Consistent with the higher accumulative incidence of extramarital coitus among married men, Kinsey observed that they had a higher active incidence (Kinsey, Pomeroy, and Martin 1948). As with married women, active incidence declined with age, actually peaking among men under twenty. Among men in the middle years, extramarital coitus constituted a smaller percentage of their total sexual outlet than it did among married women. The discrepancies between male and female maxima in sexual incidences and frequencies led Kinsey and his colleagues to the conclusion that the peak of sexual responsiveness occurs for males in late adolescence or the early twenties, subsequently declining into old age. For women, on the other hand, sexual responsiveness does not reach its maximum until the late twenties or even until the thirties, and it generally remains on a plateau for most of their lives. These patterns, Kinsey suggested, cannot be explained by anatomical differences or the physiology of sexual responses (Kinsey et al. 1953, 759–60). Nor can they be attributed to different capacities aroused by psychosexual stimuli. Many—but not all—of the differences between the levels of sexual responsiveness, Kinsey believed, derived from various hormones and their effects on physiologic activities, an issue we will later address.

Against this backdrop, it should be recognized that our population of concern here—those now in the middle years of the life course (thirty-five to sixty years old)—are representatives of very different cohorts. The oldest among them came to adolescence in the post–World War II era, the youngest in the heyday of the reputed sexual revolution. Normatively, the middle-aged have witnessed significant upheavals, distancing the youngest among them from their parents and grandparents in terms of sexual norms, if not actual behavior. To more precisely assess the bearing of sexuality on the well-being of marrieds now in their middle years, it is important to note the changes and timing of alterations in sexual norms and practices. This is predicated, of course, on the assumption that past is prologue, an assumption not unfounded in the case of sexuality but one that we later qualify.

The eldest cohort came to adolescence in the post–World War II era, a time of still conservative sexual norms. The median age at marriage was twenty for women, twenty-three for men (U.S. Bureau of the Census 1985). As parents of the later baby boomers, their total fertility rate was twice that of the younger cohort now in the middle years, whose fertility hovers around replacement level. In terms of the life course, the younger cohort was more apt to delay marriage, especially the women. Cohabitation prior to marriage was a much more common experience for the younger than the older members of those middle-aged (Spanier 1986), their numbers having quadrupled since 1960. Not only has the younger cohort reduced the number of children they have per family; they have also been more prone to remain childless altogether. A higher proportion of younger wives are in the paid labor force. The one glaring commonality of all those currently in the middle years is their experience with divorce, either as a participant in the process or as a child of divorced parents.

Although the older of the middle-aged came to maturity in a still sexually conservative period, the younger among them took part in a reshaping of sexuality of major proportions. Dating from the late 1950s and early 1960s, premarital sexual codes were radically revised. An era of permissiveness of unprecedented proportions was ushered in (Kantner and Zelnik 1972). More unmarrieds were having sexual intercourse, doing so with greater frequency, and starting at younger ages (Udry, Baumann, and Morris 1975). Accordingly, those in the younger ranges of the middle years entered marriage with considerably more sexual experience, leading us to believe there may be significant differences in their marital sexuality and their levels of well-being, an issue on which we later comment.

Sexuality and Well-Being

How does marital sexuality affect marital satisfaction and other indicators of well-being? Although the question is simple and straightforward, the answer is not so. In their pioneering study of marital relationships, Terman and his collaborators (Terman et al. 1938) found no relation between the frequency of marital intercourse and reported happiness with marriage. An association was noted, however, between marital happiness and a close correspondence in the desired and actual frequency of intercourse. Individuals indicating that their actual frequency of coitus coincided with their preferred frequency reported having happier marriages. In short, the findings of Terman and his collaborators suggest that there is no necessary, nor any linear, relation involving coital frequency and at least one indicator of well-being—marital happiness in this case.

Further complications of the relationship between marital sexuality and well-being emerge from the findings of more recent studies. One investigation reports, for example, the absence of any correlations between sexual activity, the number of arguments a couple has, and reported marital happiness, the former expected to be positively related to happiness and the latter to be negatively associated (Howard and Dawes 1976). Instead, what was found was that marital happiness was a function of the combination of sexual activity and arguments. People who argued frequently tended to have sex frequently. But what was crucial was the relative balance in (the presumably more positive) sexual activity and (the more negative aspect) of marital disagreements. Those with a positive balance perceived their marriages to be happier. These findings are consistent, of course, with exchange and equity theory, which posit that positive outcomes lead to felt satisfaction (Adams 1965; Messick and Cook 1983; Michaels, Acock, and Edwards 1986).

Another study on sex and marital satisfaction looked at two groups of married couples, one group happily married and the other unhappily so (Birchler and Webb 1977). The central finding of this study was that happily married couples had a higher frequency of sexual interaction than the unhappy couples, a finding that appears to apply across the life course. Happy couples, it also was observed, reported more joint participation in leisure-time activities, suggesting that the expression of sexuality may simply be one aspect of a larger complex of activities in which the degree of togetherness is manifested. This is indirectly corroborated by an earlier analysis of ours (Edwards and Booth 1976) in which we found that, even among relatively young married individuals, a significant minority (one-third) indicated they had ceased having intercourse for a significant period of time (median = 8 weeks). The most frequent reason given for cessation was marital discord, particularly among wives.

The Consumers' Union study, involving respondents fifty and older, also notes an association between sexual frequency and marital happiness (Brecher 1984). An even stronger relationship was observed between satisfaction with the sexual relation and being happy with one's marriage. Happily married individuals were more likely to indicate agreement with their spouse concerning the desired frequency of coitus. Frequently orgasmic wives also were more apt to report having happy marriages, providing further confirmation of the connection between sex and marital well-being.

A similar pattern of findings emerged from the survey sponsored by the Playboy Foundation and analyzed by Hunt (1974). Contrary to sexual-freedom advocates, sexual pleasure and emotional intimacy, Hunt suggests, are closely—even strongly—linked for most people. In this survey, almost the entire universe, 99 percent, of those indicating they had a mostly or very pleasurable marital sex life said they had a very close relationship with their spouse. In contrast, 60 percent of the wives and 40 percent of the husbands who had distant relations with their partner indicated that their sexual relationship was unrewarding and nonpleasurable. A noteworthy aspect of this latter finding is what appears to be a persistent gender difference: the link between sexuality and marital well-being is stronger for wives than for husbands.

One point of convergence in the sexuality of individuals in the late middle years for both sexes is the onset of a climacteric, postulated by clinicians, physicians, and psychiatrists alike (Masters and Johnson 1966; Weg 1978, 1983). Although this occurrence is discussed in detail in other chapters (see chapters by Levy, McKinlay and Feldman, and Schiavi, this vol.), in terms of marital sexuality it is important to note that the symptoms and timing appear to differ for men and women.

Among men, sexual disturbances have been found to increase with age (McCarthy 1984; Starr 1985). Impotency increases markedly for males over forty and escalates with each decade (Runciman 1978). The intensity of sexual sensation among males over forty is reduced, as is the speed of erection and the force of ejaculation. Compared to younger men, the middle-aged (at least in the latter part of this life stage) typically experience an orgasm reduced to one stage, involving a shorter orgasmic period and rapid detumescence after ejaculation. The refractory period usually increases, as is the case of the time an erection can be maintained (Weg 1978).

Among women, the climacteric may extend over a twenty-year period, with its onset generally being in the mid-thirties and occasionally extending beyond the mid-fifties (Weg 1978). Menopause and its associated physiological changes coincide with the later stage of the climacteric. As with men, the intensity of sexual response is reduced, and coitus may be painful for some postmenopausal women. Yet, in contrast to the male, females in the late middle years appear to be advantaged. As Masters and Johnson put it: "There is no time limit drawn by advancing years to female sexuality" (1966, 247).

Significantly, as far as well-being is concerned, for both sexes the climacteric tends to be accompanied by higher levels of anxiety, various negative physical complaints, and a higher incidence of depression. However, another commonality among men and women, gerontologists observe, is that there is a great deal of individualization of the climacteric and the subjective experience of it (Weg 1983). This may suggest that for most people, the climacteric has minimal importance for their sexuality and their sense of well-being. In fact, from a large community-based sample, McKinlay and his colleagues (McKinlay and Feldman, chap. 10, this vol.) have found that only a relatively small minority of men and women report having climacteric-associated problems. Among women, for example, less than 5 percent view menopause in a negative light.

The widely cited *Redbook* survey, although confined to a convenience sample of female responses, provides further corroborating evidence of the connection between sexuality and specific dimensions of well-being

(Tavris and Sadd 1977). Although no tabular figures are presented, Tavris and Sadd state that their data indicate "the higher the frequency of intercourse, the happier the wives were with their marriages and the better they rated their sex lives" (1977, 67). Sexual frequency, they further suggest, declines with age and marital duration, but the major decline occurs after the first year of marriage. Even though frequency of marital intercourse declines with age, satisfaction need not. "Across all age groups," Tavris and Sadd point out, "wives were equally likely to say they were having sex too often or not often enough" (1977, 69). One of the more noteworthy findings from this survey, though, was that almost four in ten wives felt they were not having sex often enough. Although this finding might be an artifact of the data-collection procedure, it could well be evidence of a cohort effect. It is in sharp contrast to the reports of the married cohorts interviewed by Kinsey, wherein many wives complained of having sex too frequently. None of Kinsey's respondents said their marital sex was too infrequent until the later years of marriage.

In a more up-to-date, large-scale study involving over three thousand married women and men, Blumstein and Schwartz (1983), likewise, conclude there is an important relation between the quantity and quality of sex and the well-being of couples. They write, "Married couples feel so strongly about having sex often that those who say they have it with their partner infrequently tend to be dissatisfied with their entire relationship" (1983, 201). In further commenting on the nature of the relationship between sex and well-being, Blumstein and Schwartz state, "It is hard to know whether an unsatisfactory relationship leads to less frequent sexual activity and reduced sexual pleasure or whether the problems begin in the bedroom and eventually corrode the entire relationship. From our vantage point it looks as if other problems come into the bedroom and make it less likely that the couple will want to have sex together. The low frequency then becomes a source of dissatisfaction in and of itself" (1983, 201).

As in the *Redbook* survey, rather consistent differences were found by Blumstein and Schwartz in the reports of younger and older respondents, again suggesting a cohort effect. In general, younger respondents were more liberated concerning their sexual expression, indicating an openness to experimentation and a greater rejection of a sense of exclusiveness associated with a monogamous relationship.

There is general agreement, then, that (1) sexuality and at least some aspects of well-being are interrelated, (2) coital frequency tends to decline over time, and (3) some evidence indicates younger female cohorts have greater variety and frequency of sex (although less than they would like) than their older counterparts. There are, however, two central issues we can raise with respect to these conclusions. First, it is not clear what the precise nature of the relation is between sex and well-being. The directionality, or what causes what, has never been clearly specified, although it has been the subject of much speculation (Blumstein and Schwartz 1983; Hunt 1974; Kinsey et al. 1953; Tavris and Sadd 1977; Udry 1971). Second, although the generalization concerning the temporal declines in sexual frequency is widely accepted, it remains unclear as to what accounts for the decrease. Most researchers accept this as an effect of aging, but there are other interpretations. We first address the issue of directionality and then turn in a later section to a brief discussion of some pertinent evidence bearing on the decline in sexual frequency.

An early study addressing the issue of directionality suggested that sexuality was a function of marital quality (Clark and Wallin 1965). Based on the Burgess-Wallin longitudinal study, with the final panel data obtained in 1956 and in 1958, Clark and Wallin found that wives with consistently positive marriages had a greater probability of being sexually responsive (frequency of orgasm) in the middle years of marriage than wives whose marriages were consistently negative in quality. The latter group of wives decreased in their responsiveness to a greater extent than those with positive marriages. Wives in deteriorating marriages showed a greater decrease in responsiveness than did those whose marriages qualitatively improved. This last group, contrary to expectation, did not report improvements in sexual responsiveness. In the end, Clark and Wallin concede that responsiveness may influence marital quality, suggesting that the relation between the two may be reciprocal. Their analysis, however, stops short of demonstrating that.

In discussing the issue of directionality, Blumstein and Schwartz (1983) agree that relationship satisfaction has a positive effect on coital frequency. At the same time, they suggest that the frequency of marital intercourse may have an independent effect on how couples evaluate their marriages. Hunt (1974), too, thinks the relation between well-being and sexual frequency is a reciprocal one, but the quality of existing data and its mostly cross-sectional nature have prevented researchers from empirically sorting out how the two influence each other over time. One pattern that is clear is that the relationship differs for men and women. Husbands and wives have different conceptions of intimacy. Husbands are more likely to view sex as a separate component of their relationships; wives more closely associate sexual fulfillment with marital intimacy and, hence, with the quality of their marriages (Patton and Waring 1985; Udry 1971).

Because most studies documenting the temporal decline in coital frequency are cross-sectional in design, it is extremely difficult to identify the separate effect age may have. Some of what has been observed may reflect cohort influences, period effects, or may have to do with marital duration. As we noted earlier, people who are currently in their middle years matured in qualitatively distinct sexual environments, leading us to expect some cohort and period effects.

Using data from the Duke Longitudinal Study on aging, George and Weiler (1981) contend that findings from cross-sectional research overestimate the extent of sexual decline. Stability in sexual patterns is much more marked than any changes, and the commonly observed decline is probably a cohort-related effect. George and Weiler are careful to point out, though, that mean levels of sexual activity and aggregate findings should not be extrapolated to individuals, an issue of special import to clinicians. Although they found stable levels of sexual activity to be typical, the aggregate findings masked distinct patterns of change exhibited by individuals. This included not only a decline in coital activity but also an increase in some cases, and in others it obscured the complete cessation of intercourse of a minority of the study participants (8 percent of the husbands and 14 percent of the wives over a six-year interval).

However, for persons for whom sex was of considerable importance early in life, it is likely to continue to be so as age advances (Pfeiffer and Davis 1972). A couple's pattern of sexual activity, in brief, seems to be a part of an overall lifestyle. Nonetheless, the extent to which this holds depends, among other things, on past sexual enjoyment, objective health and its subjective experience, the mental health of the partners, the maintenance of a relative level of marital satisfaction and happiness, the stress of various life events, the use of alcohol and psychotropic medications, preoccupations with activities outside the marriage, as well as husbands' and wives' definitions of the meaning of the aging process itself—including their respective interpretations of the climacteric (Hallstrom and Samuelsson 1990; Masters and Johnson 1966; Pfeiffer and Davis 1972; Starr 1985).

Our current marital instability over the life course study provides additional insight into the role of sexual behavior in the middle years in how it affects and is affected by both general well-being and marital quality (Booth and Edwards 1985; Booth, Johnson and Edwards, 1991a; Booth et al. 1984, 1985). Presently, this study involves four panels of interview data collected over a twelve-year period from a national sample of married persons ($N = 2033$ at the outset). The respondents were interviewed by telephone in 1980, 1983, 1988, and again in 1992. Of the respondents, 78 percent were successfully reinterviewed in 1983, and 66 percent of the original sample supplied information in 1988. Households were selected through a clustered random-digit-dialing procedure, and the husband or wife was chosen by a second random procedure. The completion rate was 65 percent, similar to other studies using this technique. With attrition in the sample over time, African-Americans, Latinos, younger respondents, renters, and those with low educational attainment are underrepresented in later panels but no more so than investigations using personal interviews (see Booth, Johnson, and Edwards [1991a] for further details). The study's longitudinal nature enables us to look at the issue of stability and change in sexual expression and well-being over time, a clear deficiency in the cross-sectional studies of marital sexuality. Here, we draw on the data from the first three panels.

Three particular questions in our surveys are pertinent to the above issues. The first is a general question: "How happy are you with your sexual relationship? Would you say very happy, pretty happy, or not too happy?" The other two questions tap problems in the relationship. The lead-in to the questions is, "I'd like to mention a number of problem areas. Have you had a problem in your marriage because one of you—." The two endings of concern here are "—has become less interested in sex?" and "—has had a sexual relationship with someone else?"

To gain some perspective on how middle-aged adults (thirty-five to sixty years old) differ from younger persons, and to ascertain whether those in their early middle years differ from those in their late middle years, table 1 shows the responses to our three questions for three age categories: less than thirty-five, thirty-five to forty-seven, and forty-eight to sixty.

Although less than a majority are very happy with their sexual relationship (see panel A), only a small minority are "not too happy." Females in the later part of their middle years tend to be less satisfied with their sexual relationship; those in the early middle years are more like younger women in their level of satisfaction ($p = .05$). Male satisfaction (as reflected in the number of people selecting the "not too happy" cate-

TABLE 1 Each Evaluation Category of Marital Sex
by Age and Gender (%)

A. Happiness with Sexual Relationship

	Females (N = 739)			Males (N = 466)		
Age	Very Happy	Pretty Happy	Not Too Happy	Very Happy	Pretty Happy	Not Too Happy
Under 35	48	47	5	45	52	3
35–47	48	44	8	40	48	12
48–60	40	47	12	46	45	9

B. Loss of Interest in Sex Viewed as Problem in Marriage

	Females (N = 741)				Males (N = 466)			
Age	No	Spouse	Self	Both	No	Spouse	Self	Both
Under 35	84	2	11	3	73	21	5	1
35–47	83	5	9	3	83	12	2	3
48–60	75	7	11	7	78	13	5	4

C. Sexual Relationship with Another Viewed as Problem in Marriage

	Females (N = 739)				Males (N = 467)			
Age	No	Spouse	Self	Both	No	Spouse	Self	Both
Under 35	95	3	1	1	96	3	1	. . .
35–47	94	4	1	1	92	2	4	1
48–60	97	3	. . .	. . .	98	1	1	. . .

gory) appears, on the other hand, to drop in the middle adult years. However, the differences are not statistically significant.

Only a minority (approximately one-fifth) report a problem in their marriage because of a loss of interest in sex (see panel B). Men and women appear to agree that the loss of interest is mostly on the part of the wife, a pattern of attribution contrary to that observed in most aging studies. Wives in the late middle years are more likely to report a loss of interest as a problem than are younger women ($p = .03$). Older and younger men do not differ.

An even smaller minority (approximately 5 percent) report extramarital sex as causing a problem in their marriage. When it is a problem, there is a tendency to attribute it to the spouse and to report fewer problems of this nature in late middle age. Neither trend is statistically significant. Although most people are not ecstatic with their sexual relationship, problems such as a loss of interest in sex and extramarital sex appear to have an effect on only a minority of marriages. For women, late middle age seems to be a time of greater dissatisfaction than early middle age. Among men, however, dissatisfaction appears to set in during the early middle years.

To assess the relative stability in the sex items, the scores on the three sex variables were correlated with their respective scores obtained in succeeding waves of interviews. Change was estimated by examining the means over the three time periods for individuals who were in all three waves (two waves in the case of the loss-of-interest-in-sex variable). These results appear in table 2.

As shown here, the correlations between one wave and another are high for the item tapping "happiness with sexual relationship." The correlations are lower for loss-of-interest-in- and extramarital sex. Happiness is very stable over time, but loss of interest and extramarital sex are less so. There is a statistically significant ($p < .01$) decline in happiness with marital sex and a statistically significant ($p < .01$) increase in loss of interest in sex, indicating that these factors change with marital duration. There is no significant change in problems stemming from extramarital sex over the three waves of data. With the possible exception of

TABLE 2 Means and Correlations for Three Measures of Sexual Behavior Obtained from the Middle-Aged (N = 860)

Measures	Mean	Correlations	
		Wave 1	Wave 2
Happiness with sex:			
Wave 1	2.5	. . .	. . .
Wave 2	2.4	.51	. . .
Wave 3	2.3	.42	.50
Loss of interest:			
Wave 2	.14	. . .	. . .
Wave 3	.19	.37	. . .
Extramarital sex:			
Wave 1	.04	. . .	. . .
Wave 2	.04	.42	. . .
Wave 3	.04	.30	.29

extramarital sex, these findings are consistent with most prior studies of marital quality.

How do these aspects of sexuality relate to well-being? Our survey contains two measures of general well-being and four measures of marital quality. The first measure of general well-being is the widely used social indicator: "Taking all things together, how would you say you are these days? Would you say you are very happy, pretty happy, or not too happy?" Those reporting greater happiness were assigned higher scores. The item has a mean of 1.61 and a standard deviation of .58. The second general item taps psychological distress: "In the last three years, were there ever times when you were extremely unhappy, nervous, irritable or depressed?" An affirmative response was followed by the question: "Have you felt this way recently?" Those reporting distress were coded 1, others 0. The item has a mean of .17 and a standard deviation of .38. Marital quality was assessed by four different measures. These pertain to overall happiness with the marriage, marital interaction in the course of everyday activities, frequency and severity of disagreements, and divorce proneness.[1] All of the scales have an acceptable level of reliability.

The zero-order correlations between the responses to the sex questions and the well-being items for those thirty-five to sixty years old are shown in table 3. Responses to each of the sex questions are significantly correlated with general well-being, as well as with marital well-being. All the relations are in the direction we might expect. In order to gauge the total effect on well-being, regression equations were computed with all three sex variables entered at the same time. The fourth column in

TABLE 3 Cross-Sectional Analysis of Relation between Sexual Behavior and Well-Being for the Middle-Aged

	Zero-Order Correlations (N = 860)			
Measures of Well-Being	Happiness with Sex	Loss of Interest	Extramarital Sex	R^2 with 3 Variables
Global happiness	.37**	−.27**	−.08*	.14
Depression and anxiety	−.19**	.19**	.10**	.04
Marital happiness	.54**	−.32**	−.21**	.31
Marital interaction	.31**	−.20**	−.12**	.09
Marital disagreement	−.30**	.21**	.16**	.09
Marital instability	−.40**	.33**	.31**	.22

**$p < .01$.
*$p < .05$.

table 3 shows the total variance explained. By social science standards, sexual satisfaction has a significant relationship with overall happiness, marital happiness, and marital instability.

To see whether there were age differences, we further computed sex by age (early to late middle age) interaction terms and entered them into the equations along with age and the independent variables. Only two interactions were observed: Those in early middle age had higher marital instability scores when they were not happy with their sexual relationship or had lost interest in sex. Apparently those in late middle age are less likely to consider divorce as a viable option to their dissatisfaction.

We also have examined the relation between change in sexual behavior and changes in well-being. Change scores were created by subtracting the 1980 scores from the 1988 scores. The subtraction was done so that higher scores reflect less happiness with the sexual relationship, a loss of interest in sex, and the occurrence of extramarital sex, on the one hand, and lower marital quality and psychological well-being, on the other. As may be seen from the zero-order correlations presented in table 4, changes in the two sets of variables are correlated with one another. The somewhat lower correlations in the case of extramarital sex probably have to do with the relatively low incidence of change in this variable. Although we cannot sort out the causal direction of these changes, it is clear that changes in sexual behavior are generally related to changes in psychological well-being and marital quality.

Our data also provide an opportunity to examine the influence of a

TABLE 4 Zero-Order Correlations Showing Relation between Change in Sexual Behavior and Change in Well-Being over an Eight-Year-Period

Measures of Well-Being	Decreased Happiness with Sex	Loss of Interest in Sex	Extramarital Sex
Lower global happiness	.19**	.10**	.05
More depression and anxiety	.08**	.06*	.03
Lower marital happiness	.30**	.12**	.13**
Less marital interaction	.17**	.07*	.02
Greater disagreement	.14**	.03	.06*
More marital instability	.26**	.11**	.26**

*$p < .05$.
**$p < .01$.

change in happiness with marital sex between 1980 and 1983 and on the probability of divorce between 1983 and 1988. The results of a probit analysis indicate a decline in sexual satisfaction is associated with an increase in the likelihood of divorce ($p < .01$). Similarly, a change from reporting no extramarital sexual problem to this being a problem between 1980 and 1983 increased the probability of subsequent divorce ($p < .01$).

Our findings thus confirm the interrelations between various aspects of sexuality and well-being, whether it is general well-being or specific to marriage itself. The latter tend to be lower in late middle age and are associated with greater dissatisfaction with marital sex and a loss of interest in it. Additionally, we find that over time as dissatisfaction and loss of interest increase, psychological well-being and the perception of marital quality decrease. It is even the case that loss of interest in sex is related to the likelihood of divorce, which we can take as a negative indicator of well-being.

THE ROLE OF BIOLOGY

What role might biology play in these changes in sexuality and the sense of well-being? As we have pointed out, from Kinsey (Kinsey et al. 1953) on, studies generally have reported a linear decline in the frequency of sexual intercourse as people age (Kaplan 1974; Pfeiffer and Davis 1972). But the finding, no matter its consistency or the degree of decline involved, remains unexplained in the face of what others, such as Masters and Johnson (1966), maintain to be the "mythology of declining biological potential." Physiologically, Masters and Johnson contend, people can perform well sexually into their eighth decade from birth. Why, then, does sexual frequency and other demonstrations of sexuality diminish over time?

One explanation centers on fluctuations in androgen levels over the life course. Although there may be other hormones implicated, testosterone is viewed as the key hormone regulating sexual interest in both males and females. Testosterone is produced by the adrenal gland, testes, and ovaries. Women's production is approximately one-tenth of that of men. Testosterone is highest in the morning right after awaking and decreases throughout the course of the day. It is also highest in the months of November and December, at least for men. After a rise during the adolescent years, it declines throughout the adult life course in men (Dabbs 1990). Less is known about the age-related production in women. Testosterone is reliable from day to day, month to month, and year to year (Dabbs 1990), and individual differences in testosterone levels are heritable (Meikle et al. 1988).

Higher levels of testosterone are related to mean levels of sexual activity (Morris et al. 1987; Persky et al. 1978; Udry 1988). Studies have also shown that administrations of testosterone are followed by increases in sexual activity (Sherwin, Gelfand, and Brender 1985). Changes in testosterone have been observed to occur near the time of sex. Although increases in testosterone in men have been observed in anticipation of sex, some studies suggest that elevations in testosterone are more likely to follow sexual activity than precede it (Dabbs 1992a). However, these appear to be short-term elevations and not cumulative.

On the assumption that hormonal changes occur earlier in women, Udry and his associates have challenged Kinsey's assertion that sexual declines are due solely to waning male capacity (Udry, Deven, and Coleman 1982; Udry and Morris 1978). It is their contention that female age and not male age is the more important contributor to declines in coital frequency at least during part of the middle years. The most parsimonious explanation, they suggest, is that such declines are associated with changing hormone levels.

James (1983) has argued, however, that declines in sexual frequency are nonlinear. By the end of the first year of marriage, coital frequency drops almost by half. Thereafter, the rate stabilizes for many years, taking perhaps another twenty years to halve again. Such a pattern, James suggests, is unlikely to reflect a biologically based change. The reason the wife's age is more highly correlated with the rate of intercourse, James maintains, is due to the wife's age being more closely associated with the duration of marriage than is the case with husband's age, which is more variable at the time of marriage. Be that as it may, the gradual sexual declines James reports are consistent with the gradual age-related changes in androgens.

Testosterone has a number of properties that may have a bearing on marital quality. Testosterone has been shown to have a consistent and moderately strong relation with aggression (Meyer-Bahlburg 1981), dominance (Gray, Jackson, and McKinlay 1991), antisocial behavior (Dabbs and Morris 1990), sensation seeking (Daitzman and Zuckerman 1980), and low occupational achievement (Dabbs 1992b). Uncontrolled, these behaviors are inconsistent with the subordination of self-interest and the sensitivity important to long-term intimate relations with the opposite sex.

Indeed, a study by Booth and Dabbs (1991) supports such a conclusion. Men with higher testosterone production are found to be less likely to marry and, if they do so, they are more likely to divorce. Once married, they are more likely to leave their wife for some period of time, more likely to have extramarital sex, more apt to experience a lower quality of spousal interaction, and more likely to report hitting or throwing things at their wives. Testosterone level attenuates, to some degree, three social models of marital quality: the negative relation between social class and marital dissolution; the negative relation between drug or alcohol abuse, being in trouble with the law and the inability to hold down a job and marital quality; and the positive relation between marital duration and marital stability. As testosterone decreases with age, Booth and Dabbs note, men may be less pugnacious and more desirable as marital partners.

In a study of 350 women ages 27–30, Udry, Kovenock, and Morris (1992) show that prenatal testosterone is related to a wide range of non-traditional gender role behaviors including not marrying, assigning a lower priority to caring for children, having fewer children, attaching more importance to having a career, entering male-dominated occupations, and having higher-status jobs. Although this study suggests that high-testosterone women are less apt to experience marital sex, it does not inform us in a detailed way about the testosterone–sexual expression relation in women. The range of behaviors affected by testosterone found in this study does suggest, however, that sexual expression is likely to be influenced by this hormone.

These studies indicate, in sum, that hormones do play a role in sexual expression and may be implicated in age-related declines in sexual activity. But it remains unclear as to the degree that biological and social factors interact in accounting for the decline.

The Extramarital Connection

For a significant portion of American couples, marital sex represents only a part—albeit a large part—of their total sexual outlet, which raises the question as to what influence, if any, extramarital sexuality might have on individual well-being, and what effect it may have on relationship satisfaction. These are difficult issues to assess, for in comparison to the research we have on marital sexuality—sparse as it is—there is an even greater paucity of evidence on the incidence of extramarital sex and its consequences. For one thing, its actual incidence is uncertain.

Hunt, in the early 1970s, found no change in people's attitudes or experience with sex outside of marriage from that reported by Kinsey. By the mid-1970s, however, Bell, Turner, and Rosen (1975) speculated that among the wives they surveyed, who at that time averaged thirty-five years old, as many as 40 percent would have an extramarital affair in the next decade. Contemporaneously, Tavris and Sadd (1977) reported 40 percent of the wives in their oldest cohort indicated they had had extramarital intercourse. Cumulative incidence was related to the length of marriage and to being employed, the incidence reaching 53 percent among the latter group.

In contrast, among the married individuals in the Blumstein and Schwartz study (1983), only 26 percent of the husbands and 21 percent of the wives reported they had been nonmonogamous since the beginning of their marriages. Blumstein and Schwartz do note, though, a cohort effect, with the younger wives in their survey being more apt to indicate they had sex outside of their marital relationships (no figures are provided). More recently, from an analysis of the General Social Surveys, Smith (1991) estimates about half of all married adults have had no more sexual partners than marital partners. The proportion is higher among women (65 percent) than among men (30 percent). Once more, there is some suggestion of a cohort effect, with younger marrieds being more sexually active outside of marriage (Smith 1991).

No doubt some of these discrepancies can be attributed to the differences in sampling techniques and the age composition of the samples. The one pattern on which the research literature does agree is that the active incidence of extramarital intercourse is very low (Hunt 1974; Smith 1991; Tavris and Sadd 1977). Smith recently found that only 1.5 percent of married people had sexual partners other than their spouses in the year prior to being interviewed. The evidence further suggests the number of different sexual partners people have outside of marriage is likewise low, although the number is higher for men than women. Although the precise figures vary from one study to the next, it appears that approximately 40–50 percent of the wives' extramarital experience has been confined to one person; about one-third of the husbands have a similar amount of experience (Blumstein and Schwartz 1983; Hunt 1974; Kinsey et al. 1952; Tavris and Sadd 1977). These patterns may be in a state of flux, however. Because of cohort effects, higher rates of female employment, and the greater prevalence of divorce, the younger cohort of wives in the middle years may be behaving more similarly to husbands than was the case in the past. Noting such a convergence among the younger subjects in her analysis of twenty-five hundred episodes of extramarital sex, Lawson (1988) argues that we may be witnessing a "masculinization of sex," while simultaneously undergoing the "feminization of love." Men—those married after 1970—are reducing the number of casual affairs as women are increasing the number they report.

Even though it is somewhat uncertain as to what proportion of married adults have extramarital sex and it is clear that a large percentage limit such experience to one partner, further complicating any assessment of its effect on well-being is the wide variation in its circumstances, duration, and the meaning attributed to the experience. As Reiss, Anderson, and Sponaugle (1980) have suggested, extramarital relationships vary along two major dimensions: the degree to which they are love centered and the degree to which they are consensual. Presumably, the vast bulk of extramarital relationships for men are non–love centered and nonconsensual, whereas for women they tend to be love centered and nonconsensual. The implication, of course, is the experience is a transitory one more often for husbands than for wives. A small proportion of extramarital relationships, however, are consensual in nature, involving communal sex and so-called swinging. With such variation in extramarital relationships, the meaning attributed to them is likely to be very different, as is true of their implications for well-being.

The terminology applied to participation in extramarital relationships, no matter how fleeting most are, is illuminating. Despite what seems to be the relatively high incidence of extramarital sex, our society does not treat it matter-of-factly. Our language is replete with terms such as *adultery, cheating, infidelity,* and *unfaithful spouse.* Even nonparticipants are scornfully referred to as *cuckolds.* And our religious and legal norms are filled with negative sanctions, including extramarital sex serving as the only common ground for divorce across the states and considered illegal in all but five states, being subject to a prison sentence in some instances (Sponaugle 1989). All this is based on the premise that marriage is to be an exclusive relationship with well-defined boundaries designating privileges and obligations associated with its interior and exterior. As Smith reports (chap. 3, this vol.), more than three-quarters of all Americans say that extramarital relations are always wrong. But as Neubeck (1969) some time ago pointed out, people vary in the ground rules they establish in their marriages and the boundaries may be more or less permeable, more or less open to having one's needs met by outsiders. For some, the *extra* in extramarital is merely a supplement to the satisfactions and rewards of their marriages.

Indeed, sociological research on extramarital relationships portrays those involved as anything but an aggregate of deviants. Particularly given the broad cross section of the married population involved, whatever its exact dimensions, the differences between individuals with extramarital sexual experience and those without tend to be minimal. The former tend to be somewhat more liberal, more diffuse in their sense of intimacy, to have had premarital sexual experience, to be more autonomous in interacting with the opposite sex, and to emphasize more the pleasurable aspects of sexuality (Edwards 1973; Edwards and Booth 1976b; Reiss, Anderson, and Sponaugle 1980; Saunders and Edwards 1984; Sponaugle 1989).

More to the point of our concerns here, those engaged in extramarital relations, some evidence suggests, are more dissatisfied with their sexual relationship within marriage, and sexual relations outside of marriage may be associated with some degree of marital discord (Edwards and Booth 1976a; Johnson 1970). Given the volume of divorce over the last three decades, it would appear that a great many of the extramarital liaisons are actually associated with changing partners, for a large proportion of divorces are followed by rapid remarriages.

Kinsey (Kinsey et al. 1953), in contrast, claimed that clandestine relationships caused no serious marital difficulties and had, in some cases, improved marital sexual adjustment. Hunt (1974), though, found very little evidence to support Kinsey's contention, arguing that those who report such are seeking to rationalize their behavior or are failing to accurately assess the state of their marriages. The overwhelmingly expressed need to maintain the generally secretive nature of the relations would seem to add credence to Hunt's position, but a minority (about 6 percent) do succeed in balancing their marital relations with extramarital relationships (Bell, Turner, and Rosen 1975; Tavris and Sadd 1977).

Little is known about the quality of extramarital relations themselves, and most often even that focuses only on wives. Kinsey (Kinsey et al. 1953, 432), for example, indicated that 42 percent of the wives who had extramarital experiences had orgasms more often in those relations than they did in their marriages, with an additional 34 percent reaching orgasm equally frequent in the two types of relationships. Hunt (1974), too, notes that females reach orgasms in the majority of their extramarital copulations. But, he further indicates, orgasm regularity is distinctly less in these relations than it is in marital coitus. Although the majority of men and women in the *Playboy* study indicated their experience with extramarital sex was mostly or very pleasurable, an even higher proportion rated their marital sex in the same fashion. Moreover, Hunt observed that nontraditional coital positions were used less frequently in extramarital relationships and that the range of non-coital techniques employed was more restricted. Conceding the limitations of these quantitative measures, Hunt concludes that, on balance, extramarital relationships yield "a mixture of satisfactions and frustrations, rewards and penalties that add up to less overall pleasure" than people derive from the sexual relationship within marriage (1974, 277).

Reports of jealousy, as an adverse indicator of well-being, are infrequent in accounts of the effects of extramarital relations (Brecher 1984), most probably due to the predominantly secretive nature of these relationships. When they become known, such relations often are seen as a contributing factor leading to divorce. More than one-third of Kinsey's (Kinsey et al. 1953) respondents who had been divorced perceived it to be a prime or contributory factor to the breakup of their previous marriage. Males were twice as likely as females to see extramarital activities as the reason for marital dissolution, perhaps further evidence of a double standard. The accumulative incidence of extramarital coitus, Hunt (1974) found, was two to three times higher for divorced women as it was for currently married females, a ratio consistent with Kinsey's findings. It would appear, as Kinsey (Kinsey et al. 1953, 436) observed nearly four decades ago, that Americans continue to encounter problems in reconciling the desire for a variety of sexual partners and, at the same time, maintaining a stable marriage.

CONCLUSIONS

Our review suggests several major conclusions regarding sexuality in the middle years of marriage:

1. A positive relationship does exist between select measures of well-being and sexual expression, especially coital frequency and rates of female orgasm. The strength of the relationship, however, is moderate and not nearly as strong as one might surmise on the basis of the normative definition of American marriage. This applies not only to those in the middle years but also to the young and elderly as well.

2. The expression of marital sexuality in the middle years has changed, both in terms of its variety and its frequency, with younger cohorts experiencing greater variety by employing a broader range of sexual techniques and positions and having more frequent sex.

3. Even so, the bulk of the evidence indicates that sexual activity

tends to decline with age and marital duration. However, in the absence of sudden changes in health or cataclysmic life events, the decline tends to be gradual and, on average, rather modest, following the first year or two of marriage. Moreover, the slope of any such decline appears to be less steep among the younger cohorts now in middle age.

4. Over the life course, interest in and satisfaction with sex decline, accompanied by corresponding decreases in general well-being, as well as in different aspects of marital quality. Longitudinal data firmly establish that changes in sexuality and well-being are linked to one another.

5. In the relation between well-being and sexuality, the main effect seems to run from the former to the latter. In the final analysis, though, it may be most reasonable to conclude that the relation is reciprocal. However, a minority of couples who have bad marriages have great sex lives and, correspondingly, some couples with good marriages have qualitatively poor sexual relations. This, in part, may account for why a stronger association between well-being and sexuality has not been found.

6. Despite significant changes in sexual norms and attitudes, which have had a differential effect on females, gender differences in sexuality persist. Wives tend to be more dissatisfied with sex in marriage and, as one indicator of their well-being, derive fewer rewards from marriage itself. These gender differences are more pronounced, though, in the older cohorts of women now in their middle years than among younger wives.

7. Biological change does seem to play some role in the declines in sexual activity. How much of a role it plays remains unspecified. Yet, it appears to have a more profound effect on men than women in the middle years.

8. High testosterone levels, moreover, have the effect of lowering marital quality among some men. This suggests that attention to biological factors may aid in explaining some sociological models.

9. Extramarital sex appears to be a more frequent experience among the younger people now in the middle years, and the experience of wives—in contrast to what Kinsey found—may be converging with that of husbands. Despite what appears to be greater liberation, however, the bulk of Americans continue to encounter difficulties in balancing their extramarital relations with their marital relationships.

As sound as those conclusions may be, we must note that there is a dire need for methodologically more sophisticated research dealing with marital sexuality. In particular, this concerns investigating truly representative samples of people to reflect differences in gender, race, and social class. Longitudinal studies are sorely needed if we are going to have a greater understanding of the changes that take place over time. And, finally, there needs to be a broader conceptualization and measurement of sexuality itself. For too long, researchers have given almost exclusive attention to the more objective indicators of sexuality (coitus and orgasm), neglecting the equally important subjective dimensions and the meaning people ascribe to their sexual experience.

NOTE

1. Marital happiness is assessed using an eleven-item Likert-type scale that includes seven items asking about happiness with specific aspects of marriage (extent of understanding, amount of love and affection received, agreement with spouse, sexual relationship, spouse as someone who takes care of things around the house, spouse as someone with whom to do things, and spouse's faithfulness) and four global satisfaction items (overall happiness of marriage, rating of own marriage compared to others, strength of love for spouse, and whether marriage is getting better or worse). Higher scores indicate greater happiness.

A summated scale of marital interaction was derived from respondents' reports on how often (almost always, usually, occasionally, to never) they engaged jointly in five different activities: eating the main meal, shopping, visiting friends, working on projects around the house, and going out. The 1980 mean is 14.8 and the standard deviation is 3.0. Higher scores signify greater interaction.

The disagreement scale taps the amount and severity of conflict between spouses. "Do you and your [husband or wife] have arguments or disagreements about whether one of you is doing your share of the housework?" "How often do you disagree with your [husband or wife]? Would you say never, rarely, sometimes, often, or very often?" "How many serious quarrels have you had with your spouse in the last two months?" "In many households bad feelings and arguments occur from time to time. In some cases people get so angry that they slap, hit, punch, kick, or throw things at one another. Has this ever happened between you and your [husband or wife]?" The items were z scored and added, with higher scores indicating greater disagreement. The 1980 mean is 3.9 and the standard deviation 2.2.

Marital instability represents the propensity to divorce and includes both a cognitive component (thinking the marriage is in trouble, considering the idea of getting a divorce) and actions people take on the basis of these thoughts (talking to friends or spouse about the possibility of divorce, consulting with clergy, a counselor, or an attorney, separating from the spouse, or filing a divorce petition). The scale consists of thirteen items, tapping both frequency and timing of the indicators. Because the scale is skewed, the measure is logged. The scale has a mean of .18 and a standard deviation of .37. Those who score high on the scale are nine times more likely to divorce than those who score low on the scale (Booth et al. 1985).

References

Adams, J. S. 1965. Inequity in social exchange. In *Advances in experimental social psychology,* ed. L. Berkowitz, 267–99). New York: Academic Press.

Bell, R. R., S. Turner, and L. Rosen. 1975. A multivariate analysis of female extramarital coitus. *Journal of Marriage and the Family* 37:375–84.

Birchler, G. R., and L. J. Webb. 1977. Discriminating interaction behavior in happy and unhappy marriages. *Journal of Consulting and Clinical Psychology* 45:494–95.

Blumstein, P., and P. Schwartz. 1983. *American couples.* New York: Morrow.

Booth, A., and J. Dabbs. 1991. Testosterone and men's marriages. Unpublished.

Booth, A., and J. N. Edwards. 1985. Age at marriage and marital instability. *Journal of Marriage and the Family* 47:67–75.

Booth, A., D. R. Johnson, and J. N. Edwards. 1991a. *Marital instability over the life course methodology report.* Lincoln: Univ. of Nebraska Bureau of Sociological Research.

———. 1991b. Social integration and divorce. *Social Forces* 70:207–24.

Booth, A., D. Johnson, L. White and J. N. Edwards. 1984. Women, outside employment, and marital instability. *American Journal of Sociology* 90:567–83.

———. 1985. Predicting divorce and permanent separation. *Journal of Family Issues* 6:331–46.

Brecher, E. M. 1984. *Love, sex, and aging.* Boston: Little, Brown.

Bumpass, L. 1990. What's happening to the family? Interactions between demographic and institutional change. *Demography* 27:483–98.

Clark, A., and P. Wallin. 1965. Women's sexual responsiveness and the duration and quality of their marriages. *American Journal of Sociology* 71: 187–96.

Dabbs, J. 1990. Age and seasonal variation in serum testosterone concentration among men. *Chronobiology International* 7:245–49.

———. 1992a. Male and female salivary testosterone concentrations before and after sexual activity. *Physiology and Behavior* 70:813–24.

———. 1992b. Testosterone and occupational achievement. *Social Forces* 70:813–24.

Dabbs, J., and R. Morris. 1990. Testosterone and antisocial behavior in a sample of 4,462 men. *Psychological Science* 1:209–11.

Daitzman, R., and M. Zuckerman. 1980. Disinhibitory sensation seeking, personality, and gonadal hormones. *Personality and Individual Differences* 1:103–10.

Edwards, J. N. 1973. Extramarital involvement: Fact and theory. *Journal of Sex Research* 9:210–26.

Edwards, J. N., and A. Booth. 1976a. The cessation of marital intercourse. *American Journal of Psychiatry* 133:1333–36.

———. 1976b. Sexual behavior in and out of marriage: An assessment of correlates. *Journal of Marriage and the Family* 38:73–83.

George, L. K., and S. J. Weiler. 1981. Sexuality in middle and late life. *Archives of General Psychiatry* 38:919–23.

Gray, A., D. Jackson and J. McKinlay. 1991. The relation between dominance, anger, and hormones in normally aging men: Results from Massachusetts male aging study. *Psychosomatic Medicine* 53:375–85.

Hallstrom, T., and S. Samuelsson. 1990. Changes in women's sexual desire in middle life: The longitudinal study in Gothenburg. *Archives of Sexual Behavior* 19:259–68.

Howard, J. W., and R. M. Dawes. 1976. Linear prediction of marital happiness. *Personality and Social Psychology Bulletin* 2:478–80.

Hunt, M. 1974. *Sexual behavior in the 1970s*. Chicago: Playboy.

James, W. H. 1983. Decline in coital rates with spouses' ages and duration of marriage. *Journal of Biosocial Science* 15:83–88.

Johnson, R. E. 1970. Some correlates of extramarital coitus. *Journal of Marriage and the Family* 32:449–56.

Kantner, J. F., and M. Zelnik. 1972. Sexual experience of young unmarried women in the U.S. *Family Planning Perspectives* 4:9–18.

Kaplan, H. S. 1974. *The new sex therapy*. New York: Brunner/Mazel.

Kinsey, A. C., W. B. Pomeroy, and C. E. Martin. 1948. *Sexual behavior in the human male*. Philadelphia: Saunders.

Kinsey, A. C., W. B. Pomeroy, C. E. Martin, and P. H. Gebhard. 1953. *Sexual behavior in the human female*. Philadelphia: Saunders.

Lawson, A. 1988. *Adultery: An analysis of love and betrayal*. New York: Basic.

Masters, W. H., and V. E. Johnson. 1966. *Human sexual response*. Boston: Little, Brown.

McCarthy, B. W. 1984. Strategies and techniques for the treatment of inhibited sexual desire. *Journal of Sex and Marital Therapy* 10:97–104.

Meikle, A., J. Stringham, D. Bishop, and D. West. 1988. Quantitating genetic and nongenetic factors influencing androgen production and clearance rates in men. *Journal of Clinical Endocrinology Metabolism* 67:104–9.

Messick, D. M., and K. S. Cook, eds. 1983. *Equity theory: Psychological and sociological perspectives*. New York: Praeger.

Meyer-Bahlburg, H. 1981. Androgens and human aggression. *The biology of aggression*, ed. P. Brain and D. Benton, 263–90. Alphen ann den Rijn, Netherlands: Sijhoff & Noordhoff.

Michaels, J. W., A. Acock, and J. N. Edwards. 1986. Social exchange and equity determinants of relationship commitment. *Journal of Social and Personal Relationships* 3:161–75.

Morris, N., J. R. Udry, F. Khan-Dawood, and M. Dawood. 1987. Marital sex frequency and midcycle female testosterone. *Archives of Sexual Behavior* 16:27–37.

Neubeck, G. 1969. *Extramarital relations*. Englewood Cliffs, N.J.: Prentice-Hall.

Patton, D., and E. M. Waring. 1985. Sex and intimacy. *Journal of Sex and Marital Therapy* 11:176–84.

Persky, H., H. Lief, D. Strauss, W. Miller, and C. O'Brien. 1978. Plasma testosterone level and sexual behavior of couples. *Archives of Sexual Behavior* 7:157–73.

Pfeiffer, E., and G. C. Davis. 1972. Determinants of sexual behavior in middle and old age. *Journal of the American Geriatrics Society* 20:151–58.

Reiss, I., R. E. Anderson, and G. C. Sponaugle. 1980. A multivariate model of the determinants of extramarital sexual permissiveness. *Journal of Marriage and the Family* 42:395–411.

Runciman, A. P. 1978. Sexual problems in the senior world. In *Sexuality and aging*, ed. R. L. Solnick, 78–95. Los Angeles: Univ. of California Press.

Saunders, J. L., and J. N. Edwards. 1984. Extramarital sexuality: A predictive model of permissive attitudes. *Journal of Marriage and the Family* 46:825–35.

Sherwin, B. B., M. M. Gelfand, and W. Brender. 1985. Androgen enhances sexual motivation in females. *Psychosomatic Medicine* 47:339–51.

Simpson, J. A., B. Campbell, and E. Bercheid. 1986. The association between romantic love and marriage: Kephart (1967) twice revisited. *Personality and Social Psychology Bulletin* 12:363–72.

Smith, T. W. 1991. Adult sexual behavior in 1989: Number of partners, frequency of intercourse, and risk of AIDS. *Family Planning Perspectives* 23:102–7.

Spanier, G. B. 1986. Cohabitation in the 1980s: Recent changes in the United States. In *Contemporary marriage: Comparative perspectives on a changing institution*, ed. K. Davis and A. Grossbard-Shechtman. New York: Russell Sage.

Sponaugle, G. C. 1989. Attitudes toward extramarital relations. In *Human sexuality: The societal and interpersonal context*, ed. K. McKinney and S. Sprecher, 187–209. Norwood, N.J.: Ablex.

Starr, B. D. 1985. Sexuality and aging. In *Annual review of gerontology and geriatrics*, ed. M. P. Lawton & G. L. Maddox, 97–126. New York: Springer.

Tavris, C., and S. Sadd. 1977. *The Redbook report on female sexuality.* New York: Delacorte.

Terman, L. M., P. Buttenweiser, L. W. Ferguson, W. B. Johnson, and D. P. Wilson. 1938. *Psychological factors in marital happiness.* New York: McGraw-Hill.

Udry, J. R. 1971. *The Social Context of Marriage.* Philadelphia: Lippincott.

———. 1988. Biological predispositions and social control in adolescent sexual behavior. *American Sociological Review* 53:709–22.

Udry, J. R., K. E. Bauman, and N. M. Morris. 1975. Changes in premarital coital experience of recent decade-of-birth cohorts of urban American Women. *Journal of Marriage and the Family* 37:783–87.

Udry, J. R., F. R. Deven, and S. J. Coleman. 1982. A cross-national comparison of the relative influence of male and female age on the frequency of marital intercourse. *Journal of Biosocial Science* 14:1–6.

Udry, J. R., J. Kovenock, and N. Morris. 1992. A biosocial paradigm for women's gender roles. Paper presented at the Population Association of America meetings, Denver, Colorado.

Udry, J. R., and N. M. Morris. 1978. Relative contribution of male and female age to the frequency of marital intercourse. *Social Biology* 25:128.

U.S. Bureau of the Census. 1985. *Statistical abstract of the United States.* Washington, D.C.: Department of Commerce.

Weg, R. B. 1978. The physiology of sexuality in aging. In *Sexuality and aging*, ed. R. L. Solnick, 48–65. Los Angeles: Univ. of California Press.

———. 1983. The physiological perspective. In *Sexuality in the later years*, ed. R. B. Weg, 39–80. New York: Academic Press.

Age-Related Variation in Sexual Activity and Interest in Normal Men: Results from the Massachusetts Male Aging Study

John B. McKinlay and Henry A. Feldman

This paper addresses two major questions using a single, comprehensive set of survey data. The first part answers the question, How does male sexual activity vary among men who are presently in their middle years? Here we are concerned to describe the experience of a random sample of community-dwelling men between the ages of forty and seventy. The second part addresses the question, What variables and circumstances are associated with the cross-sectional variation in sexual activity? Here we are trying to account for (not explain) the phenomena described in the first part. There is no pretense to explain why the observed patterns prevail—the cross-sectional survey method precludes this—but rather an interest in identifying what variables contribute to, or are associated with, those effects.

Although these questions have been raised before, nothing like the Massachusetts Male Aging Study (MMAS) data set has been available to address them. The MMAS is distinguished from most earlier work in at least three ways. First, most earlier work used nonrandom convenience samples, often consisting of patients presenting with sexual dysfunction. By contrast, the MMAS comprises a representative sample of community-dwelling men. Second, sexual-activity variables in the MMAS, unlike much of the work to date, are not limited to simple indices such as frequency of intercourse or masturbation. In the MMAS, sexual activity encompasses a comprehensive range of information including both self-reports of behavior or events (e.g., frequency of erection, masturbation, intercourse, nocturnal erections, pain during intercourse, and difficulty obtaining and maintaining erections) and also

Drs. Jack Rowe and Chris Longcope and Ms. Karen Yuhas, RNNP, made important contributions to the Massachusetts Male Aging Study (MMAS), especially in the development of the questionnaire for assessment of potency and libido. We also thank Drs. Irwin Goldstein, Robert Krane, and Dimitrios Hatzichristou (Department of Urology, Boston University School of Medicine) for lending medical insights regarding impotence. The research was supported by the National Institute on Aging (NIH AG-09537). Communications should be directed to Dr. John B. McKinlay.

subjective or cognitive phenomena (e.g., desires, fantasies, preferences, attitudes, and levels of satisfaction). Third, the MMAS is distinguished from earlier studies by the extensiveness of social, psychological, physiological, and anthropometric data gathered on each subject. In addition to standard sociodemographic information (e.g., age, education, employment, income, and race and ethnicity), we also gathered data on medication usage, anthropometrics (height, weight, and fat topology), lifestyle (smoking, nutrition, physical activity, and alcohol consumption), and psychological states (depression, dominance, anger in/out, social support, aspects of quality of life). Two venous blood samples were drawn for determination of cholesterol and sixteen different serum hormones, proteins, and metabolites. It was possible to include many of these variables (although not all of them, for obvious reasons) in our identification of factors associated with changes in male sexual activity during the middle years.

Sampling Procedures

Between January 1987 and February 1989, the MMAS was conducted in eleven cities and towns in the Boston area. Communities were randomly selected by use of probabilities proportional to population within each of six strata defined by community size and median income.

Men born between 1917 and 1946 (inclusive, currently aged forty to seventy) were selected at random from each community by use of official street lists, which are compiled annually under Massachusetts law. Sampling fractions were adjusted so as to produce a uniform age distribution over the three decades. Introductory letters were sent to 5,287 men, followed by a telephone call in which the in-home protocol was described and the subject was encouraged to participate. No financial incentive was offered for participation. Telephone contact was made with 4,014 respondents or their households. Among successful contacts, 1,526 subjects and 23 household members declined to cooperate. Of the remaining 2,465 sampled subjects, 756 were deceased, inaccessible, ineligible, or unable to complete the interview. A total of 1,709 respondents agreed to participate and completed the in-home protocol.

Our response rate (53 percent), although similar to those of other comparably extensive, invasive field studies on large, random, population-based samples, requires some comment. Factors working against a higher response rate included (1) lower response rates in the Northeast, coupled with a secular decline in such rates; (2) the venipuncture requirement (two blood samples) and the increase in public alarm concerning AIDS during this study; (3) the lack of financial incentive, as no token compensation could be provided; and (4) the logistic challenges of in-home data gathering early in the morning with a sample of predominantly employed men.

We examined the sociodemographic differences between respondents and nonrespondents using information from Massachusetts street lists, which constituted the MMAS sampling frame. These lists are updated annually by law and contain age, occupation, and household composition, which were assessed for reliability against interview responses before inclusion in the comparison. Our results suggested that employed men were overrepresented in the MMAS sample as compared with ineligibles, refusals, and no contacts.

The distributions of serum cholesterol, body-mass index, and blood pressure in the MMAS sample closely matched those of the National Health and Nutrition Survey of the late 1970s (NHANES II). Small discrepancies, particularly in blood pressure, were easily accounted for by the secular changes that occurred in the U.S. population during the ten years that separated the two studies.

The effects of nonresponse were further investigated by attempting to conduct brief interviews with 400 randomly selected nonrespondents in the towns that had response rates under 60 percent. Of the 400, 206 were successfully interviewed, 119 refused, 57 could not be contacted, and 19 were found to be ineligible or deceased. Compared with MMAS respondents, the nonrespondents were slightly less likely to claim that they were in good-to-excellent health (52 percent vs. 56 percent) and also less likely to report heart disease (10.2 percent vs. 12.7 percent) or cancer (1.9 percent vs. 6.1 percent). No difference was detected in the proportions reporting that their activity was restricted for health reasons ($p > 0.05$), but among those who did report such restrictions, nonrespondents were more likely to report at least twelve days of restricted activity (13 out of 18 vs. 49 out of 199). Finally, no differences were detected in reports of diabetes, high blood pressure, or arthritis or rheumatism. Thus, there is little evidence of major differences between respondents and nonrespondents that would indicate extensive nonresponse bias in the MMAS results.

Data Collection

Following the approach developed for the Pawtucket Heart Health Program (McKinlay et al. 1984), a trained field-technician interviewer visited each subject in his home, completing the questionnaire, performing physiological measurements, and obtaining blood samples within four hours of the subject's waking (in order to obtain basal levels and avoid fluctuations resulting from diurnal variability). All subjects gave written informed consent.

The subject's prescription and nonprescription medications were gathered and inventoried by the interviewer, after which the subject was asked about dosage levels and reasons for use of each medication. A comprehensive list of other nonprescription medications was also completed. Weight was measured by a battery-operated portable scale, height by a carpenter's rule, and blood pressure by a mercury sphygmomanometer according to standardized techniques (McKinlay et al. 1984). Two blood samples were drawn thirty minutes apart (to control for the pulsatile emission of hormones) and pooled for analysis of lipids and sex steroid hormones (Brambilla et al. 1991). Psychological instruments administered by the interviewer included the Jackson dominance scale (Jackson 1984), the Spielberger scales of anger expression (Spielberger et al. 1985), and the CES-D depression scale (Radloff 1977).

The remainder of the interview included items concerning health status, smoking habits, alcohol consumption, physical activity, sleep, education, employment, income, ethnicity, marital status, household composition, and social networks. More detailed descriptions of MMAS appear in Ascherio et al. (1991); Feldman et al. (forthcoming); Gray et al. (1991a, 1991b); Gray, Jackson, and McKinlay (1991); Longcope et al. (1990); McKinlay (1989); McKinlay, Longcope, and Gray (1989) and Washburn et al. (1990).

Following all other questions and measurements and after rapport had been established, the subject was given a booklet titled *Self-Administered Questionnaire,* containing twenty-three questions concerning sexual activity, including frequency, satisfaction, and erectile function. The subject was instructed to complete this questionnaire in private, seal it in an envelope, and return it when finished to the interviewer for delivery to the principal investigator. Items used in this study are listed in table 1 and rates of response in table 2.

Coding and Scaling

Serum cholesterol and serum-free testosterone were expressed in log concentration units. All psychological scales were scored in integer increments. The Jackson dominance scale had a range of 17 units (0–16). The CES-D depression scale had a range of 48 units, and the Spielberger anger scales had various ranges between 18 (anger out) and 48 units (anger expression). Age (year), waist-hip ratio, body-mass index (kg/m^2), alcohol consumption (ml/d), and exercise level (kcal/kg/d) were expressed directly as continuous quantities. General health was coded on a five-point scale (poor to excellent). Diabetes, heart disease, and hypertension were coded on a three-point scale reflecting severity: absent, untreated, and treated. Education was coded on a five-point scale, running from noncompletion of high school to study beyond bachelor's degree. Current employment, current cigarette smoking, and use of medications were treated as dichotomies.

TABLE 1 Items from Self-Administered Instrument,
Massachusetts Male Aging Study

Q2. *How satisfied are you with your sex life?*
(1) Extremely satisfied.
(2) Somewhat satisfied.
(3) Neither satisfied nor dissatisfied.
(4) Somewhat dissatisfied.
(5) Extremely dissatisfied.

Q3. *Do you currently have one or more than one sexual partner?*
(1) No partner.
(2) One partner.
(3) More than one partner. (Enter number in box.)

Q4. *How satisfied are you with your sexual relationship with your present partner or partners?*
(1) Extremely satisfied.
(2) Somewhat satisfied.
(3) Neither satisfied nor dissatisfied.
(4) Somewhat dissatisfied.
(5) Extremely dissatisfied.

Q5. *How satisfied do you think your partner(s) is (are) with your sexual relationship?*
(1) Extremely satisfied.
(2) Somewhat satisfied.
(3) Neither satisfied nor dissatisfied.
(4) Somewhat dissatisfied.
(5) Extremely dissatisfied.

(continued)

TABLE 1 *(continued)*

Q6. *Has the frequency of your sexual activity with a partner been*
(1) as much as you desire?
(2) less than you desire?
(3) more than you desire?

Q7. *How frequently do you feel sexual desire? This feeling may include wanting to have sexual experience (masturbation or intercourse), planning to have sex, feeling frustrated due to lack of sex, etc.*
(1) More than once a day.
(2) Once a day.
(3) 2 or 3 times per week.
(4) Once a week.
(5) 2 or 3 times per month.
(6) Once a month.
(7) Less than once per month.
(8) Not at all.

Q8. *How frequently do you have sexual thoughts, fantasies, or erotic dreams?*
(1) More than once a day.
(2) Once a day.
(3) 2 or 3 times per week.
(4) Once a week.
(5) 2 or 3 times per month.
(6) Once a month.
(7) Less than once per month.
(8) Not at all.

Q9. *In an average week, how frequently do you usually have sexual intercourse or activity? (Enter number in box.)*

Q10. *In an average week, how frequently would you like to have sexual intercourse or activity?? (Enter number in box.)*

Q11. *During an average 24-hour day, how often do you have a full, hard erection? (Enter number in box.)*

Q12. *During the last 6 months have you ever had trouble getting an erection before intercourse begins?*
(1) No.
(2) Yes.
(3) Have not had sexual intercourse in last 6 months.

Q13. *During the last 6 months have you ever had trouble keeping an erection once intercourse has begun?*
(1) No.

TABLE 1 *(continued)*

(2) Yes.

(3) Have not had sexual intercourse in last 6 months.

Q14. *During the last 6 months have you ever found it difficult to reach orgasm ("to come")?*
(1) Never have difficulty.
(2) Seldom, less than 25% of the time.
(3) Sometimes, about 50% of the time.
(4) Usually, about 75% of the time.
(5) Always have difficulty.
(6) Have not had intercourse in last 6 months.

Q15. *How frequently do you awaken from sleep with a full erection?*
(1) Daily.
(2) 2 or 3 times per week.
(3) Once a week.
(4) 2 or 3 times per month.
(5) Once a month.
(6) Less than once per month.
(7) Not at all in the last 6 months.

Q16. *During the last 6 months have you ever felt pain in your genitals during or after sexual intercourse?*
(1) Never have pain.
(2) Seldom, less than 25% of the time.
(3) Sometimes, about 50% of the time.
(4) Usually, about 75% of the time.
(5) Always have pain.
(6) Have not had intercourse in last 6 months.

Q17. *How often do you ejaculate by (a)* masturbation? *(b)* intercourse?
(1) Once per day or more.
(2) 2 or 3 times per week.
(3) Once a week.
(4) 2 or 3 times per month.
(5) Once a month.
(6) Less than once per month.
(7) Not at all in the last 6 months.

Q21. *How do you feel about the following statement: Men's interest in sexual activity tends to decline as they get older; that is, the older you are, the less interest you have in sexual matters.*
(1) Completely in agreement.
(2) On the whole in agreement.

(continued)

TABLE 1 *(continued)*

(3) Neutral.
(4) Not really in agreement.
(5) Completely disagree.

Q22. *Compared to when you were an adolescent (around 18–20 years), do you feel sexually aroused?*
(1) More than when an adolescent.
(2) About the same.
(3) Less than when an adolescent.

Q23. (*Men 60 years or older only*). *Compared to when you were in your 40s (around 10–20 years ago), do you feel sexually aroused?*
(1) More now than then.
(2) About the same now as then.
(3) Less now than then.

TABLE 2 Response Rates for Sexual Activity Questionnaire

Question[a]	Subjects Responding
Q2	1,661 (97)
Q3	1,629 (95)
Q4	1,358 (79)
Q5	1,359 (80)
Q6	1,581 (93)
Q7	1,661 (97)
Q8	1,658 (97)
Q9	1,625 (95)
Q10	1,607 (94)
Q11	1,610 (94)
Q12	1,643 (96)
Q13	1,647 (96)
Q14	1,651 (97)
Q15	1,654 (97)
Q16	1,636 (96)
Q17 (*a*)	1,333 (78)
Q17 (*b*)	1,306 (76)
Q21	1,640 (96)
Q22	1,633 (96)
Q23	533 (92)[b]

Note: Numbers in parentheses represent percentages.
[a]For text, see table 1. Total sample: 1,709 subjects.
[b]Total sample: 579 men age 60 and over.

How Do Male Sexual Activity and Interest Vary among Men in Their Middle Years?

Statistical Methods

To answer the question of how male sexual activity varies among men who are presently aged forty to seventy, we analyzed the cross-sectional age trend for each item on the sexual-activity questionnaire. Binary-response and multiple-choice items were treated as categorical data and analyzed by logistic regression with age as the independent variable, divided into five-year intervals to allow for linear effects. Quantitative responses (such as frequency of a particular activity or event) were grouped into discrete categories to prevent undue influence of sparse data or extreme values. (Compare, e.g., summary categories for Q15 in fig. 1 with complete range of responses for Q15 listed in table 1.)

Maximum likelihood estimates were produced, with standard error, for the percentage of each categorical response in each of the six five-year age intervals (Kleinbaum, Kupper, and Muller 1987). The null hy-

ERECTILE FUNCTION

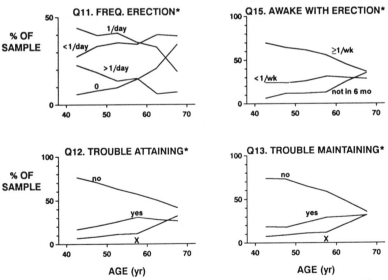

FIGURE 1. Erectile function in men aged forty to seventy, as ascertained by self-report in a random sample of 1,709 community-dwelling Massachusetts men. *Statistically significant cross-sectional age trend, $p < 0.0025$. X indicates no intercourse in last six months. Question numbers refer to table 1.

pothesis—namely, invariance across age groups as to the distribution of responses to a particular item—was tested by the appropriate chi-squared statistic from the maximum-likelihood fitting procedure, with $5k$ degrees of freedom for a k-category response. Because we performed approximately twenty of these statistical tests according to plan in the first part of the analysis, a p value of 0.0025 was taken as the critical level for statistical significance in order to ensure an overall type 1 error rate of 0.05.

The purpose of this first stage of analysis was to provide a straight-forward description of the observed cross-sectional trends in self-reported sexual behavior and interest levels. Therefore, the questionnaire items themselves were analyzed, in a form as close to the original instrument as possible, and age was taken as the sole independent variable. No confounders or correlates of age, such as health or employment, were considered at this stage.

Results

For purposes of presentation, sexual activity is divided into two broad categories: reports concerning actual events or behavior (e.g., waking with an erection or masturbation) and reports of subjective phenomena (e.g., desires, interest, and satisfaction).

Regarding actual events, figure 1 summarizes data on four measures of erectile function: frequency, waking, trouble attaining, and trouble maintaining. Older men reported lower erectile function than younger men on all four measures. The decline with age was statistically significant in each instance. The consistency of this decline across all four measures of erectile function is noteworthy. Because these are cross-sectional data, it is uncertain whether this evident decline is indeed a function of age or whether it reflects cohort differences. This perennial issue is returned to below.

Results concerning aspects of intercourse and ejaculatory function (both behavioral phenomena) are presented in figure 2. Because intercourse and the frequency of ejaculation during intercourse presuppose the availability of a sexual partner, data on the number of partners are also depicted in figure 2. The fraction of men having a partner declined significantly between the ages of forty and seventy. There was a similar and significant decline with age in the frequency of intercourse and ejaculation during intercourse, and in the frequency of ejaculation by masturbation. There was a statistically significant increase with age in the reporting of trouble with ejaculation and of pain associated with inter-

INTERCOURSE AND EJACULATORY FUNCTION

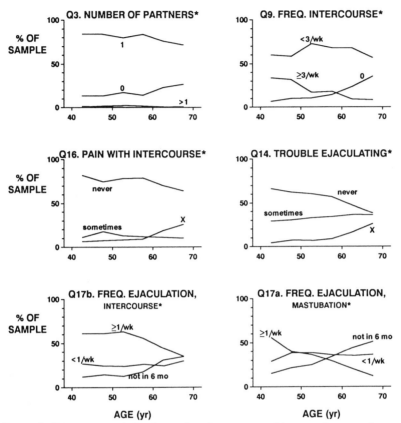

FIGURE 2. Intercourse and ejaculatory function as reported by a random sample of Massachusetts males aged forty to seventy. *Statistically significant cross-sectional age trend, $p < 0.0025$. X indicates no intercourse in last six months. Question numbers refer to table 1.

course. In sum, these reports of different sexual events and behavior evidence a clear, consistent, statistically significant association with age.

With respect to subjective phenomena associated with sexuality (fig. 3), there was again a consistent and significant decline with age in feeling desire, in sexual thoughts and dreams, and in the desired level of sexual activity. There was no evidence in these data that this decline in subjective phenomena either followed or preceded the reported decline in actual behavior or event; they appeared to occur together. The cross-sectional nature of these data precludes a definitive answer to the ques-

SUBJECTIVE ASPECTS OF SEXUALITY

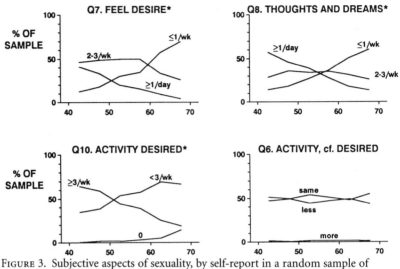

FIGURE 3. Subjective aspects of sexuality, by self-report in a random sample of Massachusetts men aged forty to seventy. *Statistically significant cross-sectional age trend, $p < 0.0025$. Question numbers refer to table 1.

tion as to what occurs first. There does appear to be strong congruence between the level of activity reported and the level of activity desired, even though it is clear that both show marked decline. In other words, there is no evidence here of a disjunction between the level of sexual activity desired and the level of activity actually reported: it is not the case that, as men age, they desire at a level that is different from that which they report.

As illustrated in figure 4, the data concerning men's level of satisfaction with their sex life, their partners, and their estimate of their partners' levels of satisfaction did not evidence the same age-related variation reported so far for other aspects of sexual activity. Despite the marked declines in actual events and behavior and in subjective aspects of sexuality, men in their sixties reported levels of satisfaction with their sex life and partners at about the same level as younger men in their forties. Of this finding at least two interpretations are possible: (*a*) men simply accommodate to the age-related declines that clearly do occur; or (*b*) the expectation of men with respect to sexual activity or desire itself declines with age. In other words, the level of satisfaction reflects the normative expectation associated with a specific age group.

SATISFACTION AND EXPECTATION

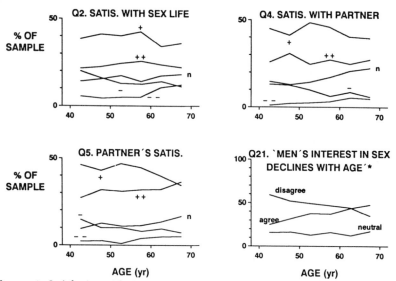

FIGURE 4. Satisfaction with circumstances of present sex life, as reported by a random sample of Massachusetts men aged forty to seventy. + + indicates extremely satisfied; + somewhat satisfied; *n* neither satisfied nor dissatisfied; − somewhat dissatisfied; − − extremely dissatisfied. *Statistically significant cross-sectional age trend, $p < 0.0025$. Question numbers refer to table 1.

The latter appears the more plausible in view of subjects' response to a question concerning their opinion of the following statement: Men's interest in sexual activity tends to decline as they get older. As shown in figure 4, the level of agreement with this statement was significantly and positively associated with the age of the subject; the older the subject, the higher the level of agreement. One can argue that expectations associated with sexual activity decline with age, along with the frequency of sexual events, behavior, and subjective phenomena, and that, consequently, levels of satisfaction in aging men change little as a result of aging itself.

An important concern is whether the trends reported above are in fact age related or whether they are perhaps due to a cohort effect. Are the forty-year-old men in the MMAS in some way different from what the seventy-year-old men were when they were forty, some thirty years earlier? Many would argue that the period from the 1960s through the 1980s was a period of such dramatic social change that the cross-sectional trend may not accurately reflect the longitudinal trend. Figure

5 summaries how respondents compared their present level of sexual arousal with what they felt when they were eighteen years old, and, for subjects over sixty, with what they felt when they were forty. Even during their forties and increasingly with age, men described themselves as less aroused than when they were eighteen years old. The older the subjects, the fewer compared their present level of arousal favorably with that at eighteen. As shown in figure 5, men in the sixty-to-seventy age band considered themselves less aroused than when they were forty. Because this result derives from a small proportion of the total sample, it is not statistically significant. However, these older men did appear to be expressing prior levels of arousal generally consistent with those characterizing the younger men. This suggests that these cross-sectional data may be reflecting a true age trend.

COMPARATIVE LEVEL OF AROUSAL

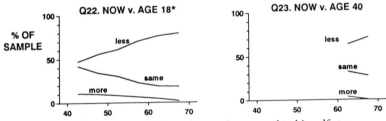

FIGURE 5. Subject's general level of sexual arousal compared to himself at a younger age, as reported by a random sample of Massachusetts men aged forty to seventy. For wording of questions, see table 1. *Statistically significant cross-sectional age trend, $p < 0.0025$.

WHAT ACCOUNTS FOR VARIATION IN MALE SEXUAL ACTIVITY AND INTEREST AMONG MEN IN THEIR MIDDLE YEARS?

Having described the way in which sexual events, behavior, and subjective phenomena vary among a cross section of men in their middle years, it remains to account for the effects observed: What factors are associated with or contribute to the variation reported? Figure 6 diagrammatically represents the many social, psychologic, anthropometric, and biomedical variables considered as possible influences on male sexual activity. For clarity, they are divided into six groups: social circumstances, health status and medical care, anthropometrics, hormones, lifestyle, and psychosocial variables.

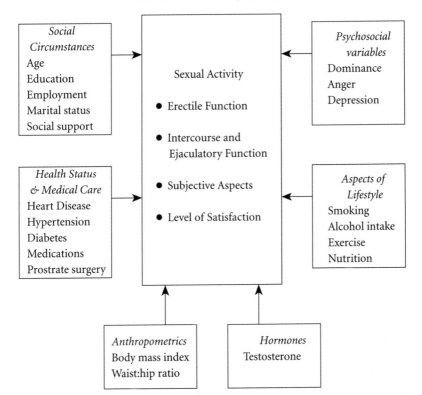

FIGURE 6. Range of social, psychological, anthropometric, lifestyle, biological, and health-status variables gathered by Massachusetts Male Aging Study and potentially influencing sexual activity.

Statistical Methods

To address the interrelationships among this large set of variables, we used methods of multivariate statistics (Kleinbaum, Kupper, and Muller 1987). First, we used multivariate techniques to condense and express the responses to the sexual activity instrument by means of a few summary variables. Second, we used similar techniques to identify a manageable set of unconfounded axes of variation among the many sociodemographic, health-status, psychological, physiological, and lifestyle variables that were collected in MMAS. Finally, we used multivariate regression analysis to establish and describe the association between the major sexual-activity variables and the various domains of independent and intervening variables.

Principal-components analysis was employed to reduce the list of more than twenty questionnaire items to a handful of statistically independent composite sexual-activity factors. Three items were inappropriate for multivariate analysis, being applicable to only a subset of subjects, and were therefore omitted from this stage of analysis. Three additional items (relating to ejaculation) were omitted because of a high rate of nonresponse, which would severely reduce the sample size available for principal-components analysis. The omission of Q4 and Q5, relating to mutual satisfaction of sexual partners, was not detrimental to the analysis, despite the obvious importance of their content, because Q4 and Q5 showed little variation with age and were strongly correlated with Q2, a general question concerning satisfaction with one's sex life (see fig. 4).

The sociodemographic, health-status, psychological, physiological, and lifestyle variables were likewise reduced to a smaller set of statistically independent factors by principal-components analysis. Quartimax rotation was employed to ensure that each variable would be strongly associated with one and only one composite factor. In this respect the rotation method resembled variable cluster analysis.

Having established a principal-components structure for the sexual-activity variables and a structure for their potential predictors, we connected the two structures by multivariate linear regression analysis. The null hypothesis of no effect was tested for each prediction factor with respect to each sexual activity factor by the usual partial F-statistic. As corroboration we conducted, for each prediction factor, a multivariate F-test of the null hypothesis of no effect on the pattern of sexual-activity factors as a whole. Because we planned in excess of forty regression hypothesis tests, a critical p value of 0.001 for statistical significance was adopted as a tight control on type 1 error. All computations were carried out with Statistical Analysis System (SAS) statistical procedures (SAS 1988).

Results: Principal Components of Sexual Activity

Of the 1,709 subjects in the MMAS sample, 1,413 had complete data on the sixteen sexual-activity questionnaire items that we selected for multivariate analysis. Principal-components analysis reduced the sixteen variables to four composite, statistically independent factors (table 3) accounting for 57 percent of the variance. Quartimax rotation produced a clean division of the original sixteen variables, such that each was strongly associated with one and only one of the composite factors.

TABLE 3 Principal Components of Sexual Activity Variables in Massachusetts Male Aging Study

Principal Component	Variance (%)	Constituent Items	Correlation[a]
S1. Involvement	22.3	Q7. Frequency of desire	0.82
		Q8. Frequency of fantasies	0.79
		Q9. Frequency of activity	0.60
		Q10. Frequency preferred	0.78
		Q11. Frequency of erection	0.69
		Q15. Frequency awake erect	0.65
S2. Difficulties	13.6	Q12. Trouble getting erection	0.82
		Q13. Trouble keeping erection	0.82
		Q14. Trouble ejaculating	0.72
		Q16. Pain during intercourse	0.42
S3. Satisfaction	12.8	Q2. Satisfaction with sex life	0.82
		Q6. Satisfaction with frequency	0.76
		Q3. Have partner	0.53
		Q12–16. Intercourse within 6 months	0.57
S4. Attitude	8.6	Q21. Disagree interest declines	0.61
		Q22. More interest than when 18	0.71
Total	57.2		

[a]With principal component.

The dominant factor, accounting for over 22 percent of variance, comprised six variables related to the subject's level of activity and interest in sex (table 3). These included physiological, psychological, and behavioral aspects of involvement in sex, all strongly correlated with one another and with their linear combination defining the first principal component ($r \geq 0.60$). For convenience we dubbed this variable S1, or *involvement.*

The second principal component (S2, *difficulty*) accounted for 13.6 percent of variance and related to functional difficulties in sexual intercourse. Erectile and ejaculatory problems were strongly associated with S2 ($r \geq 0.70$), and unspecified pain during intercourse less so.

Satisfaction (S3) accounted for 12.8 percent of variance. Strongly associated with S3 ($r \geq 0.70$) were too explicit expressions of satisfaction with the subject's sex life. Moderately associated ($r \geq 0.50$) were two objective indicators of behavior: having a partner and having had intercourse within six months of the interview.

The minor component S4, accounting for 8.6 percent of variance, was associated with the subject's opinions on the notion that sexual interest declines with age, in relation both to himself and to men in general. We dubbed this variable *attitude*.

Results: Principal Components of Predictors

Complete data were available from 1,405 subjects for principal-components analysis of twenty-one sociodemographic, health-status, psychological, physiological, and lifestyle variables. These were reduced to eight principal components accounting for 60.6 percent of variance (table 4). Quartimax rotation produced an unambiguous alignment of each original variable with one and only one composite factor in most cases; the exceptions are noted below (table 5).

The eight principal components were roughly equal in importance, none accounting for more than 11 percent of variance. Factor X1 consisted of three related Spielberger anger scales. Factor X2 involved age and three negative correlates reflecting the social circumstances that accompany aging or characterize the older cohort in this sample: lower rate of employment, less education, and lower dominance score on the Jackson scale. Factor X3 coupled repression (Spielberger's inward-

TABLE 4 Principal Components of Predictor Variables in Massachusetts Male Aging Study

Principal Component	Variance (%)	Constituent Variables	Correlation[a]
X1. Anger	11.0	Anger expression	0.89
		Anger out	0.84
		Anger control	−0.85
X2. Aging (social aspect)	9.1	Age	0.76
		Employment	−0.66
		Education	−0.56
		Dominance	−0.50
X3. Depression	8.7	CES-D score	0.72
		Anger-in	0.82
X4. Obesity	8.4	Weight:height^2	0.81
		Waist:hip	0.78
X5. State of health	7.5	General health	0.52
		Diabetes	−0.65
		Heart disease	−0.52
X6. Lifestyle 1	5.9	Cigarette smoking	0.77
X7. Lifestyle 2	5.1	Alcohol consumption	0.77
X8. Prostate surgery	4.9	. . .	0.87

[a]With principal component.

TABLE 5 Predictor Variables Diffusely Associated with Principal Components, Massachusetts Male Aging Study

Variable	Principal Component[a]	Correlation
Hypertension	X4. Obesity	0.45
	X5. State of health	−0.36
Serum-free testosterone	X2. Aging social aspect	0.41
	X6. Lifestyle 1	0.43
	X8. Prostate surgery	0.38
Serum cholesterol	X4. Obesity	0.29
	X6. Lifestyle 1	0.37

[a]See table 4.

directed anger) with depression (CES-D scale). Factor X4 reflected obesity, and factor X5 state of health. Factor X6 was the most ambiguous, carrying a strong correlation with cigarette smoking and mild correlations with serum testosterone and cholesterol as well. Two lifestyle variables, exercise and alcohol consumption, were represented in factor X7. Factor X8 was chiefly correlated with a history of prostate surgery.

A small number of variables failed to line up unambiguously with any one principal component. Hypertension was moderately correlated with both X4 (obesity) and X5 (health). Serum cholesterol was mildly correlated with X4 (obesity) and X6 (cigarette smoking). Serum-free testosterone was moderately correlated with X2 (aging), X6 (cigarette smoking), and X8 (prostate surgery).

In preliminary analyses, we found that use of medications was strongly correlated with the associated disease indices: vasodilators with heart disease, antidiabetics with diabetes, and so on. (Epidemiologists commonly refer to this phenomenon as confounding by indication.) Medication variables were deleted from the principal-components analysis because we found that their presence, by doubly representing each disease condition, caused individual conditions to be highlighted in the factor structure rather than the more conceptually useful composite factors that emerged in their absence (table 4).

Relation of Sexual Activity to Predictors

Multivariate regression analysis, relating the four composite activity variables (S1–S4) to the eight composite predictor variables (X1–X8) produced the relationships diagrammed in figure 7. The independent variables were unconfounded in this analysis because principal compo-

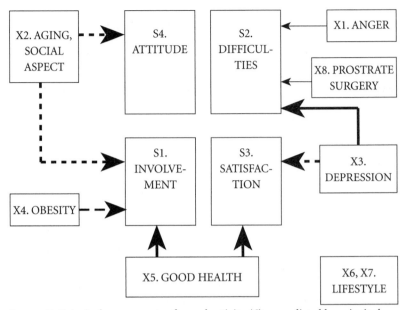

FIGURE 7. Principal components of sexual activity (S) as predicted by principal components of sociodemographic, health-status, physiological, psychological, and lifestyle variables (X). Arrows indicate statistically significant prediction by multivariate linear regression. Heavy line indicates $p < 0.001$; light line, $p < 0.01$. Solid line indicates positive effect; dashed line, negative effect.

nents are orthogonal by construction. Any ambiguity in interpretation is due to the imperfect correlation of original variables with any one principal component, or in some cases the mild correlation of an original variable with two or more principal components.

The most potent predictors were aging and its social correlates (X2), state of health (X5), and depression (X3). Aging was strongly associated with involvement (S1) and attitude toward sex (S4), negatively affecting both. Good health, conversely, had a strong positive association with involvement and satisfaction (S3). Depression strongly predicted sexual difficulties (S2) and detracted from satisfaction. Each of these regression relationships was significant at $p < 0.001$.

Relaxing the criterion to $p < 0.01$ produced a small number of additional relationships, which are depicted lightly in figure 7 to emphasize their less definite status. Obesity (X4) was negatively associated with sexual involvement. Anger (X1) and prostate surgery (X8) added to sexual difficulties. Factor X7, an ambiguous composite involving cigarette smoking, serum testosterone, and serum cholesterol, worked against the difficulties factor (S2) with $p < 0.01$, but this relationship was omitted from figure 7 because of the difficulty of interpretation. Factor X6, comprising two lifestyle variables, did not enter significantly into any regression.

We emphasize that each of these regression relationships is in the nature of a statistical association, and none of the above characterizations should be taken as implying cause and effect.

CONCLUSIONS AND IMPLICATIONS

This paper is organized in two parts, addressing separate but related research questions. In the first part we addressed the question, How do male sexual activity and interest vary among men who are presently in their middle years (between ages forty and seventy)? Having described these effects, in the second part we addressed the question, What variables account for (or are correlated with) age-related patterns in male sexual activity and interest during the middle years?

With respect to the first part we found the following:

1. There was a statistically significant and consistent cross-sectional decline with age in four separate measures of erectile function (frequency, awakening with, trouble attaining, and trouble maintaining).

2. There was clear evidence of a consistent, statistically significant cross-sectional decline with age of intercourse and ejaculatory function. Trouble with ejaculation and pain associated with intercourse both increased across the three decades considered.

3. Subjective aspects of sexuality (e.g., desire, thoughts, and dreams) also appeared to decline in frequency during the middle years. There was no evidence that such decline either followed or preceded the decline in erectile and ejaculatory functions already noted.

4. Levels of satisfaction (with one's sex life, one's partner, and perception of partner's satisfaction) changed little with age. Interest in sexual activity appeared to decline with age (along with actual behavior), so that activity levels and the levels desired and expected appeared generally congruent.

5. Whether or not a cohort effect is operating cannot be definitively addressed with these cross-sectional data. However, a comparison of present levels of sexual arousal in subjects of different ages with levels of arousal at earlier ages suggests that real age trends, rather than cohort influences, account for the results presented.

Regarding the associations discussed in the second part, we found the following:

1. Responses to the sexual activity questionnaire fell into four groups: (1) involvement; (2) difficulties; (3) satisfaction; and (4) attitude. Variables within each group were strongly correlated.

2. The independent variables fell into eight groups of roughly equal statistical importance, reflecting various aspects of aging, health status, personality, and lifestyle.

3. Physiological markers, including serum testosterone and cholesterol, were inextricably confounded with the other independent variables.

4. Aging and its social correlates, taken together, were strongly predictive of decreased involvement with sexual activity and a change in attitude.

5. Good health was associated with more involvement and satisfaction.

6. Depression and repression of anger, taken together, were strongly associated with increased sexual difficulties and less satisfaction.

These findings, from interviews with 1,709 middle-aged men randomly sampled from the general population, have important implications at several different levels. First, with respect to clinical practice, sexual decline or dysfunction is a common presenting problem in everyday medical encounters (Slag et al. 1983; Furlow 1985; National Center for Health Statistics 1988). Sexual decline may be both a symptom of existing disease (e.g., diabetes and prostate disease) and an untoward consequence of medication usage (e.g., antihypertensives and antidepressants; see Schiavi, chap. 12, this vol.); it may also be a precursor of later morbidity (e.g., cardiovascular events). Despite the prevalence and possible clinical significance of sexual decline, there are virtually no up-to-date normative data available to inform clinicians as to the usual levels of activity and interest of normally aging men (Kinsey, Pomeroy, and Martin 1948; Martin 1977). These data from the MMAS go some way to fill gaps in our knowledge of levels of sexual activity, interest, expectations, and satisfaction of normal and usually aging men during their middle years.

Second, our findings have clear implications for *health providers*. If much of the decline in activity and interest levels is attributable to aging per se (and not to para-aging phenomena), then it may be impractical to attempt the restoration of earlier levels of functioning in older men who are apparently less interested and have lower levels of expectation with respect to sexuality. Therapists, who are generally younger than their patients presenting sexual decline, and who often attribute such to para-aging phenomena (e.g., negative life events, depression, loss of partner, retirement, and occupational exposures), may be working toward unrealistic therapeutic goals. The availability of these normative data from the MMAS may help dissuade therapists from holding older patients to a level of performance and interest more appropriate to younger men (Frank, Anderson, and Rubinstein 1978).

Finally, our results clearly indicate that even though much of the decline in sexual activity and interest appears to be attributable to aging per se, a large number of social, psychological, and lifestyle phenomena taken together also contribute significantly to variation across the age range. In other words, the evident decline appears to be due to both nonmodifiable (aging) and modifiable factors. With this new information it is possible to begin to assess the relative contribution of these factors in the aging male presenting with sexual decline, in the same way that modifiable and nonmodifiable contributors are distinguished in the area of cardiovascular disease. Although it is obviously impossible to alter age, race, and family history (nonmodifiable factors), the reduction of other risk factors such as smoking, cholesterol, inactivity, and blood pressure (modifiable factors) is realistic and produces beneficial cardiovascular outcomes. With the MMAS data it may be possible to develop a health-risk appraisal to permit easy identification of individuals likely to experience sexual decline and eventual impotence. If sexual decline and impotence are precursors of subsequent disease (Bähren et al. 1988; Rosen et al., in press; Virag, Bouilly, and Frydman 1985) then such an instrument would be useful not only for clinical urology, but also as a means of identifying and intervening with men at risk for later serious health problems.

REFERENCES

Ascherio, A., M. J. Stampfer, G. A. Colditz, W. C. Willett, and J. B. McKinlay. 1991. Nutrient intakes and blood pressure in normotensive males. *International Journal of Epidemiology* 20:886–91.

Bähren, W., H. Gall, W. Scherb, C. Stief, and W. Thon. 1988. Arterial anatomy and arteriographic diagnosis of arteriogenic impotence. *Cardiovascular Intervent Radiation* 11:195.

Brambilla, D. J., S. M. McKinlay, J. B. McKinlay, S. R. W. Goldfield, and C. Longcope. 1991. Does collecting repeated blood samples improve the precision of estimated steriod hormone levels? Unpublished manuscript. New England Research Institute, Watertown, Mass.

Feldman, H. A., I. Goldstein, J. B. McKinlay, D. G. Hatzichristou, and R. J. Krane. Forthcoming. Impotence and its medical and psychosocial correlates in men aged 40–70: Results of the Massachusetts Male Aging Study. *Journal of Urology.*

Frank, E., C. Anderson, and D. Rubinstein. 1978. Frequency of sexual dysfunction in "normal" couples. *New England Journal of Medicine* 299:111–15.

Furlow, W. L. 1985. Prevalence of impotence in the United States. *Medical Aspects of Human Sexuality* 19:13–16.

Gray, A., J. A. Berlin, J. B. McKinlay, and C. Longcope. 1991a. An examination of research design effects on the association of testosterone and male aging: Results of a meta-analysis. *Journal of Clinical Epidemiology* 44:671–84.

Gray, A., H. A. Feldman, J. B. McKinlay, and C. Longcope. 1991b. Age, disease, and changing sex hormone levels in middle-aged men: Results of the Massachusetts Male Aging Study. *Journal of Clinical Endocrinology and Metabolism* 73:1016–25.

Gray, A., D. N. Jackson, and J. B. McKinlay. 1991. The relation between dominance, anger, and hormones in normally aging men: Results from the Massachusetts Male Aging Study. *Psychosomatic Medicine* 53:375–85.

Jackson, D. N. 1984. *Personality research form manual.* Port Huron, Mich.: Research Psychologists Press.

Kinsey, A. C., W. B. Pomeroy, and C. E. Martin. 1948. Age and sexual outlet. In *Sexual behavior in the human male,* ed. A. C. Kinsey, W. B. Pomeroy, and C. E. Martin, 218–62. Philadelphia: Saunders.

Kleinbaum, D. G., L. L. Kupper, and K. E. Muller. 1987. Variable reduction and factor analysis. In *Applied regression analysis and other multivariable methods,* 595–641. Boston: PWS-Kent.

Longcope, C., S. R. W. Goldfield, D. J. Brambilla, and J. B. McKinlay. 1990. Androgens, estrogens, and sex hormone-binding globulin in middle-aged men. *Journal of Clinical Endocrinology and Metabolism* 71:1442–46.

Martin, C. E. 1977. Sexual activity in the aging male. In *Handbook of sexology,* ed. J. Money and H. Musaph, 813–24. New York: Elsevier.

McKinlay, J. B. 1989. Is there an epidemiologic basis for the male climacteric? The Massachusetts Male Aging Study. In *Menopause: Evaluation, treatment, and health concerns,* ed. C. Hammond, F. Haseltine, & I. Schiff. New York: Liss.

McKinlay, J. B., C. Longcope, and A. Gray. 1989. The questionable physiologic and epidemiologic basis for a male climacteric syndrome: Preliminary results from the Massachusetts Male Aging Study. *Maturitas* 11:103–15.

McKinlay, S. M., D. M. Kipp, P. Johnson, K. Downey, and R. A. Carleton. 1984. A field approach for obtaining physiological measures in surveys of general populations: Response rates, reliability, and costs. In *Proceedings of the Fourth Conference on Health Survey Research Methods.* DHHS Publication no. PHS 84-3346. Washington, D.C.: Government Printing Office.

National Center for Health Statistics. 1988. The National Ambulatory Medical Care Survey: United States 1975–81 and 1985 trends. Vital and Health Statistics series 13, no. 93. DHHS Publication no. PHS 88-1754. Washington, D.C.: Government Printing Office.

Radloff, L. 1977. The CES-D scale: A self-report depression scale for research in the general population. *Applied Psychological Measurement* 1:385–401.

Rosen, M. P., A. J. Greenfield, T. G. Walker, P. Grant, J. Dubrow, M. A. Bettmann,

L. E. Fried, and I. Goldstein. In press. Cigarette smoking: An independent risk factor for atherosclerosis in the hypogastric-cavernous arterial bed of men with arteriogenic impotence. *Journal of Urology.*

SAS Institute. 1988. *SAS/STAT User's Guide.* Cary, N.C.: SAS Institute.

Slag, M. F., J. E. Morley, M. K. Elson, D. L. Trence, C. J. Nelson, A. E. Nelson, W. B. Kinlaw, H. S. Beyer, F. Q. Nuttall, and R. B. Shafer. 1983. Impotence in medical clinic outpatients. *Journal of the American Medical Association* 249:1736–40.

Spielberger, C. D., E. H. Johnson, S. F. Russell, R. J. Crane, G. A. Jacobs, and T. J. Worden. 1985. The experience and expression of anger: Construction and validation of an anger expression scale. In *Anger and hostility in cardiovascular and behavioral disorders,* ed. M. A. Chesney and R. H. Rosenman. New York: Hemisphere McGraw-Hill.

Virag, R., P. Bouilly, and D. Frydman. 1985. Is impotence an arterial disorder? A study of arterial risk factors in 440 impotent men. *Lancet* 1:181–84.

Washburn, R. A., S. R. W. Goldfield, K. W. Smith, and J. B. McKinlay. 1990. The validity of self-reported exercise-induced sweating as a measure of physical activity. *American Journal of Epidemiology* 132:107–13.

Sex and Sexuality in Later Life Stages

Judith A. Levy

Sex is a universal and rewarding activity that can be enjoyed throughout the life course. Its practices and delights are romanticized and celebrated in songs, theater, and art as something special for two people to do—everyone, that is, but two elderly adults. Common stereotypes, held by both the young and old, view sex and sexuality as the prerogative of youth. In contrast to their younger counterparts, older people are viewed as being sexually undesirable, disinterested in sex, and unable to perform functionally (Butler and Lewis 1976, 1986). This chapter challenges these assumptions by examining the scientific facts and popular myths that surround the interaction of sex and age. The overview draws on a small but growing body of research that investigates the sexual attitudes, beliefs, and practices common to older adults. The chapter focuses primarily on the social rather than the physiological properties of aging that influence sex and sexuality in later life.

We begin with the reminder that the lives and interests of older persons are not homogeneous. Just as they differ by characteristics such as race and social class, they also vary in their sexual orientations, life histories, sexual practices, and beliefs. Moreover, when discussing research findings about older people, it is important to define the population of whom we speak. Age norms and age gradings have changed considerably in recent years and people are considered old at a much later point in the life course than fifty years ago. Also, scientific definitions marking the boundaries of old age and the aging processes are quite broad. Masters and Johnson (1966), for example, included women from forty to ninety years old in their study of the aging female, a definition of old age that appears remarkably youthful by 1990s standards. Also, this age range depicts sexuality across a span of fifty years marked by numerous historical events and cohorts (Stanford 1984). Today's seventy-year-old person, who first experienced intercourse as a teen or young adult in the 1930s, confronted a social and sexual climate very different from that experienced by their fifty-year-old counterparts of the 1960s post-pill era. When compared to the experience of this later cohort, birth control and other barriers to unwanted pregnancies were less reliable or available. Norms and attitudes surrounding sexual behavior were more conservative and restrictive. These social factors undoubtedly affected the values, behavioral practices, and expectations of those who were reared under their influence. Thus, any discussion of aging and sex must be sensitive to the changing nature of sexual behavior across the human life course as it is situated within the social forces, events, and value structures of a particular historical period.

With this principle in mind, the following discussion is framed by a life course perspective that considers the occurrence, timing, and sequencing of the events and transitions that mark movement across life from birth to death (Hogan 1980). Within this context, sexuality is viewed as an erotic psychosocial response that can be expressed alone or with others through a variety of sexual acts that may differ in type and frequency as a specific person grows older.

Research on Sex and Sexuality

Although sexual behavior is an understudied area of scientific investigation for all age groups, researchers have been particularly negligent in the study of sexual behavior at the later stages of the life course (Levy and Albrecht 1989a). Examination of the landmark studies of sexual behavior reveal that older people largely have been ignored as a sample or subject of analyses. For example, older people were administered only a portion of the total instrument during the classic Kinsey studies and were excluded completely toward the end of the field work (Kinsey, Pomeroy, and Martin, 1948; Kinsey et al. 1953). The final Kinsey analyses contain only 126 men and 56 women over the ages of sixty out of a total sample of 18,000 adults (Starr 1985). Similarly, only 31 of 694 subjects studied in Masters and Johnson's seminal research on sexual functioning were sixty years old or older. Reports from these studies on age effects and differences are sparse and can be found only through careful gleaning of data primarily describing sex among people at earlier life stages or by generalizing findings based on younger study participants to those who are old.

A small number of more recent studies address this neglect by intentionally focusing on older persons in their sampling or focus. Although their findings are supplemented by other research studies that have received less attention, about five of these efforts form the basic core of knowledge consistently cited in literature reviews of sex and age. In one of the earliest of these investigations, Christenson and Gagnon (1965) drew on the noninstitutionalized portion of the case history files of the Institute for Sex Research to analyze face-to-face interviews with a non-representative sample of 241 white females aged fifty to seventy. Downey (1980), in a later set of analyses using Kinsey data, compared the types and frequency of sexual activity for five cohorts of men. Also recognizing the importance of understanding cohort factors, the Duke Longitudinal Studies collected medical histories, including sexual behavior, from a sample of 260 volunteers beginning in 1954 and continuing at two- and three-year intervals for a total of four data points. Starr and Weiner (1981) administered a fifty-item, open-ended questionnaire to 800 participants at senior centers in diverse geographic areas. Their respondents, who represented a wide range of socioeconomic statuses, were asked about their sexual interests, preferences, satisfactions, behaviors, and needs. Finally, 4,246 older men and women were sampled by the Consumers' Union on a similar set of sexual topics and issues (Brecher 1984).

Because of the necessity of relying so heavily on so few studies for information, a small number of scientists primarily have defined the conceptual contours and contributed the major findings for an important area of inquiry without much additional support or challenge to the seminal insight that their studies provide. This general paucity of research on sex and aging reflects, in part, the general methodological problems of studying human sexual conduct coupled with the high costs and sampling difficulties of targeting an older population (see Levy and Albrecht [1989b]). Taking into account such considerations, decisions to exclude older persons from investigations are reinforced by the commonly accepted belief that older people have little interest in sex and seldom engage in sexual behavior. Moreover, gerontology and the general study of aging have received widespread attention only in recent years in response to meeting the demographic demands of a growing aged population in postindustrial societies (Weg 1983).

Unfortunately, what little is scientifically known about sex and aging often is compromised by serious methodological flaws that challenge their validity (Levy and Albrecht 1989b). As is true of sexual research at all life stages, with the exception of Masters and Johnson (1966, 1970), most studies that include older people are based on self-reported data that potentially are subject to fabrication and problems of recall. The common sampling practice of using volunteers for sexual research typically results in a nongeneralizable sample of middle-class, heterosexual subjects who are likely to be more open and permissive in their sexual behavior than their nonvolunteering counterparts. Many studies fail to control for marital status, thus making it impossible to determine whether variations in sexual behavior are due to age-related factors or differential access to a sexual partner. Moreover, studies of sexual behavior tend to be cross-sectional rather than following age-related changes over time.

One of the great challenges of sexual research on older persons lies in teasing out age from cohort effects (Ludeman 1981). Untangling these influences requires longitudinal techniques that examine sexual behavior at major life events, stages, and transitions. Unfortunately, subject attrition undermines the findings of the few longitudinal studies that might provide these data. Half the 254 older persons enrolled in the Duke Longitudinal Study, for example, were lost to attrition. Those who remained tended to be healthy, cooperative subjects for whom follow-up access was possible (Pfeiffer 1975).

THE DEMOGRAPHICS OF AGING AS A SOCIAL CONTEXT FOR SEXUAL BEHAVIOR

The last fifty years has seen a dramatic increase in the proportion of adults who survive to old age with the result that we clearly live in an aging society. Currently, over one-fourth of the U.S. population is fifty years old or older, and about one-eighth are over the age of sixty-five (Riley 1989). In practical terms, this demographic transformation means that a growing subset of Americans potentially will live to engage in sexual activities at later life stages and within the context of changing definitions and values about what it means to be old. Although biological processes associated with normal aging have been shown to affect older people's sexual capacities negatively (Masters and Johnson 1966), three social factors appear critical in determining whether an older person is sexually active: (1) the desire to engage in some form of sexual activity, (2) availability of a suitable partner for those who desire sexual intercourse or other forms of dyadic sex, and (3) access to a viable physical and social space that permits sexual behavior to occur.

Sexual Desire among Elderly Persons

"The Golden Girls," a popular situation comedy that made its debut on television during the late 1980s, depicts the lives of four single women who are in their late fifties or older. All four women (including a great-grandmother) date and openly express interest in having sexual relationships, although to differing degrees and according to varying sets of social values. To what extent does their mutual interest in sex and their desire to remain sexually active parallel that of older people in the real world?

In contrast to the candid portrayal of sexuality on "The Golden Girls," sexual intercourse between two septuagenarians typically is considered embarrassing or aesthetically unappealing by those even willing to contemplate the act. According to the normative timetables of the life course, sexual interest should begin at mid-adolescence and reach full expression during mid-adulthood at the height of fertility and physical attractiveness. Thus, sex is something popularly believed to be the prerogative of youth. This view partly arises from traditional values that equate sexuality with procreation. Because pregnancy and childbirth are not part of the older person's experience, they are believed not to need or want sex (Weg 1985). Older persons who persist in displaying sexual interest appear off time and out of sequence in terms of their life course trajectories.

In this regard, images in the media and other forms of popular culture, such as cartoons and greeting cards, tend to portray older adults' interest or attempts to be sexual as humorous, ludicrous, scornful, or repugnant (Butler and Lewis 1986; Demos and Jache 1981). These negative views are reinforced by the popular notion that old people are too frail or functionally limited to perform sexually. Moreover, engaging in sexual behavior in old age is perceived by the general public as being perverse (Butler and Lewis 1986). The labels *dirty old man* (Fox et al. 1978) or *indecent old woman* (Driver and Detrich 1982) are applied to aging old people who express interest in having sex. Such messages are so normatively pervasive that older persons come to see themselves as sexless, unattractive, and consigned by old age to an asexual existence (Eaid 1972). Indeed, many older people feel ashamed of their sexual desires, fantasies, and interest (Burnside 1975).

Although the negative influences of ageism are an important variable that potentially can dampen sexual interest, meeting the rigors and demands of daily life also shape older peoples' sexual drives. Engaging in sex at any age requires an investment of time, psychosocial involvement, and energy. Like individuals in other age groups, older people's sexual drives may decline or die under the pressures of mental or physical fatigue, preoccupation with business interests, overindulgence in food or drink, physical illness, and fear of sexual failure (Stanford 1984). Monotony in sexual relationships, related to overfamiliarity and the predictability of sex with the same partner, also may figure in a loss of coital interest (Butler and Lewis 1986; Marron 1982; Masters and Johnson 1966). So do life events and transitions. For example, the term *widower's syndrome* refers to the temporary impotence experienced by some men on remarriage following the death of their first wives. This condition is particularly likely to occur if the former wife's prolonged illness demanded sexual abstinence (Butler and Lewis 1986).

Hormonal changes related to aging also are suspect in reducing libido, but evidence supporting this assumption is contradictory. Some perimenopausal and postmenopausal women experience heightened sexual interest (Kaplan 1974). Other evidence suggests that most women's sexual interest remains largely at preclimateric levels following menopause, although a few women experience some loss of libido (Bachmann et al. 1985). Still other findings suggest that all women experience some reduction in sexual interest as a result of reduced hormonal stimuli after age 60 (Stanford 1984). Given these conflicting reports, it may be that the physiological and social changes associated with age-related hormonal fluctuations may manifest themselves with wide, individual variation. Also, because they occur simultaneously, differentiating change in sexual interest resulting from hormonal shifts from other age-related processes is difficult unless longitudinal measurements are available. For example, contrary to a cross-sectional body of research suggesting that sexual interest in males declines in response to hormonal reductions with age, longitudinal research indicates that many healthy older men maintain their production of testosterone at levels equal to that of younger men (Harman and Tsitouras 1980). Similarly, the period that begins with the climacteric and ends in postmenopause among women occurs with differing levels of psychosocial disruption and varies widely in age of onset, duration, and conclusion. If the interweave of sexuality and the aging processes in women were to be studied longitudinally, it is plausible to expect that different menopausal trajectories would be associated with different permutations of hormonal stimuli and sexual interest.

In general, consensus exists among researchers that some level of sexual desire is felt throughout the life course (Weg 1983). Male subjects in an investigation by Pfeiffer, Verwoedt, and Wang (1969) continued to report high sexual interest at the later stages of the life course, although the interest of the women that were studied declined. Other studies, however, offer alternative evidence that both men and women experience sexual interest and desire well into their later years (Brecher 1984; McIntosh 1981; Starr and Weiner 1981).

Positive self-concepts are probably the single greatest contributor to libido. Men and women who feel food about their bodies and who perceive themselves as physically desirable are more likely to have a satisfying sexual relationship than those who do not. Women, however, are more likely to construct their self-images primarily based on judgments about their appearance; men also consider appearance but give greater weight to sexual performance (Dressen 1975; Stimson, Was, and Stimson 1981).

The knowledge and attitudes that people bring to sexual encounters also have a direct effect on the quality and frequency of their experience. Positive attitudes toward sexuality are associated with the desire to remain sexually active among older people of both sexes (Martin 1981). Meanwhile, programs that transmit sexuality education have been found to positively change and enhance attitudes about sex, sexuality, and aging among older people who carry negative images (Story 1989; Sviland 1978; White 1982; White and Catania 1982).

Availability of a Suitable Partner

While the desire for sexual activity can remain keen in later years, interest often outlives opportunity. Access to a suitable partner is consistently cited in the literature as the major factor governing the incidence and frequency of sexual intercourse and other forms of dyadic sex. By and large, opportunities for partnering are not equally distributed among all people. Although individual characteristics are important in attracting a potential partner, movement across the life course partly is characterized by a series of life events that bring about gains and losses in social relationships. The range of possibilities that offer, withhold, or demand a realignment of sexual bonds include marriage, remarriage, separation, divorce, and the death of a spouse. The relational circumstances that emerge from these events form differing opportunity structures for sex and sexual partnering. Other factors such as gender, sexual orientation, and the influence of kin and other social networks further mitigate the chances of an individual finding a suitable partner. Together, these influences help explain why the number of sexual partners per year reported per person decreases with age. Cross-sectional findings from the National Opinion Research Center's 1989 General Social Survey report a decline from 1.76 partners among those under thirty years old to 0.35 among people seventy years old or older (Smith 1991).

Marriage is the traditional social arrangement in which partnership leading to sexual activity is normatively sanctioned. Consistent with this expectation, older married people are far more likely than singles of the same age to report engaging in sexual intercourse. Masters and Johnson, for example, found that 70 percent of their married sample were sexually active (1966). In contrast, only 7 percent of single, divorced, or widowed older persons sampled in another study reported having recently engaged in sex (Newman and Nichols 1960).

Although most older people report that they believe that extramarital sex is wrong (Glenn and Weaver 1979; Reiss, Anderson, and Sponaugle 1980; Singh, Walton, and Williams 1976; Snyder and Spreitzer 1976), such relationships also offer married people the opportunity for additional partnership. Interestingly, however, they also appear to reduce the frequency of sex. In an analysis of General Social Survey data, Laumann and his associates (1992) found that people with only one partner in the last year, most of whom were married or cohabiting, reported having sex more frequently per week than those with two to four partners. Presumably, higher frequency among those with one partner reflects the increased interactional opportunities of a stable relationship as experienced within the proximity of marriage or coresidence. The effort needed to establish and manage the nonsexual, social dynamics of more than one relationship may siphon time and energy that might be otherwise invested in more frequent sexual activity with one's spouse or permanent partner.

Despite the advantages or normative expectations that surround it, marriage does not guarantee a partner for life. Health problems that develop over the course of a marriage can interfere with one or both partner's ability to engage in sex. The death of a spouse also ends marital opportunities for sexual partnership. Because men tend to have the more serious health problems in old age and women tend to marry older men, women are the more likely of the two sexes to be widowed or paired with a sexually incapacitated spouse. These health and morbidity effects on sexual partnering become increasingly pronounced with age. Nearly 34 percent of women and 7 percent of men are widowed at ages 55–69; 60 percent of women and 18 percent of men have lost a spouse by ages 75–79; and 82 percent of women and only 18 percent of men are widowed at age 85 or older (Sweet and Bumpass 1987). Not surprisingly, given these gender-based differentials, 86 percent of women who reported being celibate in one study gave their husband's death, illness, or loss of sexual capabilities as the reason (Verwoerdt, Pfeiffer, and Wang 1969).

Not all individuals, of course, marry (see Fowlkes, chap. 6, this vol.). In the United States, about 4.9 percent of men and 5.4 percent of women currently between sixty-five and seventy-four years old have remained single all their lives (Keith 1986). Others who do marry become singles again through separation or divorce. These individuals may have adapted to being without a spouse by learning to enjoy their sexuality alone, with other singles, through relationships with people married to others, or in ways that do not require a permanent partner (Weg 1985). Brecher's (1984) report of sex among an unmarried sample of adults over sixty revealed that 75 percent of men and 50 percent of women were sexually active. Similarly Starr and Weiner (1981) found that, although 47 percent of the men and women over the age of sixty that they studied were unmarried, 70 percent of their sample were still sexually active. When compared to heterosexual individuals, lesbians may have advantages over nonlesbians in old age because the number of eligible partners may exceed the number of eligible males available to heterosexual women (Bell 1971). Kelly, however, found that after the age of fifty-five the number of primary relationships among gay men decrease often as a result of the death of a lifelong lover.

In addition to the social arrangements inherent in marital status and other forms of ongoing relationships, opportunities for partnering also are governed by the cultural assumption that equates sexual desirability with such youthful features as slim bodies, flawless complexions, firm muscles, and smooth skin. By these standards, older people with their sagging bodies and facial wrinkles are no longer considered attractive or desirable. Although both sexes experience a gradual decrease in the attributes that are considered attractive, women tend to experience the loss more dramatically and earlier in the life course than men. By about the age of fifty women are seen as declining into sexual oblivion; men may still be coasting in terms of their sexual appeal (Byers 1983). Although the postmenopausal woman is quite capable of erotic responses, she typically is considered beyond her sexual prime. In contrast, the aging process may actually enhance some aspects of the older man's experience. Grey hair on a man may be considered distinguished and a sign of wisdom; on a woman, it typically is regarded as a sign of grandmotherliness, and it carries all the asexual connotations that this image implies. Because attractiveness is associated with feelings of well-being, a perceived decline in appearance can be particularly devastating for women (Stimson, Was, and Stimson 1981). Women who have undergone a mastectomy or hysterectomy are especially vulnerable to feelings of sexual unattractiveness and reduced desirability (Goodwin and Scott 1987).

Negative anticipation and steps to forestall loss of appearance in old age begin relatively early in the adult life course. Attempts to forestall the signs of age have fueled a cosmetic industry ranging from night cremes that women typically start using early in life to cosmetic surgery at later stages to remove under-eye bags, loose facial skin, and sagging posteriors. Despite the greater leeway that they enjoy, men also feel this pressure. Products such as Rogaine are used in an attempt to curb male baldness, and an increasing number of men now join women in turning to the skills of cosmetic surgeons for procedures referred to in the surgical industry as rejuvenation.

Peers (Costello 1973) and kinship ties also influence a person's chances of finding a partner. Although one in five older adults is childless (Bengtson, Rosenthal, and Burton 1990), children and other family members are another source of support or hindrance in establishing relationships that may result in sex. Although children can be a helpful influence, some children resent or discourage their older parents from establishing a new relationship (Stanford 1984). In some instances this stems from a perceived threat to their inheritance (Rubin 1966). In other cases, an older person's lover constitutes an additional source of accommodation or conflict for family members (Woods 1978). Offspring also refuse to recognize their parents' sexuality, particularly in old age (Robinson 1983). Consequently, adult children and other family members may discourage older peoples' attempts to express or act on their sexual interests.

Sexual activity also includes a range of behaviors that do not require a partner. Erotic dreams and waking fantasies represent mental sources of arousal and pleasure that can occur when one is alone. Sexual fantasies and dreams allow for an acceptable expression of forbidden wishes or substitute as an outlet for a negative sexual situation. They also provide an avenue for sexual expression when other forms of sex are unavailable. Whatever their reason, older adults appear to enjoy both forms of sexuality. Almost all the males, regardless of age, and two-thirds of the females that Kinsey studied reported experiencing erotic dreams. Another survey found that 88 percent of men and 72 percent of women in a sample of healthy people between ages 80 and 102 fantasized about sex (Crooks and Baur 1990).

Masturbation also constitutes a viable and readily available form of sexual activity that can be practiced alone. Besides serving as a sexual release in old age for both men (Downey 1980) and women (Doress and Siegal 1987), masturbation stimulates sexual appetite and contributes to the maintenance of aging genitalia (Weg 1985). It is particularly salient and convenient for older adults without partners (White and Catania 1982), an advantage that some elderly persons appear to enjoy. Christenson and Gagnon's (1965) study, for example, reports that the incidence of masturbation was highest among unpartnered older women, with 25 percent of single females still masturbating after age 70. Unfortunately, the pleasures and advantages of masturbation often are offset by personal guilt or disapproval stemming from childhood socialization to the belief that masturbation is morally wrong. In a study of thirty-two healthy males and females, only 67 percent of the men and 35 percent of the women approved of masturbation (Smith and Smith 1970).

Access to a Conducive Environment

Although sex is shown explicitly in many contemporary films, magazines, and other aspects of material culture, the actual practice of sexual intercourse tends to occur behind closed doors and without an audience. Thus, opportunities for sexual exchanges partly are governed by the availability of private space where they can occur. Most older adults presumably have little difficulty finding the seclusion needed to engage in sexual acts as the majority of people sixty-five years old or older live alone or as part of a marital dyad. This residential independence holds true even for the oldest of old. Census figures from 1980 show that one-half of women and two-thirds of men eighty-five or older live in their own homes (Longino 1988).

Although their proportion relative to the total population of older people is small, about 5 percent of persons over the age of sixty-five are in nursing homes or other long-term care facilities. Before they die, approximately 50 percent of women and 30 percent of men spend some time in a nursing home (Cohen, Tell, and Wallack 1986). Here the normative and environmental opportunities for sexual expression historically have been repressive. Research from the 1960s through the mid-1980s amply documents the insensitive and restrictive practices typically employed by most long-term care facilities to discourage or inhibit sexual relations among residents. A 1983 study showed that hugging and kissing on the cheek were the only sexual behaviors perceived by nursing staff as acceptable (Szasz 1983). Separation of married couples who engaged in sexual activities was common (Falk and Falk

1980). Few facilities provided the privacy or freedom from supervision needed for courtship or to maintain marital relationships (Lobsenz 1974), and contact with the opposite sex typically was confined to public lounges and dining rooms where staff could monitor what was going on (Kaas 1978). In addition, administrators routinely resisted offering educational programs related to sexuality, and residents themselves frequently felt uncomfortable when topics concerning sex were introduced (Starr and Weiner 1981).

These attitudes and practices appear to be changing, partly in response to legal statutes that protect the older person's rights (Patients' Rights Section 1980). Nonetheless, a legacy of former attitudes and practices appears to remain (White and Catania 1982). The problem of finding a suitable space for sex is particularly acute for older homosexual partners because homophobic attitudes and prejudice against lesbian and gay lifestyles make it difficult to establish or maintain lesbian and gay relationships within nursing homes (Kelly and Rice 1986).

Older persons who live with their offspring also may lack the privacy needed to engage in sexual behavior (Butler and Lewis 1986). This problem is exacerbated in situations of role reversal, where the adult child becomes the parent to the older person and demands that the person adhere to limits and boundaries that he or she imposes (Steege 1986; Sviland 1978).

Do Older People Really "Do It"?

When asked how often they thought that people engaged in sexual behavior as they grew older, college students in one study reported believing that frequency of sexual intercourse declines in a rapid, linear manner from age 20 and diminishes almost entirely in old age (Zeiss 1982). Ample evidence, however, shows that, despite social and structural barriers to sexual activity, sexual interest and activity persist well into the later life stages. But, exactly what is it that older people do and does it differ from younger people?

Normal Age-Related Changes in Physiology That Affect Sex and Sexuality

The physiological processes of aging are multidimensional and complex. Not all men and women experience the biological changes at the same rate, intensity, self-awareness, or attitudes. Unfortunately, many older people equate what is a normal and clinically nonthreatening reduction in sexual response related to the physiological process of aging with sexual dysfunction and impotence (Stanford 1984).

As men age, they experience change in the duration and intensity of their sexual response cycle (Masters and Johnson 1966). In contrast to the few seconds typically needed by young men to achieve an erection, during the excitement phase, older males may require several minutes of direct stimulation to achieve an erect penis. During the plateau stage, muscle tension (myotonia) may be less, and the testes may not elevate as close to the perineum as at an earlier age, but a tendency toward increased prolongation of this phase may contribute to enhanced pleasure. The orgasm phase shortens and lacks the urgency of youth. The expulsive force and volume of the seminal fluid decreases. Detumescence is of shorter duration during the resolution phase, and the refractory period takes longer before another erection can be attained.

As women age, all phases of the response cycle continue to occur but with less intensity, resulting from hormonal changes (Masters and Johnson 1966). During the excitement phase, vaginal expansion decreases and lubrication in older women may take several minutes to produce rather than the ten to thirty seconds experienced during early adulthood. In the plateau phase, the uterus elevates but to a somewhat lesser degree for those women who have completed menopause. Contractions of the orgasmic platform and the uterus continue to occur at the orgasm phase, but their numbers are reduced. Finally, entry into the resolution phase typically occurs more rapidly in postmenopausal women.

Frequency of Sexual Activity

Until recently when researchers began to appreciate the social aspects of sexual behavior, the largest body of research on sexual behavior at all life stages consisted largely of activity counts and attempts to assess functional ability couched primarily within the context of genital sex rather than the intimate sexuality of a relationship. The earliest research of this genre found low levels of sexual activity among older people, particularly when compared to their younger counterparts. Kinsey, Pomeroy, and Martin (1948), for example, reported a decrease in incidence and frequency as men aged. Meanwhile, a study of 188 healthy, highly socioeconomically advantaged married males in the Washington-Baltimore metropolitan area showed that over one-third of the sixty- to seventy-nine-year-old respondents reported no more than six sexual events within a year (Martin 1981).

More recent studies suggest that the rate of sexual behavior remains relatively stable as people age, providing that they have a partner (Comfort 1980; Starr and Weiner 1981). George and Weiler (1981), in a second wave of the Duke Longitudinal Studies, found little change in rates of activity among married people during the six-year period in which the activities of the 278 individuals in their sample were measured. The Starr and Weiner report found that sex and sexuality were a vital and valued part of the lives of the 800 individuals that they surveyed. When taken as a whole, these studies and others suggest that sexual interest and activity continue into old age, with some decline in frequency and type for some but not all older adults (Starr 1985).

Diachronicity appears to be an important key to sexual patterns in old age. People who are active in youth and midlife tend to be active later on (Corbett 1981; Irwin 1973; Pfeiffer and Davis 1972). This trend holds true even for the institutionalized older person (White 1982). Conversely, the person with little sexual activity throughout life may curb or cease sexual activity in old age (Masters and Johnson 1966). In this regard, an association has been found between feeling weak to moderate sexual feelings in youth and reports of being without sexual feelings in old age (Dressel and Avant 1983).

In sum, there appears to be some truth to the popular adage, Use it or lose it, when applied to sexual behavior. The best prospect for continued sexual activity throughout the life course rests in being sexually active without interruption (Masters and Johnson 1966). Disuse attrition occurs in periods of abstinence, making it difficult to resume sex at a later date. For example, women who have sex once a month or less may experience discomfort at penetration (Masters and Johnson 1966). Unnecessarily prolonged abstinence among men who experience chronic conditions, such as cardiovascular disease, can result in functional difficulties when they do attempt to resume activities (Byers 1983).

Effects of Illness

Arthritis, back pains, cancer and its therapies, and other disabling or chronic conditions common to aging can hinder the older person's ability to remain sexually active. Medications for arthritis, blood pressure, and antidepressants that may be prescribed for medical conditions have an inhibiting effect on sexual response and functioning (see Schiavi, chap. 12, this vol., for an extended discussion). Illness may be more problematic for men because of its effects on penile erection. In one study, the large majority of males attributed cessation of intercourse to illness-related problems (Verwoerdt, Pfeiffer, and Wang 1969).

In contrast to males, because of their receptive role in intercourse, women typically do not have the same difficulties with performance. Rather, sexual response and functioning is more likely to result from physiological changes associated with menopause, including vaginal dryness, that may make intercourse painful. The excessive fatigue, emotional irritability, and hot flashes of menopausal discomfort can interfere with a woman's pleasure in intercourse (McCoy et al. 1985). In a few instances, an unusually low estrogen level is associated with reduced coital activity (Cutler, Garcia, and McCoy 1987). An increased sex drive that accompanies the administration of estrogenic preparations may be due to the cessation of these problems rather than actual adjustment of the person's sex-steroid imbalance (Masters 1957).

Sexual problems including male impotency following a heart attack are common and usually stem from psychosocial anxiety and apprehension rather than organic causes. Both the male who experienced a myocardial infarction and his spouse may fear resuming intercourse for fear of precipitating another attack. Marron (1982) reports that the general rule in resumption of sex is about three months following the occurrence. About one-third of those who follow this guideline return to their former level of activity. The remainder undergo some permanent reduction of activity, and about 10 percent abstain permanently. Individuals, particularly men, because of their higher rates, may avoid resuming sexual intercourse out of fear of provoking another attack. Despite such fears and possible limitations, research shows that older adults develop strategies that overcome the limitations of illness and disability (Bangs 1985). These include adopting positions that avoid pressure on joints and other parts of the body where discomfort occurs (Doress and Siegal 1987). A study of thirty-two older male cancer patients who had undergone radical prostectomies, a procedure that is strongly associated with erectile dysfunction, found that only six of these patients remained totally sexually inactive over time (Spengler 1981). Thus, the majority had found means to continue some form of sexual interaction; a key element in their resumption was having a partner who perceived them as remaining sexually capable.

Sexuality becomes intertwined with the aging process both in changes related to reproduction and the infirmity that characterizes advances in old age. Men who are anxious or ambivalent about sexual activities may use the belief that sexual interest and loss of functional

ability is a natural state in old age as a welcome excuse to abandon sexual activities (Comfort 1980). Perhaps, as has been found with men,
some women may welcome menopause as a sign that sexual activities
no longer are appropriate. The belief that older persons should not engage in sex also serves the purpose of an excuse or face-saving device
for those who never did like sex, lack available partners, or have lost
their sexual capacity (McCarthy 1979).

WRITING NEW SEXUAL SCRIPTS

Frequency counts and functional measures capture only the quantity
side of sexual behavior. This measurement practice ignores the social
meanings and role that sexual behavior plays in the larger framework
of peoples' lives. Moreover, the focus on counts carries an age bias as it
applies young and middle-aged standards to the study of people later in
life (Robinson 1983). This emphasis on objective criteria does not take
into account how sex and sexuality are viewed from the perspective of
the older person (Thomas 1982). When compared to younger counterparts, older adults may be enjoying the benefits of quality over quantity
(Verwoerdt 1976).

In recognition that coitus and other sexual practices take place
within the total social context of human interaction, recent research has
turned to the social relationships of sexuality including issues of intimacy, pleasure, and bonds of human connectedness that sexual interaction can provide. In this regard, evidence suggests that most older
people find sex equally as satisfying or more so than when they were
younger, particularly when the social rewards of sex are considered
(Brecher 1984; Starr and Weiner 1981). This may hold true regardless
of sexual orientation. About half the men in a small study of gay men
reported that sex was less frequent than in their younger years but more
satisfying because of the increased emphasis on intimacy and the total
person (Kimmel 1980). From this perspective, many individuals report
that age enhances many valued components of sexual relations.

Although intercourse may become less frequent, kissing, caressing,
and more prolonged intercourse may contribute to greater satisfaction
in old age (Brecher 1984). Intimacy can result from placing greater emphasis on cuddling and manual stimulation without penetration.
Menopause, with its resulting freedom from worry about conception
and pregnancy (McKinlay, McKinlay, and Brambilla 1987), may increase
a woman's desire and enjoyment of sex. Also, the movement toward
biological and social androgyny related to hormonal changes associated

with aging may encourage older adults to expand their role concepts of appropriate sexual behavior (Rice and Kelly 1987). Both sexes may become more sensually compatible when androgyny results in men developing greater enjoyment of nongenital sexuality and in women realizing greater pleasure in genital sex (Bangs 1985).

Change in attitudes and life circumstances related to older age also may prompt new sexual behaviors and practices. Loss of a marital partner through death or divorce may result in the search for new sexual partners or realignments of long-standing unrewarding sexual practices and renewed interest in sex (Masters and Johnson 1966). Some people over sixty-five increase the number of sexual encounters (Pfeiffer 1975; Sarrel and Whitehead, 1985). Experimentation with new positions may occur, in some instances to offset physical difficulties. Sexual orientations may shift. Some women, following years of being a heterosexual wife and mother, may turn to a lesbian relationship (partnership) and perhaps join a community of women, now free to follow a previously unexpressed sexual orientation, or choose to change in response to new social circumstances (Doress and Siegal 1987; Goodwin and Scott 1987). Males also may turn to homosexual relationships in old age (Brecher 1984; Gray and Dressen 1985).

With death or divorce, older persons may find themselves back on the dating market. The person who is fifty or older typically experienced courtship and marriage prior to birth control pills and the sexual revolution. They now face the dilemma of how to be sexually active outside of marriage in a dating market that has changed considerably since their youth. Advice books such as *How to Find Romance after 40* (Grice 1985) and *Love, Sex, and Intimacy after 50* (Gershenfeld and Newman 1991) offer advice on topics that range from locating a potential person to date to handling the fears and practical problems of being sexually active. Classes and programs that focus on communication and sexual techniques enhance sexual satisfaction and increase activity (Rowland and Haynes 1978).

Perhaps one of the newer areas of advice (see Gershenfeld and Newman 1991, 253–55; Grice 1985, 281–86) concerns measures for avoiding sexually transmitted disease (STDs). Actual statistics on STDs among older people rarely are reported, perhaps because health providers and their older patients fail to recognize the importance of screening for these diseases (Ehrhardt and Wasserheit 1991). Figures from over a decade ago reported a prevalence rate of 1.5 percent for latent syphilis among older men and estimates at that time projected that 3 percent of older men were believed to be infected with gonorrhea (Felstein 1983). Meanwhile, a study that examined epidemiological trends for 1982–87 showed that 10 percent of reported cases of AIDS occurred among people fifty or older (Stall, Catania, and Pollack 1989). Most of these resulted from transfusions prior to the institution of screening tests to detect infected blood. Nonetheless, the proportion of adults over fifty with sexually acquired AIDS (both homosexual and heterosexual) occurs at a substantially higher rate than at younger ages (Riley 1989). Biological changes associated with aging may increase the efficiency of HIV transmission and decrease immune-system function (Catania et al. 1989). Also older gay men tend to reject safer sex practices (Bye 1984), although older people in general are more likely than their younger counterparts to subscribe to sexual norms that approximate safer sex (Levy and Albrecht 1989a). Over all, older people tend to have fewer sexual partners and engage in less high-risk behaviors than younger adults (see Hunt [1974]; Starr and Weiner [1981]).

For the most part, current cohorts of older individuals tend to be sexually conservative about what they view as sexually appropriate behavior. Although they appear to approve sexuality even in old age, they are less accepting than their younger counterparts of noncoital sexual behaviors such as oral sex (Story 1989). A study of one hundred women between the ages of sixty and ninety-four reported that they are still interested in sexual activity, but the majority disapproved of what they considered unusual forms of sexual behavior (McIntosh 1981). Meanwhile, the actual practice by older people of behavior considered deviant by all age groups (such as exhibitionism and pedophilia) appears negligible (Whiskin 1970).

How much of the findings reported in this chapter will hold for successive waves of older people moving through historical time and across the life course? The answer is that we do not know. New groups of aging individuals can be expected to write their own sexual scripts partially in response to the social values and forces of their era, personal biographies, and cohort influences. Intercohort shifts in age-graded life chances provide an ever-changing opportunity structure for older adults with considerable variation within cohorts over the live course. In addition, the lengthening of the life course has stretched the period spent in old age and increased incentives for retaining sexual vitality and creating new scripts. Concomitant demographic processes that have brought about the feminization of old age in postindustrial societies have created a social climate in which women and men adopt new gender roles and sexual relationships vis-à-vis one another. To further understand the intersection of age and sex, we need to look at the sexual expressions of those born at different times and at different stages of the life course over time. The challenge for research is before us.

REFERENCES

Bachmann, G. A., S. R. Leiblum, B. Sandler, W. Ainsley, R. Narcessian, R. Shelden, and H. N. Hymans. 1985. Correlates of sexual desire in post-menopausal women. *Maturitas* 7:211–16.

Bangs, L. 1985. *Aging and positive sexuality: A descriptive approach.* Ph.D. dissertation, U.S. International University.

Bell, R. R. 1971. *Social deviance.* Homewood, Ill.: Dorsey.

Bengtson, V., C. Rosenthal, L. Burton. 1990. Families and aging. In *Aging and the social sciences*, ed. R. H. Binstock and L. K. George, 263–87. San Diego, Calif.: Academic Press.

Brecher, E. L. 1984. *Sex and aging: A Consumers' Union report.* Boston: Little, Brown.

Burnside, I. M. 1975. Listen to the aged. *American Journal of Nursing* 75:1801–03.

Butler, R. N., and M. I. Lewis. 1976. *Love and sex after sixty.* New York: Harper & Row.

———. 1986. *Love and sex after 40.* New York: Harper & Row.

Bye, L. 1984. *Designing an effective AIDS prevention campaign strategy for San Francisco: Results from the first probability sample of an urban gay community.* San Francisco: San Francisco AIDS Foundation.

Byers, Joan P. 1983. Sexuality and the elderly. *Geriatric Nursing* 4(5): 293–97.

Catania, J. A., H. Turner, S. M. Kegeles, R. Stall, L. Pollack, S. E. Spitzer, and T. J. Coates. 1989. HIV transmission risks of older heterosexuals and gays. In *Aids in an aging society*, ed. M. W. Riley, M. G. Ory and D. Zablotsky, 77–95. New York: Springer.

Christenson, C., and J. Gagnon. 1965. Sexual behavior in a group of older women. *Journal of Gerontology* 20:351–56.

Cohen, M. A., E. J. Tell, and S. S. Wallack. 1986. The lifetime risks and costs of nursing home use among the elderly. *Medical Care* 24:1161–72.

Comfort, A. 1980. Sexuality in later life. In *A handbook of mental health and aging*, ed. J. E. Birren and R. B. Sloane, 885–92. Englewood Cliffs, N.J.: Prentice-Hall.

Corbett, L. 1981. The 1st sexual taboo: Sex in old age. *Medical Aspects of Human Sexuality* 15:117–31.

Costello, M. K. 1973. Intimacy and aging. *American Journal of Nursing* 75:1330–32.

Crooks, R., and K. Baur, 1990. *Our sexuality.* Redwood City, Calif.: Cummings.

Cutler, W., C. Garcia, and N. McCoy. 1987. Perimenopausal sexuality. *Archives of Sexual Behavior* 16:463–73.

Demos, V., and A. Jache. 1981. When you care enough: An analysis of attitudes towards aging in humorous birthday cards. *The Gerontologist* 21:209–15.

Doress, P. B., and D. Siegal. 1987. The potential of the second half of life. In *Ourselves, growing older*, ed. P. B. Doress, D. L. Siegal, and the Midlife and Older Women Book Project, xxi–xxvi. New York: Simon & Schuster.

Downey, L. 1980. Integenerational change in sex behavior: A belated look at Kinsey's males. *Archives of Sexual Behavior* 9:297–317.

Dressel, P., and W. Avant. 1983. Range of alternatives. In *Sexuality in the later years: Roles and behavior,* ed. R. B. Weg, 185–207. New York: Academic Press.

Dressen, S. E. 1975. The sexually active adult. *American Journal of Nursing* 75: 1001–5.

Driver, J. D. and D. Detrich. 1982. Elders and sexuality. *Nursing Care,* February, 8–11.

Eaid, C. 1972. Sex counseling for your geriatric patients. *Canadian Family Physician* 18(12): 58–60.

Ehrhardt, A. A., and J. N. Wasserheit. 1991. Age, gender, and sexual risk behaviors for sexually transmitted diseases in the United States. In *Research issues in human behavior and sexually transmitted disease in the AIDS era,* ed. J. N. Wasserheit, S. O. Aral, K. K. Holmes, and P. J. Hitchcock, 97–121. Washington, D.C.: American Society for Microbiology.

Falk, G., and U. Falk. 1980. Sexuality and the aged. *Nursing Outlook* 28:51–55.

Felstein, I. (1983). *Sex in later life.* Baltimore: Penguin.

Fox, N., A. Garland, J. Hanss, and D. Pettid. 1978. Sexuality among the aging. *Practical Nursing,* 16–41.

George, L. K., and S. J. Weiler. 1981. Sexuality in middle and late life. *Archives of General Psychiatry* 38:919–23.

Gershenfeld, M., and J. Newman. 1991. *Love, sex, and intimacy after 50.* New York: Fawcett Columbine.

Glenn, N. D., and C. N. Weaver. 1979. Attitudes toward premarital, extramarital, and homosexual relations in the U.S. in the 1970's. *Journal of Sex Research* 15(2): 108–18.

Goodwin, A. J., and L. Scott. 1987. Sexuality in the second half of life. In *Ourselves growing older,* ed. P. B. Doress and D. L. Siegal, 79–105. New York: Simon & Schuster.

Gray, H., and P. Dressen. 1985. Alternative explanations of aging among gay males. *Gerontologist* 25:83–87.

Grice. J. 1985. *How to find romance after 40.* New York: Evans.

Harman, S. M., and P. D. Tsitouras, 1980. Reproductive hormones in aging men. I. Measurement of sex steroids, basal luteinizing hormone and Leydig cell response to human chorionic gonadotropin. *Journal of Clinical Endocrinology and Metabolism* 51:35–40.

Hogan, D. 1980. The transition to adulthood as a career contingency. *American Sociological Review* 45:261–76.

Irwin, T. 1973. Sexuality in late years. *Physician's World* 1:53–56.

Kaas, M. J. 1978. Sexual expression of the elderly in nursing homes. *Gerontologist* 18:372–78.

Kaplan, H. S. 1974. *The new sex therapy.* New York: Brunner-Mazel.

Keith, P. M. 1986. The social context and resources of the unmarried in old age. *International Journal of Aging and Human Development* 23(2): 81–96.

Kelly, J., and S. Rice. 1986. The aged. In *Helping the sexually oppressed,* ed. H. Grochros, J. Grochros, and J. Fisher. Englewood Cliffs, N.J.: Prentice-Hall.

Kimmel, D. 1980. Life history interviews of aging gay men. *International Journal of Aging and Human Development* 10:239–48.

Kinsey, A. C., W. B. Pomeroy, and W. B. Martin. 1948. *Sexual behavior in the human male.* Philadelphia: Saunders.

Kinsey, A. C., W. B. Pomeroy, W. B. Martin, and P. H. Gebhard. 1953. *Sexual behavior in the human female.* Philadelphia: Saunders.

Laumann, E. 1992. Sexual practices in the general population. Paper presented at the annual meeting of the Midwest Sociological Society, Kansas City.

Levy, J. A., and G. L. Albrecht. 1989a. A review of research on sexual and AIDS-related attitudes and behavior. In *AIDS in an aging society,* ed. M. W. Riley, M. G. Ory, and D. Zablotsky, 39–59. New York: Springer.

―――. 1989b. Methodological considerations in research on sexual behavior and AIDS among older people. In *AIDS in an aging society,* ed. M. W. Riley, M. G. Ory, and D. Zablotsky, 96–123. New York: Springer.

Lobsenz, N. 1974. 1974. Sex and the senior citizen. *New York Times Magazine,* 20 January, 87–91.

Longino, Jr., C. F. 1988. A population profile of very old men and women in the United States. *The Sociological Quarterly* 29(4): 559–64.

Ludeman, K. 1981. The sexuality of the older person: Review of the literature. *The Gerontologist* 20:182–87.

Marron, K. R. 1982. Sexuality with aging. *Geriatrics* 37:135–36, 138.

Martin, C. E. 1981. Factors affecting sexual functioning in 60–79 year old married males. *Archives of Sexual Behavior* 10:399–420.

Masters, W. H. 1957. Sex steroid influence on the aging process. *American Journal of Obstetrics and Gynecology* 74:733–46.

Masters, W. H., and V. E. Johnson. 1966. *Human sexual response.* Boston: Little, Brown.

―――. 1970. *Human sexual inadequacy.* Boston: Little, Brown.

McCarthy, P. 1979. Geriatric sexuality: Capacity, interest, and opportunity. *Journal of Gerontological Nursing* 5 (January–February): 20.

McCoy, N., W. Cutler, R. Prescott, I. Campbell, and B. Clark. 1985. Relationship among sexual behavior, hot flashes, and hormone levels in premenopausal women. *Archives of Sexual Behavior* 14:385–94.

McIntosh, D. 1981. Sexual attitudes in a group of older women. *Issues in Mental Health Nursing* 3:109–22.

McKinlay, J., S. McKinlay, and D. Brambilla. 1987. The relative contribution of endocrine changes and social circumstances to depression in middle-aged women. *Journal of Health and Social Behavior* 28:345–63.

Newman, G., and C. R. Nichols. 1960. Sexual activities and attitudes in older persons. *Journal of the American Medical Association* 173:33–35.

Patients' Rights Section. 1980. Marital Privacy, 405 1121 (K[14]). In *Federal regulations guidelines for directors of nursing,* ed. M. L. Kander and K. May, 710, 711. Owings Mill, Md.: National Law Publishing.

Pfeiffer, E. 1975. Sex and aging. In *Sexual issues in marriage,* ed. I. Gross. New York: Spectrum.

Pfeiffer, E., and G. Davis. 1972. Determinants of sexual behavior in middle and old age. *Journal of the American Geriatric Society* 20:151–58.

Pfeiffer, E., A. Verwoerdt, and H. S. Wang. 1969. The natural history of sexual behavior in a biologically advantaged group of aged individuals. *Journal of Gerontology* 24:193–98.

Reiss, I. L., R. E. Anderson, and G. C. Sponaugle. 1980. A multivariate model of the determinants of extramarital permissiveness. *Journal of Marriage and the Family* 42:395–411.

Rice, S., and J. Kelly. 1987. Love and intimacy needs of the elderly: Some philosophical and intervention issues. *Journal of Social Work and Human Sexuality* 5:89–96.

Riley, M. W. 1989. AIDS and older people: The overlooked segment of the population. In *AIDS in an aging society*, ed. M. W. Riley, M. G. Ory, and D. Zablotsky, 3–26. New York: Springer.

Robinson, P. K. 1983. The sociological perspective. In *Sexuality in the later years: Roles and behavior*, ed. R. B. Weg, 82–103. New York: Academic Press.

Rowland, K. F., and S. N. Haynes. 1978. A sexual enhancement program for elderly couples. *Journal of Sex and Marital Therapy* 4:91–113.

Rubin, I. 1966. Sexual life after forty and after seventy. In *Analysis of Human sexual response*, ed. R. Brecher & E. Brecher, 251. Boston: Little, Brown.

Sarrel, P. M., and M. I. Whitehead. 1985. Sex and menopause: Defining the issues. *Maturitas* 7:217–24.

Singh, B. K., B. I. Walton, and J. S. Williams. 1976. Extramarital sexual permissiveness: Conditions and contingencies. *Journal of Marriage and the Family* 38:701–12.

Smith, J., and L. Smith. 1970. Co-marital sex and the sexual freedom movement. *Journal of Sex Research* 6:131–42.

Smith, T. W. 1991. Adult sexual behavior in 1989: Number of partners, frequency of intercourse, and risk of AIDS. *Family Planning Perspectives* 23:102–7.

Snyder, E. E., and E. Spreitzer. 1976. *Archives of Sexual Behavior* 5(3): 249–54.

Spengler, A. 1981. Sexuality and aging: The role of severe illness. Paper presented at the twelfth International Congress of Gerontology, Hamburg.

Stall, R., J. A. Catania, and L. Pollack. 1989. The social epidemiology of AIDS and HIV infection among older Americans. In *AIDS in an aging society*, ed. M. W. Riley, M. G. Ory, and D. Zablotsky, 60–76. New York: Springer.

Stanford, D. 1984. Sexuality and aging. In *Mental health and the elderly*, ed. B. A. Hall. New York: Grune & Stratton.

Starr, B. D. 1985. Sexuality and aging. In *Annual review of gerontology and geriatrics*, ed. C. Eisdorfer, M. P. Lawton, and G. L. Maddox. New York: Springer.

Starr, B. D., and M. B. Weiner. 1981. *The Starr-Weiner report on sex and sexuality in the mature years*. Briarcliff Manor, N.Y.: Stein & Day.

Steege, J. F. 1986. Sexual functioning in the aging woman. *Clinical Obstetrics and Gynecology* 29:462–69.

Stimson, A., J. Was, and J. Stimson. 1981. Sexuality and self-esteem among the elderly. *Research in Aging* 3:228–39.

Story, M. D. 1989. Knowledge and attitudes about the sexuality of older adults among retirement home residents. *Educational Gerontology* 15:515–26.

Sviland, M. A. 1978. In *Sexuality and aging*, ed. R. L. Solnick, 96–114. Los Angeles: Univ. of Southern California Press.

Sweet, J. A., and L. L. Bumpass. 1987. *American families and households.* New York: Russell Sage.

Szasz, G. 1983. Sexual incidents in an extended care unit for aged men. *Journal of the American Geriatrics Society* 31:407–11.

Thomas, L. E. 1982. Sexuality and aging: Essential vitamin or popcorn? *The Gerontologist* 22:240–43.

Verwoerdt, A. E. 1976. Normal psychology of the aging process revisited. I. Sex and old age: A further review of the literature: discussion. *Journal of Geriatric Psychiatry* 9(2): 211–19.

Verwoerdt, A. E., E. Pfeiffer, and H. Wang. 1969. Sexuality behavior in senescence. *Geriatrics* 24:134–37.

Weg, R. B. 1983. Introduction: Beyond intercourse and orgasm. In *Sexuality in the later years,* ed. R. B. Weg, 1–10. New York: Academic Press.

———. 1985. Beyond babies and orgasms. In *Growing old in America,* ed. E. Hess & E. Markson, 206–22. New Brunswick: Transaction.

Whiskin, R. E. 1970. The geriatric sex offender. *Medical Aspects of Human Sexuality* 4:125–29.

White, C. B. 1982. Sexual interest, attitudes, knowledge, and sexual history in relation to sexual behavior in the institutionalized aged. *Archives of Sexual Behavior* 11(1): 11–21.

White, C. B., and J. A. Catania. 1981. Psychoeducational intervention for sexuality with the aged, family members of the aged, and people who work with the aged. *International Journal of Aging and Human Development* 15(2): 121–37.

Woods, N. 1978. Human sexuality and the healthy elderly. In *Readings in gerontology,* ed. M. Brown, 84–85. 2d ed. St. Louis: Mosby.

Zeiss, A. M. 1982. Expectations for the effects of aging on sexuality in parents and average married couples. *The Journal of Sex Research* 18(1): 47–57.

IV SELECTED HEALTH ISSUES

Effect of Chronic Disease and Medication on Sexual Functioning

Raul C. Schiavi

Clinical studies and physiologic investigation have led to new information on the mechanisms that underlie sexual responses and to a better understanding of the consequences that medical illnesses have on the sexual functioning of men and women. Earlier emphasis on the psychological and interpersonal aspects of medical conditions on human sexuality is shifting to an increasing focus on biological processes. Implicit in much of the current literature is a simplistic unidimensional model centered on sexual performance, a view that overlooks the close interaction among the biological, psychological, and social factors that shape individual responses to chronic illness.

This selective review summarizes information on the effect of disease and medications on sexuality. It briefly considers the physiologic processes that mediate normal male and female sexual responses and then discusses the physical and psychological consequences that chronic illness, drugs, and surgical interventions have on sexuality. These conditions impair sexual function both directly—by acting on mediating physiologic mechanisms and reproductive structures—and indirectly—by limiting total body function. They also have psychological consequences that are both reactive to the organic impairment and independent from it. The effect of illnesses on individual sexual responses is influenced by psychosocial factors such as the stage of life, prior experiences and attitudes about sex, coping styles, personality characteristics, and the nature of current relationships. Regretfully, little empirical, systematic data is available on these aspects of critical importance for determining the effect of illness on sexual satisfaction.

Because the overall scope of this chapter is very broad, it precludes an in-depth discussion of the effect of chronic illness on sexuality. The reader is directed to recent publications (Bancroft 1989; Schover and Jensen 1988) and to selected references for a more extensive treatment of this topic.

Effect of Chronic Disease on Sexual Function
The Physiology of Sexual Function

A rational understanding of the clinical consequences of illness and drugs on sexuality requires knowledge about the physiology of male and female sexual responses. A central organizing principle is that sexual responses unfold in a predictable sequence of physiologic and genital changes labeled by Masters and Johnson (1966) as the "sexual response cycle." The prevailing conceptual model, on which the current nosological system of sexual dysfunctions is based (American Psychiatric Association 1987), divides this cycle into four phases: desire, excitement, orgasm, and resolution. It is postulated that these phases are mediated by specific physiologic processes and that their disruption or inhibition gives rise to distinct male and female sexual dysfunctions. The mechanisms underlying each of these phases is only briefly summarized here.

Desire. This stage is characterized by the motivation of the individual to initiate or engage in a sexual situation. Its assessment is based on the occurrence of sexual thoughts and fantasies, the interest in initiating sexual activities, and the recognition of sexual cues. Studies on the behavioral responses of hypogonadal men to androgens and physically normal men to antiandrogens have shown that the processes that mediate sexual desire are androgen dependent (Bancroft et al. 1974; Davidson, Camargo, and Smith 1979; Skakkebaek et al. 1981). The most important androgen is testosterone, most of which circulates tightly bound to a sex-hormone-binding globulin (SHBG). Only the testosterone that is free or the hormonal fraction that is loosely bound to plasma proteins such as albumin is bioavailable and capable of exerting physiologic effects. These effects take place following coupling at receptor sites located in the central nervous system and peripheral target tissues. Sexual drive may reflect not only variations in plasma testosterone but also molecular mechanisms such as threshold changes at receptor sites (Bancroft 1980). It has been hypothesized that the decrease in sexual drive and behavior associated with male aging may reflect lowering levels of bioavailable testosterone, as well as an increase in the threshold of activation of central androgen receptors (Schiavi et al. 1991). Limited empirical information is available on the central structures that mediate the behavioral effects of androgens. It is believed, mainly on the basis of animal research, that these structures are located within the hypothalamic and limbic systems (MacLean and Ploog 1962; Perachio, Marr, and Alexander 1979).

There is growing, but still conflicting, evidence that androgens are also involved in sustaining sexual drive in women (Bancroft et al. 1983; Schreiner-Engel et al. 1982). Much of this evidence is inferred from pathologic conditions or from the behavioral results of androgen administration to women deprived of their ovaries (Sherwin, Gelfand, and Brender 1985). Estrogens and progesterone do not appear to have a direct effect on sexual interest; however, estrogens may influence sexual behavior indirectly by their effect on mood, or on vasomotor symptoms, and by trophic action on the vaginal mucosa in perimenopausal women.

Excitement. The major genital changes during this phase are, in the male, penile tumescence and in the female pelvic vasocongestion, vaginal lubrication, and swelling of the external genitalia. These responses are mediated by neural and vascular mechanisms that have been almost exclusively investigated in men. It is commonly believed that penile tumescence occurs under the control of two synergistic neurophysiological pathways: a sacral parasympathetic component that mediates reflexogenic erections induced by direct stimulation of the genitals, and a thoracolumbar sympathetic pathway that mediates erections induced by visual, auditory, tactile, or imaginative stimulation (de Groat and Steers 1988; Weiss 1972). Erections are the result of the relaxation of the smooth muscles within the corpora cavernosa, which results in increased arterial blood flow to the penis. The engorgement of the sinusoidal spaces compresses the plexus of venules between the sinusoidal walls and the undistensible tunica albuginea leading to restriction in blood outflow, and to an increase in penile intracavernosal pressure. The relaxation of the cavernosal smooth muscles is thought to be controlled by cholinergic and nonadrenergic, noncholinergic mechanisms and also by the release of an endothelium-derived relaxing factor. Sympathetic nerves and alpha-adrenergic mechanism exert a tonic inhibitory control over the sinusoidal smooth muscles and mediate the detumescence of the erect penis (Krane, Goldstein, and deTejada 1989). It is assumed that the neurovascular processes that mediate genital vasocongestion in women are similar to men. There is, however, a paucity of empirical studies on the physiology of female sexual arousal.

Orgasm. Orgasm is characterized in both sexes by an acme of sexual pleasure associated with rhythmic muscle contractions of perineal and reproductive organ structures and a release of sexual tension. During the emission phase, in men, the contraction of the smooth muscles of the vas deferens, prostate, and seminal vesicles propel the seminal fluid into the bulbar urethra. This phase, which is associated with the subjective sense of impending ejaculation is under thoracolumbar sympathetic control and is mediated by release of norepinephrine acting on alpha-adrenergic receptors (Anton and McGrath 1977). Ejaculation proper, mediated by a sacral spinal reflex, occurs following clonic contractions of the striated muscles that surround the bulbar urethra, which, in turn, results in the outward projection of semen.

Although the literature is extensive, we continue to know little about the physiological aspects of the orgasmic experience in women. In contrast to men, women lacking a postorgasmic refractory period have the potential for experiencing multiple orgasms. There is still controversy concerning whether different physiological processes underlie orgasms induced by vaginal or clitoral stimulation (Singer 1973). There is also scarce and conflicting evidence in support of the claim that stimulation of a circumscribed area on the anterior vaginal wall may trigger orgasm and the emission of fluid suggestive of prostatic secretion (female ejaculation) (Goldberg et al. 1983; Ladas, Whipple, and Perry 1982). The participation of brain processes in the orgasmic response of humans has been explored with deeply implanted electrodes into the septum and limbic structures and with cortical recording techniques (Cohen, Rosen, and Goldstein 1976; Heath 1972). The extent to which central neurophysiological events are related to the nature and intensity of orgasmic experiences and to male-female differences in the refractory period is not known.

Resolution. This phase is characterized by a subjective sense of calm, well-being, and relaxation, associated with genital detumescence and, in the male, with a refractory period that increases with age. Adrenergic mechanisms appear to play an important role in the return to the prearoused physiological state (Lue and Tanagho 1987).

Systemic Effects of Medical Illnesses

Any illness that is associated with weakness, a febrile state, pain, and malaise is likely to have a generalized, nonspecific effect on sexual function. Medical disorders may also have direct actions by interfering with the previously mentioned endocrine, neural, and vascular processes that mediate sexual responses. Their effect in sexuality is frequently multifactorial, involving several physiological mechanisms in interaction with psychological processes. Aging provides an important contribution to the nature of this interaction. The stage in the individual's life cycle not only influences the probability of being affected by a specific illness but also determines his or her biobehavioral response to the medical problem. Aging is generally associated with a decrease in frequency in sexual behavior, to a lesser extent with a diminution in sexual interest, and with an increase in prevalence of sexual dysfunction (Schiavi 1990b). Considerable variability in sexual responses is noted, however, even when the effects of illness or medication are minimized as confounding variables in studies of healthy individuals (Schiavi et al. 1990). Although we remain largely ignorant about the age-related physiological and psychological factors that contribute to these individual differences, they should not be ignored in considering the information that follows because it may open up valuable areas of research and possible therapeutic intervention. We attempt here to organize the data according to the primary physiological systems involved in the effects of chronic medical illness on sexuality (see table 1). Only the organic conditions most likely to affect sexual physiology are mentioned here; psychological aspects are mostly discussed in a subsequent section.

Endocrine-Related Disorders

Surveys that have assessed the association between endocrinopathies and sexual dysfunctions have focused primarily on impotent patients (Schiavi and White 1976; Spark, White, and Connolly 1980). The reported prevalence of hypothalamic-pituitary-gonadal abnormalities has ranged widely, up to 35 percent, depending on selection factors and the nature of the clinical groups sampled. The most common hormonal problems associated with erectile difficulties are hypogonadal disorders and hyperprolactinemia (Slag et al. 1983). In certain conditions the primary pathology is in the testes, inducing a compensatory increase in pituitary LH secretion; in others there is a luteinizing-hormone decrease resulting from a primary hypothalamic-pituitary defect. The end result is a decrease in bioavailable testosterone with a consequent decline in sexual drive, secondary erectile problems, and impaired ejaculatory capacity. Diminished sexual desire and impaired sexual function are also associated with hyperprolactinemic states commonly caused by hypothalamic-pituitary tumors or medication (Drago 1984). These patients

TABLE 1 Chronic Organic Conditions Associated with
Sexual Dysfunction

Neurological:
  Central:
    Temporal lobe lesion
    Multiple sclerosis
    Parkinsonism
    Amyotrophic lateral sclerosis
    Cerebrovascular accidents (stroke)
    Trauma:
      Tumors: brain, spinal cord
  Peripheral:
    Degenerative:
      Diabetic neuropathy
      Alcoholic neuropathy
    Postsurgical:
      Radical prostatectomy
      Abdominal perineal resection
      Bilateral lumbar sympathectomy
Endocrine:
  Primary hypogonadism
  Hypogonadotrophic hypogonadism
  Hyperprolactinemia
  Thyroid disorders
  Addison's disease
  Cushing's syndrome
  Postsurgical: gonadectomy
Metabolic:
  Diabetes mellitus
  Chronic renal insufficiency
  Chronic hepatic insufficiency
Cardiovascular:
  Angina pectoris
  Myocardial infarction
  Hypertension
  Peripheral vascular insufficiency (atherosclerosis)
Anatomical:
  Peyronie's disease
  Postsurgical: genital tumors
Other systemic conditions:
  Chronic obstructive pulmonary disease
  Arthritis
  Obesity

frequently, but not always, show diminished gonadotropic and testosterone secretion.

The consequences of abnormalities in the hypothalamic-pituitary-gonadal axis for the sexuality of women is less clear-cut; there is evidence that hyperprolactinemia impairs sexual drive and arousal in women as it does in men. Thyroid disorders, especially hypothyroidism in the elderly and Addison's and Cushing's diseases are also associated with desire and arousal problems in both sexes (Pogach and Vaitukaitis 1983). The physiological process involved in the effect of abnormal thyroid and adrenal secretions on sexual functioning remains poorly understood.

Among all chronic illnesses, diabetes mellitus is the disorder most frequently associated with male erectile dysfunction (Schiavi and Hogan 1979). Pathological changes in the neurovascular processes that control erection rather than abnormalities in circulating hormones are responsible for the erectile problems of this metabolic condition. Several investigators have assessed the effect of diabetes on the sexuality of women with conflicting results (Ellenberg 1977; Jensen 1981; Kolodny 1971; Schreiner-Engel et al. 1985). We have found that type 1 diabetes had little sexual consequences; type 2 had a pervasively negative effect on sexual desire, lubrication, orgasmic capacity, and on the relationship with the sexual partner (Schreiner-Engel et al. 1987).

Chronic renal and hepatic failure can impair sexual desire and arousal in both sexes by a multiplicity of actions that include endocrine mechanisms (Levy 1983; Rodger et al. 1985; Zifroni, Schiavi, and Schaffner 1991). In chronic renal insufficiency serum testosterone is usually decreased, and prolactin is commonly elevated (Waltzer 1981; Weizman et al. 1983). Administration of bromocriptin, a dopaminergic agonist to men in hemodyalisis has been reported to decrease prolactin levels and to restore sexual interest (Bommer et al. 1979). Vascular insufficiency and uremic neuropathy may also contribute to the impairment of sexual arousal in chronic renal failure and are discussed in the following section. Psychological factors such as the patient's helplessness, dependency, and despair, the partner's response to the demands of dialysis procedure, and the provision of chronic care are important in influencing the sexual outcome of the disease (Berkman, Katz, and Weissman 1982).

Neurological Disorders

Sexual dysfunction is a common occurrence in neurologic diseases or traumatic conditions that impair the spinal cord, peripheral nerves, or the central nervous system. In the young, spinal cord injury resulting from traffic accidents, falls, and violence is the most frequent cause of sexual disability (Griffith and Trieschmann 1983). Damage to the spinal cord in the male interferes with sexual performance to a greater extent than with sexual drive (Higgins 1979). The nature of the impairment depends on the level of the injury and on whether the degree of cord destruction is partial or complete. Lesions above the sixth thoracic level may induce autonomic dysreflexia, a potential life-threatening condition with elevation of blood pressure, flushing, and sweating during sexual activity (Amelar and Dubin 1982). Lesions in the thoracic spine above T_{12} may prevent psychologically induced erections because of damage to the thoracolumbar sympathetic pathway. These individuals retain the capacity to have reflexogenic erections if the parasympathetic reflex arc located at the sacral level S_2–S_4 remains intact. Conversely, damage to the sacral cord may prevent reflex erections induced by direct stimulation of the genitalia but leave the potential for psychogenic erections relatively intact (Bors and Comarr 1960). In general, spinal cord injury impairs orgasm and ejaculation to a greater extent than it impairs erection, and partial lesions at any level are less deleterious to erection and ejaculation than complete lesions.

Although the literature is scarce, it would appear that a relatively high proportion of women with spinal cord injuries retain the capacity for vaginal lubrication and orgasm (Fitting et al. 1978). Adequate studies on the relation between the level of the lesion and the nature of the sexual impairment in women is lacking. Beyond the nature of the neurological damage, psychological and interpersonal factors are of critical importance in determining the sexual consequences of the physical disability. Adequate sexual counseling by addressing maladaptive attitudes and beliefs, helping with concerns about bowel and bladder function, and providing information about body positioning and alternate modes of sexual stimulation can be very effective in facilitating the adaptation of patients with spinal cord injuries, improving their self-esteem, and enhancing their sexual satisfaction (Mooney et al. 1975).

Medical disorders or surgical procedures that impair the pudendal nerve input from the genitalia to the spinal cord or the autonomic outflow from the spinal cord to genital structures can interfere with sexual responses. A peripheral autonomic neuropathy is involved in the pathophysiology of erectile failure in diabetes mellitus (Clarke, Ewing, and Campbell 1979) and possibly contributes to chronic alcoholic impotence (Schiavi 1990a). Surgical interventions such as radical prostatectomy or abdominal perineal resections can also result in erectile impotence or ejaculatory incompetence as a result of damage to the pelvic nerves that carry autonomic impulses to the genitalia (Cytron, Simon, and Segenreich 1987). The development of new surgical procedures that spare the prostatic nervous plexus has made possible radical prostatectomy without impairment of sexual potency (Catalona and Dresner 1985).

Multiple sclerosis and epilepsy are neurologic disorders commonly associated with sexual problems. Loss of sexual drive, erectile difficulties, orgasmic problems, or diminished genital sensitivity have been observed in men and women with multiple sclerosis, a demyelinizing condition variously involving the brain, the spinal cord, and the peripheral nerves (Lilius, Valtonen, and Davis 1976). Impaired sexual desire and arousal and, in men, deviant sexuality, have also been reported in association with epilepsy, particularly as a result of abnormal temporal lobe function (Taylor 1969). The pathogenic mechanisms in both neurologic conditions are poorly understood and likely to be complex, depending on the site of the lesions, psychological factors, as well as the medications used in their treatment. In older individuals, Parkinson's disease is frequently related to diminished sexual drive and erectile impotence (Paulson 1983). The sexual problem has been attributed to abnormalities in central monoaminergic processes, to psychological depression, and to mechanical difficulties owing to muscular rigidity.

Cardiovascular Disorders

Peripheral arterial insufficiency, coronary artery disease, cerebrovascular lesions, and hypertension are frequently associated with sexual difficulties or concerns. The underlying pathophysiology is arteriosclerosis, an age-related degenerative condition of the vascular tree that limits the blood supply to the tissues. The specific processes that contribute to sexual problems are complex, depending on the anatomical localization and degree of vascular pathology, the rate of progression of the disease, and the psychological and interpersonal factors that shape individual responses to the organic insult. As in the preceding section, much of the literature on this topic is impressionistic, inadequately controlled, and mainly focused on the male.

The development of new diagnostic procedures of vascular competence in erectile impotence has drawn recent attention to the high prevalence of lesions in the pudendal and penile arteries and in the venous outflow from the corpora cavernosa of older men with chronic disorders (Krane, Goldstein, and deTejada 1989). The frequent observation of penile vascular insufficiency in diabetes mellitus suggests that, in addition to a peripheral neuropathy, vascular pathology also contributes to the impaired erectile function (Abelson 1975). It should be noted, however, that the coexistence of vascular lesions and sexual problems in the same individual does not demonstrate pathogenesis. There are very few vascular studies of impotent patients that have included a comparison group of sexually normal individuals or that have followed prospectively the sexual functioning of men at risk for the development of vascular disease.

Numerous articles have indicated that the frequency of sexual activity decreases after myocardial infarction in both sexes. Women mainly report a decrease in sexual drive; men complain of erectile difficulties (Abramov 1976; Hellerstein and Friedman 1970; Kavanagh and Shepard 1977). A recently controlled study, however, has shown no differences in the prevalence of sexual problems between men with myocardial infarctions and a matched control group (Dhabuwala, Kumar, and Pierce 1986). Retrospective evaluation has shown that in many subjects the sexual problem had preceded the occurrence of the infarct.

The literature on cerebrovascular accidents (stroke) is sparse and inconsistent, variously reporting the occurrence of erectile impotence and decrements in sexual desire and activity in both sexes (Bray, DeFrank, and Wolfe 1981; Fugl-Meyer and Jaasko 1980). Psychological factors are likely to play a significant role in the sexual consequences of myocardial infarction and cerebrovascular lesions. These factors include fear that sexual activity may aggravate the physical disorder or precipitate death, depression, problems of self-esteem or body image, and marital difficulties. In addition, in patients with cerebrovascular lesions, muscle weakness, sensory impairment, loss of sphincter control, and speech limitations also contribute to sexual dysfunction and dissatisfaction.

The prevalence of sexual disorders in unmedicated hypertensive patients is not well known. Sexual drive is usually not affected, and, when erectile dysfunction occurs, it is probably due to arteriosclerotic lesions in the vascular supply to the penis. Most commonly, the erectile difficulties reported by hypertensive men are the result of the antihypertensive and diuretic agents used for the normalization of blood pressure (Papadopoulas 1980).

Reproductive Organ Pathology

Lesions in the urogenital track resulting in the young from traumatic accidents, or more frequently in older individuals to malignancies, can have profound sexual consequences. Surgical interventions, radiotherapy, and the use of cytotoxic agents for the treatment of cancer frequently interfere with the neurovascular and hormonal substrates of sexual function. Of perhaps greater importance are the deleterious effects of pain and psychological aspects such as concerns about survival, body image, and the partner's response to the mutilating results of surgical interventions. This literature has been recently reviewed by Schover and Jensen (1988); only the most salient aspects are mentioned here.

External genitalia. Peyronie's disease is a benign condition of unknown origin, characterized by an abnormal curvature of the penis that renders vaginal penetration difficult or painful and may result in erectile failure. Of more dramatic consequence are penile or vulvar carcinomas that require partial or total surgical removal of the penis or resection of the labia and, less frequently, the clitoris. The sexual sequelae of these mutilating procedures are profound, with sexual avoidance, loss of sexual drive, and arousal difficulties (Andreasson et al. 1986). Some women who remain sexually active, however, retain the capacity to achieve orgasmic release even after total removal of clitoral tissues. Radical surgery for bladder malignancies or for invasive pelvic cancers may require partial or total resection of the vaginal wall. The effect of this surgery on sexual function depends on the type and extent of the vaginal reconstruction and on available postoperative counseling (Schover and Fife 1985).

Reproductive structures. Surgical treatment for prostatic malignancies frequently impair sexual function (Pearlman 1980). As previously mentioned, loss of erectile capacity and retrograde ejaculation commonly occur after perineal prostatectomy that damages the prostatic plexus to the penis. Suprapubic and retropubic prostatectomy carry a lesser risk of interfering with the nervous control of erection but are also associated with ejaculatory problems (Cytron, Simon, and Segenreich

1987). Prostatic metastasis may necessitate surgical or chemical castration to prevent the trophic effect of testicular androgens on metastatic tissues. These procedures usually result in loss of sexual drive, ejaculatory failure, and secondary erectile problems. Analogous sexual difficulties are observed following bilateral orchidectomy as a result of testicular malignancies (Bergman et al. 1984). Benign prostate hypertrophy, common in older men, may induce urinary difficulties and require transurethral resection of prostatic tissue (TURP). This intervention, carried out through the urethra, is associated with the lowest prevalence of erectile problems but with a high probability of retrograde ejaculation resulting from damage of the internal sphincter of the bladder.

Breast and ovarian tumors can have profound consequences for the sexuality of women (Jamison, Wellisch, and Pasnau 1978; Maguire et al. 1978; Silberfarb, Maurer, and Crouthamel 1980). The treatment of breast cancer, the most prevalent female malignancy, includes total mastectomy, limited surgical excisions or lumpectomy, and adjuvant therapy to prevent recurrences of the malignancy. Psychological factors alone explain the deleterious effect of mastectomy on female sexual desire, arousal, and satisfaction. They encompass shame, embarrassment, impaired body image, and apprehension about the partner's response to the mutilating consequences of surgery (Kaplan 1992). Adjuvant treatment may include postsurgical radiation, chemotherapy, and administration of antiestrogen drugs. During radiation and chemotherapy, fatigue, nausea, depression, and hair loss commonly occur with nonspecific adverse sexual effects. In addition, chemotherapeutic agents may induce ovarian failure with deficient steriod production, loss of sexual drive, vaginal atrophy, and orgasmic dysfunction. Antiestrogenic agents are less toxic compounds with fewer general adverse reactions but with similar deleterious effects on female sexual function (Kaplan 1992). Hysterectomy is another surgical procedure commonly believed to impair sexual responses. There is presently no convincing evidence that hysterectomy has adverse physiological effects on female sexuality when the ovaries are left intact (Schover and Fife 1985). It may have psychological consequences, however (Roeske 1979).

Surgical interventions for abdominal malignancies of the bowel and rectum are mentioned here. Abdominal perineal resections may induce erectile failure and dry orgasms because of impairment of the autonomic nerves that mediate erection and the emission phase of ejaculation. Less evident are the effects of this surgery for female sexual responses. Inflammatory bowel disease and carcinomas of the colon and rectum may require bowel resection and the surgical construction of a permanent opening of the bowel onto the abdominal surface (ostomy). Loss of self-esteem, problems with body integrity and autonomy, fear of loss of fecal control, and concerns about the partner's reaction to the ostomy are determining factors in the effect of this surgery on male and female sexuality (Dlin, Perlman, and Ringold 1969; Druss, O'Connor, and Stern 1969).

Indirect Effects of Chronic Illness on Sexual Function

Chronic illness may impair sexual function indirectly by compromising the functional capacity of the organism to engage in adequate sexual activity. Among these conditions, usually observed in but not limited to older individuals, are arthritis, chronic obstructive pulmonary disease (COPD), and obesity. A high proportion of men and women with arthritis report problems with sexual arousal and satisfaction associated with impaired mobility, pain, apprehension, and fatigue (Ferguson and Figley 1979). Breathing difficulty and oxygen deficiency occurring during sexual activity in patients with COPD, asthma, and emphysema can also seriously restrict sexual activity, generate anxiety, and result in impaired sexual desire and arousal (Agle and Baum 1977). It should be noted here again that there are multifactorial origins of the sexual problems of patients with arthritis and COPD involving not only the effects of intercurrent illness and medications but also individual psychological responses to the progressive development of physical disability.

Effect of Psychiatric Illness on Sexual Functioning

Information about the sexual functioning of patients with chronic mental disorders is remarkably scarce. Clinically, it is commonly accepted that depression is associated with a lowering in sexual drive as part of the vegetative symptoms that characterize this illness. Several surveys of depressed men and women have provided suggestive evidence of a decline in both sexual desire and sexual behavior (Cassidy et al. 1957; Dunner, Dwyer, and Fieve 1976; Hamilton 1980). However, there are few controlled studies on unmedicated depressed patients. Mathew and Weinman (1982) observed that, in comparison with age and sex matched controls, drug-free depressed patients had both significant decreases and significant increases in sexual drive but no differences in erectile or orgasmic difficulties. In another controlled investigation, unmedicated depressed men were reported as having significantly lower sexual interest and satisfaction but no differences in frequency of sexual activity (Howell et al. 1987). It is not clear whether differences exist between patients who only experience depressive episodes and manic-depressive individuals in their depressive phase in regard to sexual functioning. Manic-depressive patients during the manic phase frequently show an increase in sexual drive and behavior (Liss 1982). Evaluating the relation between mental illness and sexual drive from another perspective, we compared lifetime psychopathology of forty-six physically healthy subjects diagnosed as having inhibited sexual desire (ISD) with thirty-six matched controls. Although all ISD subjects had normal psychological profiles at the time of the evaluation, more ISD volunteers than controls had significantly elevated lifetime prevalence rates of affective disorders. The proportion of ISD individuals with histories of major or intermittent depression alone was almost twice as high as controls (Schreiner-Engel and Schiavi 1986).

There is considerable lack of clarity about the effect of schizophrenia on sexual function. The sexual behavior and functioning of schizophrenic men and women have been variously reported as increased, decreased, impaired, or unchanged (Barker 1968; Friedman and Harrison 1984; Verhulst and Schneidman 1981; Woods 1981). As with affective disorders, there is a paucity of control investigations of unmedicated patients. Studies of schizophrenics under neuroleptic treatment (i.e., tranquilizer) have shown an increase in prevalence of low sexual desire and erectile and orgasmic difficulties in comparison to controls (Nestoros, Lehmann, and Ban 1981; Raboch 1984). Beyond the occurrence of sexual dysfunction, the sexuality of schizophrenic patients is influenced by the presence of negative symptoms such as flatness of affect, anhedonia (inability to experience pleasure), and emotional isolation; by their bizarre behavior and interpersonal difficulties; and by the occurrence of hallucinatory and delusional experiences that not infrequently have sexual content.

The deleterious effect of chronic mental illness on sexuality encompasses maladaptive developmental experiences, intrapsychic and interpersonal pathology, and the disruptive consequences of hospitalization and pharmacological treatment. The extent to which the putative central neurobiological abnormalities in major psychiatric disorders contribute to associated sexual dysfunctions remains unclear.

EFFECT OF MEDICATION ON SEXUAL FUNCTIONING

The noxious effects of drugs on sexual functioning have been increasingly recognized in recent years. However, most of this information is impressionistic, is based on case reports, and is almost exclusively focused on men. With some frequency, the reports fail to identify the phase of the sexual response that is impaired (desire, arousal, orgasm, or ejaculation) or to clearly distinguish the effects of the medication from the underlying disease. The major classes of drugs associated with adverse sexual effects are antihypertensives, psychotropic drugs, and drugs of abuse (see table 2). Several recent reviews provide detailed information of drug effects on sexual function (Biuffum 1988; Segraves 1989; Wein and Van Arsdalen 1988).

Antihypertensives

Antihypertensive agents are probably the medications most responsible for sexual problems in older individuals. Sympatholytics, diuretics, alpha- and beta-adrenergic blocking agents, and vasodilators have all been reported to induce erectile difficulties and orgasmic or ejaculatory inhibition (Lazar et al. 1984; Segraves, Madsen, and Carter 1985). The reported prevalence of sexual problems following antihypertensive treatment has varied widely, but, because the base rate of sexual difficulties in untreated hypertensive patients is not well known, it is difficult to evaluate the extent to which these medications impair sexual performance. It is presently believed that among the different groups of antihypertensives, angiotensin-converting enzyme inhibitors and calcium channel blockers are the agents less likely to cause sexual problems (Wein and Van Arsdalen 1988).

Psychotropic Agents

Antipsychotic medications, tricyclic antidepressants, monoaminooxidase (MAO) inhibitors and sedative-anxiolytic drugs may induce depressed sexual drive, erectile failure, ejaculatory impairment, or female anorgasmia (Schiavi and Luloff 1986; Segraves 1989). There are reports of restoration of normal sexual function either while on medication, following a decrease in dosage, or after switching to another psychotropic drug. It is frequently problematic to assess the relation between the medication and the sexual symptom, particularly in the context of behavioral changes associated with the psychiatric illness and the therapeutic actions of the drug. Controlled studies of the effect of

TABLE 2 Drugs Associated with Sexual Dysfunction

Antihypertensives:
  Alpha-methyldopa
  Clonidine
  Guanethidine
  Reserpine
  Prazosin
  Propranolol
  Phenoxybenzamine
  Atenolol
  Verapamil
  Diuretics
Antipsychotic agents:
  Phenothiazines (chlorpromazine, fluphenazine, thioridazine)
  Thioxanthenes (narvane)
  Butyrophenones (haldol)
Antidepressant agents:
  Cyclic antidepressants (imipramine, amitriptyline, nortriptyline)
  MAO inhibitors (phenelzine, tranylcypromine)
  Atypical antidepressants (trazodone, fluoxetine)
  Lithium
Minor tranquilizers:
  Benzodiazepines
Drugs of abuse:
  Narcotics (heroin, codeine, methadone)
  Cocaine
  Amphetamines
  Alcohol
  Barbiturates
  Nicotine
Cancer chemotherapy agents:
  Alkylating agents (chlorambucil, cyclophosphamide)
  Other chemotherapy agents (procarbazine, vinblastine)
Hormones:
  Antiandrogens
  Estrogens
  Corticosteroids
  Progestational agents
Miscellaneous drugs:
  Cimetidine
  Digoxin
  Clofibrate
  Disulfiram

psychotropic agents on sexual function are remarkably few (Harrison et al. 1986; Kowalski et al. 1985).

Drugs of Abuse

Numerous studies have disclosed a high prevalence of decreased sexual desire, erectile impairment and retarded ejaculation in the male, and orgasmic problems in the female following chronic use of narcotics such as heroine, methadone, or codeine (Mintz et al. 1974; Mirin, Meyer, and Mendelson 1980). An important problem in assessing the association between opiates and sexual function has been the absence of a reliable baseline of information during the preaddiction period. Amphetamine and codeine are two stimulants that induce a wide range of effects on sexual function (Segraves, Madsen, and Carter 1985). This diversity is likely due to differences in dose, mode of drug administration, duration of drug intake, personality characteristics, and individual psychopathology. Acute use of moderate amounts of amphetamine and cocaine orally or by inhalation may alleviate fatigue, improve psychomotor function, and reportedly have a nonspecific enhancing effect on sexual desire and satisfaction without altering sexual performance (Gay et al. 1975). Chronic amphetamine or cocaine use eventually results in a lowering of sexual drive and difficulties in sexual performance (Greaves 1972). The effect of alcohol on sexual function may also depend on the pattern of use. The commonly held notion that acute intake of alcohol at low doses may increase sexual arousal and facilitate sexual expression as a result of its central disinhibitory action or behavior has been challenged by experimental evidence. Cognitive and social factors and individual expectancy play an important role in sexual arousal responses at low to moderate blood-alcohol levels. As the blood-alcohol concentration increases, however, a significant negative relation exists between alcohol and genital responses to erotic stimulation (Rosen 1992). Chronic alcohol abuse can cause erectile difficulties with or without the occurrence of diminished sexual desire (Schiavi 1990a).

Miscellaneous Drugs

Various other drugs with diverse pharmacologic properties have been reported to induce adverse sexual reactions. They include anticholinergic agents, histamine-H_2 receptor antagonists (cimetidine), digoxin, antiandrogens, and cancer chemotherapy (Segraves, Madsen, and Carter 1985; Wein and Van Arsdalen 1983).

Despite the increased information on sexual physiology, considerable lack of clarity still exists on the mode of action of drugs on sexual function. The nature of drug response involves complex biological, psychological, and social interactions. Drugs may alter the cognitive aspect of the sexual experience; they may act on subcortical substrates of sexual desire and arousal; or they may have peripheral effects on the autonomic control of genital activity. Deleterious physiological actions on sexual behavior may involve decreased central dopaminergic or enhanced serotonergic function, peripheral anticholinergic activity, alpha-adrenergic antagonism, central nervous system depression or sedation, endocrine alterations, and direct effects on vascular blood flow. Of considerable importance in determining the sexual response to drugs are psychosocial factors such as the subject's expectations and previous drug experience, the past sexual history, the nature of current relationships, and personality characteristics. Only an approach that takes into account this multiplicity of determinants from several frames of reference may eventually explain the wide individual differences in sexual responses to pharmacologic agents.

Psychological Aspects

Dichotomous notions about organic versus psychogenic sexual disorders may lead to distorted or simplistic views concerning pathogenesis by imposing artificial constraints onto the observation of clinical phenomena. A large number of reports about the effects of chronic illness on sexuality follow a disease model with an inherent emphasis on functional deficits. They overlook the important role that psychological determinants play in shaping the individual's responses to medical illness, drug intake, and physical disability (Anderson and Wolf 1986). Although empirical evidence is grossly lacking, some generic statements may be made that cut across disease entities. Individual differences in sexual function and satisfaction are determined as much by factors intrinsic to the person or the environment as they are by specific organ system pathology. Among the factors intrinsic to the individual are psychological aspects such as coping processes, sexual attitudes and information, emotional responses, personality characteristics, and the nature of the patient's marital relationship.

The literature on coping provides a useful theoretical model for our understanding of individual variations in adaptation to medical disorders. Several investigators have assessed the effect of coping strategies on psychological adjustment in the chronically ill (Moos 1977), but little has been written relative to sexual function.

Coping has been defined "as the process of managing demands that are appraised as taxing or exceeding the resources of a person" (Cohen and Lazarus 1983). In keeping within this framework, the psychological effect of a sexual problem associated with a medical illness depends on how the individual appraises the significance of this event for his or her well-being. The sexual symptom may be perceived as inconsequential or, conversely, as a direct threat to his or her emotional or physical adjustment.

Attitudinal sets about sexuality, sexual information and misinformation, and personality characteristics play a key role in determining the type of cognitive appraisal the patient makes. There is evidence that attitudinal constructs such as liberalism, conservatism, and sexual guilt (Athanasiou 1973; Mosher and Greenberg 1969; Wallace, Wehmer, and Polodny 1974) and belief measures such as locus of control (Rotter 1966) possess predictive value for sexual functioning. In addition, sexual knowledge, information about the relation between illness or surgery and sexual dysfunction, and the availability of resources to deal with the problem are equally important factors in the appraisal of how stressful a sexual symptom is likely to be for the individual. For example, unrealistic expectations about sexual functioning in older men or ignorance that satisfying sexual interactions and orgasmic release remain possible in impotent diabetics can result in undue distress and inappropriate therapeutic decisions (Schiavi 1980). Similarly, lack of information about the deleterious effects of medications on sexual desire and arousal can augment the distress of a patient who attributes the problem to marital or psychological difficulties.

Personality characteristics are also likely influential factors in determining the patient's appraisal of a sexual symptom and the nature of the reaction to it. Recently, Byrne and Schulte (1990) have reviewed evidence on stable personality dispositions as mediators of sexual responses. Erotophobia-erotophilia is a personality trait characterized by affective or evaluative responses to sexual cues along negative versus positive dimensions. Although there is considerable evidence on the predictive value of this construct for sexual behavior, it has not been assessed yet as a mediator of sexual responses to medical illness. Finally, age and sexual experience are two important and related factors likely to influence how the sexual symptom is appraised by the patient and the resources that the individual can bring to bear in coping with it.

The perception of the sexual symptom by the patient as threatening or stressful is usually accompanied by dysphoric affect and negative emotions such as anxiety, fear, depression, or anger (Kaplan 1974). The specific concerns about the sexual problem are superimposed on the emotional reactions to the underlying medical illness and frequently become mutually reinforcing. For example, the depressive mood associated with a chronic illness may decrease sexual drive and arousal, rendering the subject at risk of erectile failure with attendant sexual anxiety, low self-esteem, and greater dysphoric affect.

Much has been written by sex therapists about the deleterious effect of performance anxiety and fear of failure on sexual behavior (Kaplan 1974; Masters and Johnson 1970). It is frequently difficult to delineate the extent to which sexual anxiety contributes to the impairment in erectile capacity associated with diseases known to affect sexual functioning. Recent empirical evidence has demonstrated that demands for sexual performance have differential effects on physically healthy, sexually functional and dysfunctional individuals (Cranston-Cuebas and Barlow 1990). In sexually dysfunctional men, according to the model proposed by Barlow (1986), performance demands lead to negative expectations and to an attentional focus on nonerotic cues, a maladaptive process that is facilitated under conditions of increased autonomic arousal. In contrast, in sexually functional men, a positive feedback loop exists, with performance demands generating positive affect and expectations, and an increasingly efficient attentional focus on erotic cues during enhanced autonomic activation. It would be of considerable interest to apply this model to the study of cognitive and affective processes in patients with sexual dysfunctions associated with chronic illnesses. At present, this promising line of research is lacking.

Coping strategies have been divided into two groups according to their function:one involves individual processes aimed at decreasing the emotional distress generated by the threat (emotion-regulating coping); the other aims at altering the environment or manipulating the conditions that generate the threat (problem solving) (Cohen and Lazarus 1983). Examples of emotion-regulating coping relevant to disease-related sexual problems are denial, rationalization, sexual avoidance, cognitive distortions, and projection of the source of the sexual difficulty onto the partner. Examples of problem-solving coping are acquiring information or seeking treatment for the sexual problem, engaging in experiences that enhance sexual arousal, and developing coital strategies that compensate for the decline in erectile capacity (Schiavi 1992).

Depending on the nature and rate of progression of the chronic illness, individual characteristics, and context, specific coping strategies may have adaptive or maladaptive consequences. When adaptive, they may contribute to self-esteem and sexual satisfaction, enhance interpersonal relations, and minimize the effect of disease on sexual behavior. When maladaptive, they may lead to poor compliance with the treatment of the underlying disease, emotional depression, marital disruption, aggravation of the sexual symptom, and unadvisable treatment interventions.

Environmental (situational) factors also play a significant role in determining how the individual appraises the onset of a sexual symptom, his or her emotional reaction to it, and the psychological processes he or she utilizes to cope with this event. Of critical importance is the partner's reaction to it, the interpersonal-emotional context in which it occurs, and the availability of counseling and support systems. The disposition of the health-care professional to inquire about this aspect of the human condition and his or her ability to provide adequate information and assistance are of pivotal importance in determining the impact of chronic illness on the patient's sexual functioning.

CONCLUSION

A considerable body of information has been amassed during the past two decades on the effect of medical illnesses and drugs, primarily on male sexual function. Although these data are based mostly on uncontrolled clinical observations, they have served to stimulate a growing interest in the physiological processes that mediate sexual responses. Much more research on both sexes is required, however, in order to form a rational understanding of the consequences that disease may have on human sexuality. This knowledge will be incomplete, and our capacity to develop effective preventive and therapeutic interventions will remain limited if future efforts do not incorporate a conceptual model that takes into account psychosocial dimensions. The research focus should move beyond current emphasis on performance deficits to address the factors that contribute to differences in individual adaptation and to ultimate sexual satisfaction.

REFERENCES

Abelson, D. C. 1975. Diagnostic value of the penile pulse and blood pressure:A Doppler study of impotence in diabetes. *Journal of Urology* 113:636–39.

Abramov, L. A. 1976. Sexual life and sexual frigidity among women developing acute myocardial infarction. *Psychosomatic Medicine* 38:418–25.

Agle, D. P., and G. L. Baum. 1977. Psychological aspects of obstructive pulmonary disease. *Medical Clinics of North America* 61:748–58.

Amelar, R. D., and L. Dubin. 1982. Sexual function and fertility in paraplegic males. *Urology* 20:62–65.

American Psychiatric Association. 1987. *Diagnostic and statistical manual of mental disorders.* Washington, D. C.:American Psychiatric Association.

Anderson, B. J., and F. M. Wolf. 1986. Chronic physical illness and sexual behavior:Psychological issues. *Journal of Consulting and Clinical Psychology* 54:168–75.

Andreasson, R., I. Moth, S. B. Jensen, and J. E. Bock. 1986. Sexual function and somatopsychic reactions in vulvectomy-operated women and their partners. *Acta Obstetricia Gynecologica of Scandinavica* 65:7–10.

Anton, P. G., and J. C. McGrath. 1977. Further evidence for adrenergic transmission in the human vas deferens. *Journal of Physiology* 273:45–55.

Athanasiou, R. 1973. A review of public attitudes on sexual issues. In *Contemporary sexual behavior:Critical issues in the 1970's,* ed. J. Zubin and J. Money. Baltimore: Johns Hopkins Univ. Press.

Bancroft, J. 1980. Endocrinology of sexual function. *Clinics Obstetrics and Gynaecology* 7:253–81.

———. 1989. *Human sexuality and its problems.* New York: Churchill Livingstone.

Bancroft, J., D. Sanders, D. Davidson, and P. Warner. 1983. Mood, sexuality, hormones, and the menstrual cycle. III. *Sexuality and the Role of Androgens* 45:509–16.

Bancroft, J., T. G., Tennent, K. Loucas, and J. Cass. 1974. Control of deviant sexual behavior by drugs: Behavioral effects of aestrogens and anti-androgens. *British Journal of Psychiatry* 125:310–15.

Barker, W. J. 1968. Female sexuality. *Journal of American Psychoanalytical Association* 16:123–45.

Barlow, D. H. 1986. Causes of sexual dysfunction: The role of anxiety and cognitive interference. *Journal of Consulting and Clinical Psychology* 54:140–48.

Bergman, B., J. E. Damber, B. Littbrand, K. Sjogren, and R. Tomic. 1984. Sexual function in prostatic cancer patients treated with radiotherapy, orchidectomy, or oestrogens. *British Journal of Urology* 56:64–69.

Berkman, A. H., L. A. Katz, and R. Weissman. 1982. Sexuality and the lifestyle of home dialysis patients. *Archives of Physical Medicine and Rehabilitation* 63:272–75.

Biuffum, J. 1988. Pharmacosexology update: Prescription drugs and sexual function. *Journal of Psychoactive Drugs* 18:97–106.

Bommer, J., E. Ritz, E. del Pezo, and G. Bommer. 1979. Improved sexual function in male haemodialysis patients on bromocriptine. *Lancet* 2:496–97.

Bors, E., and A. E. Comarr. 1960. Neurological disturbances of sexual function with special reference to 529 patients with spinal cord injury. *Urological Survey* 10:191–222.

Bray, G., R. De Frank, and T. Wolfe. 1981. Sexual functioning in stroke survivors. *Archives of Physical Medicine Rehabilitation* 62:286–88.

Byrne, D., and L. Schulte. 1990. Personality dispositions as mediators of sexual reponses. In *Annual Review of Sex Research,* vol. 1, ed. J. Bancroft, 93–117. Society for the Scientific Study of Sex.

Campese, V. M., W. R. Procci, D. Levitan, M. S. Romoff, D. A. Goldstein, and S. G.

Massry. 1982. Autonomic nervous system dysfunction and impotence in uremia. *American Journal of Nephrology* 2:140–43.

Cassidy, W., N. Flanagan, M. Spellman, and M. Cohen. 1957. Clinical observations in manic-depressive disease. *Journal of the American Medical Assocation* 164:1535–46.

Catalona, W. J., and S. M. Dresner. 1985. Nerve-sparing radical prostatectomy: Extraprostatic tumor extension and preservation of erectile function. *Journal of Urology* 134:1149–51.

Clarke, B. F., D. J. Ewing, and J. W. Campbell. 1979. Diabetic autonomic neuropathy. *Diabetologia* 17:195–212.

Cohen, F., and R. S. Lazarus. 1983. Coping and adaptation in health and illness. In *Handbook of Health, Health Care, and the Health Professions,* ed. D. Mechanic, 608–35. New York: Free Press.

Cohen, H. D., R. C. Rosen, and L. Goldstein. 1976. Electroencephalographic laterality changes during human sexual orgasm. *Archives of Sexual Behavior* 5:189–99.

Cranston-Cuebas, M. A., and D. H. Barlow. 1990. Cognitive and affective contributions to sexual functioning. In *Annual Review of Sex Research,* vol. 1, ed. J. Bancroft, 119–61. Society for the Scientific Study of Sex.

Cytron, S., D. Simon, and L. Segenreich. 1987. Changes in the sexual behavior of couples after prostatectomy: A prospective study. *European Urology* 13:35–39.

Davidson, J. M., C. Camargo, and E. R. Smith. 1979. Effects of androgens on sexual behavior in hypogonadal men. *Journal of Clinical Endocrinology and Metabolism* 48:955–58.

de Groat, W. C., and W. D. Steers. 1988. Neuroanatomy and neurophysiology of penile erection. In *Contemporary management of impotence and infertility,* ed. E. A. Tanagho, T. F. Lue, and R. D. McClure, 3–27. Baltimore: Williams & Wilkins.

Dhabuwala, C. B., A. Kumar, and J. M. Pierce. 1986. Myocardial infarction and its influence on male sexual function. *Archives of Sexual Behavior* 15:499–504.

Dlin, B. M., A. Perlman, and E. Ringold. 1969. Psychosexual response to ileostomy and colostomy. *American Journal of Psychiatry* 126:374–81.

Drago, F. 1984. Prolactin and sexual behavior: A review. *Neuroscience and Behavioral Review* 8:433–39.

Druss, R. G., J. F. O'Connor, and L. O. Stern. 1969. Psychological response to colectomy. *Archives of General Psychiatry* 20:419–27.

Dunner, D. L., T. Dwyer, and R. R. Fieve. 1976. Depressive symptoms in patients with unipolar and bipolar affective disorder. *Comprehensive Psychiatry* 17:447–51.

Ellenberg, M. 1977. Sexual aspects of the female diabetic. *Mount Sinai Journal of Medicine* 44:495–500.

Ferguson, K., and B. Figley. 1979. Sexuality and rheumatic disease: A prospective study. *Sexuality and Disability* 2:130–38.

Fitting, M. D., S. Salisbury, N. H. Davies, and D. K. Mayclin. 1978. Self-concept and sexuality of spinal cord injured women. *Archives of Sexual Behavior* 7:143–56.

Friedman, S., and G. Harrison. 1984. Sexual histories, attitudes, and behavior of schizophrenia and "normal" women. *Archives of Sexual Behavior* 13:555–68.

Fugl-Meyer, A., and L. Jaasko. 1980. Post stroke hemiplegia and sexual intercourse. *Scandinavian Journal of Rehabilitation Supplement* 7:158–66.

Gay, G. R., J. A. Newmeyer, R. A. Elion, and S. Wieder. 1975. Drug-sex practice in the Haight-Ashbury or "The Sensuous Hippie." In *Sexual Behavior, Pharmacology, and Biochemistry,* ed. M. Sandler and G. L. Gessa, 63–79. New York: Raven.

Goldberg, D. C., B. Whipple, R. E. Fishkin, H. Waxman, P. J. Fink, and M. Weisberg. 1983. The Grafenberg spot and female ejaculation: A review of initial hypothesis. *Journal of Sex and Marital Therapy* 9:27–37.

Greaves, G. 1972. Sexual disturbances among chronic amphetamine users. *Journal of Nervous and Mental Disease* 155:363–65.

Griffith, E. R., and R. B. Trieschmann. 1983. Sexual dysfunctions in the physically ill and disabled. In *Treatment Interventions in Human Sexuality,* ed. C. C. Nadelson and D. B. Marcotte, 241–77. New York: Plenum.

Hamilton, M. 1980. Rating depressive patients. *Journal of Clinical Psychiatry* 41 (sect. 2):21–24.

Harrison, W. M., J. G. Rabkin, A. A. Ehrhardt, J. W. Stewart, P. J. McGrath, D. Ross, and F. M. Quitkin. 1986. Effects of antidepressant medication on sexual function:A controlled Study. *Journal of Clinical Psychopharmacology* 6:144–49.

Heath, R. G. 1972. Pleasure and brain activity in man. *Journal of Nervous and Mental Disease* 154:3–18.

Hellerstein, H. K., and E. H. Friedman. 1970. Sexual activity and the post-coronary patient. *Archives of Internal Medicine* 125:987–99.

Higgins, G. E. 1979. Sexual response in spinal and injured adults: A review. *Archives of Sexual Behavior* 8:173–96.

Howell, J. R., C. F. Reynolds, M. E. Thase, E. Frank, J. R. Jennings, P. R. Houck, S. Berman, E. Jacobs, and D. J. Kupfer. 1987. Assessment of sexual function, interest, and activity in depressed men. *Journal of Affective Disorders* 13:61–66.

Jamison, K. R. , D. K. Wellisch, and R. O. Pasnau. 1978. Psychosocial aspects of mastectomy. I. The woman's perspective. *American Journal of Psychiatry* 135:432–36.

Jensen, S. B. 1981. Diabetic sexual dysfunction: A comparative study of 160 insulin treated diabetic men and women and an age-matched control group. *Archives of Sexual Behavior* 10:493–504.

Kaplan, H. S. 1974. *The new sex therapy.* New York: Brunner/ Mazel.

———. 1992. A neglected issue: The sexual side effects of current treatments for breast cancer. *Journal of Sex and Marital Therapy* 18:3–19.

Kavanagh, T., and R. J. Shepard. 1977. Sexual activity after myocardial infarction. *Canadian Medical Association Journal* 116:1250–53.

Kolodny, R. C. 1971. Sexual dysfunction in diabetic females. *Diabetes* 20:557–59.

Kowalski, A., P. O. Stanley, L. Dennerstein, G. Burrows, and K. P. Maguire. 1985. The sexual side-effects of antidepressant medication: A double-blind comparison of two antidepressants in a non-psychiatric population. *British Journal of Psychiatry* 147:413–18.

Krane, R. J., I. Goldstein, and I. S. deTejada. 1989. Impotence. *New England Journal of Medicine* 321:1648–59.

Ladas, A., B. Whipple, and J. D. Perry. 1982. *The G spot and other recent discoveries about human sexuality.* New York: Holt, Rinehart & Winston.

Lazar, J., J. Eisold, I. Gadson, and D. Tesch. 1984. Recognition and management of antihypertensive drug side effects. *Clinical Pharmacology and Therapeutics* 35:254–55.

Levy, N. B. 1983. Sexual dysfunctions of hemodialysis patients. *Clinical and Experimental Dialysis* 7:275–88.

Lilius, H. G., F. J. Valtonen, and F. A. Davis. 1976. Sexual problems in patients suffering from multiple sclerosis. *Journal of Chronic Disease* 29:65–73.

Liss, J. L. 1982. Compulsive manic sexuality. *Medical Aspects of Human Sexuality* 4:80–84.

Lue, T. F., and E. A. Tanagho. 1987. Physiology of erection and pharmacological management of impotence. *Journal of Urology* 137:829–36.

MacLean, P. D., and D. W. Ploog. 1962. Cerebral representation of penile erection. *Journal of Neurophysiology* 25:29–55.

Maguire, G. P., E. G. Lee, D. J. Bevington, C. S. Kuchemann, R. J. Crabtree, and C. E. Cornell. 1978. Psychiatric problems in the first year after mastectomy. *British Medical Journal* 1:963–65.

Masters, W. H., and V. E. Johnson. 1966. *Human sexual response.* Boston: Little, Brown.

———. 1970. *Human Sexual Inadequacy.* Boston: Little, Brown.

Mathew, R. J., and M. L. Weinman. 1982. Sexual dysfunctions in depression. *Archives of Sexual Behavior* 11:323–28.

Mintz, J., K. O'Hare, C. P. O'Brien, and J. Goldschmidt. 1974. Sexual problems of heroin addicts. *Archives of General Psychiatry* 31:700–703.

Mirin, S. M., R. E. Meyer, and J. H. Mendelson. 1980. Opiate use and sexual function. *American Journal of Psychiatry* 137:909–12.

Mooney, T. O., T. M. Cole, and R. A. Chilgren. 1975. *Sexual options for paraplegics and quadriplegics.* Boston: Little, Brown.

Moos, R. H. 1977. *Coping with physical illness.* New York: Plenum Medical.

Mosher, D. L., and I. Greenberg. 1969. Females affective responses to reading erotic literature. *Journal of Consulting Clinical Psychology* 33:472–77.

Nestoros, J. N., H. E. Lehmann, and T. A. Ban. 1981. Sexual behavior of the male schizophrenic: The impact of illness and medications. *Archives of Sexual Behavior* 10:421–42.

Papadopoulos, C. 1980. Cardiovascular drugs and sexuality. *Archives of Internal Medicine* 140:1341–45.

Paulson, G. W. 1983. Sexual aspects of parkinsonism. *Medical Aspects of Human Sexuality* 17:271–73.

Pearlman, C. K. 1980. Sex and the prostatectomy patient. *British Journal of Sexual Medicine* 7:31–35.

Perachio, A. A., L. D. Marr, and M. Alexander. 1979. Sexual behavior in male rhesus monkeys elicited by electrical stimulation of preoptic and hypothalamic areas. *Brain Research* 177:127–44.

Pogach, L. M. and J. L. Vaitukaitis. 1983. Endocrine disorders associated with erectile dysfunction. In *Male erectile dysfunction,* ed. R. J. Krane, M. B. Siroky, and I. Goldstein, 63–76. Boston: Little, Brown.

Raboch, J. 1984. The sexual development and life of female schizophrenic patients. *Archives of Sexual Behavior* 13:341–50.

Rodger, R. S. C., K. Fletcher, J. H. Dewar, D. Genner, M. McHugh, R. Wilkinson, M. K. Ward, and D. N. S. Kerr. 1985. Prevalence and pathogenesis of impotence in one hundred uremic men. *Uremia Investigation* 8:89–96.

Roeske, N. C. S. 1979. Hysterectomy and the quality of a woman's life. *Archives of Internal Medicine* 139:146–47.

Rosen, R. C. 1992. Alcohol and drug effects on sexual response: Human experimental and clinical studies. In *Annual review of sex research*, vol. 2, ed. J. Bancroft, 119–80. Society for the Scientific Study of Sex.

Rotter, J. B. 1966. Generalized expectancies for internal versus external control of reinforcement. *Psychological Monographs* 80:609.

Schiavi, R. C. 1980. Psychological treatment of erectile disorders in diabetic patients. *Annals of Internal Medicine* 92 (2):337–39.

———. 1990a. Chronic alcoholism and male sexual dysfunction. *Journal of Sex and Marital Therapy* 16:23–33.

———. 1990b. Sexuality and aging in men. In *Annual review of sex research*, vol. 1, ed. J. Bancroft, 227–49. Society for the Scientific Study of Sex.

———. 1992. Laboratory methods for evaluating erectile dysfunction. In *Erectile failure: Assessment and treatment*, ed. S. R. Leiblum and R. C. Rosen, 141–70. New York: Guilford.

———. 1992. Normal aging and the evaluation of sexual dysfunction. *Psychiatric Medicine* 10:217–25.

Schiavi, R. C., and B. Hogan. 1979. Sexual problems in diabetes mellitus. *Diabetes Care* 2:9–17.

Schiavi, R. C., and P. Luloff. 1986. Psychopharmacologic agents and sexual function. In *Clinical psychopharmacology*, ed. L. R. Derogatis, 303–18. Menlo Park, Calif.: Addison-Wesley.

Schiavi, R. C., P. Schreiner-Engel, J. Mandeli, H. Schanzer, and E. Cohen. 1990. Healthy aging and male sexual function. *American Journal of Psychiatry* 147:766–71.

Schiavi, R. C., P. Schreiner-Engel, D. White, and J. Mandeli. 1991. The relationship between pituitary-gonadal function and sexual behavior in healthy aging men. *Psychosomatic Medicine* 53:363–74.

Schiavi, R. C., and D. White. 1976. Androgens and male sexual function: A review of human studies. *Journal of Sex and Marital Therapy* 2:214–28.

Schover, L. R., and M. Fife. 1985. Sexual counseling and radical pelvic or genital cancer surgery. *Journal of Psychosocial Oncology* 3:21–41.

Schover, L. R., and S. B. Jensen. 1988. *Sexuality and chronic illness: A comprehensive approach*. New York: Guilford.

Schreiner-Engel, P., and R. C. Schiavi. 1986. Lifetime psychopathology in individuals with low sexual desire. *Journal of Nervous and Mental Disease* 174:646–51.

Schreiner-Engel, P., R. C. Schiavi, H. Smith, and D. White. 1982. Plasma testosterone and female sexual behavior. In *Sexology: Sexual biology, behavior, and therapy*, ed. Z. Hoch and H. I. Lief. Amsterdam: Exerpta Medica (Int. Congr. Ser. no. 556:88).

Schreiner-Engel, P., R. C. Schiavi, D. Vietorisz, J. DeSimone-Eichel, and H. Smith.

1985. Diabetes and female sexuality: A comparative study of women in relationships. *Journal of Sex and Marital Therapy* 11:165–75.

Schreiner-Engel, P., R. C. Schiavi, D. Vietorisz, and H. Smith. 1987. The differential impact of diabetes type on female sexuality. *Journal of Psychosomatic Research* 31:23–33.

Segraves, R. T. 1989. Effects of psychotropic drugs on human erection and ejaculation. *Archives of General Psychiatry* 46:275–84.

Segraves, R. T., R. Madsen, and C. S. Carter. 1985. Erectile dysfunction associated with pharmacologic agents. In *Diagnosis and treatment of erectile disturbances,* ed. R. T. Segraves and H. W. Schoenberg, 23–63. New York: Plenum.

Sherwin, B. B., M. M. Gelfand, and W. Brender. 1985. Androgen enhances sexual motivation in females: A prospective, crossover study of sex steroid administration in the surgical menopause. *Psychosomatic Medicine* 47:339–51.

Silberfarb, P. M., L. H. Maurer, and C. S. Crouthamel. 1980. Psychosocial aspects of neoplastic disease. *American Journal of Psychiatry* 137:450–55.

Singer, I. 1973. *The goals of human sexuality.* London: Wilwood.

Skakkebaek, N. E., J. Bancroft, D. W. Davidson, and P. Warner. 1981. Androgen replacement with oral testosterone undecanoate in hypogonadal men: A double-blind controlled study. *Clinical Endocrinology* 14:49–61.

Slag, M. F., J. E. Morley, M. K. Elson, D. L. Trence, C. J. Nelson, A. E. Nelson, W. B. Kinlaw, S. Beyer, F. Q. Nuttall, and R. B. Shafer. 1983. Impotence in medical clinic outpatients. *Journal of American Medical Association* 249:1736–40.

Spark, R. F., R. A. White, and P. B. Connolly. 1980. Impotence is not always psychogenic. *Journal of American Medical Association* 243:750–55.

Taylor, D. C. 1969. Sexual behavior and temporal lobe epilepsy. *Archives of Neurology* 21:510–16.

Verhulst, J., and B. Schneidman. 1981. Schizophrenia and sexual functioning. *Hospital and Community Psychiatry* 32:259–62.

Wallace, C., G. Wehmer, and E. Polodny. 1974. Contemporary community standards of visual erotica. In *Technical Report of Committee on Pornography,* vol. 9. Washington, D.C.: Government Printing Office.

Waltzer, W. C. 1981. Sexual and reproductive function in men treated with hemodialysis and renal transplantation. *Journal of Urology* 126:713–16.

Wein, A. J., and K. N. Van Arsdalen. 1988. Drug-induced male sexual dysfunction. *Urologic Clinics of North America* 15:23–31.

Weiss, H. D. 1972. The physiology of human penile erection. *Annals of Internal Medicine* 76:793–99.

Weizman, R., A. Weizman, J. Levi, V. Gura, D. Zevin, B. Maoz, H. Wijsenbeek, and M. Ben David. 1983. Sexual dysfunction associated with hyperprolactinemia in males and females undergoing hemodialysis. *Psychosomatic Medicine* 45:259–69.

Woods, S. M. 1981. Sexuality and mental disorders. In *Sexual problems in medical practice,* ed. H. I. Lief. Monroe, Wisc.: American Medical Association.

Zifroni, A., R. C. Schiavi, and F. Schaffner. 1991. Sexual function and testosterone levels in men with non-alcoholic liver disease. *Hepatology* 14:479–82.

Sexual Problems and Therapies: A Quarter Century of Developments and Changes

Richard Green

Major revisions have occurred in the identification, diagnosis, and treatment of problems in human sexuality during the past twenty-five years. Behaviors long considered to be pathological are no longer designated disorders. Many patterns of criminal behavior are now considered to fall within the purview of the treating professions. Disorders in gender as well as sexual behavior have been identified and special treatments developed. The origins of dysfunctions in sexual response have been reconceptualized and rapid interventions facilitated. New procedures have been developed for treating old problems of sexuality. New treatments within general medicine created new problems of sexuality, and considerable attention has been directed to early life sexual experience as having substantial implications for lifelong psychological functioning.

Sexual Dysfunction

Modern therapy for deficiencies of sexual arousal (the sexual response cycle) commenced with the physiological and clinical research of William Masters and Virginia Johnson (1966, 1970).

Males: General

With the 1970 work of Masters and Johnson on erectile failure, an arduous psychodynamic treatment model was displaced by a straightforward approach focused on social learning and behaviorist principles. Before 1970, multiple factors were posited as leading to erectile failure including an array of negative messages about sexuality beginning in childhood, traumatic early sexual experiences, and a vicious cycle whereby anxiety over achieving and maintaining erection interfered psychologically and physiologically with erection. The new treatment emphasized sensate focus in which nondemand, nongenital caressing with a partner, and a ban on intercourse, lessened performance anxiety.

In what has been termed *postmodern treatment* (LoPiccolo 1991) systems theory has augmented the Masters and Johnson approach. Here the sexual dysfunction (of whatever type, male or female) is seen as serving a homeostatic function in maintaining the couple's status quo. A couple that I attempted to treat recently is an example: the husband complained of erectile failure, but the two never got beyond a very preliminary phase of sensate focus, whereby they were to embrace, in nightclothes, for ten minutes. This stalemate was in consequence of a profound, mutually passive-aggressive relationship in which each partner's need to aggress against each other maintained their marriage. In one manifestation of this dynamic, both husband and wife acted to prevent sexual contact even though they sought sex therapy.

Males: Aging

The premodern message to older persons was that sex stopped by the end of midlife. Frequently, it did. The newer message was that sexuality should endure into advanced years. But this information was incomplete and resulted in sexual disability, instead of sexual death. Erectile dysfunction in older men is often the consequence of neither partner understanding the physiological changes in genital function coincident with advancing years. Although visual or fantasy stimulation was adequate for erection in earlier years, tactile stimulation becomes increasingly necessary with age. If unrecognized, couples attempting to continue previous patterns of sexuality may conclude that the male partner is impotent.

Another male dysfunction is an accompaniment of men living longer, in some cases beyond survival of their partner. Thus a more psychodynamic source of erectile failure is also coupled with the message that sexuality may continue into advanced years. When a couple has been together for decades and the wife dies, the survivor may experience unconscious guilt over initiating or enjoying a sexual relationship with a new partner. This was the presenting picture of a sixty-year-old man I saw recently experiencing what is called widower's syndrome (Hengeveld and Korzeg 1980).

Males: Physiological Intervention

In 1981, I coauthored with Gorm Wagner of Copenhagen a text focusing on emerging etiologic and treatment features associated with erectile failure—physiological and anatomical bases (Wagner and Green 1981). A decade before, Masters and Johnson pronounced 95 percent of all cases of erectile failure as psychogenic, a similar statistic having been advanced even earlier by psychoanalysts.

Newer diagnostic techniques identified an array of factors that interfered with obtaining or maintaining erection. They included previously undetected congenital vascular anomalies in the penis, atherosclerotic changes in the vessels leading to the penis, (similar to the blood-flow compromise commonly associated with heart or brain disease), hormonal abnormalities, such as low testosterone or high prolactin, and degenerative neural disorders perhaps as sequelae of chronic disease such as diabetes or alcoholism. In fact, one series of four hundred men complaining of erectile failure found that over one-quarter had a physiological basis (Melman, Tiefer, and Pedersen 1988).

Technologically based treatments derived from these insights. They included surgically implanted plastic rods (Small 1978), indwelling water-fillable tubes with an implanted reservoir (Furlow 1976), externally applied reduced air pressure to facilitate penile blood flow (vacuum pump) (Nadig, Ware, and Blumoff 1986), and injections of pharmacologically active drugs at the site of (renewed) genital action— that is, directly into the cavernous bodies of the penis (Brindley 1983).

Injectable drugs include papaverine hydrochloride, phentolamine mesylate, and prostaglandin E_1. They relax arterial and trabecular smooth muscle and permit increased arterial flow to the penis along with venous occlusion preventing outflow. These drugs are not approved by the FDA for this use. Many patients shrink from the suggestion of having a needle inserted into their penises, but, in those patients who overcome this block and begin and continue treatment (about half of referred patients), the majority report satisfaction with the results.

The vacuum cylinder draws blood into the penis and tension rings applied at the base of the penis retain the blood for tumescence. Acceptance of this device is higher than for direct injections. (See Althof and Turner [1992] for a review of these procedures.)

Notwithstanding the potential for treatment success in previously untreatable patients with a physiologically based erectile dysfunction, a dangerous development from these new insights was dichotomizing erectile failure into purely psychogenic or purely physiological. In fact, the series cited above that found one-quarter of men to have an organic etiology found only 40 percent in which an entirely psychogenic basis was identified. Thus, one-quarter were of mixed causation.

Clinicians sensitive to the need for comprehensive treatment approaches for erectile failure recognize the pitfall in overtreating physiological bases of erectile failure. For example, a man with evidence of physiological compromise—perhaps with ambiguous erection results in the laboratory where nocturnal penile tumescence was assessed during the dream phases of sleep or perhaps with a marginal penile artery–brachial artery blood pressure ratio, which indicates reduced blood flow to the penis—may also have a psychological basis for erectile failure. Bypassing this and inserting a penile prosthesis may not resolve the patient's problem, although it may permit intercourse. Further, resolving the psychological problem first may obviate the need for surgery. Mixed long-term outcomes for men with penile prostheses and their partners suggest that these treatment approaches are often unwisely implemented (Tiefer, Pedersen, and Melman 1988). There has been an emerging understanding by therapists that the partners of prosthesis candidates need to be evaluated before possible implantation and that the sexual partners should continue to be counseled after surgery.

The extent to which the treatment of impotence (usually by prosthesis) has come to middle America is illustrated by the potency-recovery centers that have popped up nationwide, advertising on television, on the radio, and in the printed media. A rider on the Los Angeles freeway system at evening rush hour can generally tell when the radio ad beginning with the attention-grabbing clarion call "impotency" has hit the airwaves, by the sudden, simultaneous swerving of hundreds of Mercedes-Benz.

Females: Orgasmic Dysfunction

The capacity for orgasm in the human female appears to have been discovered in 1966 by William Masters and Virginia Johnson. Subsequently (or consequently), the new industry of modern sex therapy emerged for treating women optimistically termed *preorgasmic* (Barbach 1974). A variety of techniques were introduced, ranging from psychological disinhibition (removing the fear of flying) to mechanically generated hyperstimulation (the vibrator).

A problem in treating orgasmic dysfunction in women is defining it. Some women are orgasmic with nonvaginal stimulation directly to the clitoris, via oral or digital contact, but never or rarely with coitus. Is this normal? Helen Kaplan wrote in 1974, "There are millions of women who are sexually responsive, and often multiply orgastic, but who cannot have an orgasm during intercourse unless they receive simultaneous clitoral stimulation." She asks, Are they neurotic? and concludes that, although treatment may be indicated in some cases, in others this is a normal variation of sexual response. A decade after Kaplan's book, a treatment program for such situationally nonorgasmic women attempting to transfer orgasm from masturbation to coitus was largely ineffective (Libman et al. 1984).

Males and Females: Inhibited Desire

The new dysfunction of inhibited sexual desire was described in 1977 (Kaplan 1977; Lief 1977) and entered the American Psychiatric Association (APA) diagnostic manual in 1980.

Low sexual drive, or hypoactive sexual desire disorder, has received considerable clinical attention and is defined currently by the APA (pending a *Diagnostic and Statistical Manual of Mental Disorders* IV revision) as "persistently or recurrently deficient or absent sexual fantasies and desire for sexual activity. The judgment of deficiency or absence is made by the clinician, taking into account factors that affect sexual functioning, such as age, sex, and the context of the person's life." Persons with inhibited sexual desire may experience sexual arousal—that is, vaginal lubrication or erection—but experience little pleasure. Others have minimal arousal and little interest in either autoerotic or interpersonal genital activity.

The etiology of low sexual desire is nonspecific. In the Stony Brook program's experience with twenty-seven cases, it was associated with depression, religious upbringing, other sexual dysfunctions, and aversion to specific sexual behaviors, including oral-genital contact or masturbation (LoPiccolo 1980).

Low sex drive gained prominence as a treatable disorder with the publication of the 1979 text by Helen Kaplan (Kaplan 1979). She reported that less than 15 percent of such patients could be treated effectively with the, by then, standard fourteen-session course of the "new sex therapy" (Kaplan 1974).

Low desire is identified and treated when the interest in sexual behavior is markedly disparate between the partners. Treatments include anxiety reduction, reducing depression, increasing sensory awareness, improving the couple's relationship, enhancing sexual and sensual experiences, facilitating erotic responses, and dealing with intrapsychic conflicts (LoPiccolo 1980).

The extent to which low sexual desire may be normal (in terms of common) is another issue. In a 1978 study of one hundred nonpatient couples, 35 percent of men and 16 percent of women complained of lack of interest in sex, and 28 percent of women and 10 percent of men experienced being turned off by sex.

Whereas inhibited sexual desire was initially a complaint more often expressed by women, a shift has occurred in the sex ratio. In the Stony Brook clinical experience during 1982–83, over half the cases were male. The increase in male sexual inhibition is viewed by some as a response to changing gender roles. "The power-balance between the sexes shifted, the man's position as the active, dominating, and initiating part in the sexual act was no longer a matter of course" (Mohl and Pedersen 1991, 245).

HOMOSEXUALITY

A colossal breakthrough in reducing the ranks of the mentally ill occurred in the early 1970s when the APA declared that homosexuality was no longer considered a mental illness (Bayer 1981). Initially, with a stroke of the pen, followed by referendum, some 5 percent of the population was cured of mental disease. Just how many gay men and lesbians had been consulting psychiatrists before this decision is conjectural, but a vast psychoanalytic and behaviorist literature serves as testament to the many who tried, most often unsuccessfully, to change the direction of their erotic orientation with dynamic therapy (Bieber et al. 1962; Hatterer 1970; Socarides 1968), or with behavior therapy (MacCulloch and Feldman 1967; McConaghy 1976). (See Green [1992] for a general review of treatment outcomes.)

The most extensive report of psychoanalytic treatment of male homosexuality was published in 1962. Although more than a quarter century old, I refer to it because the treatment outcome was heralded as showing "the most optimistic and promising results" from the perspective of modifying sexual orientation (Bieber et al. 1962). Of seventy-two men who were exclusively homosexual prior to therapy, 19 percent were reported to be heterosexual after therapy. Of thirty who were bisexual prior to treatment, half reportedly became heterosexual. Most men who reportedly emerged as heterosexual had at least 350 hours of treatment.

In behavior therapy, aversive stimuli (often electric shocks), were paired with viewing homoerotic slides. No aversion followed viewing heteroerotic slides. A 1977 review of thirty-seven studies of the treatment of 350 homosexuals (four females) concluded that "there is no evidence that aversion relief (aversive stimuli paired with homosexual erotic images), is a direct and potentially effective procedure for increasing heterosexual arousal" (Adams and Sturgis 1977).

The milieu enmeshing the homosexual person a generation ago is described by Martin Duberman: "The vast majority of gay people were locked away in painful isolation and fear. . . . Many of us cursed our fate, longed to be straight, and some of us had actively been seeking 'cure.' In my case, for a long time" (Duberman 1991, 3).

Homosexuals consulted therapists because of conflict, often experienced as guilt, over sexual behavior considered pathological, or at least a symptom of psychosexual immaturity (Freud 1953; Green 1972), fear of public disclosure and possible criminal consequences (Rivera 1991), and the penalty that employment status could be jeopardized by disclosure of deviant sexual orientation (Knutson 1980; Rivera 1991). Other motivations included insistence by family members on undertaking therapy, notably with younger patients, and the more idealistic source of motivation—the desire for the positive aspects of a heterosexual lifestyle including the prospect of marital stability and child raising.

No accurate figures exist for current rates at which homosexual men and women consult therapists. Certainly the behaviorist literature on reorienting sexual arousal patterns has evaporated (Green 1988), although psychoanalytic and eclectic reports by treatment enthusiasts continue. Examples are New York psychoanalyst Charles Socarides's work (Socarides 1978), and the newer work describing reparative therapy by California psychologist Joseph Nicolosi working at the Thomas Aquinas Counseling Center (Nicolosi 1991).

Contemporary views on treating homosexual patients are being informed by those who view homosexuality as a positive pattern of sexual expression. Psychoanalyst Richard Isay writes, "My perspective on the therapy of gay men is based on two convictions. First, gay men can live, as homosexuals, well-adjusted and productive lives with gratifying and stable love relationships. . . . My second conviction is one established by clinical experience: the effort to change the sexual orientation of a gay man is harmful to him" (Isay 1989, 109–10). Isay offers advice to homosexual men who seek therapy: "It is my suggestion . . . that if they are to unravel and untangle the internalized homophobia and other aspects of childhood development that may contribute to their low self-esteem, they must have a therapist who regards them as capable of gratifying and loving relationships as homosexual men. Guiding a therapeutic endeavor with any gay man must be the therapist's conviction that his patient's homosexuality is for him normal and natural" (Isay 1989, 126).

Many of the motivations that prompted men and women to seek therapy for conflicts regarding sexual orientation a generation ago continue, notwithstanding the increased societal acceptance of homosexuality and the fact that in contrast to the early 1960s when every state criminalized homosexual conduct. Today only half the states continue to do so (Green 1992). For younger men and women parental promotion of therapy continues, as most parents are not interested in whether psychiatry considers this sexual pattern to be a disorder. Civil disabilities persist for gay men and lesbians including employment and housing discrimination, which is legal in forty-four states (National Lawyers Guild 1989), and the unavailability of a legally sanctioned marital relationship. Finally, the pandemic of AIDS has frightened some men toward an alternate lifestyle (here, heterosexual) that carries a smaller health risk.

TRANSSEXUALISM

Treatment for transsexual males and females has emerged as legitimate medical intervention during the past twenty-five years. The first professional book on the subject was published by Harry Benjamin (1966). When I coedited the first interdisciplinary text with John Money in 1969, only two U.S. medical centers had instituted transsexual treatment programs (Green and Money 1969). Today most large cities have clinicians experienced in the preoperative management of transsexuals and a sufficient number of experienced surgeons are available for the focused body reconstruction of patients. Treatment centers exist in other countries as well, notably in Canada and western Europe.

Initially, sex reassignment was met with vociferous opposition from the medical community. In a survey I coconducted with Robert Stoller and Craig MacAndrew in 1966, transsexual clinical vignettes were presented, and various diagnostic stipulations were offered (Green, Stoller, and MacAndrew 1966). Even when the transsexual had undergone two years of psychotherapy and was judged by the treating psychiatrist to be nonpsychotic and reasonable in all other respects, less than 20 percent of surgeons (urologists and gynecologists) and only 30 percent of psychiatrists would approve the surgery. Even when the treating psychiatrist was convinced that the transsexual would commit suicide should sex reassignment be denied, the majority of physicians were unmoved.

Treatment guidelines today revolve around the one- to two-year real-life test, or the trial period of cross-gender (before cross-sexual) living. The strategy is reversible intervention before irreversible. Thus, cross-dressing and then cross-sex hormonal administration are earlier stages, along with counseling. The patient must prove, at least to her or himself, that living as a person of the other sex (opposite to the transsexual) is preferable (Standards of Care 1985). The real-life test requires employment in the aspired-for gender. This poses a dilemma for the patient because federal antigender discrimination employment laws do not protect transsexuals (Green 1986).

Although some clinicians continue to challenge the wisdom of sex-reassignment surgery for any patient, and others begrudgingly tolerate it but label it experimental (thus threatening third-party reimbursement), published cases attest to its utility. A review I coauthored in 1991 with Davis Fleming of cases published in the English language during the last decade indicates that less than 10 percent of male or female operated transsexuals regret the sex reassignment and that many show objective improvement (Green and Fleming 1991).

An apparent change in one aspect of this exotic variant of human sexuality in more recent years has been the reported sex ratio of patients. Earlier, at least three-quarters of surgical applicants were male (Green and Money 1969). Now, the ratio has altered to two to one and, in some reports, approaches parity. The initial ratio was believed to be due to several influences. From the neuroendocrine developmental perspective, the route to normative maleness and masculinity is ridden with more potholes than the path to femaleness and femininity because, in the absence of a second sex chromosome, or the absence of sex hormones, femaleness and perhaps femininity develop (Money and Ehrhardt 1972). This differential vulnerability may explain the higher rates of all sexual paraphilias among males. From the psychodynamic perspective, the male child must surmount an additional developmental hurdle not negotiated by the female—disidentification from the first intimate other person in the infant's life—a female (Greenson 1968). From the sociological perspective, the stigma attached to homosexuality has been greater for males, driving some, particularly those with a strong religious upbringing, to redefine their erotic interest in men as heterosexual through the process of sex reassignment (Hellman et al. 1981). From the surgical perspective, realistic-appearing genital reconstruction has been more feasible for the male-to-female transsexual (Green and Money 1969; Laub and Green 1978). Whereas no changes in human neuroendocrinological or psychodynamic differentiation are

known to have occurred during recent years, the stigma of male homosexuality has been somewhat attenuated, and advances in phalloplasty,
including devices to facilitate sufficient rigidity for intercourse, may
have influenced the shifting ratio.

CHILD AND ADOLESCENT GENDER-IDENTITY DISORDERS

Both homosexuality and transsexualism may have identifiable behavioral antecedents in childhood and early adolescence. A new psychiatric diagnosis emerged in the 1970s reflecting on early gender roles and
later sexual behavior. Owing in part to my clinical research (Green
1974) and participation in formulating the diagnostic manual of the
APA, children are now diagnosed and treated for gender-identity disorder (American Psychiatric Association 1980, 1987). Ironically, this new
mental disorder carries a high probability of later homosexual orientation (which, in turn, is no longer a disorder). Characteristic of this
childhood syndrome is the stated preference for being a child of the
other sex, a strong preference for dressing in clothes typically worn by
children of the other sex, a strong preference for the toys typically preferred by the other sex, and preferential role taking as fantasy characters
of the other sex (Green 1974, 1987). To view this behavioral picture as
disorder reflects several problematic features of contemporary culture
in the arena of sex roles.

We were informed a decade or so ago of a unisex (more properly
unigender) swing in the culture, notably in childhood, a change that
would eliminate traditionally gender-differentiated toys and activities
and gender-role styles for children derived linearly from the child's anatomic sex. Such a development would have had a significant effect on
gender-identity disorders. At the least, it could have erased much of the
presenting clinical picture of the disorder. For children and adults, it
may have mitigated much of the social rationale behind the stated desire
to be a person of the opposite sex, unless a cross-sex identity is primary,
derived from a neuroanatomic site, with its behavioral manifestations
secondary. However, a pivotal problem for cross-gendered young people
today is that the pediatric and early adolescent culture is essentially as
rigidly sex stereotyped as it was a generation or more ago. Cross-gender
boys are called "sissy" and "queer." Markedly cross-gender girls are also
teased. Consequently, the treatment of gender-identity disorders is potentially in tension with the ideas of those therapists or parents who see
adhesion to sex-stereotyped behaviors as undesirable.

An additional theoretical and practical complication with diagnosis and treatment of this childhood disorder is that, at least in my prospective fifteen-year study, three-quarters of such boys emerged as homosexual or bisexual men, and only the rare one emerged as transsexual (Green 1987). Although there are no prospective studies documenting the outcome for girls with gender-identity disorder, retrospective reports of childhood behavior by transsexual and lesbian females suggest that a higher proportion than average should emerge as sexually atypical (Bell, Weinberg, and Hammersmith 1981; Grellert, Newcomb, and Bentler 1982). The therapist is thus confronted with conflicting values regarding not only conformity to early gender-role expectations but also the desirability of one or another pattern of later sexual orientation, juxtaposed with the social pain experienced by cross-gendered young people and the psychological pain from being dissatisfied with the sex to which one was born. To the extent that sexual identity disorder in children persists as sexual identity disorder in adulthood, early intervention is justified in consequence of the substantial stress of transsexualism.

Treatment of adolescents with gender-identity disorder, which may represent transsexualism, elicits medical, ethical, and legal issues. The onset of puberty, especially for the male, sets in place irreversible body changes that impede social passing as an adult of the other sex should early adolescent transsexualism endure (Steiner 1985, 343). The problem here, facilitated by my other profession—law—is that, when the apparently transsexual adolescent's parents doubt that their son or daughter will remain transsexual, endocrine—let alone surgical—intervention cannot be accomplished. And, in the rare instances where parents have accepted the cross-sex destiny of their child and consent to medical intervention, should the transsexual status of the adolescent not endure the treating physician faces the prospect of a subsequent malpractice action from the adolescent patient who has reached adulthood.

Adolescence also involves an array of other problematic sexual behaviors. These include sexually transmitted diseases, including HIV infection, pregnancy, conflicts over homosexual orientation, and, although infrequently discussed or addressed, the sexual dysfunctions of nonorgasmic response and vaginismus in the female, and erectile failure and premature ejaculation in the male. Adolescence is also the typical period of onset of fetishistic cross-dressing in the male, or transvestism. Its appearance in the teenage boy typically comes as a surprise in that he was heretofore apparently unremarkable in terms of his gender-role development. Usually he was not a cross-gendered boy. Diagnosis and treatment involves distinguishing transvestism from transsexualism and homosexuality and perhaps reducing the reliance on cross-dressing for erotic arousal.

INTERGENERATIONAL SEXUALITY

A substantial new area of sexual therapy is treating persons who recall traumatic childhood sexual experiences. *Intergenerational sexuality* is the nonjudgmental term for what is typically called child sex abuse. This is an exploding area of concern in the professional literature and lay press on sex. The new field of victimology has assumed massive proportions that are not without significance in the medical, psychological, and legal professions.

Identifying and treating survivors of childhood sexual abuse began during the 1980s and has accelerated like a juggernaut. Early studies suggested the etiologic importance of childhood sexual abuse in the psychiatric problems experienced by adults. Surveys of psychiatric patients presenting to emergency rooms revealed a high percentage of (usually) women who reported some form of childhood sexual abuse. Often these persons experienced dissociative psychological states and resembled patients with posttraumatic stress disorder, described after the Vietnam War. Patients reporting a history of childhood sexual abuse were more often those with a history of suicide attempts and substance abuse (Briere and Runtz 1987).

There are methodological problems with these studies. First, they are correlational. They posit causality between recalled sexual experiences decades ago and current difficulty. Second, they often treat abuse as a dichotomous variable without accounting for the potentially different effect from one experience of fondling to repeated forced intercourse. Third, they do not account for other family variables that may be related to psychiatric outcome, such as the effect of divorce or alcohol abuse. They may not distinguish purely sexual from combined sexual and physical abuse. They do not compare the psychological outcomes of nonabused siblings. They do not control for the contribution of inheritance to the disorders of depression and substance abuse.

Another swarm of persons reporting sexual victimization as children emerged from individual and group therapy where what are described as previously repressed memories of early life sexual abuse are restored to consciousness. Often, patients, usually women with nonspecific psychological symptoms, are evaluated by therapists who interpret the symptoms as evidence of repressed childhood sexual abuse. Ultimately the patient recalls these experiences (Whitley 1991).

Other professionals who play a major role here are attorneys. One result of reports of recovery of previously repressed childhood sexual abuse experiences has been revision of statutes of limitations laws. These laws limit the time period during which an injured party may institute legal action to recover in the form of financial compensation. A recent change in California law will serve as an example: a person of *any* age may now bring suit for having been sexually abused as a child, providing that the person either discovered within the past three years that abuse occurred or, if having previously known of the abuse for a longer period, did not link the abuse with current emotional problems until the past three years. Before the alleged perpetrator is named in the lawsuit, the merit of this allegation must be attested to by both the patient's therapist and the patient's attorney (California Code of Civil Procedure 1991).

Are these memories of childhood sexual abuse valid? The well-known psychoanalytic phenomenon of screen memory is one confounding possibility—that is, a memory that is a representation of affect not based on factual history but nevertheless vividly recalled. Other potential confounds include demand characteristics—the expectations of therapists or others for the individual patient to recall abuse experiences and the self-serving blaming by the patient of a wide range of current psychological problems on an event that is sufficiently horrendous to justify emotional difficulty.

Professor Elizabeth Loftus of Washington State University, an expert on memory and eyewitness testimony, asserts, "Therapists are saying, you know, a lot of my other patients have these symptoms, and they were sexually abused. Were you?" She notes that, although patients will say no, they may later undergo hypnosis or relaxation sessions where they are urged to get in touch with those childhood memories that were blocked off (Whitley 1991, 69).

From the legal perspective, particularly when the alleged perpetrator is either very wealthy or an otherwise-estranged parent, or both, there is the possibility of outright fraud motivating the charge. From the clinical psychiatric perspective, the extent to which litigation can psychologically heal the scars of an alienated relationship, of whatever origin, is doubtful. From the research psychiatry perspective, there is the danger of an overly reductionistic view of mental disorder blaming all problems on sexual abuse, thus trivializing the complexity of human development, sexual or otherwise.

These concerns do not mean that childhood sexual abuse does not occur or that, in some cases, at least, there are not enduring sequelae that bedevil adults—problems that can be helped by therapy. For children, a 1986 review found that "in the immediate aftermath of sexual abuse, from one-fifth to two-fifths of abused children seen by clinicians manifest pathological disturbance" (Browne and Finkelhor 1986). A 1991 review agreed that clinical problems are common but concluded, "We do not know whether many of the symptoms . . . are specific to sexual abuse or whether they are attributable to other factors such as the child's level of premorbid functioning or a disturbed home environment. . . . Few studies have addressed the impact of disclosure, and specifically in what instances disclosure and subsequent intervention on the part of medical, legal, or social agencies can be expected to have . . ." (Beitchman et al. 1991).

For longer-term effects the 1986 review concluded that "adult women victimized as children are more likely to manifest depression, self-destructive behavior, anxiety, feelings of isolation and stigma, poor self-esteem, a tendency to revictimization, and substance abuse. . . . Victims as a group demonstrate impairment compared with their nonvictimized counterparts, but under one-fifth evidence serious psychopathology" (Browne and Finkelhor 1986). A 1991 review concluded that "the specific effect of the early sexual experience, independent of threat of force, or parental psychopathology, remains to be clarified" (Beitchman et al. 1992).

A related area of sexual problems has emerged with adults recalling satanic sexual abuse or ritualistic sex abuse. According to Sherrill Mulhern, anthropologist, University of Paris, "In the last decade, thousands of people, mostly women, have claimed—usually after undergoing intensive therapy—to be the victims of satanic cults. But 99.9 percent of them have absolutely no evidence." Mulhern has studied American satanic ritual abuse survivors (SRAs) and concludes after interviewing both patients and therapists, that no such abuse actually occurred, but rather "what *really* happened, happened in therapy" (Whitley 1991, 67–68).

Whereas the sequelae of genuine abuse, or the bases of delusional or fraudulent charges of abuse, demand clinical attention, this responsibility is not being met by therapists in some cases slogging their way through the courts. Recently, an organization has been founded comprising hundreds of parents who claim that they have been falsely accused of child molestation allegedly occurring decades ago that have been remembered in recent therapy (the False Memory Syndrome Foundation).

Sex Offenders

Treatment of documented, habitual sex offenders, usually pedophiles and rapists, has, in recent years, engaged a variety of strategies other than the pure punishment of prison. They include surgical, pharmacological, and behaviorist intervention.

Our understanding that the hormone testosterone, the primary male sex steroid, is the facilitating force behind male sexual motivation and function led to efforts to control or eliminate unwanted sexuality by removing or impeding that source. In Europe, a common treatment (punishment) for sex offenders was castration, surgical removal of the testes, the principal source of testosterone (Sturup 1972). In the United States, legal and other social obstacles impeded this approach. However, chemical castration emerged as an alternative with the advent of antiandrogenic drugs. These drugs temporarily block the actions of androgens at receptor sites. During the past two decades they have been used in Europe and Canada, the most widely used being the German-produced cyproterone acetate (CA) (Laschet and Laschet 1975). In the United States the FDA has not approved the use of CA, so the alternative has been medroxyprogesterone acetate, given in longer-acting form as Depo-provera (Berlin 1989).

A general overview of the effects of antiandrogen is that testosterone levels are lowered and subjective reports of erotic interest and arousal are diminished, but penile responsivity shows less change. Studies suggest that rates of recidivism, or repeated sexual offenses, are reduced with antiandrogen treatment (see review by Green [1992]).

Problems with evaluating or predicting antiandrogen treatment results include the absence of a linear relationship between testosterone level and sexuality in many men (some surgical castrates report erection and intercourse decades postsurgery), the differential effects of androgen on various components of male sexuality (marked reduction in testosterone but penile arousal retained in response to deviant stimuli), and the degree to which sexual assault, particularly rape, is aggressive, as opposed to sexual in nature (with aggression mediated less than sexuality by testosterone). Further, even when these chemical agents appear

to be effective, additional problems emerge in treating imprisoned
offenders. They include both removing prisoners from situations that
historically have placed them at social risk (i.e., women or children vulnerable to sexual assault) and enforcing continued treatment compliance on release from incarceration.

The view that deviant sexual arousal patterns are conditioned responses, reinforced by orgasm, led to a surge in behaviorist-based strategies to alter sexuality in the 1960s and 1970s. This was notably apparent in the efforts at modifying consenting homosexual behavior. But
whereas therapy for homosexuals has fallen into disfavor, in part because of the relative ineffectiveness of treatment, as described above,
and in part from the backlash against changing sexual orientation (a
consumer boycott), the treatment of sex offenders has continued.
Efforts at retraining sexual arousal patterns are part of the rehabilitation
program at several prison and treatment centers.

Behavior therapy strategies include aversion therapy, orgasmic reconditioning, cognitive restructuring, and social skills training. In aversion therapy, the patient is conditioned to associate negative stimuli
with formerly positive deviant sexual stimuli. Electrical shock is the
common aversive stimulus. This can be paired with slides or fantasy
depicting the (so far, only for the therapist) unwanted sexual activity.
In one type of orgasmic reconditioning, patients masturbate to orgasm
using fantasies of legal behavior and then immediately masturbate (usually without orgasm, as they are in a refractory period) to fantasies of
illegal behavior. In another the patient may begin masturbation to unacceptable stimuli and then switch to acceptable stimuli prior to orgasm.
The acceptable stimuli are introduced progressively earlier in the sequence. Cognitive restructuring helps patients identify antecedents of
deviant behavior and then to restructure them. For example, pedophiles
may interpret children's behaviors as seductive. In social skills training,
the sex offender is taught the skills that should facilitate effective sexual
interaction in a socially acceptable fashion. Behaviorist intervention
may co-occur with antiandrogenic intervention.

Treatment results have been mixed. Some offenders appear to demonstrate alterations in arousal patterns, at least within the prison or hospital treatment laboratory. But intolerance by the public of any repeat
offense by a previously incarcerated sex offender renders officials extremely cautious in releasing felons. Indeed, one state, Washington, has
recently declared that many offenders are not treatable and therefore
has enacted a sexual predator law that permits continued detention of

the offender beyond the term of his prison sentence (ostensibly for treatment). The law is being challenged by the state's civil liberties union as a violation of constitutionally required due process.

MEDICAL PHARMACOTHERAPY

Advances in medical pharmacotherapy, notably for treating the near-ubiquitous disorders of hypertension, anxiety, depression, myocardial deficiencies, and so forth have also had their medical downside. Male erectile compromise is a commonly reported side effect, as reported extensively by Schiavi (chap. 12, this vol.; see also, Biuffum [1988]). Thus, iatrogenically based sexual problems have been created that, in addition to causing a new area of distress for the patient, may also lead to non-compliance for taking lifesaving drugs. The general physician who is busily prescribing these new panaceas not only must be aware of sexual problem side effects but should also be skilled in sexual counseling or at least aware of appropriate resources for referral.

CONCLUSION

Whereas some atypical sexualities are less often conceptualized today as pathology, compared to a quarter century ago, others have been recognized as disorder. Overall, cultural, value-laden forces bear less weight on these determinations. The delisting of homosexuality emerged as a classic example of where cultural biases about a pattern of sexuality had been legitimated by science. By contrast, another area, not the deviation of choice of erotic partners but in the person's gender self-concept, previously regarded as a curiosity, became legitimated by science. The effect of recognizing transsexualism as a mental disorder was not altogether negative for the patient, however, in that it provided the basis for helpful medical and surgical intervention.

Recognition of the significance of childhood gender behavior for later sexual experience has focused attention on cultural perceptions of gender behavior. Bias affects treatment decisions and the role of early sexuality in the life cycle. The recognition of early life gender-identity conflict portending adult disorder was a pivotal insight. But the distinctions between gender-identity conflict and sexual identity conflict in children raises new political concerns. To what extent does the diagnosis of gender-identity disorder signify pretranssexual adult behavior? Transsexual life adjustment, even with sex reassignment, is substantially less than optimal and fits current criteria of disorder. Thus if the childhood behavior signifies sexual identity disorder, it argues for early life intervention. But if the behaviors of gender-identity disorder represent gender nonconformity, without discontent over anatomic sex, two problematic issues are raised. First, much of these children's conflict is the product of cultural demands for gender conformity. Should therapists insist on not treating the child but only the culture (including the parents who bring the child for treatment)? Second, a substantial proportion of gender-nonconforming children evolve into adults whose sexual behavior does not meet the criteria for disorder. They become homosexual or bisexual, if not heterosexual.

The explosion of reports in both the professional and lay press of child sexual abuse, frequently of a satanic or ritualistic character, raises several problems as does the epidemic identification of early life experiences of sexual abuse purporting to explain a broad spectrum of adult psychopathology. The new victimology industry has political and treatment ramifications. To an extent it is fired by antimale antiheterosexuals. To an extent it is fired by antisexual religious conservatives. To an extent it is fueled by therapists and attorneys with a personal agenda, both psychological and economic, for finding a history of sexual abuse in patients. A regrettable backlash will be that widely publicized cases of false allegations will promote a cynical cry-wolf attitude. Genuine experiences of child sexual abuse may then go unheeded.

The new victimology industry is part of the American antisexual backlash. Sexuality is recharacterized as the ultimate evil. In part a response to history's deadliest sexually transmitted disease, and in part a response to the vocal power of religious conservatives, the pendulum of sexual politics has swung to the right. Governmental censorship of erotic art, entrapment of persons induced by government officials to receive child pornography, unparalleled crackdowns on the adult pornography industry at a time when erotic videos have become a staple in the ubiquitous local video stores, and erosion of the woman's right to abortion evidence the new era of sexual conservatism. It remains an open question whether this shift will erase the humanistic progress in understanding human sexuality, described above, that has characterized the past quarter century.

References

Adams, M., and E. Sturgis. 1977. Status of behavioral reorientation techniques in the modification of homosexuality. *Psychological Bulletin* 84:1171–88.
Althof, S., and L. Turner. 1992. Self-injection therapy and external vacuum devices

in the treatment of erectile dysfunction. In *Erectile disorders*, ed. R. Rosen and S. Leiblum. New York: Guilford.

American Psychiatric Association. 1980. *Diagnostic and statistical manual of mental disorders. III.* Washington, D.C.: American Psychiatric Association.

American Psychiatric Association. 1987. *Diagnostic and statistical manual of mental disorders. IIIR.* Washington, D.C.: American Psychiatric Association.

Barbach, L. 1974. Group treatment of preorgasmic women. *Journal of Sex and Marital Therapy* 1:139–45.

Bayer, R. 1981. *Homosexuality and American psychiatry.* New York: Basic.

Beitchman, J., K. Zucker, J. Hood, G. Da Costa, and D. Akman. 1991. A review of the short-term effects of child sexual abuse. *Child Abuse and Neglect* 15:537–56.

Beitchman, J., K. Zucker, J. Hood, G. Da Costa, D. Akman, and E. Cassavia. 1992. Part II. Long-term effects. *Child Abuse and Neglect* 16:101–18.

Bell, A., M. Weinberg, and S. Hammersmith. 1981. *Sexual preference: Its development in men and women.* Bloomington: Indiana Univ. Press.

Benjamin, H. 1966. *The transsexual phenomenon.* New York: Julian.

Berlin, F. 1989. The paraphilias and Depo-provera. *Bulletin of the American Academy of Psychiatry and Law* 17:233–39.

Bieber, I., H. Dain, P. Dince, M. Drellich, H. Grand, R. Gundlach, M. Kremer, A. Rifkin, C. Wilbur, and T. Bieber. 1962. *Homosexuality: A psychoanalytic study.* New York: Basic.

Biuffum, J. 1988. Pharmacosexology update: Prescription drugs and sexual function. *Journal of Psychoactive Drugs* 18:97–106.

Briere, J., and M. Runtz. 1987. Post sexual abuse trauma. *Journal of Interpersonal Violence* 2:367–79.

Brindley, G. 1983. Caversonal alpha-blockade. *British Journal of Psychiatry* 143:332–37.

Browne, A., and D. Finkelhor. 1986. Impact of child sexual abuse: A review of the research. *Psychological Bulletin* 99:66–72.

California Code of Civil Procedure. 1991. Section 340.1. Minneapolis: West.

Duberman, M. 1991. *Cures.* New York: Dutton.

Freud, S. 1953. A case of hysteria, three essays on sexuality, and other works. *Standard edition of the complete psychological works of Sigmund Freud.* Vol. 7. London: Hogarth.

Furlow, W. 1976. Surgical management of impotence using the inflatable penile prosthesis. *Mayo Clinic Proceedings* 51:325–28.

Green, R. 1972. Homosexuality as a mental illness. *International Journal of Psychiatry* 10:77–98.

———. 1974. *Sexual identity conflict in children and adults.* New York: Basic.

———. 1986. Spelling "relief" for transsexuals: Employment discrimination and the criteria of sex. *Yale Law and Policy Review* 4:125–40.

———. 1987. *The "sissy boy syndrome" and the development of homosexuality.* New Haven, Conn.: Yale Univ. Press.

———. 1988. The immutability of (homo)sexual orientation: Behavioral science implications for a constitutional (legal) analysis. *Journal of Psychiatry and Law* 16 (fall-winter): 537–75.

————. 1989. Griswold's legacy. *Ohio Northern Law Review* 26:545–49.

————. 1992. *Sexual science and the law.* Cambridge, Mass.: Harvard Univ. Press.

Green, R., and D. Fleming. 1991. Transsexual surgery follow-up: Status in the 1990s. In *Annual Review of Sex Research,* ed. J. Bancroft, C. Davis, and D. Weinstein. Mount Vernon, Iowa: Society for the Scientific Study of Sex.

Green, R., and J. Money, eds. 1969. *Transsexualism and sex reassignment.* Baltimore: Johns Hopkins Univ. Press.

Green, R., R. Stoller, and C. MacAndrew. 1966. Attitudes towards sex transformation procedures. *Archives of General Psychiatry* 15:178–82.

Greenson, R. 1968. Dis-identifying from mother. *International Journal of Psychoanalysis* 49:370–74.

Grellert, E., M. Newcomb, and P. Bentler. 1982. Childhood play activities of male and female homosexuals and heterosexuals. *Archives of Sexual Behavior* 11:451–78.

Hatterer, L. 1970. *Changing homosexuality in the male.* New York: McGraw-Hill.

Hellman, R., R. Green, J. Gray, and K. Williams. 1981. Childhood sexual identity, childhood religiosity, and homophobia in development of transsexualism, homosexuality, and heterosexualitiy. *Archives of General Psychiatry* 38:910–15.

Hengeveld, J., and A. Korzeg. 1980. Mourner's impotence. In *Medical sexology,* ed. R. Forleo and W. Pasini, 243–48. Littleton, Mass.: Wright.

Isay, R. 1989. *Being homosexual: Gay men and their development.* New York: Farrar, Straus, & Giroux.

Kaplan, H. 1974. *The new sex therapy: Active treatment of sexual dysfunctions.* New York: Brunner/Mazel.

————. 1977. Hypoactive sexual desire. *Journal of Sex and Martial Therapy* 3:3–9.

————. 1979. *Disorders of sexual desire.* New York: Brunner/Mazel.

Knutson, D., ed. 1980. *Homosexuality and the law.* New York: Haworth.

Laschet, U., and L. Laschet. 1975. Antiandrogens in the treatment of sexual deviations in men. *Journal of Steroid Biochemistry* 6:821–26.

Laub, D., and R. Green. 1978. *The fourth international conference on gender identity. Dedicated to Harry Benjamin, M. D.: Selected proceedings.* New York: Plenum.

Libman, E., C. Fichten, W. Brendes, R. Burstein, J. Cohen, and G. Bunik. 1984. A comparison of three therapeutic formats in the treatment of secondary orgasmic dysfunction. *Journal of Sex and Marital Therapy* 10:147–59.

Lief, M. 1977. Inhibited sexual desire. *Medical Aspects of Human Sexuality* 7:94–95.

LoPiccolo, J. 1991. Post-modern sex therapy for erectile failure. *Nordisk Sexologi* 9:205–25.

LoPiccolo, L. 1980. Low sexual desire. In *Principles and practice of sex therapy,* ed. S. Leiblum and L. Pervin, 44–45. New York: Guilford.

MacCulloch, M., and M. Feldman. 1967. Aversion therapy in the management of 43 homosexuals. *British Medical Journal,* 2:594–97.

Masters, W., and V. Johnson. 1966. *Human sexual response.* Boston: Little, Brown.

————. 1970. *Human sexual inadequacy.* Boston: Little, Brown.

McConaghy, N. 1976. Is a homosexual orientation irreversible? *British Journal of Psychiatry* 129:556–63.

Melman, A., L. Tiefer, and R. Pedersen. 1988. Evaluation of the first 406 patients in urology department based center for male sexual dysfunction. *Urology* 32:6–10.

Mohl, B., and B. Pedersen. 1991. Men with inhibited sexual desire. *Nordisk Sexologi* 9:243–47.

Money, J., and A. Ehrhardt. 1972. *Man and woman, boy and girl.* Baltimore: Johns Hopkins Univ. Press.

Nadig, P., J. Ware, and R. Blumoff. 1986. Noninvasive device to produce and maintain an erection-like state. *Urology* 27:126–31.

National Lawyers Guild. 1989. *Sexual orientation and the law.* New York: Boardman.

Nicolosi, J. 1991. *Reparative therapy of male homosexuality.* New York: Aronson.

Rivera, R. 1991. Sexual orientation and the law. In *Homosexuality,* ed. J. Gonsiorek and J. Weinrich. Newbury Park, Calif.: Sage.

Small, M. 1978. Small-carrion prostheses. *Journal of Urology* 119:365–68.

Socarides, C. 1968. *The overt homosexual.* New York: Grune & Stratton.

―――. 1978. *Homosexuality.* New York: Aronson.

Standards of Care. 1985. The hormonal and surgical sex reassignment of gender dysphoric persons. *Archives of Sexual Behavior* 14:79–90.

Steiner, B. 1985. The management of patients with gender disorders. In *Gender dysphoria,* ed. B. Steiner. New York: Plenum.

Sturup, G. 1972. Castration: The total treatment. In *Sexual behaviors,* ed. H. Resnik and M. Wolfgang. Boston: Little, Brown.

Tiefer, L., R. Pedersen, and A. Melman. 1988. Psychosocial follow-up of penile prosthesis implant patients and partners. *Journal of Sex and Marital Therapy* 14:184–201.

Wagner, G., and R. Green. 1981. *Impotence: Physiological, psychological, surgical diagnosis, and treatment.* New York: Plenum.

Whitley, G. 1991. The seduction of Gloria Grady. *D Magazine,* October.

Sexual Offending and Victimization: A Life Course Perspective

Richard J. Gelles and Glenn Wolfner

Sexual offending and victimization are general concepts that cover a variety of sexual behaviors. Incest, child sexual abuse, sexual molestation, sexual assault, marital rape, and date rape are some of the more frequently used concepts that fall under the general category of sexual offending and victimization.[1] This chapter examines sexual offending and victimization using a life course perspective, which analyzes the variation in rates of sexual offending and victimization in terms of age-related stages of development.

The life course perspective has never before been applied to the discussion of sexual offending and victimization, although it has been a model commonly adopted by developmental psychologists to explain normal human development (e.g., Piaget on cognitive development, Kohlberg on moral development). We employ a life course perspective in this chapter as a useful heuristic framework from which to examine sexual offending and victimization. Two questions the reader might consider when reading this chapter are (1) Why do some people develop into sexual offenders? and (2) What factors lead an individual who becomes an offender to maintain, escalate, or desist from such behavior? Unless one adopts a life course perspective, answers to questions such as these are partial at best.

Sexual offending and victimization are conceptually distinct from other types of human violent behavior and therefore warrant a separate discussion. The psychological profile of the sexual offender differs from that of the physically abusive offender, although there is some overlap between the two. We begin with the assumption, supported by the empirical literature, that the generative causes of sexual aggression are different in type and extent from the etiological factors that lead to physical, nonsexual violence. In addition, unlike physical violence, where the rates of offending and victimization are more gender balanced, the victim of sexual violence is more often female, and the offender is typically male. Finally, although there are other factors driving the behaviors, sexual offending in its extreme, such as rape, is the ultimate degradation of a woman or child and an extraordinary abuse of power and strength. Therefore, sexual offending and victimization deserve a separate discussion, distinct from the existing analysis of the more general case of violence. That is not to say that we, in any way, minimize the extent or effect of other types of violence, nor that the distinction is not somewhat artificial, because sexual violence is often accompanied by physical and emotional violence.

We begin with an examination of the recent history of social concern and scholarly examination of sexual offending and victimization. Of central concern here is the fact that there is no unified field of study of sexual offending and victimization. A consideration of life course issues requires a review of research conducted in three largely separate fields—studies of sexual abuse of children, of rape and adult sexual victimization, and of date rape. The study of sexual offending and victimization has been constrained by significant conceptual and methodological problems and obstacles, and these are the topics we next review. Following that, we discuss theories of sexual offending, especially those that rely on a developmental framework. The final section of the chapter applies the life course perspective to a review of the data on victimization and offending by age and gender.

Historical Overview of Research on Sexual Offending and Victimization

It is perhaps now a cliché to state that the issue of sexual victimization has been long overlooked by scholars and clinicians and that the study of both rape and sexual abuse of children emerged only in the last two decades. Clinicians and researchers, including Sigmund Freud and Alfred Kinsey, had identified cases and patterns of incestuous relations in their clinical work and research on human sexual behavior. However, Freud eventually argued that his female patients' descriptions of incestuous relations were actually fantasies (Masson 1991); Kinsey minimized the importance of the data he uncovered about sexual abuse (Herman 1981).

Intensive study of rape and the effects of rape began in the late 1970s. Among the earliest, and now classic, studies of rape were Menachem Amir's (1971) *Patterns of Forcible Rape,* Diana Russell's (1975) *The Politics of Rape,* Linda Holmstrom and Ann Burgess's (1978) *The Victim of Rape,* and Susan Brownmiller's (1975) *Against Our Will: Men, Women, and Rape.* Scientific investigation and increased clinical awareness of sexual abuse began in the late 1970s, partly as an outgrowth of the increased awareness of physical child abuse and other manifestations of child maltreatment, partly as an outgrowth of the somewhat earlier concern for rape, and partly as a product of feminist concern with overall patterns of female physical and sexual victimization across the life course.

THE POLITICS OF RESEARCH ON SEXUAL OFFENDING AND VICTIMIZATION

Contemporary studies of sexual offending and victimization are heavily influenced by political and ideological issues. The emergence of rape and sexual abuse as a social issue and social problem is seen by many as primarily the result of the efforts of the women's movement, as feminists sought to raise political and public consciousness about women's physical and sexual victimization. One obstacle in the effort to place and keep sexual victimization on the public policy agenda is the tradition of blaming female victims for their sexual victimization. Thus, a main focus of the early research was on the consequences of sexual victimization. Studies that examined the consequences of sexual assault made up the vast majority of the early research efforts in this area. By contrast, studies of offenders were quite rare. Behind the closed doors of Initial Review Groups, such as the group that reviewed applications submitted to the National Institute of Mental Health's National Rape Prevention and Control Center, reviewers argued that scarce resources should be directed only to grants that examined victims of sexual assault, not the perpetrators. Studies that proposed to examine sexual offenders were routinely disapproved in the early years of federal funding of rape prevention efforts. Thus the literature on sexual offending and victimization was imbalanced for many years, with considerable research on victims and little research on offenders.

THE SOCIAL TRANSFORMATION OF SEXUAL OFFENDING AND VICTIMIZATION

In the past several years, sexual offending and victimization have captured the attention of the American public. Celebrities, including Oprah Winfrey, Rosanne Arnold, Miss America, Carolyn Sapp, and others have publicly revealed their own victimization and history of sexual abuse and date rape. Less celebrated revelations appear regularly and nearly daily on television talk shows, including discussions of sexual abuse of males by Catholic priests, Boy Scout leaders, sports coaches, teachers, and others. The Clarence Thomas confirmation hearings focused on charges by Anita Hill of sexual harassment. The date-rape trial of William Kennedy Smith and the rape trial of former heavyweight boxing champion Michael Tyson were televised live and were significant parts of the public discourse on rape and sexual assault for months. In the late summer of 1992, the media and the public debated whether comedian and film director Woody Allen's affair with Mia Farrow's adopted daughter was incest, tacky, or acceptable. Sexual offending and victimization have moved from taboo topics to matters of public and professional concern, then to social problems, and now to public entertainment. The current focus on sexuality goes beyond offending and victimization. The sex lives of both presidential candidates were grist for the media and political mills in the 1992 campaign. Nor is this a uniquely American phenomenon. The sex lives of the British royal family have been daily tabloid news in England for several years.

The social transformation of sexual offending and victimization has been enhanced by an increase in social research that has had a symbiotic relation with the emergence of what might be called a sexual offending and victimization industry.

Claims makers for the problem of sexual victimization, including social researchers, market this social problem through the use of incidence statistics. Claims makers loudly announce that there is an epidemic of sexual abuse and rape in American society. The term *epidemic* is almost always misused because claims makers cannot demonstrate a change in incidence statistics that would support the presence of an actual epidemic. A number of social scientists, some whose work is reviewed in this chapter, have argued that one-third to one-half of all women are sexually victimized during their lifetime. The lawyer and social activist Catherine McKinnon (1989) claims (without actual empirical data) that only 7.8 percent of women in the United States *are not* sexually assaulted or harassed. Although those who cite these figures argue that they capture an extensive and harmful social problem, critics argue that the statistics do not meet the normal rules of empirical evidence, and—worse—the statistics are considered unbelievable by much of the public and policy makers, thus undermining the efforts of social advocates on behalf of victimized women (Gilbert 1991).

The sexual offending and victimization industry also markets causal models and prevention efforts. The models draw heavily from feminist theory and argue that the main (and perhaps only) cause of sexual offending and victimization is male oppression of women or the patriarchy (see McKinnon [1989]; Russell [1975, 1984]).

The industry, especially regarding child sexual abuse, has also marketed interventions and solutions. For example, many of the clinicians who work with sexually abused children use anatomically detailed dolls. Thought to help very young children in describing what sexual acts they had experienced, the dolls became a marketed product and local and national social service conventions almost always include a booth in the exhibit area that sell anatomically detailed dolls to clinicians. There is, however, little evidence to suggest that these dolls actually increase the validity of children's reports of sexual abuse (Wolfner, Faust, and Dawes 1993).

Child-abuse-prevention programs have been developed and implemented in thousands of schools and school districts. The programs instruct young boys and girls about "good touch" and "bad touch" (with regard to genitals and body parts) and teach children that they should report "bad touches" and to whom. Proponents argue that these programs both raise consciousness and protect children from sexual abuse (Plummer 1993). Critics argue that there are no data to support the claims that the programs are actually effective, and there are even some unintended and unpleasant consequences of the widespread implementation of sexual-abuse-prevention programs (Reppucci and Haugaard 1989).

Social scientists, with the noted exception of outspoken critics like Neil Gilbert (1993) and N. Dickon Reppucci (Reppucci and Haugaard 1989), have refused to become involved in criticizing either the marketing of sexual offending and victimization as a social problem or the industry itself. Clearly, in the current political climate it is politically incorrect to challenge claims and theories concerning female victimization.

Ironically, the unwillingness of social scientists, the media, or others to take issue with the emerging industry, the claims makers, and the critics of the claims makers, has had the effect of neglecting important criticism concerning the current state of knowledge on intervention. For example, although critics have pointed to the methodological weaknesses of child-abuse-prevention treatment-program evaluations, they have failed to notice that programs are aimed only at the victims (mostly females). They fail to note that programs that try to alter victim behavior are probably doomed to failure because they do not address the actions of the offenders. Even feminists tend to overlook the unintended consequences of placing all the prevention emphasis on the actions of female victims and potential victims. Theories that blame abuse on male oppression are equally problematic because such theories are essentially single-variable explanations with an invariant causal factor—male oppression.

THE SOCIAL ORGANIZATION OF RESEARCH ON SEXUAL OFFENDING AND VICTIMIZATION

An analysis of sexual offending and victimization is complicated by a variety of conceptual and methodological issues. Perhaps the overriding problem is that there is actually no unified field of study of sexual offending and victimization. The study of sexual offenses and sexual victimization has grown rapidly over the last twenty years, but the topics involved have been balkanized—that is, each problem has a separate history, separate theories, and separate intervention agencies (Russell 1984). Those who study the general phenomenon of sexual abuse, or sexual victimization of children, focus almost exclusively on sexual offenses directed at children under eighteen years old, usually by an adult perpetrator. Students of rape examine sexual offenses against women from adolescence to adulthood. These two groups seldom overlap and represent not only two distinct academic and clinical circles, but two nearly distinct literatures.[2] Male victims of childhood victimization are rarely referred to in the literature, and male victims of adolescent or adult sexual offending are nowhere to be found in the scholarly literature—although there is a small literature on male rape in prison (Carroll 1974, 1982; Lockwood 1980).

METHODOLOGICAL CONSTRAINTS ON THE STUDY OF SEXUAL OFFENDING AND VICTIMIZATION

Students of rape and sexual abuse are confronted with the generic problems of studying a taboo topic (Farberow 1966; Gelles 1978, 1990). Sexual offending and victimization involve emotion-laden behavior that often takes place in private or intimate settings. There was, and continues to be, considerable victim blaming, which means that victims are reluctant to file official charges or to reveal their victimization to social scientists. Victims sometimes suffer emotional trauma, such as the rape trauma syndrome, or post-traumatic stress disorder (Kilpatrick et al. 1987) that may result in dissociative states of mind that make it impossible for them to even remember, let alone report on, their victimization.

In the early years of research in this area, investigators could only guess at what the true base rate of the various forms of sexual offense and victimization might be. The earliest guesses as to the prevailing base rates of prevalence and incidence were, as with most other taboo topics, quite low.

There are three main sources of data on sexual offending and victimization, and each suffers from its own significant limitations. These sources are (1) official report data, such as police reports of rape or state registries of child maltreatment, including sexual abuse; (2) clinical data, which constitute a major source of data on rape victimization, rape offenders, and child sexual abuse; and (3) self-report surveys, such as the National Crime Victimization Survey (NCVS). More detailed description and comments concerning these three primary sources of data are in order.

Official Report Data

There is overwhelming consensus that the official report data on sexual offending and victimization greatly underestimate the true incidence of the problems. The Uniform Crime Reports tabulated by the Federal Bureau of Investigation from data provided by more than fifteen thousand police departments include only cases of rape and sexual assault that are officially reported to the police. Obviously, this eliminates cases of rape that are not reported. Thus, acquaintance rape, or date rape, are likely to be underreported and marital rape can not even be reported as rape except in the approximately twenty-eight states that now prohibit marital rape by law. Moreover, the Uniform Crime Reports data eliminate unfounded cases of rape. Thus, rape cases that are determined by the police to be false reports are eliminated from the tabulations.[3]

Clinical Data

Clinical samples are a second major source of data on sexual victims and offenders. Clinical samples, however, tend to be small, often have inappropriate or no control or comparison groups, and are biased in their composition. Clinical samples of offenders contain only those sexual offenders who are caught. As with most other crimes, such samples overrepresent poor, minority, or otherwise socially marginalized members of society. Clinical samples of victims represent only those individuals who are willing or able to report on their victimization. Again, this underrepresents the true population of victims and, no doubt, includes a biased segment of this population as well.

Clinical samples and self-report surveys have additional problems. First, sexual victimization is not always reported immediately after the victimization experience. And, unlike physical abuse or physical assault, there are not always physical symptoms that require treatment after a sexual victimization experience. Thus, victims of sexual violence may enter therapy and thereby become part of a clinical study months— or even years—after the victimization experience. It is not altogether uncommon to hear about victims of sexual violence in childhood coming forward for help only as adults—sometimes twenty or thirty years after their experience. Thus, clinical researchers can collect retrospective data only over a one-, two-, three-, or even four- to five-decade period. There are rather obvious biases and limitations to such data.

Self-Report Data

A third source of data are self-report surveys. One often cited self-report survey is the NCVS. The NCVS (Bureau of Justice Statistics 1992) could serve as a useful correction to the Uniform Crime Reports, but even here the measure of the incidence of rape is inadequate. There is no specific question in the NCVS that asks about being the victim of rape; rather, rape is measured by responses to the item, "Did anyone *try* to attack you in some other way?" [4]

Self-report surveys that overcome the limitations of the measurement problems of the NCVS are also limited by methodological problems endemic to research on taboo topics in general, and sexual offending and victimization in particular. For example, Russell's (1984) groundbreaking and classic study of sexual exploitation was based on in-person interviews with 930 randomly sampled adult female respondents in San Francisco. Russell's response rate, however, was only 50 percent overall. The direct refusal rate (individuals who were approached and refused to be interviewed) was 36 percent. This refusal rate is high by normal standards of in-person interviewing and limits the generalizability of the study's findings.

Another methodological problem arises from the ambiguous wording of some measures used to assess the incidence and prevalence of sexual offending and victimization. Neil Gilbert (1993) criticizes Mary Koss' (Koss, Gidycz, and Wisniewski 1987) measure of acquaintance rape because of the ambiguous wording of the following two items: "Have you had a man attempt sexual intercourse (get on top of you, attempt to insert his penis) when you didn't want to by giving you alcohol or drugs, but intercourse did not occur?" and "Have you had sexual intercourse when you didn't want to because a man gave you alcohol or drugs?" As Gilbert notes, a positive response to these questions does not indicate whether duress, force, intoxication, or threat of force were present; whether a woman's judgment was significantly impaired; or whether the man purposefully got the woman drunk in order to prevent her resistance to his sexual advances. A *yes* response to these items is quite ambiguous, although it was coded as indicating that the respondent had been raped. Similar problems occur with measures of sexual abuse.

Sampling is another methodological problem. The most commonly cited prevalence data on sexual abuse, cited both by scholars and the media, is the estimate that one in five women and one in eleven males have been sexually victimized. These estimates come from David Finkelhor's (1979) self-report survey of 796 students enrolled in colleges and universities in the northeast. Virtually no one who cites these statistics qualifies them by noting that the sample was a convenience sample and not generalizable.

A final methodological issue is conceptual. There is great variation in the nominal and operational definitions of the many forms of sexual offending. This variation makes it difficult to compare the results of the various studies of sexual offending and victimization and yields wide variations in incidence estimates and contradictory findings regarding correlates and causal models. Russell (1984), for example, included the item *unwanted kissing* in her inventory of sexual abuse. Other measures involve much more restricted definitions of sexual victimization. For example, Finkelhor's definition of sexual abuse required that offenders be five or more years older than their victims. Thus, sexual abuse between age peers or similar-aged siblings would not be identified using this definition. Finally, some investigators begin their study of sexual victimization with the assumption that males cannot be victims of sexual assault and thus fail to ask male subjects about such experiences.

An additional conceptual problem is the ambiguous situation of adolescents in definitions and measures of sexual offending and victimization. Many definitions of child sexual abuse define a child as someone under the age of eighteen and thus, adolescents are considered children in studies of sexual abuse. However, when the definition of sexual abuse includes a five-year age difference between offender and victim, a large number of cases involving date rape and rape are not included in the analysis. In still other studies, adolescents are included in measures of adult sexual assault or rape. Sometimes adolescent victimization is defined as sexual abuse, and at other times it is defined as rape, depending on the investigator and the definitions used.

Judith Becker and Emily Coleman (1988) comment that the knowledge base on incest or sexual abuse is limited by the fact that few studies employ large samples, control groups, or instruments with known psychometric properties. These limitations are also applicable to the range of studies of sexual offending and victimization.

Theories of Sexual Offending

The emotional nature of sexual assault and the domination of research on both offenders and victims by the helping professions, such as psychologists, social workers, and psychiatrists, has produced a knowledge base that is heavily weighted toward intraindividual explanations of the generative causes of sexual offending and intraindividual explanations of the consequences, such as post-traumatic stress disorder. Social factors, in general, and life course variables in particular, are rarely included in either the theoretical conceptualizations or the data in the sexual offending and victimization literature. Age of offender is given only the most cursory attention by students of sexual offending. Age of victim is given somewhat more attention. The theoretical models used to examine and explain sexual offending behavior also place little emphasis on life course factors and processes.

What follows is a brief review of the theories that attempt to explain the etiology of sexual offending. Theoretical development is most advanced in the study of adult rape but less so on sexual abuse of children. Theories of sexual offending and abuse among adolescents are the least well developed.

Developmental Models of Sexual Abuse and Rape

Life span or developmental assumptions about the causes of sexual abuse, sexual assault, and rape are implicit in much of the clinical work in the field of sexual offending and victimization (Prentky, Knight, and Rosenberg 1989). Despite the use of an implicit developmental model in most clinical practice, few social scientists or clinicians have developed actual developmental theories or models of sexual offending. There is a paucity of literature on developmental factors that result in an individual becoming a rapist or a pedophile. This lack of attention to the development of offenders is in marked contrast to the volume of work written about sexual victims. This section summarizes the discussions and research on the developmental antecedents of sexual violence.

Freud. Freud ([1905] 1953) addressed sexual aberrations, infantile sexuality, and pubertal changes in his essays, *Three Essays on the Theory of Sexuality.* Freud's main proposition is that "every pathological disorder of sexual life is rightly to be regarded as an inhibition in development" ([1905] 1953, 74). According to Freud, each individual has the capacity to develop sexual aberrations, and all sexual aberrations can be traced to unfortunate experiences in children's development. Freud conceptualized five stages of psychosexual development: (1) oral, (2) anal, (3) phallic, (4) latency, and (5) genital. He assumed that, if a parent frustrates a child or prevents him from successfully navigating through these stages, a psychic scar results, whereby the child's development remains either fixated at a stage or the child regresses from a later stage to the one during which the trauma occurred. For example, if a trauma occurred during the anal stage (at two years old), sadism can result. Although Freud does not use the term *rape,* clearly sadism can be considered to be a continuum on which rape is at the far extreme.

Pedophilia (sexual abuse) was conceptualized as the result of failed Oepidal tasks during the phallic stage (from three to six years old), if a boy fails to identify with his father. This can lead, in Freud's view, to later difficulties that impair appropriate sexual identity or self-esteem.

Freud identified obstacles to normal sexual development that could result in aberrant sexuality. The first is constitution and heredity or biological predispositions. Some individuals have stronger biological predispositions to sexual offending than do others. A second obstacle is what Freud called further modification. The process that determines the specific expression of developmental and constitutional vulnerabilities continues into the adult years. There are three possible types of expression in the adult years: (1) If the relationship persists and grows stronger, it can result in what Freud called a perverse sexual life; (2) if some other components of the problematic areas are repressed, the result is neurosis; and (3) if a person uses sublimation to deal with the underlying problem, sexual energy is diverted into artistic or intellectual pursuits. Accidental experiences are the third obstacle. These can be specific traumas that release primitive behavior that a person might otherwise repress. The fourth obstacle is precocity, which refers to a premature ending of the latency stage of development. Because the development of inhibitions (e.g., guilt) is not yet complete, or because the genitals are not fully developed, precocity can lead to a development of perversions, such as incest. Finally, temporal factors refer to the order and duration of the psychosexual stages. If the order or duration is altered, then problems or perversions may result.

Thus, according to Freud's model of psychosexual development, behaviors that we term in this chapter *sexual offending* are predispositions in all of us but are inhibited through the process of normal psychosexual development. If there are disturbances in the normal developmental process, perversions and offending may result. A disturbance in any one of the pregenital stages can result in a disturbance of sexual aim (e.g., sadism or rape). A disturbance just prior to latency may result in a disturbance of sexual object (e.g., incest or pedophilia).

Socarides. Charles Socarides (1988) offers a refinement of Freud's psychoanalytic model. Socarides believes that when the stages of normal sexual development are obstructed, fixations and perversions can result later in life. Although Freud believed the period from two to six years was the critical period for obstacles or frustration in sexual development leading to sexual offending, Socarides places the critical stage much earlier in life—from eighteen to thirty-six months old. Socarides proposes that all sexual deviants have a common core disturbance that occurred between the ages of one and a half and three years.

The key developmental issue is that of object relations, the internalized way people interface with others in the world. According to Socarides, the child-mother relationship plays the key role in determining the child's object relationships. If a child fails to learn to think of himself as distinct from his primary caretaker (his mother), this sets the stage for developing sexual offending behavior. Socarides claims that individuals who have failed to successfully pass through the separation-individuation phase of childhood development develop a fear of fusion and a merging with their mother. They tend to lose ego boundaries and fear loss of self, or ego dissolution. A pedophile achieves the status of being the loved child while also being the loving mother. By engaging in sexual behavior with a child, the pedophile achieves sexual satisfaction and yearns for and desires to become the loved object that he envies in children. The male pedophile who chooses a boy victim views that child as the ideal representation of himself. If he chooses a girl, he feels less threatened by maternal engulfment because of the immaturity of the child's genitalia (Socarides 1988, 65–66).

According to Socarides, sexual sadism, or what we could call rape, functions symbolically to destroy the mother in response to an offend-er's fears of annihilation or engulfment by the mother. Sexual sadism or rape also reassures the offender against and lessens castration anxiety and reaffirms his gender identity.

Money. John Money (1986) also presents a developmental model of sexual offending. Money uses the conceptualization of "lovemaps" rather than the complex psychoanalytic assumptions of stage develop-ment employed by Freud and Socarides. A lovemap is a "developmental representation or template, synchronously functional in the mind and the brain, depicting the ideal lover, the idealized love affair, and the ide-alized program of sexoerotic activity with that lover." The lovemap proj-ects in imagery and ideation, or in actual sexual performance (Money and Lamacz 1989, 43).

Lovemaps are developed, in Money's view, between the ages of five and eight years. This is a much later stage of critical sexual development than that proposed by Freud or Socarides. Individual trauma and cul-tural unwillingness to acknowledge children's sexual development can lead to what Money calls a "vandalized" lovemap that can produce a rapist who extracts love by force. Nonviolent pedophiles also represent vandalized lovemaps. Money (1986, 21) suggests that the latter lovemap may replicate a juvenile sexual experience by reversing the ages of the participants.

A second key concept in Money's developmental theory is "oppo-nent-process learning" (Solomon 1980). This explains how someone can become addicted to what they once feared. Pedophiles can become addicted to the high that follows successful sexual acts, resulting both from getting away with the act or the sexual release of the act. A sadistic rapist can become addicted to causing pain or humiliation. Once a be-havior operates under the opponent process, it is very resistant to change.

Prentky. Freud, Socarides, and Money have developed largely theo-retical models informed by small numbers of clinical cases. Robert Prentky and his colleagues (Prentky, Knight, and Rosenberg 1989) pres-ent an empirically derived theory of sexual offender etiology. The theory is based on data collected from incarcerated sex offenders. Prentky stresses two developmental factors that are correlated with sexual vio-lence: (1) caretaker inconsistency and (2) sexual offending or abuse within the family. Children who experience or observe deviant sexual acts are more likely to develop into sexual offenders.

Ryan and Lane. Gail Ryan and Sandy Lane (1991) developed a model of juvenile sex offending that is based on the proposition that offending results from caregiver insufficiencies. In addition, childhood victimization is a key developmental feature in the process of becoming a sexual offender.

Sociological and Social Psychological Models of Child Sexual Abuse

Finkelhor's four-preconditions model. Perhaps the best-known sociological model of child sexual abuse is David Finkelhor's (1984) model of four preconditions that must be fulfilled for sexual abuse of children by an adult to occur. The four preconditions are (1) The adult must have sexual feelings for a child, or for children in general; (2) the adult must overcome his or her internal inhibitions against acting out the sexual feeling; (3) the adult must overcome the external obstacles to acting out the sexual feelings; and (4) the adult must overcome the resistance or attempts at avoidance by the child, if necessary. The four preconditions must be present if sexual abuse of a child or children is to occur. The model assumes a logical order to the precondition that begins with an adult having sexual feelings for a child or children.

The precondition model does not explain the derivation of sexual feelings or the inappropriateness of children as sexual objects. Thus, Finkelhor's theory seems to complement Freud, Socarides, or Money's theories of the development of sexual offending. In other words, early developmental frustrations create the potential for sexual offending (precondition 1), and social factors (preconditions 2–4) determine whether the predisposition becomes a behavioral reality.

Finkelhor's model also complements social learning models of sexual offending that view social learning as the key process by which some adults learn to be attracted to children (Gagnon 1977).

Sex-role socialization models. Finkelhor (1984), Russell (1984), and Judith Herman (1981) view sex-role socialization as a key process that explains the higher rate of sexual abuse of children among males compared to females. This view argues that males are not well socialized to distinguish between sexual and nonsexual forms of affection, that males are socialized to become more easily aroused by sexual activities than by fantasies than are females, and that males are socialized to be attracted to sexual partners who are smaller, younger, and less powerful than themselves.

Social learning models. As with research and theories of physical child abuse, studies and theories of child sexual abuse and rape propose an intergenerational transmission of maltreatment. Researchers tend to find an association between victimization as a child and later adult physical and sexual offenses (Finkelhor 1984; Gebhard et al. 1965; Russell 1984).

Gene Abel, Mary Mittleman, and Judith Becker (1985) explain that preferences for sexual offending are established before the initial act. These researchers propose that conditioning is initiated quite early in the life of males who become sexual offenders, and it is subsequently elaborated into a more general deviant disposition. Molesters tend to develop strong deviant sexual identities by the age of eighteen.

Another version of the social learning model is the proposition that pornography serves as the vehicle that provides the learning context for pedophiles and rapists. Pornography is thought to inspire violence against women. Some laboratory research has demonstrated that exposure to pornography with violent content increases aggressive behavior (Donnerstein, Linz, and Penrod 1987).

Still another variation of social learning theory is the theory of cultural spillover. This theory proposes that rape and sexual offending are influenced by implicit or explicit approval of violence in various areas of life, such as education, mass media, and sports. This theory argues that rape occurs as a result of spillover of violence from contexts in which it is socially approved to a context in which it is considered illegitimate and criminal (Baron and Straus 1989; Ellis 1989).

Social disorganization. Social disorganization theory proposes that crime in general and rape in particular reflect conditions that disrupt the integrity of communities and weaken the regulatory power of social norms and conditions such as migration, marital disruption, and cultural heterogeneity of the community. Thus, rates of rape are highest in communities and societies with the highest levels of social disorganization (Baron and Straus 1989).

Feminist theory. Feminist theories of rape and sexual offending propose that violence against women in general and sexual violence against women in particular is an expression of patriarchal, male-dominant social systems (Russell 1984). Rape is part of the way women are subjugated in a male-dominant society. Rape is a product of asymmetrical male-female socialization, wherein men are taught to be aggressive and dominant and women are taught to be passive and submissive.

Sex-ratio theory. Marcia Guttentag and Paul Secord (1983) propose that high sex ratios (i.e., more males than females) produce high rape rates because men use power to control "their" women or have to compete against other men for the scarcer sex. When sex ratios are high, men use their structural position of dominance to control women because high sex ratios decrease men's dyadic power. In contrast to the Guttentag-Secord hypothesis, Robert O'Brien (1991) hypothesizes that rape rates go up as women outnumber men in a population—a low sex ratio situation encourages more women to step out of traditional family roles and to pursue education and careers—hence a low sex ratio produces higher numbers of unattached women who are more likely to be controlled, and raped.

O'Brien (1991) analyzed arrest data from the Uniform Crime Reports for 1962, 1967, 1972, 1977, 1982, and 1987 and found a strong negative relation between sex ratio and rape rates (i.e., the lower the sex ratio, the higher the rape rates). In contrast, Larry Baron and Murray Straus (1989) analyzed sex-ratio rates and rape rates for each of the fifty states and found a significant positive correlation between sex ratio and rates of rape: states with more men than women have higher rates of rape. Thus, there is empirical support for both hypotheses, and the results are not clear enough to warrant a conclusion about sex-ratio theory and sexual offenses.

Evolutionary theory. The final theoretical model is an evolutionary model. One version of the evolutionary model argues that rape is an extreme response to natural selection processes. Rape is part of an overall male strategy to copulate with numerous female partners. This strategy conflicts with an adaptive female strategy of retaining control over who mates with her (Ellis 1989).

A second version of the evolutionary theory argues that rape is part of an overall pattern of male physical and sexual dominance over women. Barbara Smuts (1992) analyzed male aggression among nonhuman and human primates and proposes that male aggression, including sexual aggression, against females is functional to control female sexuality and to enhance male reproductive advantages. Males use coercion to increase the chances that a female mates with the aggressor or decrease the chances that a female mates with a rival. Variations of kin support of women, male-male alliances, male strategies for guarding mates, and male resource control result in variation in the rates of male-perpetuated physical and sexual aggression (see Lancaster, chap. 2, this vol. for more extended discussion of evolutionary theory and mate selection).

Sexual Offending and Victimization in a Life Course Perspective

A number of patterns emerge from the data on sexual offending and victimization when one uses a life course perspective. (See table 1.) These patterns must be viewed cautiously because of the significant methodological limitations with the available data and because this review has brought together a wide range of research on a wide array of types of sexual offending and victimization. Most importantly, researchers rarely distinguish between child and adolescent victims of sexual abuse or adolescent and adult victims of sexual assault or rape. Research to date has not yet clarified whether there are distinctive individual and social patterns associated with sexual offending and sexual victimization at different stages of the life course.

Age, Sex, and Victimization

The risk of victimization appears to be low in the early years of life, rises prior to adolescence, and peaks during late adolescence and early adulthood. The various self-report surveys indicate that child victimization is most likely to occur between the ages of six and twelve (Finkelhor 1979, 1984; Finkelhor et al. 1990). Offenders can be children, adolescents, or adults, with the modal offender being an adult.

The general findings of the adolescent sexual assault literature is that victims are generally victimized by dates or acquaintances. Mary Koss and her colleagues (Koss, Gidycz, and Wisniewski 1987) state that the typical college-student rape victim was 18.5 years old and was victimized by a single offender and that only 16 percent of offenses involved a complete stranger. Susan Ageton (1983) also found that the majority of adolescent sexual offenses were between individuals of approximately the same age. That is, the majority of assaults were carried out by dates or boyfriends.

The risk of victimization declines significantly after the age of thirty-five and appears negligible among those over fifty years old. David Mur-

TABLE 1 Rates and Prevalence of Sexual Victimization

	Yearly Rate			Life Prevalence (%)		
Victimized Group and Reference	Overall	Males	Females	Overall	Males	Females
Children:						
National Center on Child Abuse and Neglect 1988	2.5	.9	3.5	...	...	...
American Association for Protecting Children 1986	1.61	...	...	...	...	...
American Association for Protecting Children 1987	2.0	...	...	...	...	...
American Association for Protecting Children 1988	2.1	...	...	...	...	...
Finkelhor 1979	...	...	...	...	9	20
Finkelhor 1984	...	...	...	...	9	12
Finkelhor et al. 1990	...	...	...	19	...	...
Adolescents:						
Koss et al. 1987	...	...	...	27	...	...
UCR def. 76						
State reform def. 166						
Ageton 1983	6.8–12.7	...	...	5–11	...	...
Struckman-Johnson 1988	...	...	...	16	...	...
Adult women:						
FBI 1989	.7	...	...	...	...	...
Bureau of Justice Statistics 1992	...	.1	1.2	...	...	...
Russell 1984	26.8	...	...	44[a]	...	...
Gelles 1992 (marital rape only)	12.0	...	...	...[a]	...	...
Kilpatrick et al. 1987	...	...	...	36[a]	...	...
Wyatt 1992	...	...	...	33[a]	...	...

[a]Includes data for women 18 and older and 18 and younger.

man, Kristin Miller, and Amos Cutler (1992) examined 1,722 adult patients at the Memphis, Tennessee, Sexual Assault Resource Center. Of these patients, fifty-three (3 percent) were females fifty-five years or older. Twenty-two women were fifty-five to sixty-four years old; eighteen were sixty-five to seventy-four years old; and thirteen women were older than seventy-five years. Males are less likely than females to be victims of sexual offending at most stages in the life course, although some data on sexual abuse find that male adolescents are actually more likely to be victims of sexual abuse than are females (Finkelhor 1979). Male adolescent and adult victimization rates appear to be quite low and male victimization after the age of twenty appears to be negligible. The rates may be even lower if one questions the inclusion of all adult male–adolescent male sexual relations as abusive. Some observers are not willing to view these relationships as inherently abusive (Dickemann 1992), although we feel they are abusive because of the disparity in age and power inherent in them. The data on sex, age, and sexual victimization provide some support to those who use an evolutionary approach to explaining sexual offending. Although many students of rape have argued strongly that rape is an act of power and not a sexual act with reproductive intent (see, e.g., Brownmiller [1975]), the age distribution of sexual victimization parallels female fertility and thus indicates that there may well be a sexual and reproductive component to sexual offending, especially when it victimizes females.

Age, Sex, and Offenders

Males are disproportionately the offenders in acts of sexual violence, and young males are the most likely offenders. Female offenders tend to offend against young male victims and only anecdotal evidence exists for the claims of adult female rape offenders (Ageton 1983; Amir 1971; Burgdorf 1980; Eisenhower 1969; Finkelhor 1979, 1984; Jamison and Flanagan 1989; Katz and Mazur 1979; Katzenbach 1967; Koss, Gidycz, and Wisniewski 1987; MacDonald 1971; Russell 1984; Svalastoga 1962).

Child and adolescent offenders tend to offend against same-age victims. Adult offenders offend against victims across the life course, from children to adults. No study mentions or presents data on adolescent sexual offending in which the offender was a female.

Males tend to be the disproportionate sexual offenders against children (Finkelhor 1984). According to the American Humane Association's analysis of official reports, between 76 percent and 82.4 percent of the sexual offenders were males. *The First Study of the National Incidence and Prevalence of Child Abuse and Neglect* (Burgdorf 1980) reported that 13 percent of sexual abuse offenders against female victims were female and 24 percent of offenders against male children were female. Finkelhor (1984) reviewed case record studies and self-report studies of sexual abuse. He reports that female offenders against male victims ranged from 0 percent to 6 percent of the total number of offenders in the case studies. There were no analyses of female offenders and female children in the case studies. Self-report surveys yield higher percentages of female offenders. The range of female offenders against male children was 14 percent to 69 percent. The range of female offenders against female children was 0 percent to 10 percent. Finkelhor's (1979) survey of college students found that 16 percent of the offenders against female children were female. His second survey (1984) of a representative sample of 521 adult men and women in Boston found 15 percent of offenders against male children were female and no female offenders against female children.

Adult offenders against children tend to be young. Official statistics and self-report surveys provide data on the age of the offenders. The mean age of sexual abuse offenders was between thirty-two and thirty-three (American Association for Protecting Children 1986, 1987, 1988). Finkelhor's (1979) data from his survey of college students reported that for female victims, the mean age of offenders was 31.7; for male victims the mean age was 26.9. More than half (57.1 percent) of the offenders who victimized females were under thirty; more than 60 percent of those who victimized males were under thirty. When asked about the age of the offenders who victimized their own children, half the parents in Finkelhor's (1984) second survey reported that the offender was twenty-one years old or older. When asked about their own victimization, 79 percent of the parents said the offender was twenty-one years old or older.

Adults who victimize adolescents. We were unable to locate a distinct empirical or theoretical literature on adults who sexually victimize adolescents. In all likelihood, the patterns are similar to, and overlap with, adults who offend against other adults, especially because the data we have reviewed strongly indicate that most sexual offending is perpetrated by young males. Nevertheless, empirical validation remains unexplored in this age group.

Adults who victimize adults. Adult sexual offenders are male and young, specifically fifteen to twenty-four years old (Amir 1971; Eisenhower 1969; Katz and Mazur 1979; Katzenbach 1967; MacDonald 1971). Data collected by the National Commission on the Causes and Prevention of Violence reported 21 percent of all males arrested for rape were seventeen years old or younger; 48 percent were between eighteen and twenty-five, and 31 percent were twenty-six years old or older (Mulvihill, Tumin, and Curtis, 1969). Amir (1971) found that the median age for rapists was 19.6. A little more than one-fourth (26 percent) of the women surveyed by Russell (1984) estimated that their rapists were twenty-one to twenty-five years old. Two-thirds (66 percent) estimated that the rapists were sixteen to thirty years old.

Marital rape. Marital rape can be considered a special case of sexual offending because it is included in the criminal statutes in only twenty-eight states. David Finkelhor and Kersti Yllo (1985) report that 10 percent of a sample of 323 women said they had been forced to have sex with their husbands. Of the 644 married women interviewed by Russell (1984), 14 percent reported one or more incidents of marital rape. In our own national survey of family violence, we found that only 1.2 percent of the 2,934 married women interviewed said they were victims of attempted or completed forced sexual intercourse with their husbands in the previous year (Gelles 1992). Russell (1984) states that husbands who rape their wives tend to be older than men in nonmarital couples. In our own survey of marital rape, 60 percent of the men who attempted or completed an act of marital rape were under forty years old.

Life Course Factors and Sexual Offending

The accumulated data on sexual offending points to a developmental process among offenders. Sexual offenders may experience high rates of physical and sexual abuse as children, although the empirical support for this proposition is equivocal. Offenders tend to develop sexual fantasies and preferences prior to engaging in the initial act of sexual violence, and the eventual offensive sexual behavior then becomes merged with and is elaborated on with further sexual fantasies.

A second life course issue is that offenders tend to mature out of offending. It is unlikely that offenders desist because they have been caught and incarcerated because the arrest rate for rape and sexual abuse is so low. Thus sexual offending, like other human physical aggression, appears to be more pronounced during adolescence and early adulthood, and less likely during the later stages of adult life.

Probably because a life course perspective has not been applied to the study of sexual offending, there is no body of theory that explains how and why offenders tend to mature out of sexual offending. The study of these sexual offenses needs to consider the effect of physiological changes, hormonal changes, and aging on offenders. Clearly, declines in strength, testosterone production, and other age-related changes may help explain the pattern of sexual offending. A more sociological explanation would consider social control across the life course. It may well be that offenders either learn better control or are more deterred by the prospects of formal and informal social control as they age.

Summary

The balkanization of the field of study of sexual offending and victimization has prevented those who study it from developing even a rudimentary life course set of propositions. There have been some studies that compare adolescent and adult offenders, but in general life course issues have been ignored by those who study child sexual abuse, adolescent sexual offenses, and rape.

A review of the literature on sexual abuse, pedophilia, date rape, marital rape, and rape indicates that females are the most likely victims of sexual offending and males the most likely offenders. Although the media and some professional literature tend to dwell on the sexual victimization of defenseless young children, the available incidence and prevalence data, although fraught with methodological problems, suggest that the risk of sexual abuse and assault increases just prior to puberty. The highest risk tends to be between the ages of eighteen and twenty-four, suggesting that sexual assault of unmarried adult women by partners or acquaintances is the most common form of sexual victimization. The risk of rape drops for middle-aged and older women.

Male offending patterns follow the same patterns of all male criminal acts—rising during adolescence, peaking between the ages of eighteen and twenty-four, and then falling off after the age of thirty-five.

Although the advocacy literature on sexual victimization stresses power over women as the motive for sexual assault, the age and gender pattern strongly suggest that sex is an important aspect of sexual offending and victimization, and not merely a form of power and control.

We know very little about the characteristics of male offenders. The distinct and separate literatures imply that males tend to offend against either children or adolescents or adults. However, some data indicate that many offenders are polyperverse with considerable overlap in the ages of their victims (Abel et al. 1988).

The theoretical models of sexual offending and victimization are not well developed, and focus largely on issues that occur early in life and generate abnormalities in sexual aim and sexual object. There is little consideration of why sexual offenders tend to mature out of their patterns of offending.

A life course model of sexual offending and victimization would improve on current discussion by taking into consideration the age and gender patterns of offending and victimization and extending the conceptualization beyond developmental and interactional issues that occur prior to puberty. Mother-child interactions are far too narrow a focus for an adequate developmental model of sexual offending.

A more fully articulated developmental approach to sexual offending and victimization would consider some of the issues raised by Freud, Socarides, and Money, and integrate them with Finkelhor's preconditions. In addition, a more integrated model needs to examine the developmental issues related to victimization. Although some might argue that this would open the door to victim blaming yet again, social learning models suggest that individuals who were physically or sexually victimized are much more vulnerable to sexual victimization later in life. This focus would expand Finkelhor's ideas about preconditions by identifying developmental factors in victim vulnerability.

Finally, the age pattern of offenses argues for consideration of physiological, hormonal, and aging factors in an integrated model of sexual offending. Assessments of hormonal and physiological changes and associations with sexual offending in particular, and hormonal or physiological abnormalities specifically, as suggested by Freud, would be a profitable avenue for research.

NOTES

1. In addition, the term *sexual deviance* is applied, especially in some clinical settings, to prostitution, transvestite behavior, sexual fetishes, and transsexuals. Other behaviors labeled sexual deviance include extramarital affairs, premarital sex, man-boy love (i.e., homosexual relations between pubescent boys and older males), patient-therapist sexual relations, faculty-student sexual relations, and so on. This chapter focuses only on acts of sexual offending and victimization that involve forcible or coercive sexual assault. It is well beyond our space limitations and the current knowledge base to cover the broad spectrum of all forms of sexual deviance.

2. One important exception to the trend of separate literatures is Russell's *Sexual Exploitation: Rape, Child Sexual Abuse, and Workplace Harassment* (1984). Russell herself notes that she found a void in the literature and could not find a comprehensive review of the theories of causation of rape, child sexual abuse, or sexual harassment.

3. Rape is the only crime tabulated by the Uniform Crime Reports that does not include crimes that are later dismissed by the police.

4. The NCVS has now revised the questions used to measure rape victimization.

References

Abel, G., J. Becker, J. Cunningham-Rathner, M. Mittleman, and J. Rouleau. 1988. Multiple paraphiliac diagnoses among sex offenders. *Bulletin of the American Academy of Psychiatry and the Law* 16:153–68.

Abel, G., M. Mittleman, and J. Becker. 1985. Identifying dangerous child molesters. In *Violent behavior: Social learning approaches to prediction, management, and treatment*, ed. R. B. Stuart, 116–37. New York: Brunner/Mazel.

Ageton, S. 1983. *Sexual assault among adolescents.* Lexington, Mass.: Lexington.

American Association for Protecting Children. 1986. *Highlights of official child neglect and abuse reporting, 1984.* Denver: American Humane Association.

———. 1987. *Highlights of official child neglect and abuse reporting, 1985.* Denver: American Humane Association.

———. 1988. *Highlights of official child neglect and abuse reporting, 1986.* Denver: American Humane Association.

Amir, M. 1971. *Patterns of forcible rape.* Chicago: Univ. of Chicago Press.

Baron, L., and M. A. Straus. 1989. *Four theories of rape in American society.* New Haven, Conn.: Yale Univ. Press.

Becker, J., and E. Coleman. 1988. Incest. In *Handbook of family violence*, ed. V. Van Hasselt, R. Morrison, A. Bellack, and M. Hersen, 187–205. New York: Plenum.

Brownmiller, S. 1975. *Against our will: Men, women, and rape.* New York: Simon & Schuster.

Bureau of Justice Statistics. 1992. *Crime victimization in the United States, 1990.* Washington, D.C.: Department of Justice.

Burgdorf, K. 1980. *Recognition and reporting of child maltreatment.* Rockville, Md.: Westat.

Carroll, L. 1974. *Hacks, blacks, and cons: Race relations in a maximum security prison.* Lexington, Mass.: Lexington.

———. 1982. Race, ethnicity, and the social order of the prison. In *The pains of imprisonment*, ed. R. Johnson and H. Toch. Beverly Hills, Calif.: Sage.

Dickemann, M. 1992. Phylogenetic fallacies and sexual oppression: Review of *Pedophilia: Biosocial dimensions*, ed. Jay R. Feierman. *Human Nature* 3:71–87.

Donnerstein, E., D. Linz, and S. Penrod. 1987. *The question of pornography.* New York: Free Press.

Eisenhower, M. 1969. To establish justice, to insure domestic tranquility. Final report of the National Commission on the Causes and Prevention of Violence. Washington, D.C.: Government Printing Office.

Ellis, L. 1989. *Theories of rape.* New York: Hemisphere.

Farberow, N., ed. 1966. *Taboo topics.* New York: Atherton.

Federal Bureau of Investigation. 1989. *Crime in the United States.* Washington, D.C.: Department of Justice.

Finkelhor, D. 1979. *Sexually victimized children.* New York: Free Press.

———. 1984. *Sexual abuse: New research and theory.* New York: Free Press.

Finkelhor, D., and K. Yllo. 1985. *License to rape: Sexual abuse of wives.* New York: Holt, Rinehart & Winston.

Finkelhor, D., G. Hotaling, I. A. Lewis, and C. Smith. 1990. Sexual abuse in a national survey of adult men and women: Prevalence, characteristics, and risk factors. *Child Abuse and Neglect* 14:19–28.

Freud, S. [1905] 1953. *Three essays on the theory of sexuality.* Vol. 7 of *Standard edition of the complete psychological works of Sigmund Freud.* London: Hogarth.

Gagnon, J. 1977. *Human sexuality.* Glenview, Ill.: Scott-Foresman.

Gebhard, P., J. Gagnon, W. Pomeroy, and C. Christenson. 1965. *Sex offenders: An analysis of types.* New York: Harper & Row.

Gelles, R. 1978. Methods for studying sensitive family topics. *American Journal of Orthopsychiatry* 48:408–24.

———. 1990. Methodological issues in the study of family violence. In *Depression and aggression: Two facets of family interaction,* ed. G. R. Patterson, 49–74. Hillsdale, N.J.: Erlbaum.

———. 1992. Marital rape. Mimeographed.

Gilbert, N. 1991. The phantom epidemic of sexual assault. *The Public Interest* 103:54–65.

———. 1993. Date rape: examining the facts. In *Current controversies on family violence research,* ed. R. J. Gelles and D. Loseke, 120–32. Newbury Park, Calif.: Sage.

Guttentag, M., and P. Secord. 1983. *Too many women? The sex ratio question.* Newbury Park, Calif.: Sage.

Herman, J. 1981. *Father-daughter incest.* Cambridge, Mass.: Harvard Univ. Press.

Holmstrom, L., and A. Burgess. 1978. *The victim of rape: Institutional reactions.* New York: Wiley Interscience.

Jamison, K., and T. Flanagan. 1989. *Sourcebook of criminal justice statistics, 1988.* Washington, D.C.: Department of Justice.

Katz, S., and M. Mazur. 1979. *Understanding the rape victim: A synthesis of research findings.* New York: Wiley.

Katzenbach, N. 1967. The challenges of crime in a free society. A report by the president's Commission on Law Enforcement and the Administration of Justice. Washington, D.C.: Government Printing Office.

Kilpatrick, D., B. Saunders, C. Best, and J. Von. 1987. Criminal victimization: Lifetime prevalence, reporting to police, and psychological impact. *Crime and Delinquency* 33:479–89.

Koss, M., C. Gidycz, and N. Wisniewski. 1987. The scope of rape: Incidence and prevalence of sexual aggression and victimization in a national sample of higher education students. *Journal of Consulting and Clinical Psychology* 55:162–70.

Lockwood, D. 1980. *Prison sexual violence.* New York: Elsevier.

MacDonald, J. 1971. *Rape offenders and their victims.* Springfield, Ill.: Thomas.

Marshall, W. L., H. E. Barbaree, and D. Christopher. 1986. Sexual offenders against female children: Sexual preferences for age of victims and type of behavior. *Canadian Journal of Behavioral Science* 18:424–39.

Masson, J. M. 1991. *The assault on truth: Freud's suppression of the seduction theory.* New York: HarperCollins.

McKinnon, C. A. 1989. *Toward a feminist theory of the state.* Cambridge, Mass.: Harvard Univ. Press.

Money, J. 1986. *Lovemaps.* New York: Irvington.

Money, J., and M. Lamacz. 1989. *Vandalized lovemaps: Paraphiliac outcome in seven cases in pediatric sexology.* Buffalo, N.Y.: Prometheus.

Mulvihill, D., M. Tumin, and L. Curtis. 1969. Crimes of violence: A staff report submitted to the National Commission on the Causes and Prevention of Violence, vols. 11–13. Washington, D.C.: Government Printing Office.

Murman, D., K. Miller, and A. Cutler. 1992. Sexual assault of the elderly victim. *Journal of Interpersonal Violence* 7:70–76.

National Center on Child Abuse and Neglect. 1988. *Study findings: Study of national incidence and prevalence of child abuse and neglect: 1988.* Washington, D.C.: Department of Health and Human Services.

O'Brien, R. 1991. Sex ratios and rape rates: A power-control hypothesis. *Criminology* 29:99–114.

Plummer, C. 1993. Child sexual abuse prevention programs are effective. In *Current controversies in family violence research,* ed. R. J. Gelles and D. Loseke, 288–305. Newbury Park, Calif.: Sage.

Prentky, R., R. Knight, and R. Rosenberg. 1989. A path analytic approach to the validation of a taxonomic system for classifying child molesters. *Journal of Quantitative Criminology* 5:231–57.

Reppucci, N. D., and J. J. Haugaard. 1989. Prevention of child sexual abuse: Myth or reality? *American Psychologist* 44:1266–75.

Russell, D. 1975. *The politics of rape: The victim's perspective.* New York: Stein & Day.
———. 1984. *Sexual exploitation: Rape, child sexual abuse, and workplace harassment.* Newbury Park, Calif.: Sage.

Ryan, G., and S. Lane. 1991. *Juvenile sexual offending: Causes, consequences, and correction.* Lexington, Mass.: Lexington.

Socarides, C. 1988. *The preoedipal origin and psychoanalytic therapy of sexual perversions.* Madison, Conn.: International Univ. Press.

Solomon, R. 1980. The opponent-process theory of acquired motivation: The costs of pleasure and the benefits of pain. *American Psychologist* 35:273–75.

Smuts, B. 1992. Male aggression against women: An evolutionary perspective. *Human Nature* 3:1–44.

Struckman-Johnson, C. 1988. Forced sex on dates: It happens to men too. *Journal of Sex Research* 24:234–41.

Svalastoga, K. 1962. Rape and social structure. *Pacific Sociological Review* 5:48–53.

Wolfner, G., D. Faust, and R. Dawes. 1993. The use of anatomically detailed dolls in sexual abuse evaluations: The state of the science. *Applied and Preventive Psychology* 2:1–11.

Wyatt, G. 1992. The socio-cultural context of African-American and white-women's rape. *Journal of Social Issues* 48:77–91.

Alan Booth is professor of sociology at Pennsylvania State University. He received his Ph.D. from the University of Nebraska, where he served on the faculty as a distinguished professor of sociology before moving to Penn State in 1991. He was editor of *Journal of Marriage and the Family* from 1985 to 1991, was president of the Midwest Sociological Society in 1989–90, and was chair of the family section of the American Sociological Association in 1992. Alan Booth's past research focused on social participation and urban crowding. Since 1980 he has directed the Marital Instability over the Life Course Study with funds from the National Institute on Aging. In addition to his work on marital change, he has been conducting research on the role of hormones in competition, deviance, and family organization. Recent books include *Child Care in the 1990s: Trends and Consequences* (Erlbaum, 1992), and *Contemporary Families: Looking Forward, Looking Back* (National Council on Family Relations, 1991).

Benjamin P. Bowser is an associate professor of sociology and social services at the California State University at Hayward. He received his Ph.D. from Cornell University and has held administrative and adjunct faculty appointments at Cornell University, the University of Colorado at Boulder, Santa Clara University, and Stanford University. His research and publications have focused on race relations, community studies, AIDS, and drug abuse prevention. He is coeditor with Raymond Hunt of *Impacts of Racism on White Americans* (Sage, 1981); editor of *Black Male Adolescents* (Univ. Press of America, 1991), and *Racism and Anti-Racism in World Perspective* (Sage, forthcoming). His current research projects are on indigenous community strategies for drug-sales prevention, funded through the Robert Woods Johnson Foundation, and he is on the national syringe exchange evaluation project, funded through the U.S. Centers for Disease Control.

Benjamin C. Campbell is a postdoctoral fellow at the Carolina Population Center, University of North Carolina at Chapel Hill. He obtained his Ph.D. in anthropology from Harvard University and has been the recipient of the Hooten prize from the American Association of Physical Anthropologists. His past research and publications have been on reproductive endocrinology and adolescent sexuality. His current research includes projects in Turkana, Kenya, on male reproductive ecology and in Zimbabwe testing biosocial models of adolescent sexuality in a cross-cultural context.

John N. Edwards is professor of sociology, Virginia Polytechnic Institute and State University. He received his Ph.D. from the University of Nebraska. He held faculty appointments at the University of Nebraska and the University of Kentucky prior to joining the faculty at Virginia Tech. His research has focused on voluntary associations, sexuality, and changes in marriage and the family. Professor Edwards's most recent book (coedited with David Demo) is *Marriage and Family in Transition* (Allyn & Bacon, 1991). His current research with Alan Booth concerns marital instability over the life course, a twelve-year panel study of married American women and men.

Henry A. Feldman is senior research scientist at the New England Research Institute, Watertown, Massachusetts, and adjunct associate professor at the School of Public Health at Harvard University. A native of Oak Ridge, Tennessee, he was educated at Swarthmore College and received his Ph.D. in applied mathematics from Harvard University. He has held research and teaching positions at Massachusetts General Hospital, the National Cancer Institute, and M.I.T. as well as Harvard, where he has been a faculty member since 1979. His teaching and research are concerned with biomedical applications of mathematics, ranging from theoretical biology to medical statistics. He is currently active in the Massachusetts Male Aging Study, Pawtucket Heart Health Program, and Child and Adolescent Trial for Cardiovascular Health.

Martha R. Fowlkes is professor of Educational Leadership in the School of Education at the University of Connecticut, Storrs. From 1986 to 1992 she served as associate dean and dean of the School of Family Studies at the University of Connecticut. She holds an M.A. in social anthropology from the London School of Economics and Political Science, and a Ph.D. in sociology from the University of Massachusetts at Amherst. She has held administrative and research appointments at Smith College and was awarded research fellowships by the Danforth Foundation, the Woodrow Wilson Foundation, National Institutes of Mental Health, and the Federal Emergency Management Agency. She has written in the areas of family and work, human development and sexuality, and community and environmental sociology. Her most recent work is on intimacy and loss in "The Social Regulation of Grief," published in *Sociological Forum* in 1990.

Richard J. Gelles is professor of sociology and anthropology and director of the Family Violence Research Program at the University of Rhode Island. He received his A.B. degree from Bates College (1968), an M.A. in sociology from the University of Rochester (1971), and a Ph.D. in sociology from the University of New Hampshire (1973). He is the author or coauthor of sixteen books and more than one hundred articles and chapters on family violence. His most recent books are *Intimate Violence* (Simon & Schuster, 1989), *Physical Violence in American Families: Risk Factors and Adaptations in 8,145 Families* (Transaction, 1990), and *Intimate Violence in Families* (Sage, 1990).

Richard Green is a professor of psychiatry in residence at the School of Medicine at the University of California (Los Angeles), where he also holds a part-time appointment as a faculty member in the School of Law. He earned his M.D. degree from the Johns Hopkins University School of Medicine, and his J.D. degree from Yale University Law School. He was the founding president of the International Academy of Sex Research, and a past president of the Society for the Scientific Study of Sex. He is the author of some 130 journal articles and book chapters and author or editor of nine books. His recent clinical and research interests have been in atypical psychosexual development, gender identity disorders, and the legal aspects of sexual issues.

Jane B. Lancaster is a professor of anthropology at the University of New Mexico. She received her Ph.D. from the University of California, Berkeley. Her research and publications have been on human reproductive biology and behavior, especially on human parental investment, on women's reproductive biology or pregnancy, lactation, and child spacing, and on male fertility and investment in children. Current research with Hillard Kaplan is on male life-history strategies among a large sample of men in New Mexico. She has coedited three books on human parental investment: *School-Age Pregnancy and Parenthood* (with B. Hamburg; Aldine de Gruyter, 1986), *Parenting across the Life Span* (with J. Altmann, A. Rossi, and L. Sherrod; Aldine de Gruyter, 1987), and *Child Abuse and Neglect* (with R. Gelles; Aldine de Gruyter, 1987). She is scientific editor of a quarterly journal, *Human Nature: An Interdisciplinary Biosocial Perspective* (Aldine de Gruyter). She is also a council member of the newly formed Human Behavior and Evolution Society.

Judith A. Levy is associate professor of health resources management of the School of Public Health at the University of Illinois (Chicago). She received her Ph.D. from Northwestern University. She has held numerous positions in professional societies, including currently serving as chair-elect of the medical sociology section of the American Sociological Association. Her research and publications are in the sociology of aging, occupations and professions, AIDS, and social movements in medicine. She recently edited *Health Professions in a Changing Environment* (JAI, 1990) and coedited (with Gary Albrecht) *Chronic Illness and Disability across the Life Course* (JAI, 1991). She is the principal investigator for a five-year demonstration project, funded by the National Institute on Drug Abuse, to investigate the effects of delivering community-based social support designed to encourage street drug abusers to stop or reduce their drug use and prevent HIV transmission.

John B. McKinlay is vice president and director of the New England Research Institute, an independent research organization located in Watertown, Massachusetts. He is also professor of sociology, research professor of medicine, and professor of epidemiology and biostatistics at Boston University, and director of the

Center for Health and Advanced Policy Studies at that institution. He received his doctoral training at Aberdeen University in Scotland. He is presently the recipient of an NIH Merit Award. He has published over one hundred articles, chapters, and books in epidemiology, sociology, gerontology, and health services research.

Alice S. Rossi is Harriet Martineau Professor Emerita of Sociology at the University of Massachusetts (Amherst). She received her Ph.D. from Columbia University and has been the recipient of five honorary degrees. She held research or teaching appointments at Goucher College, the Johns Hopkins University, the University of Chicago, Cornell University, and Harvard University before joining the faculty at the University of Massachusetts. Her research and publications have been on sex and gender, social movements, and family and kinship. She was the recipient of the Common Wealth Award in 1989 for distinguished work in sociology, and the William J. Goode Book Award in 1991 for her most recent book (coauthored with Peter H. Rossi), *Of Human Bonding: Parent-Child Relations across the Life Course* (Aldine de Gruyter, 1990). Her current research is on menopause, social responsibility, gender, and sexuality, as a member of the John D. and Catherine T. MacArthur Foundation Research Network on Successful Midlife Development.

Raul C. Schiavi is professor of psychiatry and director of the Human Sexuality Program at Mount Sinai Medical School in New York City. After earning his medical degree from the University of Buenos Aires, Argentina, he obtained psychiatric training at the University of Pennsylvania in Philadelphia, and research training in neuroendocrinology at the College de France in Paris. He has held faculty appointments at the University of Pennsylvania, Cornell Medical College, and State University of New York, Downstate Medical Center. Raul Schiavi has been a member of the board of directors of Sex Information and Education Council of the United States, a council member of the American Psychosomatic Society, and president of the Society for Sex Therapy and Research. He has been the recipient of a Scientific Development Award from the National Institute of Mental Health, and the Seventh Annual Masters and Johnson Award of the Society for Sex Therapy and Research. He has served as a coeditor of the *Journal of Sex and Marital Therapy* and is on the editorial board of the *Archives of Sexual Behavior,* and *Hormones and Behavior.* He is the author of numerous articles and book chapters on the psychobiology of sexual function and dysfunction.

Tom W. Smith earned his B.A. in political science and history and an M.A. in history from Pennsylvania State University, and a Ph.D. in American history from the University of Chicago. He is widely known as an expert in survey research, specializing in the study of social change and survey methodology. Since 1980 he has been coprincipal investigator of the National Data Program for the Social Sciences and director of its General Social Survey (GSS) at the National Opinion Research Center in Chicago. He has also written extensively on virtually every aspect of survey methods; he has organized an extensive program of data quality assurance and methodological analysis on the GSS, and he edits the GSS Methodological Report Series. He has also served on the National Academy of Sciences' Panel on Survey Measurement of Subject Phenomena, on the board of directors of the Roper Center for Public Opinion Research, on the National Science Foundation's Committee on Data Sharing in the Social Sciences, and he has filled several posts in the American Association for Public Opinion Research. He is currently on the editorial boards of both *Public Opinion Quarterly* and the *International Journal for Public Opinion Research.*

Claire Sterk-Elifson is an assistant professor in the Department of Anthropology at Georgia State University in Atlanta. She received a degree in anthropology and sociology from the Rijks Universiteit Utrecht. She also received a Ph.D. in the social sciences from Erasmus University, Rotterdam–City University of New York. She held a research appointment at the National Centers for Disease Control, Center for Prevention Services. Her research and publications have been on urban issues such as substance abuse, prostitution, the homeless, and on health issues, in particular HIV and AIDS. She recently received a grant from the National Institute on Drug Abuse to study social support mechanisms among female drug users. Her recent publications have appeared in such journals as the *Milbank Memorial Quarterly, Journal of Sexually Transmitted Diseases, Urban Anthropology,* and *Human Organization.*

Sharon Thompson received her B.S. from Columbia University and has published widely on adolescence, sex and gender, and reproduction. In addition, she has published short fiction and literary criticism. She was coeditor (with Ann Snitow and Christine Stansell), of *Powers of Desire: The Politics of Sexuality* (Monthly Review Press, 1983) and currently serves on the fiction advisory board of the *Village Voice Literary Supplement* in New York. Her book *All the Way: Teenage Girls' Narratives about Sex, Romance, and Reproduction* (Hill & Wang, Farrar, Straus & Giroux) is forthcoming.

J. Richard Udry is Kenan Professor of Sociology and of Maternal and Child Health at the University of North Carolina at Chapel Hill, where he has been on the faculty since 1965. He received his Ph.D. from the University of Southern California in 1960. From 1977 to 1992 he was director of the Carolina Population Center, where he is now a fellow. He was elected president of the Population Association of America for 1994. His career research interest is the incorporation of biological factors into social science and demographic models of behavior. His current research involves the development of biosocial models of adolescent sexual behavior and women's gender roles.

Glenn Wolfner is a doctoral student in clinical psychology at the University of Rhode Island, where he is the research assistant for the Family Violence Research Program. He received his B.S.Ed. in human development and social policy from Northwestern University, and his M.A. in clinical psychology from the University of Rhode Island. He recently received the Roger Lorenz Award for Outstanding Presentation as a graduate student from the International Psychohistorical Association for his work on emotional reactions to the Persian Gulf War. He has worked as a child protective social worker for the Commonwealth of Massachusetts and is currently a court investigator for the juvenile courts. His most recent published work is on child sexual abuse and violence toward children. His current research interests are in family violence, affective and anxiety disorders, and family functioning.

Page numbers in italics refer to citations in reference lists.